Frontiers in Economic History

Economic historians have contributed to the development of economics in a variety of ways, combining theory with quantitative methods, constructing new databases, promoting interdisciplinary approaches to historical topics, and using history as a lens to examine the long-term development of the economy. Frontiers in Economic History publishes manuscripts that push the frontiers of research in economic history in order to better explain past economic experiences and to understand how, why and when economic change occurs. Books in this series will highlight the value of economic history in shedding light on the ways in which economic factors influence growth as well as social and political developments. This series aims to establish a new standard of quality in the field while offering a global discussion forum toward a unified approach in the social sciences.

Emmanouil M. L. Economou •
Nicholas C. Kyriazis

Daily Life in Classical Athens

A Socioeconomic Analysis

Springer

Emmanouil M. L. Economou
Department of Economics
University of Thessaly
Volos, Greece

Nicholas C. Kyriazis
Department of Economics
University of Thessaly
Volos, Greece

ISSN 2662-9771 ISSN 2662-978X (electronic)
Frontiers in Economic History
ISBN 978-3-031-58540-1 ISBN 978-3-031-58541-8 (eBook)
https://doi.org/10.1007/978-3-031-58541-8

This Springer imprint is published by the registered company Springer Nature Switzerland AG
The registered company address is: Gewerbestrasse 11, 6330 Cham, Switzerland

Dedicated to the memory of our friend and colleague, Professor Anastasios D. Karayiannis
And to those scholars around the globe who, like Karayiannis, have dedicated their lives so as to reveal the great achievements
of the Ancient Greeks regarding their economy

Acknowledgments

We would like to express our deepest gratitude to Assistant Professor Dr. Nikolaos A. Kyriazis (University of Thessaly, Department of Accounting and Finance) and Eleni Kekropoulou (Manager/Owner of the Enalios Publications in Greece, being also a writer) for their careful reading of the book and for providing us with their very useful insights that led to the improvement of this work.

We are grateful to Andreas Gkouvas for his tireless support on various research issues as well as to the designer Vasiliki Demopoulou for her kindness to prepare for us the wonderful images 4.1, 5.1, 6.2, 7.1, 8.6, 8.7, 8.8, 9.1, 16.1, 24.1, 29.1.

We are also grateful to Dane Kurth–Rowe for her kindness to grant us permission rights to use the beautiful coin images that are presented in the book.

Our last thanks go to our Springer editor, Niko Chtouris for all the wonderful cooperation we had with him at all the stages of book preparation, his colleague, Parthiban Gujilan Kannan, our Scientific editors of the Springer's Series, *Frontiers of Economic History*, Claude Diebolt (University of Strasbourg) and Michael Haupert (University of Wisconsin–La Crosse) for their very productive comments and suggestions and for the excellent collaboration we had with them during the publication process of this book as well as Vergine Josh Vengadalabady who as production manager handled this publication.

About This Book

The principal aim of the present book is to provide a synthetic analysis that focuses on the economic organization and the institutions that were developed and practiced in Athens during the Classical period (508 - 323 BCE), mainly during the 4th century BCE, by connecting this evidence with crucial socioeconomic and sociopolitical aspects that characterized the Athenian society. This book argues that parallel to the development of democracy, the Athenian city-state introduced a series of innovative and sophisticated (for the times) economic institutions including, among others, property rights protection, prices that were in principle determined by (what we nowadays characterize as) market forces, institutions against profiteering, a variety of banking and insurance services, measures to protect the Athenian currency's trustworthiness from fraud and forgery, and a well-developed public sector. The book also sheds light on the Athenian welfare state policy through the provision of public goods and public–private partnerships.

In general, by focusing on the socioeconomic side of the Athenian daily life the book answers to questions like: How did the ancient Athenians live? How were society and the household organized? What was the social position of women, foreigners, and slaves? How were the Athenians behaving between each other? What were their customs and traditions? How was the economy organized? Why their economy was transformed from an agrarian toward a maritime market-oriented economy? Which were their business and labor mentality and practices? How did international trade take place? Which were the trade patterns they followed?

In parallel to the above, the book examines further aspects of social life such as: how they were getting married, what they were eating, what they were drinking, how they were dressing, which were their values, ethos, and norms of behavior on various socioeconomic issues, how they were fighting against enemies, etc.

The book introduces New Institutional Economics (NIE) as a methodology of interpretation of the historical data it deals with. Thus, in actuality, it uses institutional analysis in combination with economic history. The book follows also an interdisciplinary approach, and at some specific points, it interprets various phenomena from the perspective of political science, strategy, and behavioral theory.

The arguments of the book are reinforced by a plethora of ancient sources, inscriptions found, and a large modern bibliography. The bibliography is a combination of Classical history to economic analysis.

Lastly, the book provides a set of ideas as to how the Athenian paradigm of socioeconomic organization could be seen as a benchmark for our modern societies, in order to remedy current problems such as the efficiency (or not) of economic governance institutions and their nexus to the crisis of democracy worldwide.

Contents

1 Introduction 1

2 The Athenian *Oikos* and the *Kalos Kagathos* Behavior 15
- 2.1 Scene 1: Nicomedes in His *Oikos* 15
- 2.2 General Notes 17
- 2.3 Family 18
- 2.4 Parents-Children 19
- 2.5 The *Oikos* as a "Laboratory" of Producing Social Behavior 22
- 2.6 The Social Ethics Behind the *Kalos Kagathos* Behavior 23

3 The Relationships Between Men and Women, and the Social Groups in Classical Athens 29
- 3.1 Hegeso: The Manager of the *Oikos* 29
- 3.2 Relationships Between Men and Women 31
- 3.3 The Social Position of Women 34
- 3.4 The Ideal Woman and the Right Age for Marriage 41
- 3.5 *Metics* at Athens 43
- 3.6 Slaves in Athens 44
- 3.7 Athenian Society: A Critical Appraisal 51

4 Preparations for Receiving Guests at the *Oikos* 53
- 4.1 Hegeso and Eriphyle Dress Up to Welcome Their Guests 53
- 4.2 Clothing and Footwear 54
- 4.3 Fashion and Women's Grooming 56

5 The Athenian Citizen Identity and the Administrative Organization of the Athenian City-State 57
- 5.1 Nicomedes: The Dutiful Citizen of Alopekis and the Landowner 57
- 5.2 Units of Length and Width 58
- 5.3 The Evolution of Athenian Society over Time 59
- 5.4 The 10 *Phylae* and the 139 Athenian *Demes* 61

5.5 The Alopekis *Deme* 63
5.6 The *Demesmen*, the *Demarchs*, and Their Responsibilities 63
5.7 The Title of Citizen and the Role of Censuses 65

6 The Athenian Political System's Institutions and the Manning of Posts Related to Public Administration 69
6.1 Nicomedes: The Active and Virtuous Citizen 69
6.2 The Naval Decree of Themistocles of 483/482 BCE 71
6.3 The *Ecclesia of the Demos* 73
6.4 *The Bouleutai* 75
6.5 The *Prytaneis* 78
6.6 The *Nine Archons* and the *Areopagos* Court 79
6.7 The *Heliaia* Court 80
6.8 The Judicial Process 81
6.9 The *Nomophylakes*, the *Graphe Paranomon*, the *Nomothetai*, and the *Thesmothetai* 81
6.10 The Economic Temperament of the Athenians in the Assembly 87
6.11 The *Strategoi* 89
6.12 The Draw and the *Cheirotonia* Procedures 90
6.13 Public Officials and Efficiency in the Public Administration 91
6.14 *Archai*: The Categories of Public Officials 95
6.15 The Salaries of Public Officials 99

7 Life at the *Oikos*, Individual and Public Hygiene, and Water Supply 101
7.1 Chariclea: The Turbulent Life of a Female Slave 101
7.2 General Notes 103
7.3 The *Oikos* as a Dwelling Place 103
7.4 Individual and Collective Hygiene and Quality of Life 105
7.5 Water Supply System 108
7.6 The Athenian Week and the Athenian Months 110
7.7 Measuring Time 112
7.8 The Achaean League 113

8 The Athenian Agora and the Port of Piraeus 115
8.1 A Merchant from Iberia in the Agora of Athens 115
8.2 The Athenian Agora 117
8.3 Consumer Protection and Price Control 123
8.4 The Port of Piraeus 125
8.5 *Neosoikoi* and Philon's Arsenal 126
8.6 The Athenian *Long Walls* 128

9 Ancient Greek Hospitality, Food Habits, and Grain Supply 131
9.1 Meal to Honor a Stranger 131
9.2 The Household Utensils of the Ancient Kitchen 133

9.3 Cooking, Delicacies, and Obesity 134
9.4 Dairy Products, Vegetables, Fruits, Drinks, and Spices 135
9.5 The Athenian Grain Supply Institutions 137

10 The Athenian Drachma and the Role of Money in the Economy 139
10.1 In Nicomedes' *Andron* 139
10.2 The Athenian *Drachma* and the Money Supply in the Economy 142
10.3 Establishing Unconventional Monetary Regimes: The Athenian Monetary Model, the Scottish Free Banking Regime, and the Digital Currencies Nowadays 149
10.4 The Law of Nicophon of 375/374 BCE 152
10.5 Methods of Assessing the Purity of Metal Coins in Classical Greece 154

11 The Financial Institutions of the Athenian Economy 157
11.1 Nicomedes: The Experienced Banker 157
11.2 Financial Institutions 159
11.3 The Regime of Property Rights Protection 160
11.4 Inherited Property and Testament 162
11.5 Protection of Commercial Contracts 163
11.6 *Dikai Emporikai* 165
11.7 Types of Banking 166
11.8 Lending Policy 169

12 The Financial Aspects of the Silver Mining Operations 171
12.1 Nicomedes Becomes a Winner at an Auction 171
12.2 The Board of *Poletai* 173
12.3 Laurion Silver Mining and Quarries 175

13 The *Liturgies*, the Financing of the Navy, and the Tax Regime in Classical Athens 179
13.1 Nausinicus: The *Liturgist* and the *Trierarch* 179
13.2 The *Liturgies* 181
13.3 *Eisphora:* The Taxation of the Athenians 182
13.4 The *Symmories* and the *Synteleiai* 183
13.5 The *Trierarchy* 184
13.6 The *Triremes* 186
13.7 The *Antidosis* Procedure 190

14 The Port of Piraeus, the Agora of Athens, and Their International Role in Commercial Affairs of the Times 191
14.1 Xenocrates' Purchases from the Agora 191
14.2 Pottery 192

14.3 Fabrics . . . 193
14.4 Books and Illiteracy . . . 193

15 Insurance Premium as an Institutional Mechanism of Promoting International Trade . . . 195
15.1 Nicomedes's Insurance Practices and Credit Sales . . . 195
15.2 Insurance and Interest Rates . . . 198
15.3 Credit Sales . . . 198
15.4 The *Kapeleia* . . . 199

16 Ancient Greek Merchant Marine and International Commercial Routes . . . 201
16.1 Xenocrates Prepares His Return Trip to Emporion . . . 201
16.2 Shipbuilding . . . 203
16.3 Greek Commercial Cities of the Mediterranean . . . 204

17 High Cost Made Eternal Athenian Monuments as a Sign of Economic Power . . . 207
17.1 Return to Emporion, Under the Auspices of Goddess Athena and Zeus . . . 207
17.2 High Cost Made Eternal Athenian Monuments . . . 208

18 Managing the Athenian State Finances . . . 213
18.1 A Symposion with Lycurgus for the Welfare of Society and the Polis . . . 213
18.2 Nicomedes's Symposion . . . 218
18.3 The *Theorica* . . . 218
18.4 Lycurgus: The Honest and Able *Epimeletes/Tamias Tes Koines Prosodou* . . . 219
18.5 The *Hellenotamiai* and the Allied Fund . . . 221
18.6 The *Demosion* Fund . . . 222
18.7 The *Treasury-Temples of Athena and the Other Gods* . . . 222
18.8 The *Theoricon* and the *Stratiotikon* Funds . . . 225
18.9 An Ancient *Social Contract* . . . 226

19 The Mentality of the Greek Way of War, the Battle of Chaeronea, and the Rise of Macedon . . . 229
19.1 Nicomedes: A *Trierarch* in the Navy and an Infantry Officer at Chaeronea . . . 229
19.2 The *Hoplite Phalanx* . . . 231
19.3 The *Ephebeia* and the Oath of the Athenian *Ephebes* . . . 236
19.4 The Battle of Chaeronea . . . 238

20 Taking Crucial Decisions in the Athenian Assembly and the Pivotal Role of *Paideia* . . . 241
20.1 A Special Day at the Assembly . . . 241
20.2 The Ethical Dimension of the Athenian *Paideia* . . . 244

20.3 The *Paideia* of the Athenians as an Educational Process 246
20.4 Aristophanes on the Education of the Youth 248

21 Slave Trading in the Athenian Market 251
21.1 Melanippe: An Amazonian, Given as Gift for Chariclea and Nicandros 251
21.2 The Fortifications of Attica 253
21.3 The Amazons 254

22 The Athenian Symposia 255
22.1 A Symposion for Nicandros and his Friends 255
22.2 General Notes 257
22.3 Symposia and Music 258
22.4 Neaera: The Turbulent Life of a *Hetaera* 258
22.5 The Illegal Accommodation of Non-Athenians within Athens 259

23 The Sexual Life of the Ancient Greeks 261
23.1 Phano's Dance and an Unforgettable Night for Nicandros 261
23.2 Sex Life of Men and Women 262
23.3 Sexual Principles and Habits 263
23.4 Prostitution 266
23.5 The *Hetaerae* 267
23.6 Homosexuality 268
23.7 Pederasty 270

24 The Athenian Welfare State and the Provision of Health Services 273
24.1 Young Nicandros Recovering After a Tough Fight at the *Palaestra* 273
24.2 *Pankration*: An Ancient Mixed Martial Art 276
24.3 The Olympian Truce 277
24.4 Sports in Athens 278
24.5 The Great Panathenaea and the Funding of Athletes 280
24.6 Sports and Prestige of Greek City-States 281
24.7 Greek Women and Sports 282
24.8 Athens: The First Historically Recorded Welfare State 284
24.9 Provision of Health Services 286

25 Religion and the Great Panathenaea 289
25.1 Panathenaea: Participating in the Athenian Polis's Greatest Festival 289
25.2 The Religious Consciousness of the Athenians 290
25.3 The Athenian Priests and Priestesses 292

26 Marriage and Life Expectancy 295
26.1 Eriphyle's Marriage 295

26.2 The Wedding Ritual 296
26.3 The Dowry 297
26.4 The Divorce 297
26.5 The Abortion 298
26.6 The Life Expectancy of the Athenians 298
26.7 The Lamian War (323–322 BCE) and the *Strategos* Leosthenes 299

27 The Athenian *Choregos* 301
27.1 Nicomedes: The *Choregos* 301
27.2 The Tragedy, the Comedy and the Theaters 302
27.3 Freedom of Expression 303

28 The Demosthenes Speech *on the Crown* 305
28.1 Nicomedes *on the Crown* of Demosthenes 305
28.2 General Notes 309
28.3 The Defense of the Public Interest 309

29 The Child as the New Member of the Family 311
29.1 A Mature Couple Strolls in the Acropolis at Dusk 311
29.2 General Notes 313
29.3 The Duties of the Young Mother Toward her Children 313
29.4 The Toddler's Birthday 315

30 Conclusions 317

Glossary 333

References 345

Index 361

List of Images

Image 3.1 Bust of Themistocles as a mature Greek man. Source: https://upload.wikimedia.org/wikipedia/commons/8/87/Beeld%2C_Themistocles_-_Unknown_-_20408396_-_RCE.jpg 32

Image 3.2 Ancient Greek woman. Praxilla, by John William Godward. Source: https://commons.wikimedia.org/wiki/File:Praxilla._John_William_Godward.jpg 37

Image 4.1 A Corinthian *pyxis* (fifth c. BC) and an *alabastron*. Bowls with lid, for keeping tablets of powder for makeup. Source: Image created by painter Vasiliki Demopoulou 56

Image 5.1 General topographic illustration of the state of Athens. Source: Image created by painter Vasiliki Demopoulou 62

Image 6.1 The Pnyx's podium. The Acropolis and the Lycabettus hills in the background. Source: Image owned by the authors 74

Image 6.2 The Prytaneion (round building on the left) and the Old and the New Bouleuterion, respectively (on the right). Source: Image created by painter Vasiliki Demopoulou 79

Image 7.1 View of the architectural layout of a part of a neighborhood in an ancient Greek polis. Source: Image created by painter Vasiliki Demopoulou 104

Image 7.2 Part of the water supply network of Classical Athens. Source: https://commons.wikimedia.org/wiki/Category:Ancient_Greek_terracotta_water_pipes#/media/File:1790_-_Athens_-_Finds_at_the_Evangelismos_Station_-_Photo_by_Giovanni_Dall'Orto,_Nov_12_2009.jpg 110

Image 8.1 Agora: The center of the city of Athens. Source: Uknnown creator 117

Image 8.2 Part of the ancient Agora of Athens. In the background is the Acropolis (For an important spatial illustration of the Agora of Athens, see also: http://www.thehistoryofancientgreece.com/2017/12/066-athenian-agora.html). Source: Image owned by the authors 118

Image 8.3	Map of Ancient Athens c. 430 BCE. Source: https://commons.wikimedia.org/wiki/Category:Maps_of_ancient_Athens#/media/File:Map_ancient_athens.png	118
Image 8.4	The Agora of Athens. View from the Areopagos Hill	119
Image 8.5	A spatial illustration of the port of Ancient Piraeus. Source: https://commons.wikimedia.org/wiki/File:Plan_Piraeus.svg. Retrieved by: Tomisti	127
Image 8.6	*Neosoikoi* in Piraeus. Source: Image created by painter Vasiliki Demopoulou	128
Image 8.7	Performing maintenance of a *trireme* inside a *neosoikos*. Source: Image created by painter Vasiliki Demopoulou	129
Image 8.8	The twin city-state of Athens and Piraeus through the Long Walls. (A): Athens, (P): Piraeus, (Ph): Phalerum. Source: Image created by painter Vasiliki Demopoulou	129
Image 9.1	Pots of various types. Source: Image created by Vasiliki Demopoulou	133
Image 10.1	A Lydian electrum coin of 600 BCE. Source: https://www.wildwinds.com/coins/greece/lydia/sg3401.jpg. With the permission of Wildwinds.com	145
Image 10.2	An Athenian *didrachm*. Source: https://www.wildwinds.com/coins/greece/attica/athens/SNGCop_03.jpg. With the permission of Wildwinds.com	145
Image 10.3	An Athenian *tetradrachm*. Source: http://www.wildwinds.com/coins/greece/attica/athens/sg2526.jpg. With the permission of Wildwinds.com	146
Image 10.4	An Athenian *drachma*. Source: http://www.wildwinds.com/coins/greece/attica/athens/SNGCop_043.jpg. With the permission of Wildwinds.com	146
Image 10.5	An Athenian *obol*. Source: http://www.wildwinds.com/coins/greece/attica/athens/SNGCop_053ff.jpg. With the permission of Wildwinds.com	147
Image 10.6	An Athenian *hemiobol*. Source: https://www.wildwinds.com/coins/greece/attica/athens/SNGCop_059.jpg. With the permission of Wildwinds.com	147
Image 10.7	An Athenian *tritemorion*. Source: https://www.wildwinds.com/coins/greece/attica/athens/BMC_187.jpg. With the permission of Wildwinds.com	148
Image 10.8	An *hemitetartemorion*. Source: https://www.wildwinds.com/coins/greece/attica/athens/Mionnet_26.jpg. With the permission of Wildwinds.com	148
Image 10.9	Athenian *tetradrachm* with multiple test cuts. Source: https://www.wildwinds.com/coins/greece/attica/athens/Kroll_08.jpg. With the permission of Wildwinds.com	156

Image 12.1 Interior view of silver mine at Thorikos at Laurion. Source: https://commons.wikimedia.org/wiki/Category:Mines_of_Laurion#/media/File:Mineing_Shaft_in_Throikos.jpg 176
Image 12.2 Ore washing site (below the arrow) near the theater at Thorikos, at the Laurion silver mines. Source: Image owned by the authors 177
Image 13.1 The *trireme* Olympias (bow side). Source: https://commons.wikimedia.org/wiki/File:Triere_Olympias_at_Paleon_Faliron_Museum.JPG. Permission: Public Domain 187
Image 13.2 The astern side of the reconstructed Athenian *trireme* Olympias. Source: Image owned by the authors 188
Image 16.1 Representation of a type of a merchant ship of the Classical period. Source: Image created by Vasiliki Demopoulou 204
Image 16.2 A replica of the mythical Argo, docked at the port of Volos, Greece. Source: Image owned by the authors 205
Image 17.1 Temple of Olympian Zeus (Acropolis in the font). Source: Image owned by the authors 210
Image 17.2 The famous statue of Zeus in Olympia. Painting made by Quatremère de Quincy. Source: https://commons.wikimedia.org/wiki/File:Le_Jupiter_Olympien_ou_l%27art_de_la_sculpture_antique_1.jpg 212
Image 18.1 The Opisthodomos of the temple of Athena at the Parthenon in Acropolis. Source: Image owned by the authors 224
Image 19.1 *Hoplite phalanxes* clashing with each other. Chigi vase. Source: https://commons.wikimedia.org/wiki/File:Detail_from_the_Chigi-vase.jpg 233
Image 19.2 An *hoplite* citizen-soldier. Source: https://upload.wikimedia.org/wikipedia/commons/1/1b/Illustrerad_Verldshistoria_band_I_Ill_094.jpg 233
Image 19.3 One of the authors in the Aigosthena fortress (including towers). Source: Image owned by the authors 234
Image 19.4 *Tetradrachm* depicting Alexander the Great. Kallatis mint, issued in 250–225 BCE. Source: https://www.wildwinds.com/coins/greece/macedonia/kings/alexander_III/BlackSeaHoard_038.jpg. With the permission of Wildwinds.com 239
Image 24.1 Two *pankration* athletes fighting (under the watchful eye of two *hellanodikai*). Source: Image created by painter Vasiliki Demopoulou 277
Image 24.2 Ancient Greek women athletes exercising on various sports. Source: https://commons.wikimedia.org/wiki/File:Casale_Bikini_modified.jpg#/media/File:Armerina.jpg 282

Image 27.1	View of the famous theater of Epidaurus, with the perfect acoustics. Source: Image owned by the authors	303
Image 29.1	Ancient Greek baby feeder. Source: Image created by painter Vasiliki Demopoulou	314
Fig. 30.1	The Athenian political and economic system of governance	318
Fig. 30.2	The Athenian Agora institutional setting	319

List of Tables

Table 6.1	The three levels of good administration of the Athenian public sector	94
Table 6.2	Total number of officials in the public sector in 431 BCE	98
Table 6.3	Athenian budget c. 435–330s (in *talents*)	99
Table 8.1	Public buildings in the Athenian Agora (fifth century)	119
Table 8.2	Various critical points at the port of Ancient Piraeus	127
Table 10.1	Athenian drachma and *obol* subdivisions	149
Table 10.2	Methods of assessing the purity of metal coins in Classical Greece	155

About the Authors

Emmanouil M. L. Economou is an Assistant Professor of History of Economic Institutions at the Department of Economics, University of Thessaly (Greece). He is a member of the Laboratory of Economic Policy and Strategic Planning (L.E.P.S.PLAN) at the same department. He is also a member of the Laboratory of Intelligence and Cyber-Security, Department of International and European Studies, University of Piraeus (Greece).

His research focuses on Economic History, Institutional Economics, History of Economic Institutions, International Political Economy, and Defense Economics. He is the author of 9 books (4 in English and 5 in Greek) and the editor of 2 collective volumes in acclaimed publishing houses such as Routledge, Springer, and Cambridge Scholars Publishing.

He has contributed to the international academic bibliography with 65 scientific papers. In particular, he has contributed with 41 papers in peer review quality academic journals, such as the: *Journal of Institutional Economics* (3), *Defence and Peace Economics* (2), *Sustainability*, *European Journal of Law and Economics*, *Peace Economics, Peace Science and Public Policy* (3), *Economics of Governance*, *Evolutionary and Institutional Economics Review*, *Homo Oeconomicus*, *Journal of Risk and Financial Management* (4), *Journal of Financial Economic Policy*, *Journal of Risk and Control*, *The Journal for Markets and Ethics* (*Zeitschrift für Marktwirtschaft und Ethik*), etc. He has further contributed to the international academic bibliography with 24 papers in English and Greek collective volumes.

He is also a reviewer in the following highly distinguished journals: American Political Science Review, Journal of Institutional Economics, Cliometrica, Public Choice, Peace Economics, Peace Science and Public Policy, Investigaciones de Historia Económica—Economic History Research (EHR), and Journal of Risk and Financial Management. Furthermore, he has 79 publications of Discussion Papers (64 in English, in the IDEAS RePec—Munich International Library and 15 as "ΚΟΙΔΑ" Discussion papers published by the L. E.P.S.PLAN Laboratory). He has participated in 44 International and Greek conferences.

He often writes in Greek newspapers on economic, political, historical, and defense issues.

Nicholas C. Kyriazis combines academic and business experience. He took his diploma and Ph.D. in Economics in Bonn University in Germany in 1979 and had been a visiting Professor at Harvard University with a Fulbright grant and at Trier University, respectively.

He is a Professor Emeritus at the Department of Economics, University of Thessaly, Greece, where he also served as a Chairman during the 2013–2015 period. He has published 17 academic books in English or Greek language, 62 papers in distinguished international refereed academic journals (such as the *European Journal of Law and Economics*, the *Journal of Institutional Economics*, *Defence and Peace Economics*, *Theory and Society,* and *Economics of Governance*) and 30 papers in book chapters (collective volumes).

In 2005, the President of the French Republic honored him with the France's highest decoration, the Knight of the Legion of Honor (*Chevalier de la Legion d'Honneur*) for his contribution to European integration and the preparation for the EMU as a member of the Delors-Moreau committee. He has also published many articles in journals for a wider audience and articles in the Greek press, for economic, political, and defense issues.

Previous business positions he held include (among others): Directorate General for Research of the European Parliament, advisor to the government of the National Bank of Greece, advisor to the Minister of Finance, and advisor to Minister of Defense, and he has contributed as one of the major consultants for the Greek Command, Control, Communications, Computers and military Intelligence (C4I). He was also General Secretary of the National School for Public Administration of Greece. He is currently a Vice-Chairman of the Quality Assessment Committee of the Legislative Drafting Process of the Hellenic Parliament.

Chapter 1
Introduction

Abstract This introductory chapter explains the purpose of the book and its organization. It introduces the reader to the main theme of the book: an attempt to "revive" the way of life in Ancient Athens of the second half of the fourth century BCE. It explains why this is useful and interesting not only from an (economic) historian's perspective, but also from those scholars and interested readers (in general) who wish to find answers in questions such as what system of governance is democracy, which is the nexus between democracy and economic performance, how democracy functioned in Classical Athens, and if and how can modern economic policymakers be inspired by the functioning of the Athenian political and economic institutions for improving the current institutional setting regarding governance. This introductory chapter further provides a brief description of the variety of the issues that are discussed and analyzed through the book.

Everyday Life in Classical Athens: A Socioeconomic Analysis comes as a continuation of our research, for approximately 30 years in total, on various aspects of Ancient Greece (economic and political organization, issues of democratic institutions, federalism, strategic behavior and war, etc.) through various books and published papers in international scientific journals and collective volumes.[1]

The idea of writing this particular book was triggered by our friend and colleague at the University of Piraeus (Department of Economics) Professor Anastasios Karayiannis who passed away prematurely, in 2013. This is the reason why the book in hand is dedicated to him. A. Karayiannis also made the initial research with a

[1] A part of this work on related topics is provided in the Reference list. The interested reader may also visit the following links for a more detailed overview regarding our contributions on the field:
https://mycloud.econ.uth.gr/s/sF7gcjbEjB3fAPJ
https://scholar.google.com/citations?user=n51vZYcAAAAJ&hl=en
https://www.researchgate.net/profile/Emmanouil-Economou
https://ideas.repec.org/e/pec39.html
https://www.researchgate.net/profile/Nicholas-Kyriazis
In addition, Nicholas C. Kyriazis is the author of various historical novels related to Ancient Greece. His novels, *The Shield* and *Last Love*, listed in the References section, have been translated and published in English under the pen name Nicholas Snow.

E. M. L. Economou, N. C. Kyriazis, *Daily Life in Classical Athens*, Frontiers in Economic History, https://doi.org/10.1007/978-3-031-58541-8_1

selection of information regarding the ancient literature. Additional selection of information from primary and secondary sources was of course much further elaborated by us at a later time during the synthesis of the book.

In this book we attempt to "reproduce" the way of life in Ancient Athens of the second half of the fourth century BCE. We focus on this period because at that time the political and economic institutions of democracy had become more mature, efficient, and functional, increasing the well-being of the polis's citizens, *metics*,[2] and slaves.

The difference of this book from previous ones on relevant topics is that it addresses both to the general public and to experts. It is divided into 28 chapters that cover a multitude of socioeconomic activities related to the functioning of the Athenian state (the Athenian *polis*) at that time. Each chapter in the first subsection begins with a "Scene" that is a short narrative which includes fictional characters that perform various activities of socioeconomic nature in the context of the Athenian polis, such as banking. Then, each of these small-length "Scenes" is followed by an elaboration based on the issues raised in the narrative. This explanatory analysis is of course made abiding by scientific writing standards.

Under such a way we attempt to revive the Athenian daily life of the times, by combining academic analysis with short narrative stories that describe situations and the relative socioeconomic institutions that applied at the times. These small "scenes" or "episodes" function as "snapshots" from the life of a well-to-do Athenian, the banker Nicomedes and his family.

In particular, in Scene 1, as analyzed in Chap. 2 (Sect. 2.1), Nicomedes and his family are introduced. Thus, each chapter begins with a 'scene', that is, a short fictional story (e.g., in Sect. 2.1), which is explained and further elaborated in the subsections that follow (2.2–2.6) with scientific analysis.

In Scene 2 in Chap. 3 the wife of Nicomedes, Hegeso is presented as the manager of the house, the so-called *oikos*, while in Scene 3 (Chap. 4), she, her daughter Eriphyle, and their female slave Chariclea prepare to welcome a couple to their *oikos*, where the man is a commercial partner of Nicomedes. In Scene 4 (Chap. 5), Nicomedes is presented to associate with magistrates of the local municipality to which he belongs, while in Scene 5 (Chap. 6), he associates with various members of the Athenian public administration. Scene 6 (Chap. 7) presents the turbulent life of Chariclea.

In Chap. 8, a merchant from Iberia, Xenocrates, is presented, who becomes active in the Athenian Agora, the area where market transactions were taking place, while in Chap. 9, Nicomedes offers Xenocrates a meal in his household as a way to express hospitality, where they discuss various matters, mostly of economic nature. Chapter 10 presents Nicomedes, his trusted slave Ischomachos, and Xenocrates discussing banking issues and how the Athenian "monetary policy" works in practice. Chapter 11 presents a typical day at Nicomedes's bank, followed by an analysis of

---

[2] *Metics* were alien residents of Athens. They relocated in Athens for work purposes. Most of them were Greeks, originating from other city-states. For the social status of *metics* and slaves we provide further analysis in Sect. 3.5.

the banking system of the times and the set of institutions based on which it functioned. Chapter 12 presents an auction procedure regarding the silver mines at Laurion.

In Chap. 13, an Athenian citizen, Nausinicus is presented as a *liturgist* and *trierarch*,[3] while Chap. 14 presents the wholesale purchase of products of the merchant Xenocrates from the large Athenian "international" market of the times. The next Scenes in the following three chapters present various financial institutions that had been established in the city-state of Athens such as insurance, lending at an interest rate, bottomry loans, and "credit sales." Chapter 16 provides evidence regarding shipbuilding and a voyage preparation of a commercial ship.

Chapter 18 presents a symposion that concerns a discussion with politicians and philosophers about the future of the Athenian *polis*.[4] This symposion lays out a fantastic scene, which however is based on true facts, regarding a proposal by Lycurgus, a famous Athenian statesman of the times, toward the economic reform of the Athenian public financial management. It is a historical fact that Lycurgus, together with his predecessor, Eubulus, being both high-ranking officials entrusted with the implementation of the (annual) Athenian fiscal policy, succeeded in making the Athenian economy achieve an impressive economic recovery and growth for the years 354–322 BCE during their tenure. We describe in detail how this happened.

In Chap. 19, Nicomedes is presented as a *trierarch* in the navy and as *lochagos* ("captain") in the *hoplite phalanx*, the major land army of Classical Athens and almost every other Greek state of the times. In Chap. 20, a special day in the Athenian Assembly of Citizens (known as the *Ecclesia of the Demos*) is presented, concerning the very crucial issue of choosing peace or continuation of the war against the Kingdom of Macedon under Philip II, which after the defeat of the Athenians and their allies at Chaeronea in 338 BCE became the mightiest Greek state of the times in military terms. The basic proponent of peace was Lycurgus.

Chapter 21 presents the purchase of a new beautiful female slave for assisting Chariclea as well as for providing sexual pleasures to the son of Nicomedes, Nicandros who has just returned home after finishing his military duty in one of the nearby fortresses of Attica. Chapter 22 presents a symposion, a banquet for Nicandros and his friends, where the customs and the attitudes toward love and sex of the Athenians are illustrated, while in Chap. 23 Neaera and her daughter, two famous *hetaerae* (courtesans) of the times, are presented offering their services by pleasing the symposion participants, and primarily Nicandros.

In Chap. 24, Nicandros is shown recovering at his *oikos* after being hit by an opponent in a *pankration* athletic contest held in a private arena. This chapter also provides evidence regarding the health system of Athens and connects this discussion by seeing Athens as (probably) the first ever state where social welfare policies

[3] The performer of the so-called *liturgies* was called *liturgist*. *Liturgies* constituted a kind of taxation imposed on the richest Athenians and *metics*. See further in Chap. 13.

[4] *Polis* (in plural, *poleis*) literally means "city" in Greek. It also meant the body of citizens under a city's jurisdiction. In modern times, the term is normally used to refer to the ancient Greek city-states, related to democratic regimes, such as Classical Athens. Robinson (2011) presents an extended catalogue of democratic city-states during the Classical period.

were provided in practice to the benefit of its citizens. Chapter 25 presents Nicomedes and his family to participate in the Great Panathenaea, the great religious and social celebration of the polis. Scene 25 describes the ritual of the marriage of Eriphyle, with Leosthenes, the latter great general of Athens during the Lamian War of 323 BCE.

In Chap. 27, Nicomedes is presented as *choregos*, that is, the financier (sponsor) of the theatrical works for the Great Dionysia festival (to honor the God Dionysus), and in Chap. 28, he is presented as one of those magistrates who judged the dispute between Demosthenes and Aeschines, which led to famous speeches, *Against Ctesiphon* by Aeschines and the responsive *On the Crown* by Demosthenes, of which especially the latter (of Demosthenes) is considered a masterpiece of rhetorical art.

Finally, in Chap. 29, Nicomedes and Hegeso are shown going up to the Acropolis to worship the famous statue of the goddess Athena at the Parthenon temple and then to muse from there at dusk.

Mainly thanks to the speeches of the orators during the period 340–330 BCE that our book refers to, i.e., toward the end of the Classical Period, that is, the period between 508 and 323 BCE, we know much more about the daily life of the Athenians, the *metics*, the slaves who lived permanently, as well as the foreign merchants who lived temporarily in the famous polis, compared to the previous century. The speeches of the orators help us "reconstruct" the functioning of the Assembly and the other state institutions as well as the popular courts.

In principle, our main arguments are based on a synthesis of evidence which derives from (i) the findings of modern literature (based on a number of publications in various books, scientific articles in journals and collective volumes), (ii) ancient sources, and (iii) evidence from inscriptions found. We then combine this evidence with economic analysis and behavioral science theory, where possible, and arrive at our own conclusions.

It should be noted that one of the most difficult tasks we had to deal with in this new book was the proper synthesis of the available information which was scattered on a plethora of ancient and modern sources. Then, this information had to be analyzed and assessed accordingly and then placed at proper points throughout the book so as to function as a coherent and integrated whole.

Another challenging task we faced was to trace the appropriate degree of using the interpretive tools of modern research, so as to interpret ancient phenomena, under an institutional economics perspective. In fact, there is an ongoing debate in the international bibliography concerning the degree that modern interpretative tools of economic analysis can be used to explain the functioning of ancient economies. Previous research such as Engen (2010), Lyttkens (2013), Bresson (2016a), and von Reden (eds.) (2022) and the recent book of Economou (2024) provide an extensive analysis regarding the limitations and potentialities of performing research under such a perspective.

In such a context, inevitably, our analysis is connected to the so-called *primitivists* vs *modernists* debate regarding the status of the ancient economy, which is dated back to the so-called Bücher-Meyer controversy. Karl Bücher, historian and economist, and advocate of the *German Historical School*, viewed the ancient Greek economy as small-scale, lacking sophistication, reliant on home production, and practicing self-sufficiency at the city-state level. By contrast, Edward Meyer, a proponent of (British) economic liberalism, considered it as complex in its organization and structure—in many aspects, comparable to contemporary advanced economies (Bresson 2007, 2014, 44–45, 2016a).

The *modernist* view, which continues the tradition of Meyer, argues that free-market economic principles and concepts derived from Classical and Neoclassical Economics, if treated cautiously, can be used for the correct interpretation of the functioning of the ancient Greek economy.

Engen (2010, 5) adds that the debate between "primitivists" and "modernists" in the late nineteenth century and early twentieth centuries morphed into the opposing camps of "substantivists" and "formalists." A significant reason for this dichotomy should be attributed to the work of Karl Polanyi in the 1940s and 1950s, culminating in the wide acceptance of the primitivist-substantivist "model" proposed by Finley (1973). However, Engen (2010) notes that during the last decade of the twentieth century and the first decade of the twenty-first century, a plethora of studies have put into doubt Finley's model into question and that we have to acknowledge that the ancient Greek economy was much more complex and dynamic than previously realized.

In fact, there is a plethora of modern evidence that advocates that the Athenian (and the ancient Greek in general) economic institutions were much more advanced than what was thought in earlier times by (mainly) Marxist-oriented historians such as Finley (1973, 1983, 1985), Austin and Vidal-Naquet (1980), and de Ste Croix (1981), who like Bücher accepted the primitivist view regarding ancient Greek and the Roman economy by extension.

According to Reibig (2001) the *primitivists* vs *modernists* debate remained inconclusive. However, Economou (2024) explains that the majority of scholars in the last 30 years have convincingly argued that the Athenian state implemented in practice much more advanced economic institutions than the *primitivists* thought. A literature review on the debate is provided by Finley (1979), Reibig (2001), Bresson (2007, 2016a), Tridimas (2019), and Economou (2024), among others. For the corrective view in favor of the "modern structures" that characterized the ancient Greek economy, important contributions are provided by eminent authors such as Andreades (1933), Rostovtzeff (1941 [1953]), Cohen (1992), Figueira (1998), Amemiya (2007), Bitros and Karayiannis (2006, 2008, 2010, 2013), Ober (2008, 2011, 2015a, b), Engen (2010), Lyttkens (2010, 2013), Bresson (2016a, b), Harris et al. (2016), O' Halloran (2018), Leese (2021), von Reden (ed.) (2022), and our own.[5]

[5] See again the related links we provide in ftn. 1, as well as various relative contributions of us in the field, which are presented throughout this book and in the reference list, such as Arvanitidis and Kyriazis (2013), Economou (2020, 2023, 2024), Economou et al. (2015, 2021a, b, 2022a, b), Economou and Kyriazis (2015a, b, c, 2016a, b, 2017, 2018a, 2019a, b, c, 2021a, b, 2022a, b), Halkos and Kyriazis (2010), Halkos et al. (2021, 2022), Kyriazis and Zouboulakis (2004), Kyriazis

This is also verified by the papers of two recent collective volumes: *The Cambridge Companion to Ancient Greek Economy* edited by S. von Reden (2022), and the earlier excellent collective volume with the title: *The Ancient Greek Economy: Markets, Households and City States*, edited by E. M. Harris, D. M. Lewis, and M. Woolmer in 2016.

Furthermore, a plethora of modern authors convincingly argue that the *New Institutional Economics* (NIE) methodological approach as a branch of economic analysis presents great potential in efficiently interpreting ancient economies with modern theoretical concepts. For an analytical discussion on this, one can read, among others, Frier and Kehoe (2008), Bresson (2016a), Gauthier (2022, 295), von Reden (ed.) (2022), and Economou (2024). Lyttkens (2013) adds that the application of the NIE in the case of the Athenian democracy is a very good methodology for three main reasons: (i) it helps explain what went on in ancient times, (ii) the lessons from the past regarding *institutional change* are often applicable to the modern world, and (iii) we can learn more about the potential and limitations of economic theory. Von Reden and Kowalzig (2022, 347–348) add that:

> Over the last twenty years, New Institutional Economics (NIE) has been a highly influential model in the study of the Greek and Roman economy... NIE approaches have changed the agenda of ancient economic history. NIE has sidestepped the long-standing conflict between 'primitivist' arguments of economic stagnation and 'modernist' views of market development and replaced it with a shared focus on the complex mechanisms of economic processes relative to local institutional arrangements. Crucial for this turn has been its focus on institutions, that is, above all, social norms and legal frameworks.... We suggest that NIE offers a fruitful conceptual matrix for asking new questions—with or without the answers necessarily staying within the NIE model.

Following this current trend, this book analyzes various aspects that are related to the daily economic life of the Athenians during the last sub-period of the Classical times, under an economic analysis perspective through the lenses of NIE.

What is also important is that, from the very beginning, we declare that this book does not argue that the status of institutions in the last period of Classical Athens such as property rights, banking services, or insurance contracts had exactly the same function as nowadays. We could be accused of being victims of *historical anachronism* on this basis, that is, chronological inconsistencies regarding how one interprets people, events, language terms, and customs from different periods. By contrast, this book supports that institutions which form the basis of the capitalist structure of modern societies also existed in Greek antiquity, even if in practice they were applied in simpler forms compared to nowadays.

Furthermore, this book accepts the very essence of three very important contributions, those of T. Amemiya's (2007) *Economy and Economics of Ancient Greece*, C.H. Lyttkens' (2013) *Economic Analysis of Institutional Change in Ancient Greece*, and E.M.L. Economou's (2024) *Economics in Classical Athens: Organization, Institutions and Society* who convincingly argue that **economic analysis and**

(2006, 2007a, b, 2009, 2012), Kyriazis and Metaxas (2010), Kyriazis and Karayiannis (2011), Kyriazis and Economou (2013, 2015a, b, 2019, 2021), and Kyriazis et al. (2014).

modern methodological tools and concepts on economics can be applicable to the case study of Ancient Greece. Tridimas (2013, 2020), Acton (2014), Bergh and Lyttkens (2014), O' Halloran (2018), Bitros et al. (2020), Izdebski et al. (2020), Leese (2021), and von Reden and Kowalzig (2022), among many others, accept this approach by providing further supportive and persuasive arguments. Bresson (2016a, 345) characteristically writes that:

> ....Economic analysis allows us to account for a number of phenomena observed in ancient Greece that cannot be explained using only the theoretical tools available at the time. However, one must not neglect the question of the form taken by discourse on foreign trade in the Greece of the city-states.....

For the synthesis of the book, we made use of more than 400 bibliographic references, cited at various points throughout the book. These references are not exclusively historical ones. Many of them are related to various disciplines of economic analysis such as economic history, NIE, international political economy, and behavioral economics. This is due to this book giving special emphasis on how the economic institutions of the Athenian democracy functioned in practice and how they shaped the society's preferences, attitudes, and behavior as a whole.

We try to describe the daily life in Athens, from the point of view of an Athenian of the times, with his/her own manners and customs, beliefs, and perceptions, which are often different from ours on a plethora of issues, such as the social status of women, slaves, etc. This was also the most difficult part of our book. And we hope that we did this cautiously so as to avoid the problem of *historical anachronism*.

We emphasize on issues of socioeconomic and cultural life, which have been less discussed in other books. We also argue that modern democracies still have much to learn from the ancient and especially the Athenian one. For example, according to C.H. Lyttkens (2013, 3) which applies modern NIE methodologically, in order to interpret the political and economic events of Greek antiquity:

> By focusing on ancient Athens we can look into the mechanisms that produced a remarkable male democracy, made it successful and kept it going for more than a century. We can contemplate the interaction between **institutional change and economic development. We will see the value of an economic rational-actor framework** (emphasis by the authors) that helps explain what might otherwise appear as a set of divergent developments. The archaic and classical periods in ancient Greece are fascinating in that **seldom in human history has the pace of change been so dramatic** (emphasis by the authors). The outcomes have wielded a long-lasting influence, in particular on Western society and how that society views itself. Ancient Greece is also a magnificent laboratory for those interested in economic and political institutions....

From the whole analysis of our book we consider that we can draw a basic conclusion: Athens, after the second phase of the Persian Wars (480/479 BCE), essentially evolved into an informal hegemon among its numerous allies,[6] but most

[6]According to Figueira (1998, 52) the Athenian Alliance, known also as the Delian League, comprised more than 316 members states, with Athens being the leader and hegemon among them. See also Figueira and Jensen (2019) for the mechanisms, the financing, and the morality of Athenian hegemony in the fifth and fourth centuries BCE.

importantly, it gradually became "a school and a pioneer of the politico-economic and institutional changes and developments of all Greece," as Thucydides claims (*History*, 2.41.1-4).[7] The tendencies and the behavioral procedures that prevailed in Athens significantly influenced the respective tendencies and practical actions in the rest of the Greek world of the Classical period, as happens nowadays with the USA and its allies around the globe.

Perhaps the most crucial qualitative elements regarding the success of the Athenian democratic paradigm were a combination of values related to:

- The development of advanced financial institutions for the times that went hand in hand with the general rise of economic prosperity of the Athenian polis and the well-being of its citizens
- A well-functioning *direct democratic* system of governance[8]
- The operation of state institutions under the rule of law[9]

In modern times, the great American President Abraham Lincoln in a speech on November 19, 1863, in Gettysburg to commemorate the fallen at the famous Battle of Gettysburg in the American Civil War (July 1–3, 1863) described this type of governance as "Government of the people, by the people, for the people." In accordance to this, the "father of victory" of World War II, Sir Winston Churchill, while being himself an advocate of the ideals of freedom through the model of British parliamentarism, before the outbreak of World War I did not avoid admitting that:

> It is well that the democratic nations of the world—the nations ... where the peoples own the Government and not the Government the people—should realize what is at stake. The French, English and American systems of government by popular election and Parliamentary debate ... are brought into direct conflict with the highly efficient imperialist bureaucracy and military organization of Prussia. That is the issue ... no sophistry can obscure it. (Quinault 2001, 205)

On December 1941 speaking in the US Congress, he confirmed again his belief on Lincoln's relative motto, when he argued that:

> I was brought up in my father's house to believe in democracy. 'Trust the people' that was his message ... Therefore I have been in full harmony all my life with the tides which have flowed on both sides of the Atlantic against privilege and monopoly and I have steered

[7] We elaborate on this, among others, in Kyriazis and Zouboulakis (2004), Kyriazis (2007b), Kyriazis and Metaxas (2010), Kyriazis and Karayiannis (2011), Kyriazis et al. (2014), Kyriazis and Economou (2015a), Economou and Kyriazis (2019a, 2022a), Halkos et al. (2022), and Economou (2024).

[8] See, among others, Manville and Ober (2003), Ober (2008), Cartledge (2018), and us in Economou and Kyriazis (2019a) on this. The Athenian democratic institutional setting regarding decision making was different in comparison to the current parliamentary/Western-type democracies.

[9] See, among others, Lanni (2006) and Harris (2013) on this.

confidently towards the Gettysburg ideal of 'government of the people by the people for the people (*ibid.*, 201).[10]

But rearranging the terms, what does it mean in practice, "government of the people, for the people, by the people"? It means that the Athenian citizens were "masters of themselves" and that political decisions were not determined by organized elites from behind the scenes, backstage or not, and lobbies or minority groups behind organized state administration mechanisms, according to the definition of Max Weber ([1922], 1978), including political parties. Thus, any kind of "elite paradigm," or "democratic elitism" according to the definition of Putnam (1976) among others, was not accepted according to the ancient Greek democratic ethos and practices. Phenomena of corruption or the creation of organized minorities that could "capture" the democratic institutions and public administration, what is known nowadays as *regulatory capture*,[11] was almost impossible to happen. In ancient democracies, limited access political groups were not allowed to pursue the interests of their members as if democracy were based on hereditary oligarchies or what is known as "bureaucratic elites" as defined through the seminal contributions of Robert Michels,[12] Max Weber, and Robert D. Putnam, among others.

Diamond (2007, 119), whose research has focused on issues on democratization, has wisely described these degenerative trends regarding the quality of democracy nowadays:

> There is a specter haunting democracy in the world today. It is bad governance-governance that serves only the interests of a narrow ruling elite. Governance that is drenched in corruption, patronage, favoritism, and abuse of power. Governance that is not responding to the massive and long-deferred social agenda of reducing inequality and unemployment and fighting against dehumanizing poverty. Governance that is not delivering broad improvement in people's lives because it is stealing, squandering, or skewing the available.

And of course, there was no "professionalization of politics" as is the case of today's parliamentary democracies worldwide. In other words, the ancient Athenian democrats felt that their actions had an impact on both themselves and their fellow citizens, and this made them more aware, conscious, and responsible before selecting between different policies or proposals in the Assembly. For this reason, Manville and Ober (2003) characterize Athens as a "Company of Citizens" because

---

[10] For these sayings from Churchill's speeches on the quintessence of democracy, see among others Quinault (2001).

[11] *Regulatory capture* refers to a form of corruption of authority that occurs when a political entity, policymaker, or regulator is co-opted to serve the commercial, ideological, or political interests of a minor constituency, such as an ideological group. This theoretical concept is a branch of *public choice theory* and is mostly related to the *economics of regulation*. See Stigler (1971), Laffont and Tirole (1991), and Levine and Forrence (1990), among others, on the issue.

[12] Michels (1915) envisaged the famous *iron law of oligarchy* which states that all complex organizations, regardless of how democratic they are, eventually degenerate into "oligarchies." Michels observed that since no large and complex organizations can function purely under a *direct democracy* perspective, power within an organization will always get delegated to individuals within that group, either being elected or not.

it expanded and strengthened the concept of "belonging" to a community (citizens), making this perspective an unbreakable reality. Manville and Ober characteristically write (pp. 82–83) on this that:

> Cleisthenes and his colleagues transformed the existing status of 'being an Athenian.' They gave it deeper meaning, with language and passionate rhetoric celebrating the values of freedom and equality. They also made citizenship more reliable by formalizing the procedure of membership enrollment and certification. In so doing, they were reversing previous aristocratic governance practices based on keeping people in a state of insecurity about their membership in the community The reformers ended the traditional system under which elite rulers could arbitrarily decide who was *really* an Athenian and kill or exile as political enemies anyone they decided was 'un-Athenian.' Now it was not some elite ruler but your fellow citizens as a community who guaranteed for you your status of citizenship. You became a citizen through a vote by the citizens, and no one but your fellow-citizens could ever take citizenship away from you. The formalization of that status created a new and stronger sense of individual security. That in turn allowed for the growth of the deep mutual trust on which a true company of citizens must be built.

In other words, the Athenian democrats believed and wanted to "defend the system" if necessary, under the reasoning of Weingast (1997), precisely because they felt i) that it was really worth for them to participate in political processes, such as the *Ecclesia of the Demos*, the *Boule* (Council of the Five Hundred),[13] the *Heliaia* (popular courts), and the rest of the *archai* (the public administration posts), etc.: (i) because they felt that in practice their participation had a real impact on their lives and (ii) that through this operating framework they could really hope to improve their financial well-being and achieve their social status upgrade.

According to Demosthenes (*Against Neaera*, 59.88) the *demos* of Athens (the Athenian people) was the dominant source of power in the polis under the laws it has set. In *Against Timocrates* (24.152) Demosthenes further argues that the polis is governed according to the laws and the decrees[14] decided by the citizens themselves. In actuality, Demosthenes in the above two passages describes what eminent Nobel Laureate K. Arrow (1950, 339) characterizes as **"citizen's sovereignty."**

Osborne (1985, 9, 10, 20) adds that the polis was in fact the body of the citizens; the citizens were the center of gravity of the polis while at the same time they had political and social interaction within their *demes* (municipalities). The polis embraced the interests of all of them. **It was therefore very difficult to isolate the interests of the citizens from the goals of the polis**. Apathy of the citizens for the affairs of the polis was low, in contrast to modern-day democracies around the globe. A characteristic example is the recent elections in modern Greece (June 25, 2023) where 47% of the voters abstained from the voting procedure. What is

[13] From this point on, we will use the word "Assembly" denoting the Assembly of Citizens / *Ecclesia of the Demos* and the word "Council," denoting the *Boule* / Council of the Five Hundred.

[14] To distinguish between *laws* and *decrees* regarding the political system of governance in Classical Athens, see Schwartzberg (2004) and Canevaro (2018). Lambert (2012) has provided us with an excellent collection of inscribed Athenian Laws and Decrees between 352/1 and 322/1 BCE.

important to bear in mind is that, according to estimations,[15] this apparent lack of interest in participating in the recent elections should be attributed to the fact that they were convinced that there was no longer any point in participating, meaning that nothing would change in their lives for the better. This is of course a very worrying situation that is related to the wider discussion on the quality of democratic institutions and the crisis of parliamentary democracy at a global scale (Barber 2003; Economou et al. (eds) 2022a).[16]

By contrast, in Classical Athens there were no experts in political matters, although a portion of citizens showed more interest in politics than others. That is why the Athenian democracy has justifiably been described by many as the best of all that took place in the history of mankind.[17]

In contrast to the above description, democracy nowadays is based on the indirect participation of citizens on politics through the intermediation of political parties. There is a plethora of authors from various disciplines which argue that, under a specific set of institutions, elements of *direct democracy* for modern societies around the globe are not a far-distant utopia and can be applicable in practice under certain conditions. For example, Altman (2019) argues that citizen-initiated mechanisms of direct democracy can strengthen democracies' normative foundations—freedom and equality among citizens. Altman further demonstrates how citizen-initiated mechanisms of direct democracy empower citizens, defuse violence, and break through some of the institutionalized barriers to accountability that arise in representative systems.[18]

Internet technology and social media with platforms such as Facebook, Twitter, Viber, Instagram, and TikTok have already paved the way so that people around the globe have become familiar with social networking techniques. The idea of an "electronic Pnyx" with the help of information and communication technology (ICT) in political and governance processes should not be considered as an

[15] See: https://blogs.lse.ac.uk/greeceatlse/2023/07/03/the-2023-greek-elections-were-an-exercise-in-disillusionment/

[16] Various authors such as North and Thomas (1973), North (1981), Olson (1982, 1993), North et al. (2009), Acemoglu and Robinson (2013), Bergh and Lyttkens (2014), and Economou and Kyriazis (2019a) have focused on the nexus between efficiency in democratic governance and the quality of the state economic institutions. In Georgiou et al. (2015), we provide a literature review on the nexus between democracy, political stability, and economic performance, while others such as Lauk (2014) and Runciman (2015) connect the crisis of democracy to the various crises that historically occur in the capitalist system.

[17] There is a view among some scholars or political thinkers that in actuality the Athenian democracy was not a true democratic regime due to the fact that women did not have political rights or due to the usage of slaves in the economy, etc. This view, which is related to the quality of democratic governance, can be questioned however for a series of reasons. We elaborate on this issue in Chap. 3 below.

[18] One can consult the works of Barber (2003), Cronin (1999), Fishkin (2011), and the discussion as provided by us, among others, in Economou and Kyriazis (2019a), Bitros et al. (2020), and Economou (2024) regarding this. See further the papers in the collective volume, *Democracy in Times of Crises*, in Economou et al. (2022a).

impossible prospect as various authors have argued so far. Many recent studies that link ITC technology to democracy, such as those of Moreno-Jimenez and Polasek (2003) and Qvortrup (2007), confirm the truth of this view. After all, using the Internet for e-voting on policy issues is already a reality in a wide range of country examples, with many variations.[19] Other authors argue that in modern states where *direct democracy* institutions are applied, economic performance is higher, at least at some degree, with less waste of public money (Feld and Savioz 1997; Cronin 1999; Matsusaka 2005a, b).[20]

The most important component on which the Athenian state was based were the citizens themselves, each one behaving as an individual and at the same time all acting together collectively as a coherent whole, contributing to the (smooth) functioning of the state on its daily actions. And this was the result of the face-to-face Athenian society of the times. De Romilly (1994), Kyriazis and Economou (2015a), and Economou and Kyriazis (2019a) provide an elaboration on this.

Characteristic in this respect is the view of Lucian (*Anacharsis*, 20.1.9) which takes us to the beginning of the sixth BCE century. Lucian presents the views that were in existence at his time regarding the way of educating the youth, through the mouths of the Athenian philosopher, legislator and reformer Solon, and the Scythian Anacharsis, a rather mythical person. Regarding the city-state and the reason for its operation, Lucian writes the following as expressed through the mouth of Solon:

> So you must first hear briefly our views on the polis and its citizens. We do not consider buildings, such as walls, sanctuaries and the *neosoikoi*[21] to be the polis. These are a kind of body, fixed and immovable, to receive and protect citizens. We give all the weight to the citizens, because they are the ones who fill the polis, plan and execute everything and protect it, as the soul is for each of us. (ancient text translated by us)

Contrary to the above views of the ancient and modern philosophers, in modern democracies, including the modern Greek one, parliamentary elites are forced to turn on shaping governing political coalitions, because each separate party simply does not gather the required percentage of vote to rule autonomously. This is a serious sign of democracy in crisis; the peoples around the globe are increasingly turning their backs on these political formations precisely because they believe that, in essence, these parties, in their present form, function more as unions that satisfy the interests and preferences of their group members or their *political clients* as against the interests and preferences of the people as a whole.[22] Phenomena such as *regulatory capture*, the inefficient bureaucratic structure of the public

[19] https://en.wikipedia.org/wiki/Electronic_voting_by_country

[20] For arguments for or against introducing *direct democracy* mechanisms of governance nowadays, see also Zittel and Fuchs (eds) (2007), Bitros et al. (2020), and Economou et al. (2022a).

[21] *Neosoikoi* were naval shipsheds for the purpose of maintenance and safekeeping the Athenian warships, when they did not operate at sea, as for example happened during the winter. See further in Sect. 8.5.

[22] *Clientelism* is another serious corrosive problem regarding the quality of modern democracy nowadays. It is related to political support by individuals or groups of people, often involving implicit or explicit *quid pro quo* procedures.

administration, and *clientelism* as defined above, as well as *democratic elitism*, *democratic deficit*, the *principal-agent problem*,[23] *rent-seeking*,[24] *information asymmetry*,[25] the undue influence of *special interests and pressure groups*,[26] and, of course, Arrow's (1951) *Impossibility Theorem*,[27] are all related to the so-called crisis of democracy, around the globe nowadays, which is a *parliamentarism* crisis in principle.

Regarding the issue of *democratic deficit*, which is of course directly related to the crisis of democracy, Barber (2003, ix–x) in the 20th edition of his provocative book *Strong Democracy: Participatory Politics for a New Age* characteristically argues that:

> The democratic deficit that was becoming apparent in the 1970s has become far more widespread, both within the United States and beyond its shores. The number of nominal democracies has continued to increase—which nation does not today affect to call itself a democratic regime?—but the number of nations in which democracy is seriously practiced remains restricted and cannot even be said with conviction to always include the United States.

In contrast to nowadays, the epicenter of the developments in the democracies of antiquity was the citizen himself as an individual who operated as an active component of the politico-economic system in favor of the public interest. North et al. (2009) characterize such a society as an *open access society*, which in a nutshell means the creation of economic and political organizations and structures that favor fair competition between individuals acting individually or collectively, which makes such a society more developed and prosperous in the long run. More specifically, such societies are characterized by:

- Free access to economic, political, religious, and educational activities for all citizens providing that they meet a number of formal requirements
- The fact that the state supports organizational structures open to all citizens

---

[23] According to the great father of the American nation Benjamin Franklin the interests of the citizens are aligned with those of the politicians who govern them very rarely, something that is also confirmed by A. Downs (1957) in his important work *An Economic Theory of Democracy*. Franklin (2005, 87) writes characteristically:

> Few in public affairs act from a meer view of the good of their country, whatever they may pretend; and, tho' their actings bring real good to their country, yet men primarily considered that their own and their country's interest was united, and did not act from a principle of benevolence

[24] Such a situation occurs when an entity seeks to gain additional wealth without any reciprocal contribution. It is often related to government-funded social services and social service programs. See Krueger (1974) and Tullock (1989).

[25] *Asymmetrical information*, as defined by the seminal work of Akerlof (1970), happens in situations where some parties have more information regarding an issue than others. It is considered a major cause of market failure. For the implementation of this concept in the case of Classical Athens, see Economou and Kyriazis (2022a).

[26] Olson (1965, 1982) has explained how concentrated and well-organized interests are able to use the political process for their benefit, at the expense of larger groups that are less well-organized.

[27] This theorem in short states that a clear order of voter's preferences cannot be determined while adhering to mandatory principles of fair voting procedures.

- The rule of law being impartial to all citizens
- Only the state having a monopoly on the exercise of coercive persuasion (even if through the use of force)

For North et al. (2009) such structures characterize modern societies while from the past they singled out the cases of Classical Athens, Rome (before it became an empire), and the Renaissance states of Northern Italy. In these case studies we could add, among others, the ancient Greek democratic federations, with the Achaean and the Aetolian Leagues being the most characteristic cases of all of them,[28] as well as the Old Swiss Confederacy (1291–1798 AD), the United Provinces (Dutch Republic), and England since the sixteenth century onward (Kyriazis et al. 2018; Economou and Kyriazis 2019a). Throughout this book, elements of *direct democracy* and *open access society* emerge.

In this book, we consciously chose to present fictional scenes that strongly link the element of economic activity with various aspects of the Athenian social life. An important element regarding this book is the nexus between democracy as a political process and economic prosperity. We argue that the success of the Athenian politico-economic regime of the times should be attributed to the inseparable intertemporal nexus between:

- Political stability and political freedoms through democratic governance
- Economic freedoms and market type of economic institutions and practices (even if in a primordial form)
- The rule of law

We have interpreted this nexus as *economic democracy* in Kyriazis and Zouboulakis (2004) and Kyriazis (2007a, 2009), a term adopted also by Patriquin (2015, 82) who states that:

> If Athenian democracy teaches anything it is that struggle for relative equality on the 'material plane' is essential if we are to move beyond forms of public decision-making that disproportionately benefit society's elite. In short, economic democracy is a necessary prerequisite of political democracy. Without the former, the latter cannot exist.....At the height of the democracy, Athenian citizens had their hands on both economic and political power. Today, most citizens have neither economic nor political power. Material resources are increasingly concentrated in a small number of households, and most governments are reluctant to challenge the market 'logic' that fuels this inequality.....

For all the above reasons, we consider that the study of ancient democracy, focusing here on the Athenian one, is always relevant and a beacon for the modern ones. We hope that with the analysis that follows we revive again, to a greater or lesser extent—it is up to the reader to judge it—time, space, and various historical characters and events after approximately 2350 years!

---

[28] For federalism in Ancient Greece, see Larsen (1968), Mackil (2013), Beck and Funke (eds) (2015), Cartledge (2020), and our own in Economou et al. (2015), Economou and Kyriazis (2015a, b, c, 2016a, 2018a), Economou (2020), and Kyriazis and Economou (2021), among others.

Chapter 2
The Athenian *Oikos* and the *Kalos Kagathos* Behavior

Abstract This chapter deals with the organization of the Athenian *oikos*, i.e., the family, the family's property, and the house. It explains the relationships between the family members, such as between parents and children, describing their responsibilities, rights, and obligations. It describes the *oikos* as a laboratory where various types of social behaviors were formed and developed. It also describes the morals of society, by explaining that the highest duty of both the family and society as a whole was to create virtuous citizens who would be imbued by high moral standards, such as honesty, patriotism, and altruism. These morals could ensure a good quality and dignified life for the members of the society as a whole. This chapter introduces us to the general behavioral role models of the Athenians of the time. This is important because it provides an image of the Athenian society and indirectly explains the reasons why the Athenians shaped their economic relations in the ways that can be further explained extensively in the following chapters.

2.1 Scene 1: Nicomedes in His *Oikos*

Nicomedes made his morning routines and went down to the kitchen of his *oikos*, where his wife Hegeso and his daughter Eriphyle were waiting for him, sitting at the table.

Absent from the *oikos* was Nicomedes' son, Nicandros, who served his military duty, the *ephebeia*, as it was called, in the fortress of Rhamnous, near the region of Marathon, at short distance from the sea.

The housemaid, a slave, called Chariclea had set the table for the family's morning quick meal.

Eriphyle, with a smile of satisfaction reflected on her face, rose from the table and kissed her father on the cheeks as soon as he came down the stairs, from the *andron*, and Nicomedes returned a kiss on her forehead.

He marveled at his daughter. At the age of 15 she was gradually changing from a girl to a beautiful woman. They should start thinking about her marriage. He had to confer with Hegeso on this, so as to identify a proper family and a suitable son-in-law. They should have no difficulty, for Eriphyle would be a bride who lacked

E. M. L. Economou, N. C. Kyriazis, *Daily Life in Classical Athens*, Frontiers in Economic History, https://doi.org/10.1007/978-3-031-58541-8_2

nothing: originating from a good family, with a large dowry, and she was beautiful herself.

Eriphyle was already within the usual marriageable age for Athenian women. Nicomedes wished to plan her future prudently, with the help of the gods. In the forthcoming symposia that he would attend, he would take care of finding out which families had unmarried sons, learning about their character, their financial position, seeing them, talking to them, and judging for himself. He loved his daughter, and would like to see her happy, married with a *kalos kagathos* young man of her social position. He would not marry her off to a more mature man, perhaps a widower, or an unattractive youth, as was sometimes done with young women who were not supported by good dowry.

He drank warm milk from the goats they kept in the *oikos* at the back of the yard, ate a boiled egg from their coop which Chariclea had collected in the morning, also bread leavened by herself and baked in their oven, cheese, and finished his short meal with two dry figs. All these products were the production of Nicomedes' estate itself, the size of about a third of a *plethron*.

Enough until the evening meal. After all, if he was hungry, he would buy something from the shops of Agora.

– What are you up to do today? Hegeso asked him

He told her that he was going to settle first some pending matters he had with the *deme*, mainly to pay a municipal fee that he had forgotten, not because he was insolvent, but because his many obligations at his bank filled his thoughts and he simply had forgotten.

Then he would go to the Agora at his bank, for some meetings with some merchants, who were interested in asking him to insure their goods, which then would be transported by sea on a merchant ship for them to be sold in the Kimmerikon, Nymphaion, and Pantikapaion, cities found in distant Kimmeria which was also called Tauris.

Nicomedes told Hegeso that he was planning to invite friends for a new symposion to be held at his *oikos*. He could start by first inviting Lycurgus, a prominent Athenian statesman of the times, and then, some other friends of him.

Nicomedes got up, greeted his wife and daughter by kissing them on the forehead, and left the *oikos*.

It was a beautiful day in early summer, in the month Scirophorion.

He decided to walk to the Agora instead of taking his horse. He was not in a hurry. His associate, formerly a slave and now a freed man, a *metic* called Ischomachos, had set out in the morning, at sunrise, to open the bank which was in the center of the Agora. Ischomachos lived with the family he had created with a former slave, Eudokia, in an *oikos* in another *deme*, not very close to his master's.

The district where Nicomedes lived in the Alopekis *deme* was considered "expensive." It was mainly inhabited by well-to-do Athenians.

Ischomachos had been in the bank's service for 20 years already. He had been chosen and trained by the father of Nicomedes and through the years he had become very experienced and capable. Nicomachos, father of Nicomedes, had freed

Ischomachos 5 years ago, when he had withdrawn from the bank. He handed over the reins to his son and fled for a quieter life in one of his estates in Mesogeia. Ischomachos was now a kind of shareholder in the bank, and a *metic* in Athens.

Perhaps at some point he would acquire the enviable position of an Athenian citizen. The citizen's status to former slaves was given in special cases of high contribution by a *metic* or foreigner to the prosperity of the Athenian polis. Nicomedes would support him and there was some chance that he would succeed, due to the fact that as a slave of Nicomachos and then Nicomedes he had shown great conscientiousness, respected the laws of the Athenian state, was always consistent in his tax obligations, and honored the gods and the customs of the polis, while, and very importantly, he had also participated in the defense of the polis as a rower in a *trireme*. There was, after all, the example of Pasion.

Nicomedes walked from his *oikos* to the Agora.

* * *

2.2 General Notes

The Greek cities of Kimmerikon, Nymphaion, and Pantikapaion were located in distant Kimmeria, also known as Tauris, which coincides with today's Crimea (annexed by Russia since 2014). Pantikapaion was located roughly on the borders of the present-day known city of Kerch in Crimea.

We analyze Lycurgus as a fourth-century eminent Athenian statesman in Sect. 18.1.

Scirophorion coincided with June, according to today's calendar.

We determine Nicomedes' *oikos* at about a third of the *plehtron*. This means that it was about 300 square meters by today's measurement. We return to this discussion regarding the size of the Athenian houses in Sect. 7.3.

For the social status of the *apeleutheroi* (freed men), see further Sect. 3.6.

Our main hero's name, Nicomedes, is a composite word which derives from the words *nike* (victory) and *meidomai* (properly take care of). Thus, Nicomedes is the person who prepares accordingly himself/his army, etc., for achieving victory. Various Greeks like our hero bore the name, such as Nicomedes (458–457 BCE) a Spartan military commander being also a scion of the royal Agiad dynasty, as well as Nicomedes IV Philopator, king of Bithynia from c. 94 to 74 BCE. He was the first son and successor of Nicomedes III of Bithynia.

The name Hegeso, the wife of Nicomedes, is literally interpreted as "she, who leads." At the National Archaeological Museum there is the so-called Grave Stele of Hegeso, dated between ca. 410 and ca. 400 BCE, most likely sculpted by Callimachus, a renowned architect and sculptor of the times. Lady Hegeso was a real person, daughter of Proxenos. We were inspired by her name and we adopted it in our Scenes.

2.3 Family

It is known that the first stimuli for social behavior that a person receives originate from his family environment. The family is not only intended to bring together two individuals of different sexes with the aim of perpetuating the species. Much more than that, a network of obligations and rights of its members is created, based on principles that, in general, apply to the society as a whole. If, for example, the families that come together to form a society have as a principle that the child be freed from its family's bonds when it reaches the age of 15, it is very difficult for every new family that lives within such a social environment not to follow the same principle.

As bonds of blood and the cohesion that is created between the family members are two key family elements, so was also the case with the society built by the Athenians; they were conscious that they were originating more or less, from the same blood ties since they had formed their local *demes* and later their city based on the union of genera or clans that had intermingled. They already knew from the time of the Trojan War and Theseus (mid-thirteenth century BCE)[1] that they were an independent and indigenous society and would have read in Homer's *Iliad* (9.63) the words of Nestor that a society without brotherhood and laws is a voracious society which is constantly in civil wars.

This knowledge of their common past led them to firmly believe that they were, by blood, "genuine children" of the polis, who had been indigenous people and had not come from another place (Demosthenes, *Funeral Speech*, 4–5; Isocrates, *Panegyricus*, 4.24–25). They had fully accepted and trumpeted that they had founded the most ancient city with a native population (Euripides, *Ion*, 29–30, 585–90; Herodotus, *Histories*, 1.56–9, 7.163; Lycurgus, *Against Leocrates*, 83).

In fact, at the end of the sixth century (around 507–505 BCE) Cleisthenes had the brilliant idea to strengthen the political consciousness of his fellow citizens by mixing groups of people, from different socioeconomic classes, professions, and places of residence by creating 10 new artificial *phylae* ("tribes") (Aristotle, *Athenian Constitution*, 20.4, 21.5). That is why there were people from different *demes* belonging to the same genus (Demosthenes, *Against Neaera*, 59.61).

Perhaps, if one wishes to characterize the greatest achievement of the institution of the family in one word, it would be altruism. This innate affinity of one member of the family to another comes either from the unconscious influence of the *consanguineous gene* or is the result of the common effort for survival, or of the feelings of attraction that are progressively developed by symbiosis. The feelings shared by

[1]Contrary to researches which claim that the Trojan War took place around 1100 BCE a large number of scholars believe that these events happened about a century earlier. Ancient Greek writers give a range of dates for the events of the fall of Troy ranging from 1334 to 1150 BCE. A famous mathematician and geographer of the third c. BCE, Eratosthenes estimates that this significant event took place in 1184 BCE, while Herodotus in 1250 BCE. D'Amato and Salimbetti (2011) have estimated these events to have taken place sometime around the end of the thirteenth c. BCE or at the beginning of the twelfth.

family members such as love, interest, and attention are also expressed through altruism toward one another. These expressions are easily amplified and diffused among family members to achieve a common goal.

The Athenians' trust in the ties and nature of the family was the cohesive link of a prosperous and growing polis. Perhaps this was one of the main reasons why the Athenians were very sparing in granting the status of Athenian citizen to non-Athenians. Thus, they did not wish to include in the citizens' lists of the polis new citizens who had not contributed anything (in advance) to its achievements but only wanted to enjoy what others created. Under one sense, they sought to avoid the *free-rider* problem as advocated by modern economic theory and to uphold their principle that **each citizen first has obligations to fulfill ex ante for the polis and then can enjoy what the polis provides**. For this reason, anyone who did not pay his debts to the public lost his political and other rights granted by the polis, while he could not exercise any public duty that might have been assigned to him, for example, being a councilman in the Council of the Five Hundred (see below).

2.4 Parents-Children

The first people a person faces when he/she opens his/her wings for the journey of life are his/her parents, close relatives, and friends. Entering life, even from his/her school days he/she is confronted with other people with whom he/she is forced to express a certain behavior. The Athenians, knowing that for the orderly functioning of their society it was essential to define certain rules, "patterns and protocols of behavior"[2] toward one another, they diagnosed general tendencies caused by the particularity of each person's behavior and pursued through many ways, from persuasion and teaching, to punishment, to direct the citizens to actions that would not create social effervescence and tensions. Parent–child relationships were highly coordinated in (i) maintaining the unity of the family members and (ii) forming a behavior that would benefit the family as a whole, being also useful to the children who were gradually being integrated into the polis's social structures.

In their everyday life, Athenian parents, with the father in the fore,[3] treated their children on the grounds of "congenital obedience" to them. This reduced the parents' anxiety about the dangers their children would face by their participation in social

[2]For the important role that habits, rules, and routines play in shaping human behavior and the course of societies throughout history, see North (1981, 1990) and again Hodgson (1997). Hodgson (1997, 664) recognizes that:

> Rules are conditional or unconditional patterns of thought or behaviour which can be adopted either consciously or unconsciously by agents. Generally, rules have the form: in circumstance X, do Y....

[3]Who was not only responsible before the law for his family but was largely the one who provided the necessities of life.

life, since obedience to their will or advice, they hoped, would act as a deterrent against any such dangers (Demosthenes, *Against Theocrines*, 2).

Children learned from a very early age that they belonged to an *oikos* and due to this they participated in various ceremonies within the *oikos*. They also learned that their behavior and actions had a direct impact on the social standing of their parents and other family members. They had to fully respect their parents and it was frowned upon by society for the child to criticize the father's decisions or actions (Lysias, *Against Philon*). Even in the extreme case where, according to the customs of the Athenians, the child (mainly the son) was at loggerheads with his father, after the latter's death he/she was not allowed to show disrespect to the deceased; he/she was obliged to offer the customary contributions to the deceased. In case his/her father had left a testament, the son/daughter had to accept it (Demosthenes, *Against Boeotus 2*, 40.47). This respect for parents and especially for the father and his decisions may have been a creation of the authority of older males aimed at strengthening the family bond and seems to have been tacitly accepted by the younger family males since they would also be thinking about their own similar situation after some decades.

But beyond these, it seems that the selfish tendency of parents goes even further. Parents' motivation to give birth was also the future financial and other retributive rewards they would expect to receive from their children. The couple wished to have children and mainly boys, since they hoped the latter would take care of them in future needs and illnesses (Xenophon, *Oeconomicus*, 7.12–3). That's why even those who didn't have children of their own made sure to adopt a boy, especially if they had separated from their other relatives such as siblings (Demosthenes, *Against Neaera*, 58–59). From a young age, parents taught their children that those who did not treat their parents with respect and did not meet their material and other needs were socially reprehensible (Lysias, *Against Agoratus*, 91).

To reduce the risk of children rejecting their parents, there was a law that sentenced children to deprivation of their civil rights if they were proven in court to have abused their parents (Andocides, *On the Mysteries*, 1.74). This was a sign of social disrepute which entailed significant implications for the person who did not prove himself in society as a good son to his parents. It is worth noting that those citizens, who had completed their 30th year of life, and were about to serve the polis from some demanding public post, no matter how more or less important was, they went through the *dokimasia* procedure, an evaluation process where the Council of the Five Hundred checked in advance the skills, abilities, and behavior of these candidates and excluded those who did not possess a proper behavior to their parents.[4] The argument for this exclusion was based on the following logic: since a person, while naturally inclined to love his parents, nevertheless does not pay attention to them when they need him, how would it be possible for one to believe that this particular person would respect a more vague entity such as the motherland? (Demosthenes, *Against Aristogiton 1*, 25.66).

[4] We analyze this issue in more detail in Sect. 6.4.

Of course, it cannot be neglected that the desire for children is also a product of a biological imperative (*selfish gene* theory[5]) that makes parents having the anticipation that their life will continue even after death. It is also a conscious decision to avoid loneliness. These motivations would surely affect the mental world of the average Athenian to become a parent. But apart from these, the feeling of ownership was something that was also taken into account in the pursuit of biological continuity, mainly from the side of the man.[6] The father usually prepared a written testament dividing his property among his blood children (Lysias, *Against Diogeiton*, 6).

If there was not a written testament due to a sudden death, the children of a deceased man still inherited his property, an intertemporal practice that still applies nowadays, so that the deceased could be sure that what he had worked hard for would not be lost. There was a law that in strict order of priority defined those who inherited someone. First came his children. If he had sons and daughters, the sons came first with the provision to marry off their sisters by giving them a dowry from the father's property (Demosthenes, *Against Macartatus*, 43.51). Then followed the male close relatives, i.e., the brothers of the deceased, the nephews, etc., according to the descending family relationship by blood (Demosthenes, *Against Leochares*, 44.11–14; *Against Macartatus*, 43.17–18). This was a legal classification of relatives who had claims to inheritance.

In case the Athenians did not have a genuine heir (i.e., their own natural child) they could proceed with the adoption of one. The adopted sons should not waste the property they inherited since they were accountable to the other blood relatives of the deceased. However, the children who were direct biological descendants of a man could dispose of the paternal property they inherited as they wished. The relevant legislation is noted by Demosthenes and probably had existed since the laws of Solon (Demosthenes, *Against Leochares*, 44.49, 44.67–68). But apart from the issue of inheritance, the father usually let his children know about his debtors and creditors before he died as well as for any money he owed to the state (Demosthenes, *Against Timotheus*, 49.42). **If the deceased had debts to the public, these were paid first and then the children took over the inheritance** by accepting any other burdens he had (Demosthenes, *Against Boeotus 2*, 40.22; *Against Callippus*, 17–18). This applied to both male and female relatives. Schaps (1979, Chapter 5) offers several cases of women who had undertaken to pay off debts either of their father or of their husband. The fact that the law recognized such a right is directly linked to the issue of protection of private property, as the law recognized the right of the wife or daughter-in-law to conduct lawful legal financial/commercial transactions on behalf of her relatives.

---

[5]This theoretical concept states that the more two individuals are genetically related, the more sense (at the level of the genes) it makes for them to behave cooperatively with each other. See Dawkings (1976).

[6]We analyze the pivotal role of property rights protection regarding the success of the Athenian economic system in Sect. 11.3.

It is not known whether or not the children had the right not to accept inheritance, as is the case with the current provision of the legislation. Also, the father could divide his property among his children (Demosthenes, *Against Macartatus*, 43.19) as a means of financial support (Lysias, *On the Property of Aristophanes*, 19.40).

2.5 The *Oikos* as a "Laboratory" of Producing Social Behavior

The Athenians had developed an institution, the *oikos*, which was larger than that of the family in the narrow sense, i.e., husbands and children. The *oikos* was an entity made up of people with kinship ties. The *oikos* also included material goods and slaves. It also had a continuity regardless of whether the children had in turn started families of their own. The reference to the ancestral *oikos* was fundamental for the Athenians, who learned from a very early age that their fate was completely connected to the well-being of all the members who made it up.

For example, if the headman of the *oikos*, known as *kyrios*,[7] had to pay a fine to the polis, it would come from the property of the *oikos* as a whole; thus, this affected all members. In general, if any member of the *oikos* did not have the appropriate social behavior or he/she was engaged in illegal acts, this caused a social outcry and the consequences were suffered by the *oikos's* members as a whole (Demosthens, *Against Neaera*, 59.1). On the other hand, if the head of the *oikos* undertook large financial expenditures in favor of the polis, this had a positive impact on all the *oikos* members (Isaeus, *Apollodorus*, 7.32). This mentality resulted in a serious internal control of the actions and behavior of the members of the *oikos*, so that they all behave in a socially acceptable manner, which was the best way to secure the overall affluence of the *oikos* in the long run.

Therefore, the *oikos* was the social group within which the whole life of its members revolved around. The income, risks, and losses of the entrepreneurial and other pursuits of the *oikos* members had a direct impact on its overall prosperity. These entrepreneurial or other activities could also be carried out either inside it or in another area of Attica, even in the silver mines where a member of the *oikos* could potentially work as an entrepreneur (Andocides, *On the Mysteries*, 1.38). Thus, in reality, the *oikos* could also be seen as a self-employed group of individuals operating as a single entity, as producers and consumers.

[7]In Classical Athens, the *kyrios* was the head of the *oikos* being responsible for his wife, children, and any unmarried female relatives. *Kyrios* had to arrange the marriages of his female relatives, prepare their dowries, and represent them in court, if necessary. Ideally a woman's *kyrios* would be first her father and then her husband. Under other circumstances, a son, son-in-law, or a more distant relative might take guardianship. When Athenian women married, their husband became their new *kyrios* (Pomeroy 1995).

2.6 The Social Ethics Behind the *Kalos Kagathos* Behavior

Athenian society in Classical times, due to its relatively small population size, compared to today's chaotic mega-cities worldwide, was considered, more or less, a *face-to-face society*, at least for a period before the significant rise of its population due to the economic growth that took place at various times during this period.[8]

This practically means that there was a high degree of interaction between its inhabitants, and the constant friction between them created the conditions for cultivating values such as trust, companionship, and "same-mindness"—concord among them, known as *homonoia*, but also knowledge about the characteristics of everyone's behavior. Each specific citizen's attitude toward his family or the city was well known by his fellow citizens who were members of the same *phratry* or his neighbors in the area he resided in[9] or as relatives who belonged to the same *deme*. His morals and actions were known to his fellow citizens and it was difficult for him to deceive them when he assumed public office (Bitros et al. 2020; Economou 2024). A key element of the *kalos kagathos* man was *philotimia* (a sense of honor). According to Xenophon (*Oeconomicus*, 14.10), an honorable man was considered one who:

> wants to be praised and honored, and toiled where he should and to risk and abstain from illegal profits

W. Jaeger ([1939], 1967, xxiii) summarizes *kalos kagathos* behavior as:

> the chivalrous ideal of a complete human personality, harmonious in mind and body, foursquare in battle and speech, song and action.

The model of citizen life that the Athenians had formed over time and the experiences they had acquired for the smooth functioning of their society and democracy was well-defined and detailed. They had clearly understood that the good or bad character of an individual was based on the morals, customs, habits, and routines that the individual followed in general, as well as on the laws of the polis as accepted by the larger body of citizens (Demosthenes, *Erotic Essay*, 61.35). For this reason, in the courtrooms, the litigants (either citizens or *metics*) in order to convince the judges to make a favorable decision for them emphasized their earlier honest life based on their character and behavior. The *kalos kagathos* characterization was given to those who showed prudence, bravery, skills through education,

[8] That economic growth was achieved during that period is verified by authors such as Morris (2004), Ober (2008, 2015a), Burke (2010), Tridimas (2013), Economou and Kyriazis (2016b), Harris (2016), O' Halloran (2018), Bitros et al. (2020), Leese (2021), von Reden and Kowalzig (2022), and Economou (2023), among many others. This is also verified by the analysis of this book in the following chapters.

[9] A *phratry* was a group of people within a tribe who had a common ancestor. *Phratries* (in plural) are attested in a wide range of Greek states. Ionian Greeks, including Athenians, conceived this institution as part of their Ionian heritage. Within Athens, *phratries* (in plural) played a prominent role in social and religious life, particularly in the major festival of Apatouria. Only citizens were enrolled in *phratries*.

altruism, and having been engaged in socially acceptable occupations (Demosthenes, *Funeral Speech*, 60.17, 60.27) and were also compassionate and philanthropic in the past. The last two elements laid the foundations of a society characterized by *homonoia* and not by fratricidal conflicts (Demosthenes, *Against Aristogiton 1*, 25.81, 25.89).

It should not escape us that only the Athenians, as Pausanias informs us (*Description of Greece*, 1.17.1), had an altar for mercy in their Agora. Apart from these characteristics, youths to be considered *kaloi kagathoi* should be beautiful not only in body but also in soul, be brave but not brazen, be pleasant when talking, be gentle, and show respect to others (Demosthenes, *Erotic Essay*, 61.1, 61.8, 61.13). These codes of behavior are intertemporal virtues that apply even today (at least, in principle).

The Athenians further proceeded to adopt codes of behavior that would motivate a person to live by these standards. That is why they introduced many incentives for someone to follow this lifestyle. The most important thing was social recognition and reward.[10] In other words, they told a person that if he behaves in this way toward others and the polis, not only will they applaud him, but also honor him and thus he would acquire one of the greatest goods for man; reputation and fame. So much did the Athenians honor fame that, as Pausanias informs us (*Description of Greece*, 1.17.1), they had erected statues in their polis in honor of fame as well as of *aedo* (shame, modesty, respect).

Since the time of Homer and Hesiod one's reputation had been emphasized as his most valuable social characteristic. Hesiod (*Ways and Means*, 763–764) characteristically wrote that the fame is not lost at all, "because fame too is some god." Fame was highlighted by the Athenians not only as a reward for an individual's efforts but also as a means of setting an example for others. Social esteem (honor) was attributed to a person who enjoyed it, under the context of the polis. Within the concept of honor co-existed motivation and reward (Thucydides, *History*, 2.43–2.44). Honor was a reward since social recognition was the most important reward of a successful life.

Xenophon (*Oeconomicus*, 11.1–2) outlines this ideal type of *kalos kagathos*: he should spend his life in the following activities and behavior: He participates in the activities in the market, the Agora, and does not stay at home, he educates his wife excellently (7.2–10) with special teachings, his behavior toward his wife and especially his love of justice act as models for her, he takes care of his property diligently (11.8–9), he has full knowledge of all the working activities that are taking place in his estates (12.18), he trains the *oikonomos* ("steward") of his property to manage it properly, and he sets incentives (reward-punishment) for every worker and slave to increase and improve his performance (12.4–5, 13.11–2). He should also take care of his health (11.11), avoid laziness (11.15), be temperate in eating and drinking, be just in his dealings and decisions (11.22), be honorable and not

---

[10]For a practical implementation of this logic on environmental matters, see Economou et al. (2023). See further the related discussion in the next pages.

avaricious (14.10), not to have a tendency to blame others (11.22), and to practice the art of rhetoric (11.23). He should also refrain from any *banausos* art and occupation such as coppersmiths and dyers because such activities destroy the body and therefore the soul (4.1–3). A *banausos* work, known also as *banausikos*, means "vulgar and 'illiberal' work, mostly related to manual laborers or artisans. Such a situation 'deforms the body or the mind.'" According to Aristotle (*Politics*, 1341 a7, 1337 b7), *banausos* meant "cramped in body" and "vulgar in taste." And of course, no reason for men to help with housework (Aristophanes, *Lysistrata*, 880–885), as is still the case even today around the globe, to a large extent.

In line with the above, the Athenians deliberately set up social incentives to induce individuals to serve various purposes, such as the welfare of their fellow citizens. They never missed an opportunity to constantly recall the great achievements of ancient warriors and heroes, which they mythologized and used as teachings by incorporating them into the works of poets, tragedians, and historians (Demosthenes, *Funeral Speech*, 9). It is as if they were saying, using the words of Lysias (*Against Philon*, 31.30):

> Recall to your minds what reason you can have for honoring those who have proved themselves good servants of the State and for dishonoring those who serve her ill. In either case the distinction has been made not so much for the sake of those who have come into the world, as of those who are yet to come, in order that they may strive to become worthy by studious effort, and in no single direction may attempt to be base.

Also, in various ways the Athenians showed that a man's good reputation (due to his virtuous way of life) was also inherited in children (Lycurgus, *Against Leocrates*, 127). In addition, they erected statues or marble stelae in prominent places in the Agora to commemorate and chronicle acts in favor of the community such as the tyrant slayers Harmodius and Aristogeiton (Lysias, *Against Agoratus*, 13.72).

For great deeds they did not miss an opportunity to recall the contribution of those involved to the prosperity and glory of the polis (Aristophanes, *Knights*, 565–70, 1325–30). Athenians did not only honor the valiant fallen on the battlefields (Thucydides, *History*, 2.34; Xenophon, *Hellenica*, 2.4.17; Lycurgus, *Against Leocrates*, 50) but also the citizens who in any way benefited or glorified the polis such as the Olympian winners (Demosthenes, *Against Theocrines*, 66). To the benefactors of the polis that had been chosen according to strict criteria, the Athenians erected a bronze statue in the Agora and provided them with food for free in the Prytaneion or gave them a *stephanon* (crown) or the *metics* became *isoteleis*, meaning to be taxed under the same status as the citizens (Demosthenes, *On the False Embassy*, 19.330; *Against Aristocrates*, 23.65, 123.145, 23.211; Lysias, *Against Nicomachus*, 30.26–27; *Defence Against a Charge of Subverting the Democracy*, 25.6). This further meant that they were exempted from the *xenikon* tax, which was an extra tax paid by *metics* or foreigners.

The Athenians had as their motto that the *golden crown* of the polis was the most honorific element that an individual could enjoy and not the expensive goods he possessed (Demosthenes, *Against Timocrates*, 24.183; Demosthenes, *Against Androtion*, 22.8; Lycurgus, *Against Leocrates*, 139). The polis crowned those wealthy Athenians who proved themselves *agathoi* (virtuous) citizens and spent much of their wealth in favor of the polis (Isocrates, *Antidosis*, 15.94) and for its glory (Demosthenes, *Against Androtion*, 22.76). In addition, generosity and helping friends was rewarded by society by enhancing a person's good reputation (Demosthenes, *For Phormio*, 36.59). For this reason, the benefits that someone provided to the polis such as financing a *trierarchy*[11] or serving his military duty, etc., were very often emphasized in the courts (see, e.g., Demosthenes, *Against Conon*, 54.44). In accordance with the above, the Athenians were not only interested in their own reputation but also in the one they would leave to their descendants (Thucydides, *History*, 4.18.5; Isocrates, *Panegyricus*, 4.76). There are many such recorded cases, such as the case of someone who tried to illegally usurp his half-brother's name because his father's name was accompanied by a good reputation (Demosthenes, *Against Boeotus 2*, 40.15).

Regarding the *kalos kagathos* behavior in his *Epitaph* (Funeral Speech) (Thucydides, *History*, 2.37), Pericles emphasizes that in Athens everyone lives as he pleases, without anyone, not even the state, interfering in his way of life. His intention to offer his life and defend his motherland is also a matter of personal will.

Social morality was based on the concept of justice which strengthened unity in the polis, while tolerance of injustice harmed it. Generalized morality in the society was expressed by the citizens in various ways. As a consequence, the Athenians believed that the moral standing of citizens was lowered if society praised those who harmed their fellow citizens and their polis, more than its benefactors (Lysias, *For Polystratus*, 20.32). If someone did not have the appropriate behavior, a "social" mechanism of bringing him back to the accepted norms was public outcry which could also include the members of his *oikos* (Demosthenes, *Against Neaera*, 59.1).

The creation of "social ethics" was the goal of the Funeral Speeches, the best known being given by Pericles which became a source of inspiration for later ones such as the "Epitaph" delivered by American President Abraham Lincoln for the dead of the Battle of Gettysburg, on November 19, 1863, during the American Civil War. Funeral Speeches were delivered in late October-early November, i.e., at the end of the annual war season, and women could also attend them. Besides Pericles (Thucydides, *History*, 2.35–2.46) other related speeches included those of Lysias for the dead of the Corinthian War (395 BCE), Demosthenes for Chaeronea, where he also fought (338 BCE), Hyperides on the dead of the Lamian War (322 BCE), and references of Socrates by Plato (*Menexenus*). Demosthenes (*Funeral Speech*, 60.1.) explains the meaning of sacrifice in favor of the society as a whole and for the motherland:

> After the State decreed that those who repose in this tomb, having acquitted themselves as brave men in the war, should have a public funeral, and appointed me to the duty of delivering over them the customary speech, I began straightway to study how they might receive their due tribute of praise; but as I studied and searched my mind the conclusion forced itself upon me that to speak as these dead deserve was one of those things that cannot

[11]For *trierarchy*, see Sects. 13.2 and 13.5–13.7.

be done. For, since they scorned the love of life that is inborn in all men a**nd chose rather to die nobly than to live and look upon Greece in misfortune, how can they have failed to leave behind them a record of valor surpassing all power of words to express?**.....

The Athenians therefore tried with these Funeral Speeches, being public ceremonies, to honor their heroes and to justify their acts of self-sacrifice, so as to motivate others to do the same, if the necessity arose, as well as to console their relatives.

Chapter 3
The Relationships Between Men and Women, and the Social Groups in Classical Athens

Abstract This chapter deals with various important societal issues, such as the relationships between men and women, the social position of women, and who was considered the ideal woman in the Athenian society of the times. It also analyzes which was perceived as the ideal age for marriage between men and women. Furthermore, it also analyzes the roles of *metics* (alien residents who resided in Athens for work purposes) and slaves and concludes with a critical appraisal regarding the functioning of the social relationships within the Athenian society.

3.1 Hegeso: The Manager of the *Oikos*

Shortly after Nicomedes left for the Agora, Chariclea and Eriphyle went upstairs, to the *gynaikonites*, where Hegeso was waiting for them.

– Chariclea sit down!
– I am hearing you ma'am.
– I don't need to tell you about the established ones. You have been doing them with care and diligence for so many years. However, as you know, this evening Nicomedes will host a friend of his, a merchant from Chios at the *andron*, together with another merchant, Athenaeus. They will talk about business and from what he told me yesterday before we went to sleep, the merchant from Chios and the Athenian want Nicomedes to finance the purchase of wine and its transfer from Chios with a loan. The cargo consists a large amount of wine. The transport presents some risk, but as this wine is in high demand, originating from certain famous Chiot vines, it will be sold dearly, and my Nicomedes and the other two merchants aspire to make quite a fortune.
– I wish so mother! Because for my birthday I would like you to buy me that nice blue *peplos* from Artemis's store in the Agora. I really liked it when we spotted it, passing from her store the other day. It is a bit expensive of course...
– This is very expensive, my dear, not just expensive....Hegeso replied.

E. M. L. Economou, N. C. Kyriazis, *Daily Life in Classical Athens*, Frontiers in Economic History, https://doi.org/10.1007/978-3-031-58541-8_3

– Her father has a weakness for her and he will buy it, Chariclea commented and continued:
– And who is this Athenian merchant?

Hegeso focused her gaze on hers and said:

– Epiphanios!
– Oh Gods! answered both Chariclea and Eriphyle spontaneously with an expression of disapproval.
– And he will carry us here this wife of his... Chariclea commented, with her tone of voice suggesting strong reluctance.
– Oh Gods! There is no other gossiper in the Asty like her![1] Eriphyle replied.
– Um, isn't her name Eulalia? Her name means that she 'speaks well', with a fair judgement. But, contrary to this, what that particular Eulalia really does is gossiping all the time, criticized Hegeso ironically.
– Normally she should be called Alalia, Eriphyle commented mockingly. Her mouth should be sewn shut and she should never speak again at all....
– I wish so! Chariclea commented.
– That's exactly why I want you to do your best, added Hegeso. Clean up very well both the *gynaikonites* and the *andron* and prepare the dishes so that when they come, everything should be ready. I don't want to give them an excuse to badmouth me to the other well-to-do ladies in polis.
– Don't worry ma'am! Everything will be as it should be, Chariclea replied.
– As soon as we all return from the Agora, we will immediately get to work.
– Yes, but we should also pass by that shop of Artemis to tell her not to sell that blue veil to anyone else, until my father buys it for me, Eriphyle said, with a tone of anticipation in her voice.
– Your mind always revolves around such things.... On new clothes.... We're getting lost here! Hegeso commented, with a fair amount of exaggeration of course.
– Calm down, my lady! said Chariclea.

Hegeso continued in the same tone:

– Also, Chariclea, prepare our bath, and notify the hairdresser Elpinike, to be here in the early afternoon. And don't forget to take the eggs from the henhouse and milk our new goats, commanded Hegeso.

* * *

[1] In the Athenian polis.

3.2 Relationships Between Men and Women

Athenian society, like most ancient and modern societies, was male-dominated. The ancient Greeks believed that there were natural biological differences between the sexes that decisively determined their distinct roles in society. The male-warrior and the female-nurturer were the dominant roles (see, e.g., Xenophon, *Oeconomicus*, 7.19–20; Aristotle, *Nicomachean Ethics*, 1162a. 23–26).

The Athenians had explicitly clarified the division of tasks in life related to the biological distinction between male and female. Athenian life was dominated by the belief that nature prescribes the abilities and characteristics of the individual while social life perfects them. Therefore, one should do what he/she was created for, so that he/she becomes more efficient and increases his/her pleasure by engaging in activities that satisfy him/her (Plato, *Republic*, 433a). Based on this belief it was justified why men had different duties than women.

The man had the primary responsibility of providing his family with the means of preservation. He was also responsible to defend his motherland against the enemies and try to extend the boundaries of his motherland and its sphere of influence. It should not be overlooked that at that time many military encounters had as their starting point the conquest of new territories and the expansion of the polis' production potential, mainly in agricultural and livestock goods (Xenophon, *Oeconomicus*, 5.7). In the perception of the Athenians and the rest of the Greeks of the times, this justified that the male population was "legitimized" to fully take into their own hands all the political processes and decisions. This does not mean that Athenian women were not considered to be citizens. In many texts they are referred to as citizens of Athens as well, a title not given to *metic* or freed women (Isaeus, *Ciron*, 8.43; Isocrates, *Plataicus*, 14.51; Demosthenes, *Against Eubulides*, 57.43).

The Athenian female citizens, on their part, participated in the various rituals of the polis and were responsible for various religious ceremonies that strengthened their consciousness of their common origin and the sense of distinction from those women who were foreigners, freed, or slaves. The male Athenians, on the other hand, although they were divided into categories according to their income purely for tax reasons, were actively involved in the management and day-to-day operations of their enterprises, whether these were related to agriculture-livestock, land or maritime commerce, or manual work in local workshops. They themselves actively participated in these activities with the help of their slaves or hired workers who were either citizens or *metics* also living in Athens.

Xenophon devoted several chapters in his work *Oeconomicus*, such as in 7 and 8 to describe the duties of men and women, granting the dominant role to the man. He thus expressed the belief of the median Athenian of the times, through the mouth of Critobulus when he informs Socrates that the man must educate his wife in the management of the household by explaining her the ways she should behave inside and outside the *oikos* (Image 3.1).

Image 3.1 Bust of Themistocles as a mature Greek man. Source: https://upload.wikimedia.org/wikipedia/commons/8/87/Beeld%2C_Themistocles_-_Unknown_-_20408396_-_RCE.jpg

Xenophon argued that if the man treats and teaches his wife in an efficient way then he will have a happy *oikos*, but if he does not do this, then his wife will spoil it (*Oeconomicus*, 3, 11). In other words, the man is to blame for what his wife is and does, and as argued by Aristotle (*Politics*, 1254b, 14–16) the man is the ruler and the woman the one who must follow his advice and wishes in the *oikos*. This info is related to codes of behavior in the male-dominated society that existed at that time. Aristophanes further informs us in the *Clouds* the verse tale of Strepsiades with his spoiled well-to-do and spendthrift wife, and his spoiled son who in their folly almost destroyed his *oikos'* budget, filling their household with debt. Here Aristophanes emphasizes the necessity for the woman to be prudent in the management of the household's financial resources.

Perhaps with the excuses that the man holds a shield and defends his *oikos* and the motherland and that he is mainly engaged in securing the livelihood of the *oikos*, he should therefore have the right and the ability to be a citizen and actively participate in making social and political decisions. The woman, who originally lives introverted, was not considered to be entitled for such a role; for this reason her rights as a citizen were represented by a male relative, husband, father, or brother.

The exclusion of women extended to other spheres of social life. The man, because he does not give birth himself, and because he could have doubts about the paternity of the child, took care to establish customs, habits, institutions, and even laws that limited the woman's opportunities to make love with someone other than her husband.

The men had discussed among themselves the argument that the man's polygamy is in accordance with his nature and a sign of his masculinity and it is something positive, while the woman's is a sign of their vanity and estrus, characteristics that only had a negative impact. In this way, they vilified any man who had a wife that others also enjoyed, while they honored the one who kept her for "exclusive use."

Whether or not this comes as men's drive for ownership and power over women, or a mechanism to curb male uncertainty about children and love, it was a concept that dominated Athenian society. That is why the median Athenian woman, at least of the middle and upper class, had her own apartment in the couple's shared *oikos*, known as *gynaikonites*. In principle, she was not allowed to socialize with other men outside their family circle. In the dinners that the men had with each other, the aim was not for different families to get to know each other. Only men participated and not their wives (Lysias, *On the Murder of Eratosthenes*, 1.23) perhaps because they knew that with the gaiety and the flow of wine the passions would be unbridled. That is why they took in their company only slave-women and *hetaerae* (courtesans), where the latter, for a fee, were willing to participate even in orgies, having intercourse with other men as well, even slaves (Demosthenes, *Against Neaera*, 59.24, 59.33–34, 59.48).

A woman's ability to give birth was another male–female dividing point. The Athenians—like most men until recently—believed that it was only the woman's fault if she did not bear children, and it was she who determined the sex of the child. We know how many marital dramas around the world were happening based on this view till recently, which has medically proven to be false and misleading. As we know today, the man is also responsible for fertility and is the one who determines the sex of the child. But at that time this strong prejudice had been so deeply instilled in the society individuals that they had deified fertility with a female gender (Hera, Demeter). Accompanying this fear of men was the message that had been passed on to society that virginity is a key qualification for a woman's marriage. By depriving women of premarital sexual relations, they believed, on the one hand, that they had many possibilities the children to be born would be theirs and thus their property would be bequeathed to a direct blood descendant, and on the other hand, they were not forced to come into sexual competition with others in terms of the emotions women would feel (intensity of sexual pleasure).

They had convinced each other, and probably had convinced their wives too, to consider virginity and her moral behavior, apart from her beauty, of course, as a kind of "dowry" of even the poorest woman (Demosthenes, *Against Neaera*, 59.112). The Athenians had been cultivated with such conviction that virginity was something sacred and essential, especially for women who would be priestesses, although many of the goddesses they believed in, such as, of course, Aphrodite, did not possess such a thing. They made the priestesses in the temples take an oath to the gods with implications for their personal lives and that of their families that they were virgins and "undefiled" (*ibid*., 59.78). The establishment and social acceptance of premarital virginity was also reinforced by the prospective groom's parents for the same reasons, i.e., gene continuation, bequeathing property to immediate blood relatives, and reducing sexual competition. That is why the daughter was married off by her family and especially by her father—although we do not know if her mother played an implicit but important role—preferring a person who enjoyed social esteem and wealth (Lysias, *On the Property of Aristophanes*, 19.12–14; Demosthenes, *Against Boeotus 2*, 40.12).

In his *Oeconomicus*, Xenophon tries to lay down normative assumptions and principles for people toward the ideal life. We read that men should believe that god (i.e., nature) has given human creatures two characteristics that differentiate them according to their sex: boldness in men and affection in women, both sharing equal capacities for memory and care (Xenophon, *Oeconomicus*, 7.22–27).

Despite Xenophon's teachings on a perfect division of labor between men and women according to their physical characteristics, abilities, and temperament, in practice this was not always the case. For example, there are also cases attested where Athenian women with the help of slaves participated even in business activities in the market, such as producing textiles for sale.

In principle, the lady of the *oikos*, with the help of one or more maids, weaved the wool and produced the clothes intended for everyone who lived in the *oikos* (Xenophon, *Oeconomicus*, 7.6, 10.10–11; Plato, *Laws*, 7.805–806; *Lysis*, 208d; Aristophanes, *Lysistrata*, 535–538). Representations on vases depict women engaged in these various activities, which leads us to assume that in the fifth century weaving was still primarily a domestic activity. The situation seems to change at the beginning of the fourth century. Such a change is probably due to the consequences of the Peloponnesian War and the consequent desolation of the countryside, the abandonment of the land, and the search for new sources of income.

The case of Aristarchus, as presented to us by Xenophon (*Memorabilia*, 2.7.), is revealing. Aristarchus who lost his fortune after the end of the war accepts Socrates' advice to employ the women of his family in weaving and sell his products, which he does, now earning a living. The Athenians of the times who had female labor at their disposal, even as slaves, managed to profit from the products of their labor [e.g.,, see Plato (*Alcibiades 1*, 1.126e) and *Lysis* (208d) as well as Aeschines (*Against Timarchus*, 1.97)]. Workshops like that of Aristarchus seem to have increased during the fourth century to meet the increased demand in the market, as shown by a related statement of Plato in the *Republic* in verse 373c.

3.3 The Social Position of Women

In this Scene we introduced Hegeso as a worthy wife who manages her *oikos* efficiently. The position of women in society is obviously a key issue, starting from the simple reasoning that women made up at least half of the population of people living in the polis of Athens. Most likely, the number of women either in terms of its socioeconomic dimension (citizens, *metics*, slaves) or in terms of age—old women, younger and capable of having children (whether working in the Agora or being engaged in the management of their *oikos*), girls—would exceed the male, even marginally, as in times of unfavorable war outcomes a part of the male Athenian population was lost on the battlefields, such as during the disastrous Sicilian Campaign or the Athenian defeat at the Battle of Chaeronea.

In the previous subsection, various aspects of the limitations that women experienced at the level of social life were mentioned. Aristophanes (*Ecclesiazusae*, 785–95; *Peace*, 980–90) created an image of introversion of women whose constant preoccupation "with the affairs of the *oikos*" is presented in his works, and Xenophon conceptualized an ideal form of the wife of the middle and upper economic class, assigning her specific tasks and roles. Characteristically, Thucydides (2.45.2) reproducing Pericles's Funeral Speech says that:

> And since I must say somewhat also of feminine virtue for you that are now widows, I shall express it in this short admonition. It will be much for your honour not to recede from your sex and to give as little occasion of rumour amongst the men, whether of good or evil, as you can.

However, opinions among historians differ regarding the rest of the rights and limitations that women faced (Economou and Kyriazis 2019c). As observed by Pomeroy (1995, 58), who has diligently dealt with the position of women in Ancient Greece, contrary to those who argue that the position of women did not differ much from that of a female slave in an (Ottoman) harem, other historians argue that despite any disadvantages, the median Athenian (and Greek in general) woman was neither secluded to her *gynaikonites* nor excluded from a great number of social activities. Pomeroy further argues that earlier historians were reluctant to believe that Athenians treated their wives like the gentlemen, of well-to-do European families in the twentieth century.

One important criticism regarding the ancient democracy is that only men had political rights and that women, foreigners, and slaves were excluded from them. The counterargument is based on three main points: Firstly, it is a matter of interpretation whether or not women were considered citizens in the most general sense of the term. In the previous subsection, we referred to Isaeus (*Ciron*, 8.43), Isocrates (*Plataicus*, 14.51), and Demosthenes (*Against Eubulides*, 57.43) who describe Athenian women as citizens, like men. There are, in addition, a number of extant inscriptions, such as Fr. 11(FHG, IV, 358 = *Athenaios*, XIII, 577b) whose interpretation reinforces the view that women were also considered to be citizens, while Athenaeus (*The Deipnosophists*, 577c) refers to the legislative proposal of a citizen, Aristophon, who proposed (probably at the beginning of the fourth century) to consider as illegitimate any children not born of an Athenian (citizen) woman.

These legal arrangements of the Athenians imply that the status of a citizen also included the element of heredity, in the sense that a citizen was considered to be one who completed his military service (*ephebeia*) but also who is entitled to become a citizen if both his parents were citizens. A proof of this is the so-called Law of Citizenship of 451 BCE, according to which Pericles introduced one of most striking proposals which provided that henceforth citizenship would be conferred only on children whose mother and father both were Athenians. Previously, the offspring of

Athenian men who married non-Athenian women were granted citizenship (Plut. Per. 37.2–5; Aristot. Ath. Const. 26.4). The Athenian aristocracy in particular had tended to marry rich foreign women, as Pericles' own maternal grandfather had done.[2]

Secondly, given that women only got the right to vote in 1919 in the USA and the UK, and only after World War II in Switzerland, etc., could one argue that there was no truly democratic country anywhere before 1919, so countries like the USA, the UK, France, Switzerland, Greece, etc. were not democracies before 1919? So, what were they?

Thirdly, black slavery was abolished in the UK and France in the late eighteenth and early nineteenth centuries, in the USA after 1865, and in Brazil in the 1880s. By the same logic, the USA was not a democracy before 1865, notwithstanding the constitution of 1787, etc. And if it wasn't democracy, what was?

It is therefore a mistake to transfer present definitions of institutions in order to describe earlier times, especially when these institutions were not functioning in exactly the same way as nowadays. The criteria of the degree of democracy in a society are institutional and concern the participation, without exclusion, of large social groups in the political process, based on commonly accepted criteria, for example, Athenian or non-citizen.

Another serious issue concerns women's property rights. Athenian women (and apparently *metic* women too) did not have such strong property rights as men, compared to some Doric cities such as Sparta and the Cretan Gortyna where women's property rights were equal to that of men (Fleck and Hansen 2009). However, Schaps (1979) through a thorough presentation of historical facts demonstrates in practice that women, in principle, did have property rights, which the state had to protect. For example, women-wives became *epicleroi*, i.e., they legally controlled their husband's estate when he died, in favor of their son(s) until they came of age (Image 3.2).

In one notable extant incident, Archippe, widow of the former slave and later extremely wealthy citizen, Pasion, had been introduced to all aspects of her husband's banking business before he died. She then was actively involved in his bank's activities before and perhaps after his death. Pasion had left as a dowry to Archippe the non-inconsiderable sum of one *talent* (6000 drachmae). Subsequently, Archippe was also involved in a legal confrontation with her son, a would-be usurper, who tried to appropriate 3000 drachmae of her assets. It is important to bear in mind (in terms of justice and equality between men and women) that Archippe was judicially vindicated through a court's decision in the end (Cohen 2002, 110, ftn. 37).

[2]For the motives behind the Law of Citizenship of Pericles, convincing answers are further provided by Lyttkens and Henrik (2018) as well as the following hyperlink:

http://www.perseus.tufts.edu/hopper/text?doc=Perseus%3Atext%3A1999.04.0009%3Achapter%3D9%3Asection%3D3%3Asubsection%3D1

Image 3.2 Ancient Greek woman. Praxilla, by John William Godward. Source: https://commons.wikimedia.org/wiki/File:Praxilla._John_William_Godward.jpg

Another equally crucial issue concerns the education of women. According to the established view, there was no institutionalized education for women, and whatever knowledge, in terms of knowledge of writing, reading, and mathematics they had, came from relatives, friends, and other (educated) women in their environment. Pomeroy et al. (1999) support the generally accepted view that the main education of women concerned the knowledge of managing the *oikos*, as Xenophon in *Oeconomicus* eloquently describes. However, there are instances of ancient texts that testify that there were clearly cases of women who knew how to write and read, such as in Lysias (*Against Diogeiton*, 32.14–18) where it is reported that a mother of children successfully defended in an Athenian court the valuable property of her children from their uncle, Diogeiton, who tried to usurp it. On another occasion in Euripides' work, *Hippolytus*, in verses 856–881 the heroine appears to know how to read and write.

Furthermore, some vases testify that women have been trained in music and dance by outside teachers. Characteristically, the British Museum in London hosts a red-figured *hydria* (water-jar) which shows a woman reading and three attendants. In addition, the Louvre Museum in Paris hosts another interesting archaeological finding, an Attic red-figure *lekythos* (type of ancient Greek vessel used for storing oil, especially olive oil), ca. 435–425 BCE from Boeotia where a Muse is reading a scroll. Moreover, in the National Archaeological Museum of Athens there is a red-figure *hydria*, ca. 440–430 BCE which depicts Sappho reading one of her poems to a group of three student-friends.[3] If the woman's position was indeed so limited, these pictorial representations in vases could not be explained.

What was probably happening is that it was to the interest of men to have their wives learn even rudimentarily how to read and write, so that they could better manage some of the financial affairs of their *oikos*, such as purchases of goods and services, supplies, ad payment of services, when the *kyrios* was absent either for a long time, e.g., in war, or even for a short time, e.g., he was in the Agora to buy or sell products or even to discuss and comment on the current socio-political affairs, or finally, to attend the Athenian Assembly or the courts or other public offices.

One could of course claim that the household duties were handled by the slaves when the husband was absent. But who remained the main person in charge of the *oikos* when the *kyrios* was absent in the Agora or elsewhere? It should be mentioned that many households of well-to-do families employed an *oikonomos*, a manager of the household and of the servants who worked to produce goods and services for the *oikos* (Xenophon, *Oeconomicus*, 3.1.3, 21). Similar views regarding the necessity of a competent manager of the property and organization of the production of a (prosperous) *oikos* were also formulated by Aristotle (*Oeconomics*, 1344b.20–30, 1345b.5–12). Again, however, the existence of *oikonomos* does not exclude the possibility that women knew how to read and write. In the less well-off families who could not afford to hire an *oikonomos*, the male husbands would have every reason to teach their wives to read and write, even rudimentarily, in order to ensure in the best possible way both the internal management of the *oikos* and the efficient transactions with its suppliers.

In practice, the introverted role of a woman in her *oikos* did not hold in the cases of women of the lower economic classes who had to work outside the *oikos* to make ends meet by also participating in the buying and selling of goods and services in Agora or elsewhere. Many of them, due to poverty, were forced to produce themselves and trade whatever they could, from hair ribbons to herbs and grasses (Aristophanes, *Lysistrata*, 445; Demosthenes, *Against Eubulides*, 57.30–31). Poor women were forced to work, for example, as babysitters, etc. to support their own family. Also, others who had been widowed managed their *oikos* (Aeschines, *Against Timarchus*, 1.170). In addition, both male and female slaves could go shopping in the Agora without any restrictions if that was the will of the gentlewoman of the *oikos* they belonged to.

Harris (2002), Bresson (2007, 268–276), and Johnstone (2011, 22, 40) report the existence of *pantopoleia* where a variety of goods, from edibles to *hoplite* equipment, were available, something like today's grocery stores or supermarkets. There were also workshops which employed as many as 10 or more persons, free citizens, men and women, *metics* or slaves, as well as handicraft enterprises of pottery,

[3] See these wonderful images through the following links:
https://www.britishmuseum.org/collection/object/G_1885-1213-18 and
https://commons.wikimedia.org/wiki/File:Muse_reading_Louvre_CA2220_n2.jpg
https://en.m.wikipedia.org/wiki/File:NAMA_Sappho_lisant.jpg

carpentry, bag factories, shoe factories, etc., agricultural products, bakeries, fishmongers, and kitchens with ready-made food (where people could be hired so as to provide various services such as to prepare meals in an *oikos* to organize a symposion). Other shops included wine shops, musical instrument workshops, perfume shops, shops of women's ornaments, spice shops, etc. Various foodstuffs were traded, such as figs, grapes, pears, apples, loquats, lamb tripe, liver and spice stuffing, honeycombs, chickpeas, cow's milk and various other dairy products, myrtle berries, lamb, as well as processed products. Of course, services were provided as well, such as florists. Many of these services were provided by women, while there are also recorded cases where parents and children worked together, such as Euxitheus and his mother selling ribbons (Schaps 1979, 20, 50; Cohen 2002, 105).

The next logical step is the following: would it be possible for all this multitude of professional and commercial activities and provision of services by women to take place if they did not know, even rudimentarily, how to read and write? Since the majority of the transactions of the times were moneyed, if they didn't know, they would be at risk of being constantly defrauded when transacting and selling their goods and/or services, thus losing wealth or being stolen.

Our conclusion is that, even indirectly, it can be proved that a significant part of the population of women, at least certainly those medium to low-income women who did not live permanently in the *oikos* but worked in the Agora, **would have to be able to read and write, at least to some extent,** in order to be capable of meeting the requirements of their participation in the activities of Agora and not to become victims of continuous exploitation and injustices.

Apart from this extroverted activity due to work, apparently, and contrary to the common perception, the Athenian women were not so much confined to their *oikos*. In principle they were tasked with organizing and carrying out many religious ceremonies. For example, they went to the sanctuary of Demeter in Alimos *deme*, for a 3-day festival of Thesmophoria held in Pyanepsion month (October/November) as a fertility festival (Lysias, *Against Eratosthenes*, 12.19). Furthermore, they were cooperating with each other, such as with neighbors and friends (Aristophanes, *Acharnians*, 253; *Lysistrata*, 638–647).

They paid visits to their female friends, provided assistance to each other (Aristophanes, *Lysistrata*, 5–10), and had the right to take private walks. The unmarried young women had the right to leave the *oikos* only if they were accompanied by a slave-maid or by their parents or by an elderly relative. They could go and bring water to their *oikos* and they could freely wash clothes in rivers or lakes (Euripides, *Electra*; Aristophanes, *Lysistrata*, 320–335). They were visiting their relatives who were in prison (Andocides, *On the Mysteries*, 1.48; Lysias, *Against Agoratus*, 39–42), they were accompanied by their male relatives to the courts to elicit the sympathy of the judges (Aeschines, *On the Embassy*, 2.152), and they actively participated in the preparation of the funerals of their family members. **They could also access the Agora with the company of a slave that belonged to their *oikos*** (either a man or woman).

They even participated in the polis' Funeral Speeches (Thucydides, *History*, 2.45), and they were buried with honors, as we are informed by the honorary columns that have been found in the Kerameikos with characteristics such as that they would be missed by all, that they were intelligent and gentle in their manners, etc. (Cohen 2000, 45). What is also important in terms of equality of rights between sexes is that women also had the right to attend the theatrical performances as we know from an anecdote about the first performance of the Eumenides by Aeschylus: When the Chorus of the Erinyes[4] appeared on the scene, it was so terrifying that pregnant women miscarried on the spot (Anonymous, *Vita Aeschyli* 9 (TGF 3 T Al.30–32). Theaters could also be seen as an important process of socialization between citizens.

Besides these, they served as *hiereiae* (female priestesses) in many temples even on the Acropolis (Herodotus, *Histories*, 8.41.3). They were allowed to accompany their dead relatives to the grave, only up to the second degree of consanguinity. They also participated in women's special religious ceremonies related to family and fertility such as Thesmophoria, thus strengthening the bonds between each other. And of course, they could interact normally, without discrimination with men when they themselves were in the Agora of Athens and Piraeus (Vlassopoulos 2007, 42).

Thus, the social status of the average Athenian woman may not have resembled the relationship of the calm Socrates to the dynamic Xanthippe, as described by Plato in *Phaedo* (Diogenes Laertius, *Lives of Eminent Philosophers*, Book II) and Xenophon in *Symposion*, but it is certainly not correct to argue that the general rule of the times was that women were confined to their *gynaikonites* and engaged in specific activities such as knitting, without enjoying an important series of events of social life, in the same way that men enjoyed them.

In any case, the above evidence refutes the arguments of those who (by focusing on specific ideas of ancient philosophers such as Aristotle) use even the term misogyny, i.e., hatred and racist prejudice, to describe the situation that prevailed in Ancient Greece regarding how men treated women. To argue about a general status of misogyny in Ancient Greece is completely groundless and the product of biased research. Characteristically, Xenophon in *Symposion* (9.2) writes:

> This girl's feat, gentlemen, is only one of many proofs that **woman's nature is really not a whit inferior to man's** (emphasis by the authors), except in its lack of judgment and physical strength. So if any one of you has a wife, let him confidently set about teaching her whatever he would like to have her know.

Katz (1992) rejects the prevailing view that women lived something like "prisoners" inside their *gynaikonites*. On the contrary, as already analyzed, it seems that women had full discretion in the management of their *oikos* as long as their husband was absent, but also several possibilities to participate actively in social life, such as in religion. There is no evidence that women felt like being imprisoned and unhappy in their *gynaikonites*. Countless performances with scenes of childbirth, women with their children, and women mourning at the grave of their child testify that Greek

---

[4]Female underworld deities of vengeance in ancient Greek religion and mythology.

women loved their children very much and were proud of their role as wives and mothers in the *oikos*. The *gynaikonites* existed as a tradition since the Mycenaean period. They continued to exist in the Hellenistic period, they were preserved during the Byzantine period (330–1453 AD) and in the Greek-Orthodox churches during the Ottoman rule period of mainland Greece (1453–1821). Some *gynaikonites* installations were still in use till some decades ago in traditional Greek-Orthodox churches.

A woman's *gynaikonites* should not be seen as a prison, like the oriental harems: it was the space in which a woman was active to perform two serious tasks: To raise her children by imbuing them with arete and high moral standards, and to manage the oikos in the absence of her husband. It was up to the intelligence of each woman of the times if *gynaikonites* could function as her personal prison, or not. After, we think that an intertemporal axiom is that a society is so conservative for both men and women as much as they allow it to be. Even under the most rigid dictatorships and the dark Middle Ages, there were people who stayed, insubordinate to these dark social regimes. Under a wider concept, almost 2½ thousand years from the time we are examining, the *gynaikonites* still exists both for men and women whose minds remain closed in front of knowledge, *kallos* (as a concept that includes natural beauty and mental virtues), cultural progress, and open-mindedness.

As a final comment, the position of women in the Greek world was much better compared to the other ancient peoples of that time. Moreover, in Sparta the position of women was almost equal to that of men as girls from an early age had the right to education, to hold property, and to participate in sports activities, just like boys, etc.

3.4 The Ideal Woman and the Right Age for Marriage

According to Xenophon (*Oec*., 2.13) women should get married at a very young age. Due to this norm, a very young woman had not time to learn many things from her mother regarding the *oikos* management. She had to be further taught and educated by her husband. Her responsibilities contained to understand that her joint symbiosis with her husband meant also unification of their properties (7.13), to follow commonly accepted standards of life, i.e., to be prudent (7.15), to assist in increasing the *oikos's* property (7.16), to supervise and direct the tasks to be done in the *oikos* and those who perform them (slaves), to try to save resources for the *oikos* (7.35-6), implying that her management should be characterized by the avoidance of wasting the *oikos* resources, to try to be the "leader" of the *oikos* and treat the slaves and workers accordingly (7.39), to ensure that all objects in the *oikos* (such as tools) would be in proper order (8), to train the servants according to their abilities in various tasks (9.11-2), to supervise what is done in the *oikos* (9.14-5, 10.10), to also contribute to various works of the *oikos* (10.11), not to beautify herself with provocative colors, and not to display her physical qualities with various tricks such as high heel shoes (10.2–3).

Xenophon in *Oeconomicus* (3.10–12) explains that if women are trained well by their husband they can be very effective in the management of the *oikos*, and the opposite. He writes that:

> '....I can also show you that husbands differ widely in their treatment of their wives, and some succeed in winning their co-operation and thereby increase their estates, while others bring utter ruin on their houses by their behaviour to them."
>
> "And ought one to blame the husband or the wife for that, Socrates?"
>
> "When a sheep is ailing," said Socrates, "we generally blame the shepherd, and when a horse is vicious, we generally find fault with his rider. In the case of a wife, if she receives instruction in the right way from her husband and yet does badly, perhaps she should bear the blame; **but if the husband does not instruct his wife in the right way of doing things, and so finds her ignorant, should he not bear the blame himself**? (emphasis by the authors)'

Athenian perceptions of women vary: from the "vixen" Xanthippe who "torments" Socrates, according to Aristophanes' exaggeration, but who nevertheless presents an image of an emancipated woman, like the women in Aristophanes' *Lysistrata*, to the wise Diotima, from whom Socrates learned much according to Plato's *Symposion*, and of course Pericles' valuable advisor, companion, and later wife, Aspasia of Miletus a famed *hetaera* of her times and previously Lamia, another influential *hetaera* being the companion of Themistocles. This is also illustrated by the role of women in ancient tragedy such as those of Sophocles, where the authors show respect and admiration for women, or in *Antigone* with the superb verse 523, where Antigone asserts that: "I was not born to hate but to love," centuries before the preaching of Christianity as reflected in the well-known saying of the Gospel "love one another."

Xenophon in *Oeconomicus* (3.12) presents the ideal wife, who has learned to run the household well:

> Is there anyone to whom you commit more affairs of importance than you commit to your wife?

asks Socrates, and Critobulus responds:

> There are few or none, I confess

Later (verses 3.14–15) Socrates tells Critobulus that he will introduce him to Aspasia, of Pericles whom Socrates apparently knew and admired suggesting that Socrates has high regard for Aspasia and recognizes in her a number of important insights:

> .... I will introduce Aspasia to you, and she will explain the whole matter to you with more knowledge than I possess. I think that the wife who is a good partner in the household contributes just as much as her husband to its good; because the incomings for the most part are the result of the husband's exertions, but the outgoings are controlled mostly by the wife's dispensation. **If both do their part well, the estate is increased; if they act incompetently, it is diminished** (emphasis by the authors)...

On the issue of marriage age for both sexes, the general trend was that men married between the ages of 24 and 30 and women between the ages of 14 and 18. In the fourth century BCE, the philosophers Aristotle and Plato raised the age limit somewhat. Plato (*Laws*, 6.785b) considered years 16–20 for a woman and 30–35 for a man as the appropriate period for getting married, while Aristotle (*Politics*, 7.1335a) suggests the 18th year for a woman and between 35 and 37 for the man. In any case, we speculate that the age difference between the couple remained quite discrete because it was believed that the man should have some experience of life that would be useful for him to ensure happiness and prosperity for his young wife and *oikos* in general. In an earlier period, the age limits were somewhat different.

According to Hesiod (*Ways and Means*, 695–699) the man should not be much younger than 30 years and the woman should be in the fifth year of puberty, i.e., around 15–17 years, while Solon believed that the proper time for a man to marry was between the ages of 27 and 34 (Garland 2008). According to the social norms of the times, the prospective groom should be *kalos kagathos*, the ideal of the ancient Greeks. The *kalos kagathos* possessed *arete* (virtue), the main elements of which were valor, justice, and especially, prudence.

3.5 *Metics* at Athens

In Athens there were a significant number of foreigners, mostly Greeks, who wanted to live there for work purposes. As Plutarch informs us (*Solon*, 24) that it was Solon who introduced the institution of the *metic* by inviting people who had substantial technical knowledge to offer to the polis, such as capital and know-how. Peisistratus implemented further this policy by increasing the number of *metics* gathered in Attica even if without having the required technical knowledge. Many *metics* distinguished themselves in the fine arts and literature, and many proved successful businessmen who undertook important public expenditures, under the so-called *liturgies* institution (see further in Sect. 13.2). Some of them engaged in the financial sector of the times, mostly to international commerce and banking activities and played an important role in the Athenian economy.

The institution of *metics* operated throughout the ancient Greek world (Osiander 2007, 47). *Metics* had no political rights and were obliged to live by adopting the customs and the habits of the Athenians, by obeying also the laws of the polis. They paid the so-called *metoikion* or *xenikon*, 12 drachmae for men and 6 for women because they were not citizens of Athens (Gabrielsen 2013, 337, 341). The underaged children of a family of *metics* were exempted from *metoikion*. If the *metics* for any reason did not pay the *metoikion*, the laws were very strict: the polis had the right to temporarily imprison them, expel them, or even sell them as slaves.

In general, the *metoikion* should not be seen as a burdensome sum of money, and was, according to our own interpretation, the price imposed on *metics* by the Athenian state for the fact that, as non-citizens, they themselves used the infrastructure of the Athenian state and achieved financial benefits through their working activities in the polis. From an economic perspective, *metoikion* could also be seen as the “renting” of state infrastructures to “unauthorized users” (Economou 2024, 258).

As "authorized users" were, of course, considered all the legal native male citizens who acquired this status at the age of 20, but also women.

The male *metics* had to participate in the military operations of the polis of Athens, if the occasion required it. During the fourth century, when shortages of manpower were observed among the Athenians, *metics* were more often used in light military corps, but mainly at sea as oarsmen in the *trireme* warships, as due to their frequent participation in naval trade, they often showed excellent navigation skills (Lyttkens and Gerding 2022, 188). The *metics* had also the right to participate in the festivals of Athens, and in the symposia, like the Athenian citizens, without any discrimination, as we understand from the people who took part in Plato's dialogues in general and from other *metics* like the orator Lysias who became an important figure of the Athenian society.

3.6 Slaves in Athens

Slaves, in Classical Athens, were the lowest social and economic class in the hierarchy and non-existent as political entities, with no rights or obligations to the polis beyond those to their masters. Such a slave status prevailed in all poleis of antiquity, with the more oppressive being cases like the Laurion mines slaves, or the *helots* of Sparta and the *penestai* in Thessaly.[5] Oppressive slave regimes were also those of Ancient Rome (*latifundia*) or later that of the blacks of the American South before the American Civil War,[6] and unfortunately, those continued to exist at least until the nineteenth century AD.

The slaves known as *douloi* were usually not Greeks but came from the so-called barbarian countries (such as Illyria, Kolchis, Scythia, Syria, Caria, and Lydia). It was possible that some of them were Greeks who were sold as prisoners after a war (Kyrtatas 2011, 93). They were used in housework, in the *oikos's* activities (agricultural, commercial, etc.), and as workers in the workshops throughout the polis and the port of Piraeus, etc. For example, slaves were used in workshops owned by free men such as textile manufacturing, shoemaking, carpentry, blacksmiths, goldsmiths, trade, agriculture, and animal husbandry. They could even be rented out by their master whether he was an individual—entrepreneur or the polis itself, to people who wanted their services for a price (Xenophon, *Ways and Means*, 4.17–24), such as the public slaves that the Athenian polis' authorities could rent to the private sector, to various consortia of individuals who were active in the mining operations in the silver mines (Van Alfen 2011, 9).

Slaves were important for the success of the Athenian economy in Classical times. In general, most Athenians and *metics* saw them primarily as a source of

---

[5]Tridimas (2023) provides an economic explanation of the different slavery regimes between Athens and Sparta.

[6]For the harsh life conditions of the black slaves in the American South, one can read, among others, the novel of Harriet Beecher Stowe, *Uncle Tom's Cabin* or, *Life Among the Lowly*.

income. This is not to deny that there were also cases where masters saw their slaves as partners in business and even as friends. State-owned slaves of Athens worked under very harsh living conditions in the silver mines of Laurion, as well as in the marble quarries, such as in Pentelikon mountain. If this group of slaves is excluded, the position of the remaining slaves whose owners were Athenians (as privates) was clearly better than that of the slaves of the above cases such as the Roman *latifundia*.

This is evidenced by the fact that, due to the unfavorable living conditions, state-owned slaves in the above cases staged continuous rebellions with requests starting from demands for better treatment, up to the request for their complete liberation, as happened in Rome in the period 73–71 BCE with the great revolt of slaves and other socially oppressed people under the leadership of the Thracian origin Spartacus. On the contrary, in Athens during the Classical and Hellenistic periods, there was never a social revolution, either of the popular strata or of the slaves, against the political-economic regime, simply because the conditions of living, integration, and "fermentation" of the slaves that were owned by privates in Athens in the fourth c. BCE were far better than the above cases.

Athens of the fourth century had developed into an international commercial and cultural metropolis-cosmopolis of the Mediterranean.[7] Cartledge (2002, 163) writes that there was no attested competition in Attica between slave-run estates and peasants'. These peasants often worked together with slaveholders in the same fields and farms in a symbiotic way "like the horse with the carriage." Ancient Athenian society of the times (and consequently the Greek one as a whole) was not completely classless, but it would be wrong to interpret it in terms of "class struggle," as suggested by the Marxist intelligentsia and those historians who tried to view ancient Greek society through Marxist spectacles; see, for example, emphatically, de Ste Croix (1981).

Various local uprisings of slaves took place indeed. For example, according to Nymphodorus of Syracuse, an itinerant ethnographer who lived in the third century BCE, there was an uprising of slaves in the island of Chios at the turn of the fourth c. BCE led by a slave named Drimakos. Chios had a formidable naval power at the time. More characteristic cases of revolts with a socioeconomic character took place in the Hellenistic period (323–146 BCE) in the Achaean and the Aetolian federal leagues' territories during the time of the Spartan King Cleomenes III. The basic demands in these uprisings were the redistribution of land and debt abolishment (Rostovtzeff 1941, 206–208, 210–214; Mendels 1982; Economou 2020).[8] But there is no tangible evidence to interpret these events as "class struggles."

Male and female slaves, when entering an *oikos*, followed an initiation ceremony similar to that of a wife entering into her husband's *oikos*. The education of slaves

[7] This international dominant role of Athens over its allies in the Eastern Mediterranean is highlighted in more detail in the following chapters.

[8] In Economou and Kyriazis (2019a, 159–164), we referred to the social uprisings in Medieval Europe, focusing on the High Middle Ages in England. Many of the demands of the insurgents, such as Wat Tyler and John Ball in 1381, were similar to those of the various uprisings of the Hellenistic period.

was not aimed so much at improving their character, which was left to the strictness of Athenian laws, as at acquiring specific technical skills usually related to their master's activities in the *oikos* or the Agora.

But why were there variations regarding the treatment of slaves?

First, it was up to their owners whether they would allow them more or less freedom in the exercise of various activities of social life. The Athenians had realized early on that the driving mechanism that activates a person is the incentive provided to him/her, while what controls him/her is the fear of severe punishment. Perhaps Athenian society is unique in that slave masters consciously instituted incentives to improve the lives of their slaves providing that the behavior and activities of the latter best served the interests of the former. There are numerous cases where masters not only entrusted the management of their *oikos* or businesses to slaves but also freed them if they were satisfied with their contribution to the *oikos*. For example, with the consent of their owners, slaves acquired the right to engage in economic activities, such as in banking, and hold personal property even if this property, in principle, belonged to their owner (Cohen 2000, 132–145, 151; Kyrtatas 2011, 106). With this "legal" property it was possible, under strict conditions, even to buy out slavery and become *apeleutheroi* (freed citizens) a situation which functioned as an important incentive for them to be honest and competent in their duties toward their masters.

In the international academic literature, there is a dispute among experts regarding the question of the legal rights of the *apeleutheroi*. Most argue that the *apeleutheroi* enjoyed rights corresponding to those of the *metics* because they too were obliged to pay the *metoikion*. However, Pseudo-Xenophon's (*Constitution of the Athenians*, 1.10) and Plato's (*Laws*, 915a4) classifications of the *apeleutheroi* regard them as a separate social category. This complicates matters. Aristotle (*Politics*, 3.1277b) considers that an *apeleutheros* was neither a *metic* nor a foreigner. However, in special cases, an *apeleutheros* or his children could be socially "upgraded" and become citizen, especially if his actions undeniably benefited the polis, as was the case with Pasion.

There were different social regimes of "upgrading" former slaves, who could become either *apeleutheroi* or according to Zelnick-Abramovitz (2005, 10) who provides an extensive analysis of all the types of manumitted slaves in the ancient Greek world, *exeleutheroi*, concerning manumitted slaves who were former citizens who were then completely disengaged from their masters, although still being socially inferior to both *metics* and citizens.

The case of Pasion (430–370 BCE) is a typical example of social progress. Pasion was originally jointly owned by the bankers Antisthenes and Archestratus, who had a bank at the Piraeus, the harbor 5 miles out of Athens. It is presumed by many that his place of origin was Syria or the Levant in general, when in circa 440 BCE vast numbers of Syrian slaves were brought to Greece through Phoenician ports, Tyre and Sidon. Initially Pasion became an *argyramoibos* (money-changer). *Argyramoiboi* (in plural) according to Cohen (1992, 18–19), Bitros et al. (2020, 30–32), Economou and Kyriazis (2021a), and Economou (2024, 168–169) dealt with the exchange of currencies and precious metals. Pasion firstly became a freed man (and *metic*) and then a citizen.

As a citizen he continued his banking business with great success. Pasion amassed a fortune of 30 *talents* during his lifetime, as he enjoyed 6000 drachmae a year from the shield-making factory he owned alone (Demosthenes, *For Phormio*, 36.11). He benefited Athens by offering 1000 shields and 5 *triremes* (which cost a total of over 5 *talents*, 30,000 drachmae, when the daily wage in the early fourth century BCE was 1–1.5 drachmae).[9] The Athenians rewarded him by making him a citizen. He died as the richest Athenian of his time, **a wonderful example of social progress independently of his nationality or place of origin.** In the advanced economies of the Western world nowadays this practice is considered an important motive for attracting people with exceptional skills from around the globe, to offer their services in the local economy which provides them with equal social and business opportunities to the natives.

Highly skillful *metics* and slaves were in high demand at the time. This is, of course, an intertemporal phenomenon. For example, when France made its first steps toward industrialization in the eighteenth to nineteenth c. AD, its policymakers of the times favored the importation of highly skilled craftsmen from England, to be employed as foremen, who brought their skills to the textile industry in France, and this should be seen as "technology transfers," under a modern Schumpeterian perspective.[10] The number of English craftsmen working in France in 1822 was estimated at 15,000.

Lysias (*For Callias*, 2–4) highlights another aspect of freeing a slave: he considers that this possibility could be exploited by the slaves themselves. He cites the case of Callias a *metic* who was accused by his slaves of sacrilege. Lysias claimed that slaves could easily lie in the hope that their denunciation might be seen as a contribution to the polis, and thus, the polis would nominate and make them *apeleutheroi* as a reward.

Xenophon (*Oec.*, 10.18, 5.16, 12. 4-5, 15-6, 13. 11-12) suggested that male slaves should be trained by their master in the tasks they could work more efficiently, and to be given food and clothing according to their performance. He also suggested that whoever entrusts a slave with the management of his enterprise should give him special training so that he learns how to manage his subordinate workers—slaves (*Oec.*, 12.4). It was very important that the *kyrios* (the slave owner) knew how to treat his slaves in order to encourage them to increase their productivity (in modern terms), as well as assign them tasks according to their knowledge, skills, and abilities (Aristotle, *Politics*, 1255b, 35–40; 1277a, 40–45, 1329a, 5–10). A *kyrios* of slaves was supposed to supervise the work of the slaves and estimate their productivity

[9] 6000 drachmae were equivalent to one *talent*. It was a very high sum of money as, according to Loomis (1998, 241, 243) who has extensively studied the issue of wages in Ancient Greece, the daily wage of an unskilled laborer in the fifth c. BCE amounted to 1 drachma, while in the fourth, to 1.5 drachmae.

[10] See analytically the seminal work of Schumpeter (1934) on this.

according to their skill and industriousness. In fact, it was thought that the *epistates* (supervisor of the slaves), if he was efficient in his supervisory duties, increased the revenues to his master's business (Demosthenes, *Against Aphobus 1*, 27.24, 27.29). These ancient texts, and especially Xenophon's *Oeconomicus*, describe practical tips so that the management of an *oikos* (and by extension, of an enterprise in the market) meets (in principle) some of the key principles of universal managerial techniques, which according to the seminal analyses of F. W. Taylor (1911) and H. Fayol (1949, 1967) are, among others, based on planning, organizing, commanding, motivating, coordinating, and controlling the production process.[11]

Although there was a strong dependence in the personal treatment of slaves by their masters, the behavior of the latter should not have been *banausic* on the slaves, because this could cause social outcry (Pseudo-Xenophon, *Constitution of the Athenians*, 10.10–11; Demosthenes, *Against Meidias*, 21.46). Plato (*Laws*, 777 D-E) recommends that the master treat the slaves humanely.

As a general principle, the torture of a male or female slave was not permitted, and any death of a male or female slave caused by misbehavior, management, or torture by his master was punishable by law. If the slave was killed by a citizen or his master, the penalty imposed on the abuser was exile, but not death. The murderer was tried by a special court even if he had no relatives (Demosthenes, *Against Evergus and Mnesibulus*, 47.55, 47.59, 47.70–72; Lycurgus, *Against Leocrates*, 66). However, the torture of a slave could occur in practice when a court deemed it necessary, i.e., subjecting them to torture to testify in court, which was not the case for free citizens.

In other words, as Demosthenes mentions (*Against Androtion*, 22.55; *Against Timocrates*, 24.167) the torture of slaves could be allowed if this could lead to an important testimony in the courts; slaves and especially those who worked in one's *oikos* were considered to be subjects of secret information. That is why they were allowed to be tortured by order of the master or the court, to testify what they knew about a subject. In fact, the testimony following the torture of a slave was considered by the court as "the most accurate evidence" (Demosthenes, *Against Onetor*, 30.37). Common tortures were whipping, turning the mill in place of the donkey, etc. (Lysias, *On the Murder of Eratosthenes*, 1.18; Demosthenes, *Against Timotheus*, 49; *Against Neaera*, 59.123–124; *Against Olympiodorus*, 48.16–18). This does not mean that they were subjected to such severe torture that their lives were endangered, but if this was the case and harm was caused to the slave, the polis should compensate the owner (Lysias, *On the Olive Stump*, 7.34).

More generally, the Athenians viewed slaves as people who did not have a high sense of responsibility to the polis, although this may not have been true. This is also shown by the fact that although some of them were literate (Demosthenes, *Against Aphobus 1*, 27.3, 27.11) they were not trusted by the Athenian politico-economic

[11]It would be very interesting to study Xenophon's views, as reflected in his *Oeconomicus* and *Ways and Means* from the perspective of F. W. Taylor's and H. Fayol's works. But this requires an exclusive and extensive analysis that cannot be provided here.

regime to undertake posts in the operation of the state machine, not even as copyists of texts (Demosthenes, *Against Timocrates*, 24.179). Slaves were considered people who "were steeped all their lives in injustice and had committed great crimes" (Lysias, *For Callias*, 5.3).

On the other hand, slaves were to some extent able to enjoy a number of privileges, such as participation in family religious activities and in symposia. They could praise the gods of their choice. But apart from this relatively good treatment of slaves by their masters (Aristotle, *Economics*, 1344b, 28–30), the Athenians were quite proactive and incentivized their efficiency and obedience to their masters and the laws of the polis; there was always the possibility where quite a few slaves could achieve the status of *apeleutheroi* by their masters. In various times these newly made *apeleutheroi* proved to be capable entrepreneurs by providing income to their masters and the polis as a whole, whereas they also helped effectively the polis in its battles with other states. In return, the Athenian state could conditionally "upgrade" their social status, in special cases (Bitros and Karayiannis 2006).

One characteristic example of efficiently utilizing highly skillful slaves is banking. Managing a bank required high skills and was a highly responsible task; however, the Athenian bankers allowed skilled slaves to practice this profession (Isocrates, *Trapeziticus*, 17.12). For example, as already mentioned, the slave Pasion had taken over the management of his master's bank, made it very profitable with his skills, and thus achieved not only to become *apeleutheros* but also to make his own bank. The same happened with his slave Phormion (Demosthenes, *For Phormio*, 36.30).

Apeleutheroi, who from this moment on held the status of a *metic*, had the right to build their own "*oikos*" by taking a wife, usually also a freed woman (Demosthenes, *For Phormio*, 36.28–29), and to engage in some productive or commercial activity while taking care of their family. There were also slaves who were allowed by their master to live alone with their family in a separate *oikos* and to practice some profession with the only obligation to pay their masters a specific amount of money (Hyperides, *Against Athenogenes*, 3.9; Demosthenes, *For Phormio*, 36. 37). Furthermore, from inscriptions found at Delphi before 150 BCE various cases of ownership of property by male slaves (368 cases) and female slaves (123 cases) have been attested (Schaps 1979, 7). Euripides (*Ion*, 853–856) justified this treatment of slaves in Athens on the basis of their own behavior and activity by emphasizing:

> There is one thing in slavery that brings shame, the name; in all other respects **a good slave is no worse than the free-born** (emphasis by the authors).

The frequent involvement of slaves in entrepreneurial activities and court cases (Demosthenes, *For Phormio*, 36. 6) proves the significant economic role of slaves in Athenian society (Cohen 2000, 108–9).

On the other hand, the attempt of the Athenian political and economic regime to implement a so-called effective "slave management policy" could not overcome some obvious limits. By leaving the responsibility of slaves to their masters, the polis did not seem to have had any list of all of them, except of course those belonging to the polis (see, e.g., Demosthenes, *Against Neaera*). The number of slaves in Athens was large, compared to the body of the citizens and therefore they represented an important source of wealth. According to Economou's (2024, 282) estimation, given that the total population of Attica in the fourth century did not exceed 300,000, it can be assumed that the number of *metics* amounted to approximately 25,000, but with an increasing trend and the number of slaves would have been about 150,000–155,000 and was higher than that of citizens.

To neutralize any possible rebellion, the Athenians, in contrast to the Spartans, developed their quality of life, at least to some degree, without treating them as in Sparta, Thessaly, or Rome. With this they not only increased their effort and ability to work but also their obedience and peaceful coexistence with the citizens. There is strong evidence regarding the Athenian case where free citizens, *metics*, and slaves worked together efficiently in important projects such as the construction of Erechtheion, the Temple of Athena Polias on the north side of the Acropolis in Athens, and, **equally important, they received the same pay**. This is emphatically recognized by Pseudo-Xenophon (*Con.*, 11.1–2) who writes that:

> If anyone is also startled by the fact that they let the slaves live luxuriously there and some of them sumptuously, it would be clear that even this they do for a reason. For where there is a naval power, it is necessary from financial considerations to be slaves to the slaves in order to take a portion of their earnings, and it is then necessary to let them go free. And where there are rich slaves, it is no longer profitable in such a place for my slave to fear you. In Sparta my slave would fear you; but if your slave fears me, there will be the chance that he will give over his money so as not to have to worry anymore. For this reason we have **set up equality between slaves and free men, and between *metics* and citizens** (emphasis by the authors). The city needs *metics* in view of the many different trades and the fleet. Accordingly, then, we have reasonably set up a similar equality also for the *metics*.

Plato (*Republic*, 563b), Pseudo-Xenophon (*Constitution*, 10.10.2), and Cartledge (2002, 163) provide supportive evidence as proof of the rightness of the above passage. And Vlassopoulos (2009, 348) emphatically writes that in Athens of the times slaves and freemen exercised the same professions and this meant that it was often necessary to accord slaves an extensive freedom of movement and initiative. This practically made it impossible to differentiate status solely on the basis of profession or living conditions. For example, there were Athenians who due to their poor or cheap clothing resembled many slaves in their outward appearance. Thus, a number of slaves were in a position to take advantage of this blurring of identities to escape detection, avoid maltreatment, and create better conditions for themselves.

As a final comment, the Athenian choice of providing some rudimentary safeguards for the human rights of slaves has not so much to do with the potential loss of income for his master and the polis in general, as with the sincere effort of the Athenians to form a society where there would be no extremes in the relationships between the people who lived in it. It is not at all far from the truth that the Athenians really wanted to build a humanist society for all. Thus, it seems that views, even of Aristotle (*Politics*, 1254a, 25–30, 1254b, 20–30; *Eudemian Ethics*, 1241b, 20–5) who proposed to regard slaves as non-rational beings and as exclusively involuntary means of production who had no hope of a better life in society, were not accepted by the majority of Athenians, as a general principle and common practice.

3.7 Athenian Society: A Critical Appraisal

Undoubtedly, Athenian society and its organization were patriarchal with strong father-master authority over women, children, and slaves. On the other hand, women could enjoy, at least to some extent, their "individual kingdom" in their *oikos*, and the children enjoyed the protection and help of the father and the polis. As far as the slaves who belonged to individuals are concerned, their fate was not completely a polis matter or a choice of their master. They themselves could also claim a "window of opportunity" based on their own personal effort to progress and evolve through the institutional setting of the Athenian society. At least, to some extent.

After all, the Athenian polis was the most populous in Classical Greece of the times, with a variety of people living in it who were anything but alike. In addition to the citizens who were the decision-makers in the polis, there were also *metics*, slaves (mostly of non-Greek origin), visitors, and entrepreneurs living in the polis for a while. Among them there were philosophers, architects, etc. There were people from other parts of Greece who gathered in this economic and intellectual center of Greece (Isocrates, *Antidosis*, 15.171–172) for a variety of reasons, even for tourism! Due to the rise of its population, Athens was gradually being converted from a face-to-face society into a mega-polis and it was therefore understandable that not everyone knew each other, even the citizens. That is why their legal system encouraged and supported written financial agreements since not everyone was sure about the identity and character of the individuals who were being called upon to transact (Hyperides, *Against Athenogenes*, 3.13).

This trend was increased due to the large dispersion of citizens, *metics*, and slaves in the various *demes*, mainly during the fourth century where due to professional obligations or marriages, they lived in a different deme from the one to whom they initially belonged (Demosthenes, *Against Eubulides*, 57.9–13). Also, the landed property of the Athenians could have been dispersed among many *demes*. This movement of individuals from one *deme* to another weakened personal contact between them (Demosthenes, *Against Polycles*, 50.8). But, on the other hand, they had several opportunities to socialize either by participating in the Assembly meetings, who were taking place approximately 40 times a year,[12] or in the courts or in the Agora or in the theater. In other words, it was not a purely impersonal society like today's mega-cities such as modern Athens, Rome, Berlin, London, New York, or Shanghai. All of them, either Athenian citizens or *metics* or freed people and slaves, male and female, had one thing in common: **they lived under the customs and laws of the Athenian state which applied to all without discriminations**.

[12] See Economou (2024, 31) on this, and the relative supportive evidence we provide therein.

Furthermore, the Athenian state, under certain conditions, rewarded with the institution of *enktesis*, i.e., the right to own land, those foreigners who possessed specialized knowledge of trade and who with their long-term activity had benefited the polis (Burke 2010, 397; Engen 2010, 192–197). This was an important stimulus for them so as to work efficiently.

As a final comment, all the people in Attica, whether they were born from Athenian parents or were *metics*, visitors-tourists, or slaves, shared more or less the same way of life, the Athenian way of life. We have no information about ghettoization of people, nor about their perfect integration. Even if it is accepted that one out of three who lived in Attica was of Athenian origin, all the others had largely embraced and adopted the Athenian social, economic, legal, and political principles, and not by coercion as in other societies, but by their free will, except of course the slaves who, however, seem to have come to terms with these values.

Metics were coming to Athens, aspired to achieve their own "Athenian dream" of the times. Here of course we paraphrase the famous motto, the "American dream," coined by James Truslow Adams, an American writer and historian back in the 1930s, which was related to a package of values reflecting the American ethos of the times such as representative democracy, liberty, equality, freedom for making individual prosperity and protection of private property, the rule of law, upward social mobility for oneself and his family, achieved through hard work in a capitalist society with few barriers.

By offering further evidence, in the following Scenes throughout this book, it will be argued that the origins of these values, ethos, and institutions should be traced back to Classical Greece and the Athenian city-state.

Chapter 4
Preparations for Receiving Guests at the *Oikos*

Abstract This chapter refers to the preparations, on the part of the women of the *oikos*, to receive guests. It further presents clothing and footwear items, as well as women's grooming items. A society proceeds with such amenities, only when it has already managed to cover its basic needs; therefore, it exhibits signs of economic development and prosperity.

4.1 Hegeso and Eriphyle Dress Up to Welcome Their Guests

Hegeso returned from the Agora with Eriphyle and Chariclea, the latter carrying the shopping. Eriphyle immediately ran to her room to flaunt in her mirror the new *epiblema*[1] her mother bought her.

– The one who persists, wins! she monologued looking in the mirror wearing the *epiblema*.

With her persistence, she had managed to convince her mother to buy her a beautiful addition to her outfit. She was certainly happy. She would wear it to public events that she would attend with her family. Excluding her family, Eriphyle wanted her best friend Agne, with whom she had a friendship since childhood, to see it first. She left her room and ran to the *gynaikonites*, where her mother had retired to begin preparing her beautification to receive the guests of Nicomedes, the entrepreneur Epiphanios and his wife Eulalia. Her mother had already managed to bathe and wash her hair.

– Mother, look! Does it suit me? Eriphyle asked, looking forward to receiving a positive response.

Eriphyle made a quick circle around herself, to present her mother the new *epiblema* with the tunic she was wearing. The *epiblema* had a nice deep yellow

[1] Shawl.

E. M. L. Economou, N. C. Kyriazis, *Daily Life in Classical Athens*, Frontiers in Economic History, https://doi.org/10.1007/978-3-031-58541-8_4

color background, decorated with many meanders, one continuation of the other, in black color. After completing her spinning motion, she bowed slightly with a smile of satisfaction, as if she were an actor in the theater, seeking applause after her personal performance. Her pale blue tunic, combined with the *epiblema*, created a nice color contrast.

- You are a little goddess, an Aphrodite! Hegeso said approvingly, admiring the color contrast of the clothes, perfectly suited to her daughter's toned and lithe body, which had obviously changed noticeably, and was no longer a body of a little girl but of a young woman.
- You are beautiful like Hera, oh mother!
- So, your father is Zeus? Hegeso replied and continued: If so, I hope he won't throw lightning bolts and burn us when he finds out, and gets angry, how much the *epiblema* you bought costs, because you always go and get the most expensive clothes!
- The most expensive, but also the best, oh mother! Come on mother! You seem to know nothing about the laws of the Agora. Sit down and let me explain!
- Oh really? How do you know these laws my daughter? Hegeso replied with a bit of an irony in her voice.
- Father explained them to me! Let me explain them to you: A product that is of high quality is in high demand by the citizens, because they like it and prefer it. But because so many people want it, sellers understand this and raise its price! After this, only the privileged can purchase it.
- I see!

Eriphyle continued:

- The father, as a well-to-do Athenian and capable banker that he is, will find a way to cover the cost of the *epiblema*. Besides, if we are both beautiful, it is good for his work, which is related to the outwardly good testimony, the prestige but also perhaps, to some extent, with the nice appearance... of him and his family...
- Ma'am, it's Elpinike, the hairdresser downstairs, waiting. Shall I tell her to come up to the *gynaikonites*? asked Chariclea.
- Yes, and tell her to come straight here immediately and not start gossiping with you! Tell her to hurry up!
- Well ma'am, don't stress yourself like that! There is a plenty of time till early afternoon when the guests will arrive, Chariclea replied.

* * *

4.2 Clothing and Footwear

The existence of many statues and paintings on vases and pottery provides us with a fairly representative picture of the clothing and footwear of the Greeks of the Classical Period. As for the color issue, the clothes were not only white, but according to traces of colors on statues and from inferences based on vases, the fabrics worn by the ancient Greeks were quite brightly colored and the clothes were elaborately decorated. There were, as today, different types of clothes and color choices depending on the situation (death, religious ceremony, etc.) or professions or identity (priests, etc.). Changes in the fashion were taking place, although it was not as frequent and short in time as in other periods (Hellenistic or Roman period). But the adoption of a new fashion in clothing was apparently caused by the rich and was followed by the rest of the socioeconomic classes only if their economic potential rose as well.

Men and women wore an inner garment, either a *peplos* or a *chiton*, and an outer garment, the *himation*. Some of the most well-known types of clothes were the following:

- The *peplos*: it was made of wool and worn by women. It was rectangular-shaped and worn over the tunic. It was applied to the body with the help of a *porpe* and/or a belt. If one pulled the *peplos* up, the upper part appeared as a separate blouse and this was called *kolpos*.
- The *perone* or *porpe*: It was a straight, long pin used to fasten the outerwear worn by both women and men. The pin was used mostly by women to fasten their *peplos*.
- The *strophion*: It was a soft belt that a woman could wear under her garment and tied around her waist.
- The *himation*: Long cloth that was wrapped around the back and chest and fastened to the right shoulder. It was worn by both men and women.
- The *chiton*: It is the so-called tunic. It was worn by both men and women and was made of linen. Sometimes it had sleeves and sometimes it didn't. Men preferred short tunics for freedom of movement, while women often wore a tunic long to the feet, the so-called foot tunic.
- The *chlamydia*: It was a short cloak worn by men. It fastened with a buckle on the right shoulder and covered the entire left arm. It was mainly worn by soldiers, travelers, and teenagers.
- The *epiblema:* It was the shawl worn by women over the veil or tunic. They wore it when they left the *oikos* and it was made in different colors. The *strophion*, a type of undergarment, and the *epiblema* could also be worn externally.
- The *perizoma*: It was a triangular-shaped loincloth worn as an undergarment by men and women. The *perizoma* may also be called a strap or thong.
- The *petasos*: A leather hat worn by teenagers that had a strap to tie under the jaw. There was also a *petasos* for women which was taller than that for men.
- The *diadema*: It was a strip that held the hair of men and women and was tied around the head.
- The *sandals*: They were the shoes of the ancient Greeks, which they wore outside the *oikos* and were made of leather. In addition, they wore boots and other footwear, while inside the *oikos* they moved around mostly barefoot, although there was also a shoe that served as today's slippers.

4.3 Fashion and Women's Grooming

Classical period women used a wide range of cosmetics, including various perfumes, which they placed in special small, narrow, and tall amphorae, usually elaborately painted, called *alabastra* or *alabastrons* (sing., *alabastron*). They also used another type of vase, with a lid, for ointments called *pyxis*. Ladies used creams to whiten their cheeks. They also used white ointment as a cosmetic and dyes for eyebrows and eyelashes, etc. (Image 4.1).

Image 4.1 A Corinthian *pyxis* (fifth c. BC) and an *alabastron*. Bowls with lid, for keeping tablets of powder for makeup. Source: Image created by painter Vasiliki Demopoulou

Chapter 5
The Athenian Citizen Identity and the Administrative Organization of the Athenian City-State

Abstract This chapter highlights the characteristics of the conscientious citizen, who should have been the model of every Athenian. The chapter also presents the administrative division of the city-state of Athens into 139 *demes* (municipalities), as well as the duties of the mayors. Finally, it deals with the key elements a citizen of Athens should have been characterized of.

5.1 Nicomedes: The Dutiful Citizen of Alopekis and the Landowner

Nicomedes greeted Hegeso and Eriphyle and, as he had said, set off for the town hall to settle three issues before going to his bank.

His *oikos* was about four *stadia* from the town hall, and from there it would take Nicomedes about half an hour at a relatively brisk walk to reach the location in the Agora where the banks of the polis were housed.

He arrived at the town hall of Alopekis known as *demarcheion*. He first wanted to pay the municipal tax he had forgotten to pay the previous month to the *deme's* treasury. He waited for two other citizens to be served and after a while it was his turn.

– Hello Hilarion!
– Hello Nicomedes! How are you? replied the municipal treasurer.
– I am fine!

Nicomedes then paid and explained that he forgot to pay the municipal tax on time due to many other obligations he had, and that it will not happen again. The treasurer replied that he did not need to worry, that these things happen, and that there is no problem, since the honesty and financial solvency of Nicomedes was known to everyone, as he told him. Nicomedes also wanted to see the civil servant who dealt with the land register of the *deme*. The time was approaching for Eriphyle to be married, and Nicomedes wanted to know some technical details about two estates he owned in Mesogeia. It was a vineyard and an olive grove. He had acquired the vineyard as a dowry when he married Hegeso while the olive grove was inherited

E. M. L. Economou, N. C. Kyriazis, *Daily Life in Classical Athens*, Frontiers in Economic History, https://doi.org/10.1007/978-3-031-58541-8_5

by him from his father and grandfather. It was about four *plethra* square in length and breadth. He planned to give them both as a dowry to the groom who would marry his beloved daughter.

Unconsciously, perhaps, he wanted to give Alopekis' estates to Eriphyle, so that he might be able to keep her with her husband, there, in this *deme*, so that in the future, she would stand close to Hegeso, her mother, when she would be in old age. Nicandros would of course also have to look after his parents in their old age, a duty to any *kalos kagathos* citizen. But Nicomedes felt that the girl, Eriphyle, could contribute to her mother more, for a series of reasons he had in mind.

Nicomedes properly arranged the matter of land registry so that he could transfer the estates at any time if he wished. The last issue that had to be resolved in the *deme* concerned his military duties. He wanted to know what rank and with which of his fellow citizens he would serve in the event of a new war with Macedon or any other potential enemy.

To find the answer, he asked the mayor himself.

The *deme* and the polis held him in high esteem. So, if a new military confrontation took place, he would probably serve as a *taxiarchos*[1] in the polis's *hoplite phalanx.*

Nicomedes felt joy and pride, and a big smile crossed his face as he unconsciously raised his head slightly, a sign of pride he really felt at that moment. He would therefore continue his great family tradition of rendering high-ranking military officers for the benefit of society and the country.

- Thank you very much mayor, he answered. I intend to organize a symposion with important personalities of public life in the near future and I will invite you because I want your opinion on some very serious issues that we will discuss about the future of our polis.
- Thanks, Nicomedes, be sure I will come anyway, the mayor responded.

* * *

5.2 Units of Length and Width

The distance was measured through the so-called *stadia* which were equivalent to 600 *podes* (feet). A subdivision of the *stadium* or *stadion* was the *plethron*, which corresponded to 100 ancient Greek *podes* or to 1/6 of the *stadion*, roughly 30 m. Although there were some slight differences in the measurement of the *plethron* between the Greek city-states, the generally accepted view was that a *plethron* roughly corresponded to 30 m in length.

When the ancient Greeks wanted to measure areas such as fields, they referred again to the *plethron* which was called square *plethron*, i.e., to $30 \times 30 = 900$ square

[1] "Brigadier general" under a modern approximation.

meters, based on today's measurement, although the word "square" was not used. The *plethron* was used as a unit of measurement also at a later time, in the Byzantine Empire.

5.3 The Evolution of Athenian Society over Time

Primitive Greek society, whose origins are lost in the depths of time, was first formed by the unification of consanguineous families that expanded to include other neighboring families due to material (increased production and exchange) and other needs (defense against the enemy).

Then the *phratriai* were formed. A *phratry* (in sing.) in ancient Greek society was considered any socio-political group of people who were made up of "people of the same blood" who had a common progenitor and were characterized by common values, standards, and rules of behavior, to serve specific purposes. Etymologically, the word comes from the word *phrater-phrator*, which means "brother," as the members of a *phratry* were considered to be "brothers" to each other or otherwise "siblings." Since each small group joined the *phratriai*, we had the evolution of society as an organization of different interests converging on an ultimate goal: the best possible meeting of the needs of all groups (families). In order for the society to function and achieve its purpose as a whole, its members would have to introduce and accept some basic principles. One of them—perhaps the most basic—was what type of laws would prevail in their relations with each other. This would be formed based on the needs of their society as a whole. That is why Aristotle declared that "man is a social and political being" (Aristotle, *Nicomachean Ethics*, 1162a.23–26, 1169b.21–23; *Politics*, 1.1253a.3, 3.1278b.25–30).

Gradually the Greek society, evolving through the Bronze Age period (approximately 2800–1550 BCE), the Mycenaean period (1550–1100 BCE), the Geometric or Homeric period (1100–750 BCE), also known as the "Dark Ages," the Archaic period (750–510 BCE), and the Classical period (508–323 BCE) which we analyze here, developed an administrative structure. According to Thucydides (*History*, 2.15) the unification of the villages located in Attica under the leadership of the (mythical) Theseus constituted the state of Athens. The inhabitants were settled in villages and *demes*, the latter functioned as separate social and political entities (Osborne 1985, 64, 188), and therefore democracy first emerged from the *demes's* communes and then spread to the polis.

Draco (ruled 621–594 BCE) established some kind of primitive democratic institutions of governance after granting civil rights to those who could buy their own *hoplite* type of weaponry, mainly the shield and spear (Kyriazis and Economou 2015a; Economou and Kyriazis 2019a, chapter 1). His type of government was based on the election of state magistrates according to the value of their property. Solon then took over the government of the polis. There are various historians who recognize that an early form of democratic government was actually introduced by the socioeconomic and political reforms of Solon in 594. If we consider that Draco's introduction of the institution of the Assembly and Solon's polity was a "proto-democratic" form of governance, then Athens undoubtedly maintains the primacy in the introduction of the oldest democracy ever, as a set of specific political institutions. But there is no doubt that Cleisthenes introduced democracy as a fully fledged regime in Athens, in 508 BCE.[2]

Regarding the socioeconomic stratification of the Athenian citizens, Solon proceeded with the so-called *seisachtheia*, which meant the policy of writing off the debts of low-income citizens as a necessary measure to restore the social legitimacy of the Athenian state in the perception of its citizens. Through *seisachtheia* the possibility of converting a free citizen into a debt slave was abolished by granting a general amnesty to those who had been enslaved or sold as slaves abroad. It could be seen as a *positive sum game* situation, under a modern interpretation, where the total gains are higher than the losses.[3]

Until his death (probably in 507 BCE) Cleisthenes institutionally reorganized the Athenian state: initially, he maintained Solon's institutional reform of dividing Athenian citizens into four social classes according to their income dynamics rather than by their descent. The upper and wealthier classes were the *pentakosiomedimnoi*,

[2]It should also be mentioned that from time to time various authors claim that democracy, as a political system, was not actually discovered in Classical Greece, but in earlier times in various civilizations from the Eastern societies, such as in Ancient Mesopotamia or even China! Authors such as Jacobsen (1943) and his successors are responsible for this erroneous view. For reasons of space we cannot analyze this topic here; see, however, Economou and Kyriazis (2019a). In fact, such views come as a sequence of a wider revisionist trend in the international bibliography which is unfortunately growing. Being subjected to the current trends of political correctness worldwide, such bibliography tends to systematically downgrade the cultural achievements of the Hellenic civilization, which is one of the oldest European cultures. Greek cultural achievements are presented, to a large extent, as "imports from Asian, Middle Eastern and African societies." This trend has reached such a point of misinformation even in mass media. For example, among many other cases, a new TV series launched by Netflix in 2023 even presents the Macedonian-born Cleopatra, last queen of the Hellenistic Kingdom of Egypt, or the Mycenaean Greek warlord/hero Achilles, who were both demonstrably Greek and white, as persons of African origin! These revisionist *afroasianist* authors reach the point to argue that even democracy as a political system was not invented in Classical Greece but this political system has "Afro-Asian roots" (sic!). Eminent historians such as Lefkowitz (1996, 1997, 2008), Thornton (2000), and Hanson and Heath (2001) deconstruct these preconceived notions which systematically intend to downgrade the value added of the ancient Hellenic civilization and culture to humanity. Unbiased academic analysis proves that the first ever democracy, as a political phenomenon and system **with organized political, judicial, and economic institutions**, introduced and flourished in practice successfully, in the Classical and the Hellenistic periods of Greece. For the development of democracy in Classical Greece, see, for example, Raaflaub et al. (2007) and for the institutions and the functioning of democracy in practice, see authors such as Thorley (1996), Ober (2008), and Cartledge (2018).

[3]For the great deeds and reforms of Solon such as *seisachtheia* one can read, among others, Aristotle (*Ath. Const.*, 5.2), Plutarch (*Solon*, 14.3), Thorley (1996, 9), Cartledge (2011, 67), and van Wees (2013). For the rationale, economic parameters, and ultimate goals of the *seisachtheia*, see among others van Wees (2013).

those who had a wealth of 500 *medimnoi*.[4] The next social class was the *triacosiomedimnoi* known also as *hippeis* (horsemen), with an income of 300 *medimnoi*, which were financially capable to buy, breed, and maintain a horse. The third class was the *diakosiomedimnoi*, or *zeugitai* or *hoplites*, with an income of 200 *medimnoi* which mainly consisted of the free peasants, who at the same time composed the main body of the *hoplites* as the income they enjoyed gave them the potential to purchase the military equipment to participate in the *hoplite phalanx*.[5] The last and most populous class in the social pyramid was that of the *thetes*. It was the class with the lowest income compared to the above (Aristotle, *Athenian Constitution*, 7.3; Plutarch, *Solon*, 18.1–2).

5.4 The 10 *Phylae* and the 139 Athenian *Demes*

The next major innovation of Cleisthenes, which progressively caused radical changes in the organizational structure of society within the framework of the newly established democratic polity, was the subordination of all citizens to ten new artificial *phylae* (tribes), which administratively consisted of 139 *demes*, in which each citizen belonged to according to the location of his *oikos* within the polis.

The ten new Athenian tribes were Erechtheis, Aegeis, Pandionis, Leontis, Acamantis, Oeneis, Cecropis, Hippothontis, Aeantis, and Antiochis. Cleisthenes chose this so as to "disengage" the citizens from the four older Athenian *phylae* which were controlled by the old traditional aristocratic families, within the previous political regime of aristocracy or oligarchy. Each tribe included, as an administrative division, areas from (i) the hinterland known as the *Mesogeia* (presented as (M) in Image 5.1), (ii) the urban/urbanized area of the city of Athens known as the *Asty* [presented as (A)], and (iii) the coastal area of Attica known as *Paralia* [presented as (P)] (Hansen 1991, 103; Tridimas 2011, 61).

The most important Asty *demes* were Alimous, Kolonos, Piraeus, Phaleron, Alopekis, Kydathinaion, Melete, Lakiadai, Koile, Euonymos, Kollytos, and Skambonidai. The main *demes* of Mesogeia were Dhekeleia, Aulon, Cholargos, Kifisia, Phlya, Athmonon, Leukonoe, Ekali, Sphettos, Aphidnai, Acharnai, Phyle, Eleutherai, Oenoe, Paiania, and Pallene. Among the numerous Paralia *demes* the most important were Thorikos, with a large preserved theater, in the northern of today's Laurion, both of which were very rich in silver deposits to be exploited, as well as Aexone, on the site of nowadays Glyfada, Rafina, Brauron (in which there was also an important cult site of the Goddess Artemis), Eleusis (where the famous Eleusinian Mysteries were taking place), Marathon, Thria on the site of today's

[4] The *medimnos* was a vessel which functioned as a unit of measurement mainly for agricultural products. Its capacity was 52–59 current liters. At the time of Solon one *medimnos* had a value equivalent to one drachma.

[5] We analyze in brief the *hoplites* and the *hoplite phalanx* in Sect. 19.2.

Image 5.1 General topographic illustration of the state of Athens. Source: Image created by painter Vasiliki Demopoulou

Aspropyrgos, Anaphlestos on the site of today's Anabyssos, Phrearrioi near Anabyssos, and Myrhinnous. In the place of the current settlement of Porto Rafti were the *demes* of Steirias and Prasiai, while a little further in the north, between Steiria and Brauron were Lamprae.

Around 400 BCE apparently due to population growth and economic development that was progressively taking place, Attica numbered 174 *demes*: 164 in the countryside and 10 in Athens (Lysias, *Against Philon*). This is clear evidence that the Asty (main city) of Athens was the urban heart of the state, even if a large part of Athenians did not reside in the city of Athens but in adjacent *demes* and settlements. All these people were going to Athens—center every day for work reasons, and then, were returning to their home.

Every new child that was born was registered in the *phratry* of his father on the feast of Apatouria (month of October). When a young man turned 18, he was included in the polis register with his name, his father's name, and the *deme* he belonged to (Demosthenes, *Against Boeotus* 2, 40.4–5, 40.9). Each of the ten *phylae* was required to keep detailed records of those citizens who served in the army as cavalrymen (Lysias, *For Mantitheus*, 16.6). The *demes* compiled and kept local citizen registers as well, known as *lexiarchika grammateia*. A general revision of the *lexiarchika grammateia* known as *diapsephismos* could be conducted in all the 139 *demes*, whereby non-citizens who had tried to deceive the *deme*, pretending to have the status of citizen, were expelled from the list, sometimes after a trial before the Heliaia court. The appropriation of citizenship was being prosecuted with a regulation known as *graphe xenias*. The guilty were punished by deprivation of their freedom and the Athenian government could sell them as slaves, a very severe punishment.

The above evidence is important because it proves that in the Athenian state there were organized censuses, so that at any time, the local *deme*, or the state itself through the *deme*, could know the situation of each citizen (place of residence, age, and whether married or single, being father or not). Also, each tribe preserved detailed conscript data: year of enlistment and corps, type of rank, e.g., horseman, *hoplite*, *psilos* (lightly armed), *thetes* (sailor-rower in *trireme*), or naval officer. In fact, it maintained elements that nowadays one can look for in a modern registry office service.

5.5 The Alopekis *Deme*

Alopeki or Alopekes was an ancient *deme* of the Antiochis *phyle* which took its name from the mythical Antiochus, son of Heracles and Meda, daughter of Phylantas. Alopekis was located about 11 or 12 *stadia*, i.e., about 2–2.3 km from the settlements to the east of the city center, not far from Cynosarges (Aeschines, *Against Timarchus*, 1.99). The exact location of the Alopekis *deme* has not yet been precisely identified. Modern researchers place its center in the border area between today's Daphne and Agios Demetrios. It is very likely that this declarative characterization of the specific *deme* came from the fact that its inhabitants worked in crafts related to the processing of fur from foxes or sheepskin. But there were also many other residents who worked at Alopekis as stonemasons and ironsmiths. Alopekis *deme* was also one of the most important seats of the aristocratic family of Alcmaeonidae, which had a very distant historical past regarding the developments that from the Archaic period to the Classical period contributed to the emergence of the democratic reforms of Cleisthenes, who was originating from it. In the period 508–307/306 BCE the *deme* participated with 10 members in the Athenian Council.

5.6 The *Demesmen*, the *Demarchs*, and Their Responsibilities

The *demarchs* (mayors) were an institution founded by Cleisthenes. At first, they were elected for a 1-year term probably by vote in a local municipal assembly but probably around 451/0 their election process was taking place by lot (Thorley 1996, 43, 45–6). Those candidates who participated in the lottery by the citizens of the *deme* should have first passed some type of inspection regarding their moral status and their contribution to the polis.

The *demarchs* represented their fellow citizens in various religious ceremonies; they distributed the *theorica*[6] to the citizens of the *deme* and collected the taxes and debts of individuals to the *deme*. From the evidence available to us it appears that *demarchs* were not necessarily members of a high-income class and were not naturally "mayors by profession" (Osborne 1985, 53). This means that the criterion for assuming their duties was not their financial situation. Also, the *demes* had the responsibility to check whether a series of candidates met the criteria to become members of the Athenian Council. The *demes* also chose those citizens who were about to undertake a *liturgy* based on their property and wealth, as well as the individuals who would man the fleet in general. The *demes* even covered the funeral expenses of citizens in need (Osborne 1985, 139). Consequently, a fairly decentralized administrative system was in place in the Athenian state, where *demes* supplied the Athenian Council and the Heliaia courts with manpower (*ibid.*, 75–82).

According to Economou (2024, 36), each *demarch* together with his associates and staff had the following important responsibilities:

- To manage income and expenses of the *deme* in collaboration with the *tamias* (treasurer) of the *deme*.
- To maintain a reliable registry of all citizens. This was important because it was directly linked to citizenship.[7]
- To maintain a reliable cadastral register regarding the rural land properties of the *demesmen*.[8]
- To prepare and organize a series of festive (and non-celebratory) events, such as offering the official sacrifices to the gods in collaboration with the priests of the temples
- To supervise and take care of the preparation of theatrical performances
- To collect rents from the leased municipal lands
- To collect state taxes (upon request)
- In case of war, to contribute to the state regarding the recruitment of the *hoplites* for the land army and sailors (*thetes*) for the naval forces, and sometimes to collect extraordinary taxes on behalf of the state
- To contribute to the selection process of the members of the Athenian Council that corresponded to each *deme* (by population criteria). If more candidate Councilmen were presented, then the *deme* should probably proceed with a lottery procedure to elect the Councilmen

[6]For the *theorica* institution, see Sect. 18.3.

[7]Therefore, like every institutionally developed state in history, the Athenian one kept census data. The Athenian public administration knew the exact number of its citizens, and through them, probably had a fairly accurate picture of the number of slaves and *metics* residing in the polis. Foreigners were only allowed to stay in the polis for a certain period of time and for a certain reason, e.g., trade, ambassadorial delegations, etc.

[8]The existence of a form of cadastre shows how well organized the Athenian state was.

- To supervise the creation of inscriptions with the names of those who benefited the *deme*
- To carry out anti-flood works in their area of responsibility (Demosthenes, *Against Callicles*, 55.17, 55.20)
- To be the representative of the *deme* in the courts, when no one else had been assigned with this
- To be the link of his *deme* with the other *demes*

5.7 The Title of Citizen and the Role of Censuses

The reason why after the Law of Citizenship introduced by Pericles the Athenians conferred the title of citizen only on children born of a marriage where both parents were proven Athenian citizens (Demosthenes, *Against Eubulides*, 57.17, 57.30) may have been that they did not want to mix their own manners, customs, and traditions with the habits of others. Such a thing, they feared, would distort democracy and the laws that accompanied it. For this reason, they demanded that a punishment should be imposed if a male or female citizen cohabited with a foreigner illegally, that is, pretending that his/her partner was a native Athenian, although she/he was not (Demosthenes, *Against Neaera*, 59.16–17, 59.52, 59.89).

When a new child was born, the child's father did not immediately announce the birth to the tribe, but announced this 10 days later, when he was fairly certain that the infant would live (Demosthenes, *Against Boeotus 1*, 39.22). Members of the *phratry* knew early on and certified whether a child was born of Athenian parents (Demosthenes, *Against Neaera*, 59.59–60, 59.63), so it was not easy to register a foreigner as a citizen in a *deme*. The entry in the censuses was requested by the father (Andocides, *On the Mysteries*, 1.124) not only to express in this way the role of the head of the family, but also to delimit his heirs. A person could not be an Athenian citizen unless he could prove it, when required. He had to be referred to as a member of a genus which was associated with groups of individuals bound together by common religious ceremonies. Thus, a newly born child had to be registered in the *deme* to which it would belong in the future to be recorded in its registry files. Hence it was not easy to falsify evidence regarding a person's Athenian origin.

The Athenian polis gave many incentives and freedoms to its citizens who wished—always according to its laws—to live and be active in it. It must be also admitted that in the period after the end of the Peloponnesian War and the Second Athenian Alliance (378–355 BCE), there was a noticeable decline in the morals of its citizens. Various officials of the *demes* as well as citizens, in general, appeared who, with various tricks, tried to illegally register foreigners in the registers of the *demes*. For example, the incident with Agoratus is typical, who with his complaints led, during the rule of Athens under the Thirty Tyrants,[9] to the killing of prominent citizens. He was trialed in 398 and proved to have forged state decisions making him a citizen, when in fact he was the son of slaves (Lysias, *Against Agoratus*, 18–20, 73–75).

Regarding the Law of Citizenship of Pericles, this law became known as the *Law of Citizenship*. Under a rational-actor perspective, Lyttkens and Henrik (2018) reveal that there are also hidden financial and political motives behind its adoption. More specifically, they argue that three key sets of actions that Pericles introduced, the introduction of payments to jurors, the law of citizenship, and the implementation of large building projects (see also Sect. 18.3), could easily have been motivated by the need to strengthen his position vis-à-vis his great political rival, Cimon. There were also at least two recorded censuses to clarify the legal citizenship (or not) of citizens, one in 445 BCE under Pericles and the other in 346 BCE. These two censuses may be the earliest in recorded history; it is evident that the belief of those who believe that the organization and registration of citizens, in ancient forms of censuses, was valid only from the period of the Roman Empire onward should be reconsidered.

The Athenians hoped that with the censuses they would reveal all the people who had illegally entered into the body of citizens in various ways. For any such case they had introduced the so-called *graphe xenias*, a law against anyone who unlawfully exercised the rights of citizenship. If convicted, such a person was sold as a slave and his property was confiscated by the state (Demosthenes, *Against Eubulides*, 57.6–7). Of course, this was a very severe punishment. But we believe that the Athenians introduced it because they wanted to eliminate any falsification in their electoral procedures in the Assembly, due to people who illegally voted.

In fact, in a related trial that took place in 345 BCE for the revision of the lists of citizens, a number of people were found illegally registered in the polis catalogues due to various situations. Rich foreigners were found buying off *demes's* magistrates and secretaries through bribery for that purpose. There is a case where 5000 drachmae were offered for that purpose, a very high price, which was considered usual though for such a type of illegal act (*ibid.*, 57.25, 57.29). Another similar illegal practice was buying off witnesses who falsely attested that those concerned were Athenian citizens. This, for example, was the case of a famous *hetaera* with the name Neaera who was accused of illegitimately claiming the rights of Athenian citizenship in favor of herself and her daughter (Demosthens, *Against Neaera*, 59.13).

Under these legal specifications, the Athenians severely punished those foreigners who were caught to have illegally acquired *isoteleia*, i.e., to pay taxes with the same status as the rest of the (well-to-do) Athenians, but also those who helped them (Demosthenes, *Against Neaera*, 59.124). Furthermore, the Athenians did not want citizenship rights to be given to the corrupt and the sons of slaves in exchange for some money they would give for that purpose (Demosthenes, *On Organization*,

[9]The Thirty Tyrants formed an oligarchic government of 30 people, which abolished Athenian democracy after the end of the Peloponnesian War. It lasted 8 months, in 404 BCE.

13.24). This would have undermined the quality of their democracy. The right of citizenship was granted to foreigners under the following conditions and procedures, based on laws: First of all, the candidate deserved the title of citizen because he offered great services to the polis so far. In addition, his citizenhsip rights had to be ratified by the Athenian Assembly and at least 6000 citizens should vote in favor of him by secret ballot. Each citizen was then allowed to express his objections to the merit of the candidate citizen or on the ground of cheating the body. There have also been recorded cases where, following a complaint, the citizenship rights were removed from a foreigner (Demosthenes, *Against Neaera*, 59.89–92). Lastly, those who eventually became *isoteleis* did not have the right to be elected among the *nine archons*[10] or undertake priestly office.

In another, case, an exceptional one, retrieved by Demosthenes (*Against Neaera*, 59.94–106), the Athenians had given the title of citizen en masse to the surviving Plataeans after they had been attacked by the Lacedaimonians (Spartans) in the early years of the Peloponnesian War for the great military assistance they offered to Athens. An Athenian with the name Hippocrates proposed, and it was accepted (after 427) by the Athenian popular Assembly, that the particular Plataeans should be divided into *demes* and *phylae* and have, as long as they lived, the right of *isoteles* citizen. However, first they also had to be examined if they were really Plataeans **and friends of the Athenians** and then their names should be inscribed on a stele on the Acropolis so that their direct descendants would have the same equal rights. If they married an Athenian woman and had children, the latter would have full rights as future citizens.[11]

As a final comment, we believe that the Athenians should not be considered simply selfish or unhumanistic because they did not include non-blood relatives-citizens in their citizen ranks. This policy was their method of "protection"—at least they thought in this way—for not relaxing the social consciousness and the societal goals they had developed.

[10]This post is further analyzed in Sect. 6.6.

[11]Canevaro (2010) provides an analysis of various aspects of this decree of awarding citizenship to the Plataeans.

Chapter 6
The Athenian Political System's Institutions and the Manning of Posts Related to Public Administration

Abstract This chapter analyzes in detail the political institutions of decision-making as well as the public offices in Classical Athens. A key element of the success of the Athenian political system and the system of public administration was that citizens should have been active in participating in the related processes of running the state institutions. It also explains why most public offices were chosen by lottery, while some (a few) were chosen by appointment instead of lottery.

6.1 Nicomedes: The Active and Virtuous Citizen

Nicomedes, being an active citizen and an ardent democrat himself, firmly and unwaveringly believed in Pericles' view that "the citizen who does not participate in the commons is useless."

He had read these ideas and was inspired by reading the Funeral Speech written by Thucydides, more than a century ago, as a eulogy for the Athenian heroes who fell on the battlefield during the first year of the genocidal Peloponnesian War.

He admired this work; he characterized it as "the blessing of Athens" and as a "practical manual of the Athenian mentality," as he considered that everyone, either Athenian or foreigner, by reading it, could easily, quickly, and comprehensively perceive the greatness and the spirit of Athens, through its morals, values, and political institutions.

Nicomedes' family had a long tradition of civic participation in the polis affairs, not only because the political system of Athens demanded the active participation of citizens in the commons, but because his ancestors had shown a special zeal for public life and public affairs. Nicomedes' distant great-grandfather, Nicodemos, had been *eponymous archon* in 483–482 BCE when the famous Themistocles Naval Decree was voted by the citizens, which transformed Athens from a mainly agrarian economy to a maritime and commercially extroverted one.

Before going to his workplace, the specialized area of Agora where the *pagkos* of his bank with Ischomachos, his trusted bank employee, was located, he decided to pass first through the Bouleuterion and the Prytaneion also known as the Tholos, to address a number of his friends, who served the polis as public officials.

E. M. L. Economou, N. C. Kyriazis, *Daily Life in Classical Athens*, Frontiers in Economic History, https://doi.org/10.1007/978-3-031-58541-8_6

He was well-networked and knew a large number of his fellow citizens not only because the very nature of the Athenian political system networked many different citizens from different *demes*, communities, and *phratries*, but also because he himself took an active interest in the polis matters, believed in its institutions, and moreover, and equally important, was distinguished by innate sociability.

He knew so many citizens by their names, and just as importantly, he was similarly known to so many, either associates, clients, and friends, or others, whom he did not know or remember, and he did not imagine that they knew him personally.

In addition, and most importantly, his integrity and morals were almost universally praised, both by his fellow citizens and by his associates and foreign merchants, but also by the ideological factions that supported either the democratic or the oligarchic circles of the polis.

Nicomedes had in the past once been a *bouleutes* (a Councilman) and twice a public official, serving the critical position of the *ten logistai*, i.e., as an auditor of the financial transactions of public officials in critical public posts. He had been chosen for this crucial post by the Athenian Council itself, because he had many years of experience in commercial and entrepreneurial activity and knew very well how the Agora laws were functioning in practice, including all the relative internationally accepted accounting and auditing practices.

Nicomedes never faced false accusations of maladministration by opportunists or slanderers, which always existed, because it was rather clear that anyone who sought to harm him would ultimately be harmed himself; state institutions such as the Council and the courts did accept complaints for maladministration or corruption against citizens who were public officials, but if these were not proven, accusers faced serious legal consequences, such as paying substantial fines. The state posts of the ten *logistai*, the *ten euthynoi*, and the *ten synegoroi* were considered pivotal for the proper administration of the "public sector," such as the effective collection and management of the state's public revenues and the effective fight against corruption, two key elements for the proper functioning of both the Agora and the state institutions. If these were achieved, at least to a satisfactory degree, even if not optimally, they ensured the well-being of the citizens, through the higher economic performance of the polis' administration as a whole. In such a case, a significant degree of trust between the citizens regarding the state institutions and democracy was forged.

Nicomedes never hesitated to submit blameless and impartial reports without reckoning that in one case, with a report of him, he condemned with a very high fine, 500 drachmae, a fellow citizen being also a personal friend of his since childhood, Agathon, who contrary to his name, meaning being naïve and pure, he proved *atimos* (dishonored) when, by incontrovertible evidence, revealed by Nicomedes, he attempted to bribe some members of the board of the so-called *poletai*, in order to win, at a humiliating price, a license to mine silver from public land, in a specific location in Laurion, something that would harm the public. Nicomedes exposed him, together with his accomplice, one of the *poletai*, as it was later proved by the courts in Heliaia. Both paid a heavy price: the event became known and they were labeled *atimoi* (dishonorable men). Since this was a serious offense, they were then deprived of their political rights and thus became finger-pointed in society.

Agathon of course never spoke to Nicomedes again. The dignity of the latter did not allow him to seek a channel of communication between the two men, and thus the childhood friendship, which had lasted until the years of their maturity, had now definitively faded away. This incident had been engraved in Nicomedes' memory, because sometimes, he also recalled with nostalgia the nice memories of true friendship he shared with Agathon in the past.

He then decided to stop by the Metroon as well and greet Dion, a friend of his who was serving that year as a *nomophylax* with six other civil servants there. At that moment, as he approached the Bouleuterion, two magistrates, Epiphanios and Androcles, passed in front of him. They were greeted.

With Androcles they were good friends and exchanged, for years, frequent visits to each other's houses. Androcles was pro-oligarchic and pro-Macedonian, but Nicomedes truly believed in the right of free speech that was related to the right for free circulation of ideas, and despite their several disagreements, they remained friends.

Nicomedes next went to the Bouleuterion, where, among other things, he was informed by his friends about the proposals to be discussed for the next Assembly of citizens, which also happened to be an *Ecclesia Kyria* (a key citizen's Assembly).

* * *

6.2 The Naval Decree of Themistocles of 483/482 BCE

With the defeat of the Persians at Marathon, in 490 BCE, the Persian danger to Greece was temporarily averted. But gradually more and more rumors began to flare up, which then became very serious indications that the Persian Empire was conducting major war preparations, mobilizing huge military forces from all the lengths of the vast empire, as well as logistical support, in order to carry out a very large-scale campaign for the conquest of Greece.

But in Hellas, some great men, like the Athenian Themistocles, were monitoring these developments with vigilance. In 483/482 BCE something happened, which, as if a *deus ex machina*, was to reshape the context of the imminent military confrontation between Greeks and Persians, which was only a matter of time as to when it would take place. A new large deposit of silver was discovered in the area of Laurion where the Athenians were exploiting silver mines. Themistocles, proving that he possessed the "yeast" of the great leaders of history, immediately realized that this was a unique opportunity that should not be missed by putting into practice his grandiose plan, which as it turned out, was a strategic plan to save Hellas. In particular, in the Athenian Assembly the question of the management of this money would be raised. One view, supported by conservative pro-oligarch circles, with Aristides as their main representative, was to distribute the money to each citizen, where each would be allocated separately 10 drachmae per year, or roughly half a monthly salary. Themistocles, however, wanted this money to be used for the construction of warships (*triremes*) in order to face the Persian invasion.

After intense behind-the-scenes actions, which contributed to the *ostracism*[1] of his main political opponent Aristides, Themistocles finally succeeded in implementing his naval program and the most important reason was because he managed to get the *thetes*, i.e., the lowest economic class of the social pyramid, on his side, promising that if they supported his proposal in the popular Assembly, he would offer them steady work as civil servants-rowers of the navy, so that their social status would be radically upgraded through the operation of the state (see further, among others, Economou (2024, 54–73) and the references we provide therein).

Apart from the genius stratagems of Themistocles, which proved decisive for the Greek victory in terms of human resources, the victory at Salamis should primarily be attributed to the *thetes*. Therefore, on the well-known dilemma of *Public Choice* theory, under an economics perspective, "butter or guns," the Athenians were not at all intending to negotiate: they clearly selected a war preparation policy, for the salvation of the motherland. The Athenian strategy was based on the simple reasoning that, in order to have health, education, and social benefits, etc., you must first of all still "have" your own state. Themistocles persuasively convinced his compatriots regarding the correctness of such a view. Themistocles did not utilize only the economic motives in favor of the *thetes* in case they would accept his proposal. He also managed to affect the decision of the Delphi Oracle who proposed that the salvation of the polis would be achieved through the construction of "wooden walls."[2] He cleverly manipulated a religious order, by cleverly convincing the majority of his compatriots that Pythia was speaking metaphorically and such kind of walls was, in reality, building warships. Herodotus (143.2–3) writes that Themistocles:

> Correctly understood, the gods' oracle was spoken not of the Athenians but of their enemies, and his advice was that they should believe their ships to be the wooden wall and so make ready to fight by sea. When Themistocles put forward this interpretation, the Athenians judged him to be a better counsellor than the readers of oracles, who would have had them prepare for no sea fight, and, in short, offer no resistance at all, but leave Attica and settle in some other country.

[1] Ostracism was a process where any citizen who was considered dangerous to the possible overthrow of the democratic regime could be exiled for 10 years from the Athenian state. This citizen who received more than 6000 votes from his fellow citizens suffered his expulsion from the polis. Voting was done by writing the name of the candidate citizen to be ostracized, on a fragment of a clay vessel called *ostracon* (Plutarch, *Aristides*, 7.5; Thorley 1996, 83–84; Hansen 1991, 35–36; Forsdyke 2005; Christ 2006, 47; Osiander 2007, 49; Fröhlich 2013, 254).

[2] For the great stratagems of Themistocles, that led to the beyond any expectation Greek victory at Salamis, see Plutarch (*Themistocles*), Strauss (2004), and the recent papers of Economou et al. (2022b) and Platias and Trigkas (2022) among others.

The Themistoclean naval program was undoubtedly a colossal task: the Athenians had to employ more than half of their free citizens in the new necessities of the program: new professions related to the sea and shipbuilding emerged and others were much more developed, such as shipwrights, carpenters, metalworkers, and blacksmiths and new labor specializations were required such as the construction of high-quality spare parts for the *triremes*, the machining and construction of the rams of the *triremes*, sails, etc. (Gabrielsen 1994; Tridimas 2013; Acton 2014; McArthur 2021).[3]

Neoria (dockyards) were located in Piraeus, whose flourishment coincided with the time of Pericles. The most important were the large *neorion* of Zea (today's Pasalimani) and the smaller ones of Munichia (today's Microlimano) and Kantharos (the cove opposite the Piraeus metro station). Inside the *neoria* were *neosoikoi* (shipsheds). During the fourth century, the *neoria* of the polis of Athens had the ability to host up to 500 *triremes*, a very large number. Other famous *neoria* were those of Samos, Corinth, Corfu, and Syracuse, etc.

From an economic standpoint, this new strategy of "turning toward the sea" contributed to the significant transformation of the Athenian economy: from a land-based economy, to manufacturing, the "secondary" sector of production, construction, and the further development of financial institutions, as will be further explained in detail in the next Scenes. After repelling the Persian threat, Athens went on the counterattack[4] and founded in 478 BCE the First Athenian Alliance in order to limit the Persian influence in the wider Greek geo-economic and geopolitical sphere of influence.

6.3 The *Ecclesia of the Demos*

Pericles' opinion that "the citizen who does not participate in the commons, is useless" is attributed by Thucydides' *History* (2.40.1).

Archaeological evidence has retrieved many speeches delivered in the Athenian Assembly, for example, the *Philippics* and *Olynthiacs*, covering the period from 355/4 to 341 BCE.

The main decisions concerning the state (war, peace, economic policy, public works, etc.) were taken in the Assembly where all citizens over the age of 20 could exercise, through *isegoria*, **the right to speak freely in the Assembly and everywhere else as well as the right to vote in political procedures** (McAuley 2013,

[3] For the transformation of the Athenian economy due to the Themistocles's Naval Decree, see also our own contributions, such as Kyriazis and Zouboulakis (2004), Kyriazis (2006, 2007b), Halkos and Kyriazis (2010), Kyriazis and Metaxas (2010), Kyriazis and Karayiannis (2011), Economou and Kyriazis (2017, 2019a), Economou et al. (2022a), and Economou (2023, 2024).

[4] As they did after the sixteenth c. AD the United Provinces and England who faced victoriously the greatest power of the time, the Spanish Empire. See, among others, Economou and Kyriazis (2019a) and Kyriazis et al. (2018) for a further analysis on this.

Image 6.1 The Pnyx's podium. The Acropolis and the Lycabettus hills in the background. Source: Image owned by the authors

180). In practice, the Athenian citizen was deciding to speak to the Assembly after he was 30 years old (Lysias, *For Mantitheus*, 16.20). The 20 years limit was the recognition of the individual as a citizen of the polis who defends it with his body; the 30 years limit marked the beginning of his social and political maturation.

The Athenian Assembly met in the fourth century (at least) 40 days a year, in all-day scheduled meetings. According to Aristotle (*Athenian Constitution*, 43.4–6), the Athenian Assembly met four times every *prytany*. The first meeting in every new *prytany* was called *Ecclesia Kyria*, where very important matters were discussed. Extraordinary meetings of the Assembly were also taking place, if circumstances required it, called *ecclesiai synkletoi* (Harris 1991).[5] Minimum number of mandatory meetings during the year was 10 (Thorley 1996, 30). The meetings of the Assembly were taking place in the Pnyx hill. To be valid, the presence of at least 6000 citizens was required. Pnyx's seating capacity may have been anywhere from 6000 to 13,000 people, while Flacelière (1959) argued that it had the required space that could host even as many as 20,000 citizens (Image 6.1).

From 403/2 BCE onward, the participants in the Assembly received through the institution of *ecclesiasticon*, initially one *obol* as a remuneration for their participation in its workings, but also as compensation for the loss of income to those who abstained from their work in order to participate in the Assembly. This was adopted by the Athenians after a proposal made in the Assembly by a politician named Aghyrrios, as an incentive because after the end of the Peloponnesian War there had been a tendency for citizens to abstain from the workings of the Assembly, with the risk of not filling the quorum of 6000 participants. Then Heracleides, a citizen of Clazomenae, a city-state of Asia Minor, who then came to Athens and faithfully served the polis, and for this he was honored by the polis with the status of a citizen, counter-suggested two *obols*, and then Aghyrrios finally counter-proposed three *obols* (half a drachma) which the Assembly finally accepted (Arist., *Ath. Const.*, 41.3). Next, in the time of Aristotle (384–322 BCE), the *ecclesiasticon* was

[5] In this respect, Harris disagrees with Hansen (1977, 2007) who challenged the mainstream view and instead argued that, in actuality, the *ecclesia synkletos* was one of the four meetings held during a *prytany*.

increased to 1 whole drachma which was equivalent to 2/3 of an average daily wage in the fourth century (see Loomis 1998), to encourage participation in the Assembly. One drachma concerned the "normal" assemblies. When one of the planned *ecclesia kyria* was taking place the daily compensation of the participants increased to 1.5 drachmae, exactly the same as the average daily wage (Sinclair 1991, 117; Hansen 1991, 150; Tridimas 2017).

Even if an Athenian attended on average only half of the main Assembly gatherings, it means that he devoted 20 days of his time to the politics-administration of the state, and so we believe that this process progressively created in the Athenians' minds an affinity and a sense of moral obligation to participate in the state administrative and political procedures. Also, since the 500 Councilmen were elected each year out of a total of 30,000 citizens in the fourth century, almost every Athenian would have served at least once as a councilor in his lifetime.

A key component of the well-functioning democracy in the fourth century, which was less radical and prone to demagogues than in the fifth century[6] was citizen's *paideia* (an educational process that included both technical knowledge and the cultivation of moral standards to citizens). In terms of institutional arrangements, the most important was the *graphe paranomon* which was established at the end of the fifth century, probably with the re-establishment of democracy in 403 BCE. It essentially provided that any proposal made either from a citizen or the Council that reached the Assembly must have been "constitutional," that is, it would not have come contrary to the current legal regime.[7] Also, accountability of state magistrates was a very important process in Athens,[8] and this was also one of the key reasons for the well-functioning of democracy at the time, in contrast to many modern democracies, where the accountability of politicians or public magistrates is essentially non-existent and ordinary citizens cannot appeal against them on political grounds, in cases such as violations of the public interest, violations of the constitution, etc.[9]

6.4 *The Bouleutai*

The main responsibility of the Athenian Boule (Council) and its members, the *bouleutai*, was (i) to prepare the issues to be discussed on various state policy issues, the so-called *probouleumata*, that is, in essence, bills proposed for approval or rejection by the Assembly of citizens, (ii) to provide auditing services regarding

---

[6] See Halkos et al. (2022) on this.

[7] We analyze the *graphe paranomon* further in Sect. 6.8. We further analyze the importance of *paideia* in Sects. 20.2 and 20.3.

[8] See Fröhlich (2013), Bitros et al. (2020), Economou (2023), and our analysis in Sect. 6.13 on this.

[9] However, it's comforting that in some countries and states, such as Switzerland, Uruguay, and various American states, the institution of *recall* is applied, where a politician can be recalled before the end of his term through a referendum "from the bottom up."

the proper functioning of the public administration through bodies such as the *logistai* and the *euthynoi*,[10] (iii) to provide the executive branch of the Athenian "constitution," that is, the *prytaneis* (see below in Sect. 6.5).

The Athenians did not unconditionally accept anyone who had been chosen by lot for membership in the Council. Each of the 500 candidates who would form the annual body of the Council for the next year would have to go through the *dokimasia*, a process where a committee derived from the outgoing Council examined whether the candidate held citizenship legally or not, and whether or not his overall past in the public sphere and especially his qualifications and morals were the proper ones (Ober 2008, 156–157). Furthermore, any outgoing Councilman had the right to challenge his replacement if he considered that this candidate did not meet the required qualifications.

The most important issue to be investigated by the committee who held the *dokimasia* was related to the overall code of behavior of a candidate in the past. He would have to reside in the polis and have taken an active part in situations that were related to the polis' prosperity (such as defending the motherland as a part of a military duty) unless there was some important reason that prevented him from doing so. He should not have put his personal interest above the polis or acquired wealth by exploiting the needs of his countrymen and especially the poor. He should not have remained uninvolved in the efforts of his fellow citizens to preserve or restore democracy and confront every internal enemy who wanted to overthrow it, including external enemies who sought to enslave or defeat Athens. He should not have shown cowardice regarding these issues. He should not have harmed the polis in any way, nor any of his fellow citizens, and he should have actively supported his own family and his parents' needs. The reason is that if he had not done so, how would his fellow citizens expect him to take an interest in favor of the state affairs? The above mean that his previous actions as an individual and as a citizen should have convinced his fellow citizens before allowing him to undertake office (Lysias, *Against Philon*, 31.10–12, 31.14, 31.24, 31.33; *For Mantitheus*, 16.3, 16.8, 1612, 16.15). "Your actions of yesterday, today and those expected tomorrow determine your future in the polis"; this must have been the motto of the Athenians to prepare the citizens for making decisions for the common good.

Anyone who wished to become a public magistrate such as a Councilman should have not by any means offended the public sentiment, as was determined by the prevailing morals. For example, when he was young he was not supposed to play dice or get drunk or have fun without measure (Lysias, *For Mantitheus*, 16.11). Such bad habits could harm his overall health progressively. After all, disabled men could not man state posts (Lysias, *On the Refusal of a Pension*, 24.4–13, 24.22). Furthermore, he had to care about his sisters, to get them endowed, or to help them if they were left unmarried and widowed (Lysias, *For Mantitheus*, 16.9–10). He should also take care to arrange properly the burial of his parents (Lysias, *Against Philon*, 31.20–21).

[10]For these crucial posts, see Sect. 6.13.

In addition to the above, the candidate for becoming a Councilman, who had been selected for this post by the *deme* to which he belonged, should also willingly wish to live such a way: to accept to participate in the good and bad moments of his polis (Lysias, *Against Philo*, 31.5, 31.9). In other words, the new Councilmen should try to serve the interests of their polis with all their power. So, if someone, while being an Athenian, resided in another polis or lived serving and pursuing only his own interest, he was not considered to meet the conditions for Councilman. After being chosen, each one of the selected Councilmen swore an oath and then was accepted to the Bouleuterion (*ibid*., 31.2). Here again is another practice that is followed also by modern states, which has its origins in Ancient Greece: A public servant, before undertaking his duties, has to take an oath as an ex ante commitment that he will perform his duties diligently until their completion.

The general concept of the operation of the Athenian public administration was that it was the duty of state officials to follow the law. Each year the new members of the Athenian Council swore to carry out their duties according to the laws. The *nine archons* of the polis were bound to recite a similar oath (Aristotle, *Athenian Constitution*, 55.5). The Councilmen, when assuming their duties, took an oath that they would defend with all their power the public interest and would not turn a blind eye to offenses that might be committed even by their relatives or friends in the future. They also swore that they would denounce anyone who did not have the qualifications and morals to serve the polis. Judges were also taking an oath before undertaking their duties (Harris 2013, chapter 3). This included also generals. From Deinarchus' speech *Against Philocles* (2.3) we learn that in 323 BCE an acting general with the name Philocles stood trial for accepting bribes and this was interpreted as an act of breaking the oath, which was a punishable condition.

The meetings of the Councilmen took place in the Bouleuterion, where all the deputies were housed. Meetings were taking place every day, except for holidays. In the Bouleuterion the Councilmen prepared the laws to be submitted to the Assembly.

Why were the Athenians so cautious in choosing their public magistrates?

The answer is that they wanted meritocracy to prevail in their polis by accepting only men who would have the will and the proper qualifications to contribute effectively on its administration. By selecting those who had demonstrated positive characteristics, it was as if they were saying: "you see that those who behave as good citizens and good people are rewarded by the polis." This encouraged citizens to live up to the standards of *kalos kagathos* behavior in the hope of being rewarded by becoming Councilmen or public magistrates, which was considered a very honorable status for every citizen and came as recognition of his worth by his fellow citizens (Lysias, *Against Philon*, 31. 25). The approval or rejection of a citizen for the position of a Councilman was also related to his external appearance, to some extent. However, the previous honest life of the candidate was what was primarily being evaluated during the *dokimasia* procedure (Lysias, *For Mantitheus*, 16.18–19).

Even in the case that during the *dokimasia* it was judged that a citizen did not have the required qualifications and morals for the position of a Councilman, that person had the right to appeal and ask to be judged also by Heliaia. In this way, among other things, the Athenians showed that they greatly respected the individuality of the citizens; thus, the possibility for a better judgment was also an option. This means that the state itself considered that every citizen, if he wished so, was entitled to a second review regarding any unfavorable judgment with which he was judged by a public body; in this case, certain executives of the Council who (potentially) evaluated him unfavorably. Apparently, as a safeguard of objective justice, the Athenian political-administrative system allowed each citizen to request a re-evaluation of his candidacy, not by the same institution, but by another (courts) as a mechanism to increase the state's impartiality regarding its affairs with the citizens.

Transparency, impartiality, and low level of corruption in public administration are a key prerequisite for achieving efficiency in the long run, and it is a core issue in advance economies around the globe nowadays (see in detail Rothstein (2011) on this). The Athenians had well-understood this. This process, along with many others that have already been mentioned, is yet another proof of the high level of democratic procedures that were followed by the Athenian system of governance in terms of transparency in decision-making. It also proves that the wish of the Athenians was to staff the public administration with the best executives, in terms of abilities and morals.

6.5 The *Prytaneis*

The *prytaneis* constituted the "government" of the Athenian democratic regime for 1/10 of the calendar year. Each day one of the *prytaneis* was chosen by them as "chairman" of the *prytanic* council where he assumed the duties of the head of the *prytaneis* or *epistates*, from sunset of one day to sunset of the next (Aristotle, *Athenian Constitution*, 43.3; Schwartzberg 2004, 312). Therefore, any citizen could become *epistates of the prytaneis*, and for one day a year he assumed duties comparable to those of a head of state. If an Assembly happened to be held that day, this magistrate presided over it (Thorley 1996, 25–28).

Image 6.2 depicts a series of public buildings which were located on the southwest side of the Agora, related to the governance of the polis. On the left is the Prytaneion or Tholos (circular building); on the right is the Old Bouleuterion and behind this building is the New Bouleuterion, where the meetings of the Athenian Council were taking place. The Prytaneion housed the *prytaneis*, the 50 members of the 500-member Council, who were on round-the-clock duty to deal with any state emergencies. The Prytaneion also functioned as a dining area for the Councilmen.

The Old Bouleuterion dates from the end of the sixth century BCE. It was used to accommodate the members of the Council. The building consisted of a large chamber with a capacity of 700 citizens. The New Bouleuterion was built shortly before 412/411 BCE. It replaced the earlier building, in order to serve the expanding needs of the state and remained in use until the Roman period. It was rectangular, with windows and amphitheatrically arranged wooden benches. After the

Image 6.2 The Prytaneion (round building on the left) and the Old and the New Bouleuterion, respectively (on the right). Source: Image created by painter Vasiliki Demopoulou

construction of the New Bouleuterion, the Old one was used as the Metroon, the storeroom for state archives. It also accommodated the sanctuary of the Mother of the Gods.

6.6 The *Nine Archons* and the *Areopagos* Court

The institution of the *nine archons* was a remnant of the aristocratic era, which the citizens nevertheless respected and honored for traditional reasons. This office was essentially stripped away during the period of democracy after the reforms of Ephialtes and Pericles where its former judicial powers were transferred mainly to the popular courts of Heliaia, but also to the Council and the Assembly.

However, the *nine archons* still held a position of prestige during the period of democracy. They were entrusted with the duties of presiding at meetings of various courts for certain cases and drawing the lots for the judges. After the end of their term they all became lifelong members of the Areopagos. The latter was linked to the Athenian governing council during the Archaic period, but after 462 BCE Areopagos was limited to a court that judged only homicides (Tridimas 2011, 61).

The process of the election of the *nine archons* was as follows: ten candidates known as *prokritoi* were chosen by lot from each tribe and one of them was finally selected by lot. As each tribe provides the state with one candidate *archon*, then they should add up to 10, not 9 as protocol dictated. Accordingly, 1 of the 10 was designated as *grammateus tois thesmothetais*, assigned with secretarial duties. The *nine archons* included:

- The *eponymous archon*, who was considered the honorary "head of the state of Athens," its "first citizen." In practice, his authority was of a typical nature. However, it served as a way of reference for dating events and situations: "This happened when *eponymous archon* was . . . ."
- The *archon basileus* who maintained the role of "honorary second" in the citizen hierarchy of the Athenian state.
- The *polemarch*
- The *six thesmothetai* and their secretary (for them, see further in Sect. 6.9)

6.7 The *Heliaia* Court[11]

The Heliaia court was manned by ordinary citizen-judges chosen by lot the day before the trials, for reasons of transparency. Various buildings were used as courtrooms. The 6000 judges appear to have rarely met in plenary session. The only known plenary session is the case of the desecration of the Eleusinian Mysteries in 415 BCE. Heliaia usually met with a smaller composition and the number of judges varied according to the nature of the cases. Every day there were four judicial bodies, one of 201 judges, two bodies of 401, and one of 501 judges who tried various cases (Avilés and Mirhady 2013, 213). There were also other bodies of different composition. Lysias (*Against Agoratus*, 35) refers to a case where 2000 (+1) judges voted in the late fifth century.

The legal system of Classical Athens had intelligently chosen the number of members of the judicial bodies to be odd (uneven) so as to ensure that there would not be a problem of equality of votes in the decision of the judges. For example, in the (extreme) case where in a court of 201 members, 101 *heliastai* decided to acquit the accused, while the other 100 decided to punish him, the result, even marginal, could issue a decision (acquittal).

The Heliaia met on all working days except the last 3 days of each month and the working days of the Athenian Assembly. Almost never, however, did all ten sections of Heliaia work at the same time. The *hegemon* who presided over each court collected the complaints and the cases to be tried and determined by lot in which department, by which judges, and in which courtroom the case would be trialed. As there were no lawyers, the accused undertook his/her own defense with the help of a single friend or relative. Many times, the accused commissioned the writing of a speech for his/her edict to a professional logographer such as Isocrates or Lysias, etc.

The time of orations was limited by a hydraulic timer, known as the *clepsydra*. This was a clay container that was filled with water, with a stopper at its base. At the beginning of each speech, the stopper was removed and time was counting down until the water ran out. The *clepsydra* ensured equal time for litigants in the courts

[11] For the functioning of the courts and the administration of justice in Classical Athens, see Hansen (1991), Lanni (2006), and Harris (2006, 2013).

and orators in the Assembly. The vote was secret. Judges received as compensation 2–3 *obols* per court day.

6.8 The Judicial Process

A lawsuit was introduced by a preliminary hearing, held before a judge. Oaths were exchanged by the plaintiff and the accused, with the former swearing that the accusation was true and the latter having the right to either admit it or deny it. The defendant could file a counterclaim or objection. Then, the case was referred to a specific court to be tried on a specific date, and its numerical composition was proportional to the importance and gravity of the matter, reaching 601 judges in the fourth century. The duration of any trial could not exceed 1 day and there was no second and third degree of justice. In the trials, witnesses were examined and relevant documents were presented, such as previous decrees, like in the trial *On the Crown*, the most famous judicial oration of Demosthenes, delivered in 330 BCE.

The judges were drawn before the day of the trial so that there was no time and no possibility of influencing them in advance. Citizens who often appeared as accusers were called *sycophants*, a term with a negative connotation, because they could blackmail other citizens with the threat of accusation. To avoid this parasitic behavior, the Athenians had enacted that when an accuser received less than one-fifth of the votes of the judges in favor of the accusation, he was himself sanctioned, and had to pay a heavy fine (Lyttkens et al. 2018).

The court members voted directly after the end of the trial, without consultation among themselves (as is the case with today's jury courts). The vote was secret and each member of the court received two different "vouchers," which he placed secretly in a wooden and a copper ballot box called *kleroterion*. Those of the wooden ballot box were considered invalid, the bronze ballot box valid, so the condemning and acquittal votes of the bronze ballot box were counted for the result. There was a *kleroterion* in front of each court. If the decision was a conviction, the accuser could propose one sentence and the accused another, as Plato testifies about the trial of Socrates. The judges then voted again on the two proposals.

6.9 The *Nomophylakes*, the *Graphe Paranomon*, the *Nomothetai*, and the *Thesmothetai*

A specialized body, the *seven nomophylakes* (the protectors of the law) were responsible for protecting the documents of the laws that were legislated by the Assembly from destruction and forgery, and for this purpose, they had full access to the Metroon, otherwise called the *nomophylakion* (Lanni 2006). According to Aristotle (*Politics*, 3.6., 4.4., 8.4., 25.2) and an important inscription attributed to

Philochorus (FGrH $_{328F\ 64B.b}$) the institution of *nomophylakes* was introduced into the Athenian polity with the reforms of Ephialtes in 462 BCE. From the fourth c. BCE, a large collection of laws was archived in the Metroon. Two other relevant institutions existed with the aim of protecting the laws of the state from possible forgery and falsification: the *grammateus epi ta psephismata* (the "secretary on decrees") and the *grammateus epi tous nomous* (the "secretary on laws"). Among other things, these two officials had to oversee the non-alteration of the laws and decrees inscribed in various stelae throughout the polis (McAuley 2013, 189).This means that the administration of justice followed specific procedural rules, based on existing written laws and resolutions, as is the case today. This evidence is very important because it proves that the Athenian judges judged based on an existing framework of laws. Avil'es and Mirhady (2013, 211, 217) add that from the end of the fifth c. BCE judges swore to judge *kata ton nomon*, that is, "according to the (existing) laws," and their final judgment would be based on them. The same was true for the other public officials as well; they had to perform their duties based on the applicable legislation (Fröhlich 2013, 259).

The laws through which the judges adjudicated and which had to be taken into account by both parties (the litigants) were announced in public *stelae* (columns) in important and well-known places, such as the Areopagos court and the Acropolis so that every citizen had easy access on them. Listing of laws in public much frequented places served as a reminder to citizens to shape their behavior accordingly, knowing at the same time the consequences of possible delinquency (Schwartzberg 2004, 312–313, 319). According to Andocides (*On the Mysteries*) if a law was not exposed to public view, it had no legal force. This tradition of publicly stating the laws so that they are widely known to the citizens dates back to the constitutional reforms of Solon of 594 BCE and has been maintained ever since.

Regarding the *graphe paranomon*, in the fifth century BCE, the Athenians made a series of strategic mistakes that undermined significantly both the economic strength and geopolitical power of their state, as well as the quality of functioning of the democratic institutions. There were decisions with great fiscal cost that were taken with the consent of the Athenians in the citizens' Assembly, such as the siege of Potidaea in Chalcidice (Northern Greece), in 432 BCE, shortly before the start of the Peloponnesian War, which according to Thucydides (*History*, 2.70.2., 3.17.2.) cost 2000 *talents*, a large sum of money.

At that time the Athenian and allied fleet numbered 250 *triremes* in full operational use in various theaters of operations (100 *triremes* on patrols in Attica, Euboea, and Salamis, and 100 en route to the Peloponnesus). Thucydides again informs us about the naval operations in Potidaea in the period 431–428, where each Athenian sailor received about one drachma per day. From the above it can be deduced that the operational cost of using 250 *triremes* was about 50,000 drachmae per day and for 240 days a year (assuming 8 months' service as the *triremes* would not be manned in winter due to adverse weather conditions at sea) cost 12,000,000 drachmae, that is, 2000 *talents*. This was a huge fiscal cost, which Athens covered: (i) In the fifth c. BCE from the contributions of the member states of the Athenian Alliance, (ii) in the fourth c. BCE from the *Tameion ton Stratiotikon* (Military Fund), since this was founded in 373 BCE, and (iii) during all the Classical period, from the sums of money the polis could borrow in emergencies from the *Treasury-Temples of Athena and the Other Gods*.[12]

Another disastrous choice was the Sicilian Campaign (415–413) whose cost exceeded 3000 *talents* per year as well as the killing of the Athenian admirals after the victorious Naval Battle at Arginusae in 406, on the charge that they had not collected the Athenian sailors found at sea, after mismanagement of the situation, but also due to an unfortunate coincidence, bad weather that greatly hampered the possibilities of rescue, resulting in a total loss of 25 *triremes*. Diodorus Siculus does not refer to losses in manpower but to the loss of ships. 25 *triremes* would be manned by approximately 5000 personnel in total. The death punishment of the polis' experienced and capable generals due to this event depleted the polis of capable high-ranking military officers and was a key reason for the Athenians' defeat in the Peloponnesian War (McAuley 2013, 188). A short time later, in 405 BCE, the Athenians suffered a devastating strategic defeat at Aigos Potamoi (in today's Dardanelles, Hellespont Straits) by the Spartan fleet that surprised them under the highly capable admiral Lysander. After this failure, Athens and her allies lost the war. This was followed by the brief overthrow of the democratic regime by a short-lived pro-Spartan oligarchic regime, the so-called Thirty Tyrants, which led to terror and chaos and was finally overthrown by the ardent democrat, General Thrasybulus.

The fact that the Athenians could vote through the Assembly for 40 times a year directly and democratically made the Athenian system of governance and administration of justice too volatile, and thus, susceptible to constant changes, which sometimes, due to their radicalism and flexibility, led to wrong choices such as the death of Miltiades, the ostracism of Aristides, Themistocles, and Cimon, the Sicilian Campaign, the foolish and frivolous killing of the able Athenian generals after the Naval Battle of Arginusae, etc. (Halkos et al. 2022). Thucydides (*Hist.*, 1.70.2–3) characteristically writes on this:

> The Athenians are addicted to innovation, and their designs are characterized by swiftness alike in conception and execution; you have a genius for keeping what you have got, accompanied by a total want of invention, and when forced to act you never go far enough. Again, they are adventurous beyond their power, and daring beyond their judgment, and in danger they are sanguine; your wont is to attempt less than is justified by your power, to mistrust even what is sanctioned by your judgment, and to fancy that from danger there is no release.

The Spartans, on the other hand, claimed to be wise, because they had learned not to despise the laws, and had the self-control not to disobey them, also because their

[12] The key role of these funds in financing the extraordinary fiscal needs of the Athenian state is highlighted in detail in Bitros et al. (2020) and Economou (2024, 177–189) but also in the explanations of Scene 17, and especially in Sect. 18.7.

political system was stable and its institutions unchanged for over four centuries (Thuc., *Hist.*, 1.18.1).[13]

According to Hansen (1974, 50) and MacDowell (1975, 74), after the upheaval of 403 BCE, the Athenians wanted to make the constantly changing legislative framework of the state less possible, hoping that in this way they could prevent the hasty, wrong, and sometimes disastrous decisions made by the Assembly in some cases.

Apparently, they understood that tightening the framework through which a process of changing a law or laws could take place was a necessary condition to ensure the smooth functioning of democracy and to avoid future major mistakes regarding strategic decisions. It is true that the Athenians had already recognized this problem since the fifth century and tried to remedy it by reinforcing the *nomophylakes* with an additional important duty; they were appointed by the Council in order to check in advance whether a proposed law was compatible with the previous ones (Xen. *Oec.*, 9.14). Only after the *nomophylakes* and the Council approved a proposed law it was further forwarded to the assembly for approval or rejection. Furthermore, if a law was already accepted by the Assembly and thus became a state law, it could be annulled ex post if the Council and the *nomophylakes* considered it as "unconstitutional," i.e., contrary to applicable laws (Schwartzberg 2004, 319). Here is clear the provision for a *checks and balances* mechanism[14] with a veto right against an Assembly's decision. Sparta also had *nomophylakes*, but fewer, five in number. Consequently, checks and balances mechanisms were not only a phenomenon of Athens, but were also practiced by other Greek states.

This in turn means that until 462 BCE the decisions of the Assembly could not be challenged by any other institution of the state; therefore, democracy was more radical since the Assembly had absolute and unique jurisdiction in passing laws. But, due to the above reasons that led to wrong critical decisions, such as the Sicilian Campaign, it appears that the Athenians decided to introduce an additional institution so as to achieve better outcomes in making their democracy less radical. In particular, in 403 BCE they introduced the so-called *graphe paranomon* for that purpose. Essentially, this institution demanded that any law proposal that would reach the Assembly should be "constitutional"; i.e., it would not contradict the existing legal status. Of course, Athens did not have a written constitution like today's. The examination of the proposed laws was conducted preliminary by the *prytaneis*, and afterward any citizen could appeal against a citizen-law initiator (called *ho boulomenos*) if he considered that his proposal was illegal and could be harmful to the state.

---

[13] For the Spartan political institutions and their functioning, see Cartledge (1987) and us in Halkos et al. (2022).

[14] Checks and balances are various procedures set in place to decrease the risk of centralization of power by one authority over the other. For example, the US government practices a system of checks and balances through the establishment of the executive branch, the legislative branch, and the judicial branch. Congleton (2012) described the evolution of political institutions in Europe during the last several hundred years, where division of power was a key element for their evolution, where no branch of government could act independently without the cooperation and coordination of others.

For example, any citizen "A"' could sue citizen "B" if he believed that "B" proposed the introduction of a law that would harm the state as a whole (Hansen 1991; Schwartzberg 2004, 319). If the accuser who introduced a *graphe paranomon* against a proposal to the Assembly did not collect at least 20% of the votes among the judges studying his objection, he was fined 1000 drachmae, a very high amount considering that, according to Loomis (1998), the average salary in the fourth century was between 1.5 and 2.5 drachmae. Moreover, the accuser had no right to instigate such legal proceedings again in the future. The same amount of money was imposed on the accuser-plaintiff if he withdrew his accusation (Lyttkens et al. 2018). This constitutional settlement of the Athenians seems very important because it was linked with penalties for those who sought to abuse the legal institutional tools of transparency by trying to abuse state institutions (Assembly, specific parts of the Council and courts).

The *graphe paranomon*, when finally accepted, was so powerful constitutionally that it could overturn even a decision previously made by the Assembly (Hansen 1991, 205–208; Lyttkens et al. 2018). Hansen (1974, 1976, 1991, 205–208) further argues that the *graphe paranomon* replaced ostracism as a means of disciplining Athenian politicians in the institutions of the state and that between 403 and 322 BCE, 35 cases of *graphe paranomon* have been recorded.

It has to be mentioned that there was also a stricter version of the *graphe paranomon*, the so-called *graphe nomon me epitedeion theinai* related only to laws (not decrees). It had to do with the right of every citizen to accuse a *boulomenos* who proposed a law or managed to already pass a law through the Assembly, which according to the accuser was either unconstitutional or was accepted although the correct legal procedures were not followed. In that case, the *boulomenos* phased a trial and if he was convicted his punishment was much more severe than *the graphe paranomon*, he could even be sentenced to death (Dem., *Against Timocrates*, 24.138; Schwartzberg 2004, 320).

In addition, at the end of the fifth century, probably in 404 BCE, two new specialized bodies were introduced, the *nomothetai* and the *six thesmothetai* (Hansen 1991; Harris 2013, 244–245). Lanni (2006, 145) based on Demosthenes (*Against Timocrates*, 24.20–23) argues that the body of the *nomothetai* was formed not in 404 but in 399 BCE. This group of magistrates *nomothetai* was drawn from the annual group of judges serving in the Heliaia courts. A board of *nomothetai* could be large: Demosthenes reports that in 354/3 BCE, Timocrates passed in the Assembly a decree setting up a board of 1001 *nomothetai* and ordering the Council to assist them in their work effort. Their main responsibility was to certify that any new law to be proposed by the Council or any individual should not conflict with existing laws (Hansen 1991; Lanni 2006, 145–147; Harris 2013, 244–245). They also aimed to oversee whether there were duplications, contradictions, or ambiguities or whether in the legal system there were still "inactive" laws, in the sense that they were not actually used in practice. In such cases they could submit their corollaries at the first annual meeting of the Assembly, where all laws were re-examined before being accepted (again) as valid.

If there were indeed duplications and relative inconsistencies, the proposed laws were rejected. The *nomothetai* was actually a two-tier body where the first chamber of judges (elected by the Council) had the right to propose new laws while the second chamber of 500 judges (elected by the *demes*) in collaboration with the Athenian Council voted on whether it would ratify newly passed laws to become state laws (Lanni 2006, 145). Harris (2013, 244) characteristically adds that in the fifth century BCE, the constitution of the Athenians placed that power in the hands of the Assembly, whereas in the fourth century, in the hands of both the Assembly and the *nomothetai*. The *nomothetai* could be summoned under three circumstances:

- If the Assembly called for revisions of the laws
- If an individual proposed a change in the laws
- If the six *thesmothetai* (see below) undertook a scrutiny of the laws respectively (Arist.*Athenian Constitution*, 55.1; Dem., *Against Timocrates*, 24.20; Aeschin. *Against. Ctesiphon*, 3.38)

To sum up, in contrast to the fifth century practice, in the fourth c. BCE the Athenians accepted a checks and balances system regarding law-making. Of course, one should not be given the wrong impression that the Athenian citizens were deprived of their ability to make law proposals. *Demos* remained the superior institution concerning law and political decision-making. Characteristically, Harris (2013, 244 ftn. 78) argues that:

> Even though the *nomothetai* gave final approval to the laws in the fourth century, it was the Assembly that initiated all laws and submitted them to the *nomothetai*. Their authority derived from the citizens of Athens, which is why they were called the laws of the Athenians (not the laws of the *nomothetai*).

The fact that the *nomothetai* could either produce or reject new laws, or not approve proposals for *graphe paranomon*, does not mean that the Assembly did not remain the main law-making body of the state. It is just that through the *nomothetai*, the Athenian democratic regime became more "moderate," that is, less radical and volatile than that of the fifth century (Kyriazis and Economou 2015a; Halkos et al. 2022). Harris (2013, 244–245) adds that it would not be correct to adopt the view that the powers of *nomothetai* as legislators are indicative of oligarchic governance practices.

For their part, the *six thesmothetai* was an institution with similar or complementary duties to those of the *nomothetai*. According to Aeschines (*Against Ctesiphon*, 3.38–3.40) this body consisted of six of the nine members of the *nine archons*, i.e., not including the following three: *archon*, *archon basileus*, and *polemarchos*. The duties of the *six thesmothetai* were to review the laws annually, identify if there were inconsistencies, overlaps, or invalid laws, and if so, instruct the *nomothetai* to rectify them (Schwartzberg 2004, 320). In such a case, the Assembly authorized the *nomothetai* to resolve the problem (Lanni 2006, 147). In addition, the *six thesmothetai* determined the sessions of the courts and the date of trial of each case and conducted the lottery of the judges. Citizens could also appeal to them for any *eisangelia* case[15] or an appeal against a decision of the Council or the courts and for a *graphe paranomon* case. This means that the duties of both the *nomothetai* and the *thesmothetai* were correlated. The *grammateus of thesmothetai*, as his title suggests, held the position of secretary to the *nine archons*. He worked closely with the *thesmothetai* and kept the proceedings of their meetings and the agenda of the topics to be discussed.

As a final comment on the above, it can be argued that the Athenians through the introduction of the above institutions attempted to make their democracy less radical so as not to undermine the effectiveness of the system of laws by often abusing it through the trend to change the overall set of laws.[16] Furthermore, what is of importance in terms of citizens' active participation in the polis's affairs is that the Athenian practice to protect the "Constitution" by eliminating any attempts to introduce "unconstitutional" laws was not only implemented through the official state institutional mechanisms, that is, the *nomophylakes*, the *nomothetai*, and the *thesmothetai*, but also by encouraging citizens' initiatives through the *graphe paranomon* and the *graphe nomon me epitedeion theinai*. Thus, there was a two-tier mechanism for defending the "Constitution": efficient state institutions as well as the active participation of citizens who could act as the "watchful eye of the state."

6.10 The Economic Temperament of the Athenians in the Assembly

The Athenians of the fourth century had therefore become much more rational in decision-making regarding politics than the Athenians of the fifth century and were not easily swayed by promises. Policy proposals in the Assembly should, in principle, be always reasoned and costed and only in this way had a chance of being approved. In principle, proposals should be made by experts, such as Demosthenes' proposals for the deployment of rapid reaction force to deal with the Macedonians before Chaeronea. All these proposals should be strictly costed (Kallet-Marx 1993; Samons 2000; Kyriazis and Economou 2015a; Ober 2015b).

An Athenian politician-orator who would consciously speak in the Assembly with populist promises risked facing serious consequences. Difficult proposals, whether of fiscal nature, such as the Naval Decree of Themistocles in 483/2 BCE, or the fiscal expansionary programs of Pericles (middle of the fifth century) and those of Eubulus and Lycurgus (toward late fourth c. BCE), or monetary policy issues such as the Nicophon's Law of 375/4 BCE, were prudently approved.

---

[15] For the *eisangelia* procedure, see Sect. 6.13.

[16] For further analysis on this subject, which we cannot exhaust here, see our own in Halkos et al. (2022) and in detail the specialist historians, Hansen (1976, 1991), Schwartzberg (2004), Harris (2013), Canevaro (2018), and Lyttkens et al. (2018).

Conversely, others that were not sufficiently justified, or exceeded the financial capabilities of the Athenian public, such as certain war-like proposals of Demosthenes, were rejected.

It was a common belief among Athenian citizens that public money should be managed wisely. Aristotle (*Politics*, 1314b4-5; *Oeconomics*, 2.1.15 and 2.1348b) explicitly states that the public expenses of the state should not exceed the public revenues; therefore, **the budget of the Athenian state should be balanced, according to the laws** (Bitros et al. 2020, 3, 53, 215; Economou and Kyriazis 2021b; Economou 2024, 211, 256). Although the opinions differ in the international literature, however, important academics in economics argue that balancing budgets is a necessary and desirable policy for an economy because budget debt, which is the cumulative sum of previous debt-producing fiscal measures, causes macroeconomic side effects. When this happens, in order for the governments to deal with it: (i) they greatly increase taxation, causing disposable income suffocation in households and non-performing loans to businesses, and (ii) they devalue the economy's currency one or more times. If this happens on a regular basis it may pose serious fiscal risks regarding the smooth functioning of an economy in the long run and the nation's potential prosperity.[17]

It seems that the Athenians had understood and formed a collective understanding that future fiscal deficits, if left uncontrollable, would lead to much suffering (Bitros et al. 2020; Economou and Kyriazis 2021b; Economou 2024, 260–263). The ancient Athenian policymakers might have understood, to some extent, what nowadays is known as *fiscal discipline*, advocated by eminent scholars such as Alesina and Perroti (1996), which is also a dominant trend of the current EU economic architecture. For example, if one reads the official site of the European Central Bank, he/she will read, among others, the following:[18]

> Fiscal policies have a significant impact on economic growth, macroeconomic stability and inflation. Key aspects in this respect are the level and composition of government expenditure and revenue, budget deficits and government debt. Fiscal discipline is a pivotal element of macroeconomic stability. The need for fiscal discipline is even stronger in a monetary union, such as the euro area, which is made of sovereign states that retain responsibility for their fiscal policies. There are no longer national monetary and exchange rate policies to respond to country-specific shocks, and fiscal policies can better cushion such shocks if they start from a sound position.

A characteristic example of mismanagement of public economics is modern Greece during the 1981–2010 period where governments followed populist fiscal policies in

---

[17] In Bitros et al. (2020) through technical analysis and terminology, we pose the central issue of the continuous rise of debt around the globe, through a counterproductive mixture of monetary policy that governments implement through their Central Banks. We focused on the Fed's policies, which affect not only the USA but also, to a great extent, the global monetary and fiscal order. We have also argued that possible failures in the American banking system are not impossible, like those that happened in 2023, such as the cases of the Silicon Valey Bank, the Silvergate Bank, and the Signature Bank.

[18] https://www.ecb.europa.eu/mopo/eaec/fiscal/html/index.en.html

combination with corruption scandals and clientelist phenomena that led to continuous public deficits, that finally had as a consequence the public debt to skyrocket. This had resulted in the so-called *memoranda* agreements, which were in actuality austerity measures imposed by the European Union's (EU) institutions and the IMF on the Greek government of the times, with the view to restructure the economy (Kyriazis and Economou 2016; Economou and Kyriazis 2018b). Unfortunately, this led to a great economic recession for all the 2010–2018, followed by an additional recession due to the negative macroeconomic side effects of the COVID-19 pandemic. The Athenians of the Classical times could give wise consultancy to modern Greeks regarding how they should deal with their fiscal policy in the long run.

The question of the efficient management of public finances and good governance is also raised by Xenophon (*Memorabilia*, 3.4.7–12.), who reproduces for us a dialogue between Socrates and Nicomachides on the issue of good governance, where Socrates argues that effective governance is required in both the private and public sector.

6.11 The *Strategoi*

As already mentioned, not all administrative positions of the Athenian state were filled by lot. Initially, the *strategoi* (generals) were chosen from citizens registered in the *demes*, one from each tribe for an annual term. The next step was that they were selected by the citizens in the Athenian Assembly as a whole not by lot but by majority voting, based on their military merit and prowess. Their term of office could be renewed, like that of Pericles who served in this critical post for 15 consecutive years. Military experience was the most important criterion for the election of generals (Demosthenes, *On the False Embassy*, 237).

One of the 10 *strategoi* oversaw the effective implementation of the *trierarchy* which the well-to-do citizens were assigned to perform. The Athenians had retained the title of *strategos* for their fleet commander(s). In addition to Themistocles, Cimon, and Pericles, some of the most important political figures of the fifth and fourth centuries BCE were also *strategoi*, such as Nicias, Alcibiades, Cleophon, Thrasybulus, and Conon (in the fifth century) and Timotheos, Iphicrates, Phocion, and Habrias during the fourth c.

This choice of the Athenians seems almost self-evident: for this important post specialized knowledge of military tactics was required since, in case of war, the very existence of the polis was at stake, and the outcome was determined by how efficient the Athenian choices at the military level were. This was directly connected with the issue of selecting the most capable generals. There were of course also wrong choices such as the case of General Charis who commanded the Athenian troops poorly at Chaeronea. The frequent change of public opinion on some subject, as, for example, the appropriateness of a general, was an admitted weakness of the system of selecting public magistrates. A typical example is the case of Theramenes, who was given excessive positions as a general and he undermined the democratic regime

(Lysias, *Against Agoratus*, 13.9–10). Capable *strategoi*, upon completion of their military duties, were also often involved in politics (Kyriazis and Economou 2015a; Economou and Kyriazis 2022b).

6.12 The Draw and the *Cheirotonia* Procedures

In Bitros et al. (2020), Economou et al. (2023), and Economou (2024, 291–292) we highlighted the organization of the Athenian state in terms of providing a series of public goods and services in order to ensure the well-being of its citizens, a mentality that can only be found in organized state services. One service of such was the *epimeletes ton hydaton*, who was responsible for the efficient working of the water supply system, the functionality of the fountains, as well as the purity of the water.

The basic principle for choosing the lottery process in selecting public magistrates was that it ensured equal opportunities and *isonomia* among the citizens, and it was a fundamental practice for a democratic state. *Isonomia* meant equality before the law (Cartledge 2022; Economou et al. 2022b).[19] Eminent economist and philoshoper F.A. Hayek (1960) in his book *The Constitution of Liberty* defined *isonomia* as "the equal application of the laws to all."

Our claim that some specialized positions of public officials of the Athenian state, known as the *archai*,[20] were not chosen by lot, but by appointment by either the Assembly or the Council or both in cooperation with each other, is also confirmed by Aristotle (*Athenian Constitution*, 42.2, 43.1), and Aeschines (*Against Ctesiphon*, 3.29) describes the existence of public offices which were filled by mainly *klerotoi* (magistrates elected by lot) but also by *cheirotonoi* (magistrates appointed by vote in the Assembly). According to Aeschines, all these magistrates were subjected to auditing. The majority of public offices were filled in by lot instead of appointment by the Assembly or the Council. Aristotle (*Politics*, 1317.b15-1318.a3) verifies the above views of Aeschines by arguing that some posts required experience and skill; thus, they could not be filled in by laymen. According to Aristotle (*Athenian Constitution*, 42.2, 43) these special posts included (see also Lewis 1997, 212):

- The *10 Strategoi*
- The treasurers of the *Theorikon* and the *Stratiotikon* funds (see further in Sect. 18.8)
- The *epimeletes epi ton hydaton kai ton krounon* (see Sect. 6.13)
- The *sophronistai* and *kosmetai* (see further in Sect. 20.3)
- The judges of *dikai emporikai* (see further in Sect. 11.6)
- The *epimeletes tes koines prosodou*, the head of the Athenian fiscal administration, introduced during the fourth century (see further in Sect. 18.4)

[19] To this particular point we do not accept Hansen (1991, 359) who argues that *isonomia* was not related at all to equality before the law.

[20] Which according to Hansen (1991, 216, 220, 222, 240, 313) amounted to about 700 state posts.

6.13 Public Officials and Efficiency in the Public Administration

In order to assume a public office, which according to the customs of the polis, was considered to be an honorary situation, the selected citizens should not maintain financial suspense with the Athenian state.

Like the case of Councilmen, the majority of these state positions were of a 1-year term. Magistrates who held these positions were accountable for their mistakes and fines could be imposed on them in case of mismanagement. For example, those citizens who had been chosen, due to property criteria, to serve as *hippeis* could receive some kind of subsidies (under a modern interpretation) from the polis, because the maintenance of the horse with its stables, etc. was a relatively expensive process. If the chief of the tribe (who was a public official, entrusted with his duty) had made a mistake in the registration of the horsemen of his tribe and had provided them with more subsidies than he was entitled to, **he had to reimburse the public treasury with money from his personal property** (Lysias, *For Mantitheus*, 16.7). This is important since it proves that the operating philosophy of the Athenian public administration linked the wrong exercise of a public post to economic impacts on an individual level, to the careless public official himself.

The Athenians had distinguished between compulsory service for the polis and voluntary conscious service, where the latter was the most important and should characterize those who held government positions. In the words of Lysias (*For Polystratus*, 5), we read:

> …My own opinion is that it is not men of his character who are guilty of wrong in such situations, but some holder of a few offices who has not held them for the best advantage of the city. For our city was not betrayed by her good magistrates, but by her dishonest ones...

From the above it can be deduced that efficient administration of the Athenian public administration was considered a great goal because through this mentality, *isonomia*, justice, and well-being among its citizens were ensured. Aeschines (*Against Ctesiphon*, 3.205) mentions even the existence of a specific law of the state (*ton ton ypeuthynon nomon*) that clearly referred to the duties of civil servants (Harris 2013, 148). In 392 BCE for example, significant corruption and bribery of public officials had been observed (Lysias, *Against Epicrates and his Fellow Envoys*, 27.3; *Against Ergocles*, 28.9–10). And since corruption and bribery were very strongly denounced, the punishment of the abusers was severe, and this was considered as fair law arrangement (Lysias, *Against Ergocles*, 28.13).

Both the Councilmen and the public officials, and especially those who held positions related to the management of public money, were fully accountable at the end of their term and required by law to submit a full account of their deeds. They underwent a detailed examination regarding the way of managing the funds that they handled. This process was called *logodosia*. According to it, each public official had to prove that he exercised his duties based on accepted regulations and on the basis of good morals, etc. This process of examining the annual (financial) reports of both the Councilmen and the public officials was undertaken by a specialized committee of auditors, who were themselves public officials and elected by lottery.

They were called, *ten logistai*. This committee subjected each official to a thorough inspection for the way he performed his duties. They were being scrutinized for possible embezzlement, bribery, or mismanagement. The *ten logistai* were assisted in carrying out these checks by another committee called the *ten synegoroi* which was similarly elected by lot. The *ten logistai* were elected one from each tribe. According to Aristotle (*Ath. Const.*, 48.3), they were also members of the Council. Both of these committees, which were composed of highly experienced and specialized officials in financial matters and procedures, were empowered to undertake these duties by the Council (Costouros 1978; Schwartzberg 2004, 312; Fröhlich 2013, 261; Bitros et al. 2020, 39–46; Economou 2024, 238, 244, 250–253).

Within 30 days the *ten logistai* and their ten assistants had to reach a verdict on the deeds of the public official(s) they examined. The decisions of these auditors had to be issued within a relatively short period of time so as not to hinder the process of handing over and receiving duties between the forthcoming public officials and their predecessors. The verdict-reports of the *ten logistai* were then transmitted to the court of Heliaia. The court, with the *ten logistai* being present, decided either to finish the process of the examination of the magistrate(s) in case everything seemed normal or to refer them to trial, based on the *ten logistai's* findings in case they found financial irregularities (Lysias, *Against Nicomachus*, 30.3). The *ten logistai* were therefore responsible for the audit procedure which dealt only with the financial aspects of the public officials' transactions. This was the end of the first phase of the audit of public officials.

But there was also a second phase: any citizen could appeal to the council of *ten euthynoi*, which functioned as a second-tier auditing body of the state, and denounce a public official within 3 days after the completion of the audit of *ten logistai*, making very specific and reasoned complaints and accusations against this particular public official (Aeschines, *Against Ctesiphon*, 3.18–3.22.; *Ath. Const.*, 48.3–5; Demosthenes, *On the Crown* 117; Fröhlich 2013, 261; Harris 2013, 27). Then the *euthynos* who was in charge to investigate this particular case (usually being of the same tribe with the accused) if he considered that the charge was indeed serious and justified had to refer it to the "*demes's* judges." It is not entirely clear what the duties of the latter were, but they were probably assigned to examine the deeds of public magistrates that belonged to the same *deme* as them. In the event that the charge concerned a lawsuit against a public official, the *euthynos* in charge had to refer it to the *thesmothetai* (Aristotle, *Athenian Constitution*, 48.3–5; Costouros 1978, 47; Sinclair 1991, 79). Then the *thesmothetai* were obliged to bring the case to trial. Charges, if proven, could concern one or more public officials engaged in a specific public service in which an audit was conducted and irregularities were found (Ober 2008, 157). Penalties were then imposed for maladministration and financial mismanagement, even on *demes* as a whole (Harris 2013, 75).

Essentially, the second audit phase contributed to making the audit process of public officials more complete and thorough. Charges that could arise in this second phase included but were not necessarily limited to *klope* (embezzlement), *dora* (bribery), and *adikia* (unjust behavior). The latter was apparently a less serious offense than the other two: conviction for *adikia* attracted a simple fine, while embezzlement and bribery were punishable by a tenfold fine. Therefore, the Athenians punished negligence, because it was the duty of the public official to be honest and perform his duties with care and responsibility, but much more, they punished deceit and the conscious pursuit of fraud.

The mechanism of denunciation from an individual against a public official was called *eisangelia* and could be conducted not only through the *ten euthynoi* but also in every *Ecclesia Kyria* if the accuser had something serious to report. The accused could defend himself either before the Assembly or the courts (Aristotle, *Athenian Constitution*, 61.2). If the Assembly felt it could handle the impeachment case itself, then it could decide to consider the case in a special meeting, something that happened indeed in important cases, or, alternatively, to refer it to the courts (Thorley 1996, 31). For example, the infamous trial of the generals after the naval Battle of Arginusae in 406 was the result of *eisangelia* and shows the power of the Assembly over the officials of the state, but also its ability to produce decisions with binding legal effects regarding a specific case or fact. According to the Athenian "constitution," it was not only the Assembly that could provide a judgment regarding an *eisangelia*, but also the Athenian Council (Arist., *Ath. Const*, 61.2; Harris 2013, 28). If the Council voted against the public official, the matter was referred to the courts for trial.

In addition, every citizen had the right to report any other citizen to the Areopagos court on four very serious offenses: (i) for attempting to overthrow democracy, (ii) treason against the state, (iii) bribing and corrupting public officials, and (iv) ill-treatment of the orphaned children who lost their parents due to war, and the women who were either *epicleroi* or in general were considered afflicted (Thorley 1996, 31).

It should also be mentioned that there was also the institution of *apocheirotonia*, similar to *eisangelia*, where any citizen could denounce to an *Ecclesia Kyria* any public magistrate for mismanagement, on the condition that he also provided the necessary proofs validating his accusations, then asking for a vote in the Assembly for the revocation of the duties of this particular public magistrate (Arist., *Ath. Const.*, 43.4; 61.2; Hansen 1991, 220–221; McAuley 2013, 186). If the charge was substantiated, the public official was referred to trial, and he was temporarily suspended from office until the Heliaia court had heard the charge brought against him for misconduct in office. If the result of the trial was negative, he was subsequently subjected to the sanctions of the law. The best-known case of *apocheirotonia* is that of Pericles in 430 BCE, when he was deposed from the duty of *strategos* and fined. Equally crucial was the *apocheirotonia* of the generals who commanded the Athenian fleet during the Arginusae naval battle, who then were put on trial and sentenced to death.

The first conclusion from the above analysis concerns that there were distinct roles among the institutions of the Athenian public administration, even if somehow, they seem to have been mixed with each other. Essentially, good administration was based on three levels as mentioned in Table 6.1:

Table 6.1 The three levels of good administration of the Athenian public sector

Audit:	*ten logistai, ten synegoroi, ten euthynoi*, all appointed by the Council
Denunciation:	*ten logistai, ten euthynoi*, Athenian Assembly, Athenian Council, Areopagos, and private citizens through the *eisangelia* and the *apocheirotonia* procedures
Judicial:	Heliaia, Athenian Assembly

The second conclusion is related to the *eisangelia* and the *epicheirotonia* procedures which means that, institutionally speaking, the citizens themselves were, to some extent, the guardians of the institutions, protecting the state from delinquent behaviors through the possibility of reporting such behaviors to the relevant state auditing bodies. Thus, in reality, the system of efficient administration was not only limited to the exclusivity of state auditing mechanisms, but it was also up to the citizens themselves to contribute with any knowledge or information they possessed to the defense of the "Constitution," the laws and the transparency of the state. Any complainants had to have strong evidence to support their accusations, because otherwise they ran the risk of being branded as sycophants, and the possible conviction for sycophancy in a court of law carried very severe penalties. It must be admitted that there were also cases under which various citizens were extorted under the threat of being sent to the courts (Plutarch, *Aristides*, 26.1). However, these were the exceptions to the rule.

In addition to the procedures of *dokimasia* and *euthyna*, audits regarding the proper performance of the duties of public officials could be carried out at any time during their term of office (Osiander 2007, 71), apparently as special and extraordinary audit. If both the committees of the *logistai* and the *euthynoi* found that a civil servant did not fulfill his duties properly or was bribed, he was punished very severely: depending on the offense, he was labeled *atimos*, and as a consequence there was an *aeschine* (public condemnation), the imposition of a very high fine, even the confiscation of his property and in very serious cases, deprivation of his political rights, or even death penalty. Depending on the magnitude of the offense, the Council could fine the public official up to 500 drachmae, a high amount of money,[21] or at its discretion to, appoint prosecutors, and refer the case to Heliaia to impose a higher penalty. Thus, dishonest public behavior (illegality and corruption) entailed very serious social and economic-financial consequences.

Thus, with the processes of *logodosia*, *euthyna*, and *eisangelia* public officials were strictly monitored regarding the proper performance of their duties and faced severe penalties if they disobeyed the laws or did not fulfill their duties properly. According to Aeschines (*Against Ctesiphon*, 3.21.) any civil servant who had not yet submitted the accounts and his deeds to the *ten logistai* had no right to leave the country, to make an offering to the Gods, and to change the status of his property. This is a practice that is also met in modern economies.

[21] We remind the reader that the average worker in the fourth century received a daily wage of about 1.5 drachmae.

Therefore, no Athenian public official could hand over his office to the next public official who would replace him without undergoing and successfully passing the established auditing procedures as to how he and the other members associated with the post he served responded to their duties, especially those related to the management of public funds. There was no exception for any public official regarding the above procedures, not even for the *strategoi* (Hansen 1991, 222–224).

As a final comment, the fact that the penalties for mismanagement or corruption were so high demonstrates how important was for the Athenians to defend the public interest (in relation to the general welfare of society) against actions that might harm it. This is an intertemporal axiom. Nowadays, it is considered that effective governance can be achieved by radically combating corruption phenomena in public administration and in general. Furthermore, corruption reduces FDIs and causes significant problems to the distribution of wealth in the economy (Mauro 1995). The reverse also applies.

On the other hand, the state itself honored those public officials who achieved effective performance of their duties (Harris 2013, 27–28). Thus, the Athenian society offered rewards to efficient and honest civil servants, such as public praises, recognition, and first or honorary seats in the theater, and in general, provided positive incentives for state institutions to function properly. Here again we notice an intertemporal practice that applies to both the Athenian and the modern advanced economies around the globe, providing incentives to (state or not) employees for ensuring their working efficiency and honesty. There is a vast modern bibliography on the issue and here we mention only the seminal works of Taylor (1911) and Fayol (1949, 1967) as well as Gibbons (1998) as proof on this. Athenians had managed to achieve an effective management of their public administration, what was known as *dioikesis* (see also Economou 2024).

6.14 *Archai*: The Categories of Public Officials

The Athenian state/constitution, the so-called *Athenaion Politeia*, functioned effectively thanks to the support of a series of public bodies manned by a significant number of citizens. We speculate that due to the many cases and the complexity of the issues that the Five Hundred Councilmen had to deal with on a daily basis, they would not have had enough time to engage in other activities, in contrast to the members of the Heliaia courts (6000 members) who apparently had more available time to practice their personal professions when they had not been selected, by lot, to try a case for that day.

This is because the Council had also auditing duties; the Athenians had decided to entrust the Council with the supervision of the public officials. Thus, the Council became the watchful eye of the state and its main coordinating body (Rhodes 1972, 104–105; Pritchard 2015). Rhodes (1972, 89) characterizes the Council as generally responsible for the financial well-being of Athens. As already mentioned, according to Aristotle (*Athenian Constitution*, 24.3) there were at least 700 public officials, known as *archai*, in addition to the magistrates and councilmen. Andreades (1933), Hansen (1980), Pritchard (2014), Bitros et al. (2020), and Economou (2024) provide a detailed description of them. Some of these public posts were:

- The *ten trieropoioi*, one from each of the ten Athenian tribes, who oversaw the shipbuidling of warships.
- The *hieropoioi*, a type of civil servants responsible for preparing religious ceremonies.
- The *ten athlothetai*, with a 4-year term, who were responsible for the preparation of the athletic contests and the procession at the Great Panathenaia.
- The *four epimeletai ton mysterion*, for the supervision of the sanctuary of Eleusis.
- The *syggrapheis*, a special committee of experts elected by lot at the *deme's* level with the task of submitting, in collaboration with the Councilmen, the *probouleumata* to be discussed and decided in the Assembly.
- The *ten astynomoi*, who were also chosen by lot at the *deme's* level. They were responsible for maintaining order and cleanliness in the Athenian polis. Half of them had duties in the Asty in Athens and the rest in the port of Piraeus. Their duties also included the supervision and prohibition of any "spatial arbitrariness" by private individuals at the expense of the public interest. In such a case, various types of fines were foreseen, such as in houses, balconies with shutters which were illegally extended on the road. For health reasons, they were responsible for the collection of animal manure to be transported outside the polis. They also supervised the removal of any dead bodies (Aristotle, *Athenian Constitution*, 50; Economou et al. 2023). Under their jurisdiction there were also armed Scythians and Thracians slaves, who performed police duties, as is the case with police authorities in modern societies. These armed slaves were known according to the type of weapon they possessed (e.g., bow, truncheon) and according to their homeland (e.g., Scythians and Phrygians).
- The *peripoloi* were made up of conscripts through the institution of *ephebeia*, between 18 and 20 years of age who took charge of guarding the walls and fortresses of the polis.
- The *ten toichopoioi*, one from each tribe, who were in charge of the maintenance and repair of the city walls.
- The *five odopoioi*, who were in charge of maintaining the city's road network to an excellent condition.
- The *ten hieron episkeuastai*, who were concerned with the maintenance of the treasury-temples.
- The *neoroi* or *guardians of neorion*, responsible for the security of the Athenian ports and their facilities and equipment, also being elected at the *deme's* level (McAuley 2013, 181).
- *The epistatai*, who were supervisors of the construction of public works (2–5, depending on the project). They were appointed by name by the Council from the lists of citizens. When large sums had to be spent on the construction or maintenance of public buildings or projects, their approval by the Assembly was necessary (Papazarkadas 2011).

- The *epimeletes epi ton hydaton and ton krounon* who supervised the distribution of water and the cleanliness of the springs.
- The *gynaikonomoi*, whose task was to oversee women's morals in order to protect public modesty.
- The state public secretaries known as *epigrapheis*, *anagrapheis*, etc.

Regarding the management of public finances, the Athenian Council had to oversee that public expenses did not exceed public revenues to ensure a **balanced state budget** as has already been mentioned, since this was a general fiscal principle that the Athenians accepted as a state policy. For this reason, the Council cooperated closely with a series of competent economic and technical state authorities in order to ensure the optimal level of efficiency in terms of the collection of public revenues of the state. The most important of these posts were:

- The ten *hellenotamiai* treasurers, who were in charge of collecting the financial contributions from the Athenian Alliance member states
- The treasurers *of the Temples of Athena and the Other Gods*
- The *tamias epi to Theorikon* (the treasurer of the *Theoricon* Fund)
- The *tamias epi to Stratiotikon* (the treasurer of the *Stratiotikon* Fund)[22]
- The *ten apodektai* (cashiers) who were responsible for ensuring the collection of most of the state's annual revenues. They also kept lists of persons indebted to the state, made entries of all monies that were paid in, and erased the names of the debtors from the lists.
- The *ten poletai*, elected at the *deme's* level, who were responsible for the allocation of import and export duties, the concession of mining exploitation to individuals or consortia of entrepreneurs, the rental of sacred estates, etc. (Papazarkadas 2011, 55).[23]
- The *ten epimeletai tou emporiou* and the *ten agoranomoi* who oversaw the smooth functioning of the market: prices to be normal, the quality of the products to be the proper one, and that coins that were circulated within the economy to be unadulterated (Aristotle, *Athenian Constitution*, 51; Fröhlich 2013, 259).
- The *ten metronomoi*, whose responsibility was to ensure that the weights and measures by which sellers priced their goods were correct and fair. This is how they fought against profiteering (Johnstone 2011, 54; McAuley 2013, 181).
- The *ten sitophylakes* (five in Athens and five in Piraeus) who were charged with the proper management of wheat's circulation in the economy (Aristotle, *Athenian Constitution*, 51).

Table 6.2 is a composition of Aristotle (*Athenian Constitution*, 24.3) and Andreades's (1933, 264) sources as is retrieved by us in Economou (2024). It is an approximation of the number of public officials that the Athenian state budget had to pay on the eve of the Peloponnesian War. Of course, it has to be acknowledged

---

[22] For the above three categories of funds we elaborate on Sects. 18.5–18.8. See also in detail Bitros et al. (2020) and Economou (2024).

[23] See further in Sect. 12.2.

Table 6.2 Total number of officials in the public sector in 431 BCE

State post	Number
Heliaia courts judges	6000
Councilmen (Five Hundred)	500
Archai (various state officials in general)	700
Officials abroad	700 (?)
Guardians of neorion	500
Guards of the Acropolis	50
Cavalry	1200
Infantry (*hoplites*)	2500
Archers	1600
Fleet: 20 *triremes* and 20 tribute collection ships[a]	6000
Other groups	(?)
Total	≥20,000

[a]Andreades (1933, 219) believes that except a squadron of 20 *triremes* with patrol duties, whose manpower was 4000 men (sailors and officers) the Athenian fleet was comprised of an extra squadron of 20 *triremes* of 2000 manpower, which was charged with the collection of tribute by the allied states of the Delian League. Obviously, the ships of this extra squadron were suitably configured to carry large storage areas other than personnel and sailors

that the ceilings for infantry (2500), archers (1600), and fleet (6000) could be met only in cases where the Athenian state found itself in full combat action, while the possibility that the Heliaia courts were to judge a case in full composition was very rare, as already mentioned in Sect. 6.7. Thus, in actuality, Table 6.2 presents the maximum potential number of public office holders, which only existed in very rare and special cases.

Table 6.3 exhibits the Athenian state budget c. 435 to 330s based on Ober (2015b, 499). It provides a synthesis of information based on his own estimations as well as those of Hansen (1991), Pritchard (2012), and Gabrielsen (2013).[24]

All the above evidence proves that the Athenian polis was an organized state that in practice exercised a series of important institutional functions with the objective of ensuring *eunomia* (law and order) and a high standard of living for its inhabitants. The confirmed existence of these institutions does not justify those who (still) dogmatically support the view that the Athenian state had rudimentary structures of state organization.

[24]For further relative estimations, see Lyttkens (1994), Amemiya (2007), Kyriazis (2009), and Economou (2024).

Table 6.3 Athenian budget c. 435–330s (in *talents*)

	c. 435	c. 425	c. 370	354	c. 340	330s
Public spending						
Military	400	1500	350	130	200	400
Government/law	100	100	100	75	100	120
Festivals	100	100	100	100	100	150
Welfare	50	50	40	30	50	100
Building	350	100	75	0	50	200
Total	1000	1850	665	335		970
Public revenues						
General	1000	1500	600	130	400	1200
Mint (maximum)	300	100	50	150	100	150
Total	1300	1600	650	280	500	1350
Loans (internal)	250	250	–	–	–	–
Surplus or deficit	300	0	−15	−55	0	380

6.15 The Salaries of Public Officials

With reference to the public sector, with which we are dealing here, it should be mentioned that the payments of public officials were not the same for all services and tasks but were also significantly influenced by wages in the private sector, depending on knowledge and skill of the economic agents in the market. The available evidence shows that there was a fixed pay for civil servants per day: one drachma. In general, we have reports of an increase or decrease in the level of wages of civil servants and therefore of the prices of goods (Loomis 1998, 232–233, 238–239, 254). When market wages rose, there was an almost simultaneous appreciation in the price of products, as modern economic theory maintains. For example, the wages of civil servants increased in the period 450–432 BCE due to an increase in Athenian public revenues from allied contributions and decreased later in the period 413–412 due to war expenditures. It is obvious that depending on the circumstances that prevailed, the reduction of public revenues also brought about a reduction of wages in the public sector, for example, in 350–349 due to war in Euboea.

Judges were paid from 460 BCE one or two *obol*s per day, and in 425 their pay increased to three *obols*. There is also evidence for wages to the *epistatai* for the whole year (annual salary) and for the members of the Assembly. The *epimeletes epi ton hydaton kai ton krounon* were paid in 440–439 BCE 1 drachma per day (*ibid*., 10, 12). The *ten synegoroi* received 1 drachma (*ibid*., 18). In the period 335–322 the *ephebes* (see Sect. 19.2 about them) received as ration four obols (*ibid*., 52).

The private school teachers were paid per course and not per day (*ibid*., 62-4, 74-5) in an amount commensurate with their knowledge. The priests received a wage for the whole year (*ibid*., 78). Musicians and singers for public ceremonies were paid according to their skill per task, and so were sculptors (*ibid*., 96, 102). There were various ways of remunerating workers who worked for the public, such as by the number of hours they worked, payment including or not the raw materials they used, including or not transportation costs in the workplace from at least 450 BCE (*ibid.*, 104–5, 115). The *epigrapheis* were paid according to the size of the inscriptions they created (*ibid.*, 121–122, 158, 161).

Chapter 7
Life at the *Oikos*, Individual and Public Hygiene, and Water Supply

Abstract This chapter begins with an account of the turbulent life of a female slave, but further focuses on various aspects regarding life in the Athenian *oikos*. Then expands on issues such as how personal and public hygiene was ensured, as well as the city-state's water supply, which were important for the quality of life of the Athenians.

7.1 Chariclea: The Turbulent Life of a Female Slave

Chariclea went with her pitcher to draw water from the well of Nicomedes' mansion.

Chariclea had gone through many hardships until she found a family, like that of Nicomedes and Hegeso, who, from the first moment, surrounded her with love, understanding, and compassion.

In that sense, she was a very lucky female slave.

Her story seemed like a heroine in the tragedies of Aeschylus, Sophocles, or Euripides, but her owners knew little about her past. She came from a well-to-do family from Patras, a city-state in Northern Peloponnesus, and when she was 17, already of "marriageable age," she met a young man, Demon, a little older from her, from nearby Aegion at a festival in honor of God Apollo which took place in Patras.

The movement of citizens and goods remained relatively easy between the two member-city-states, even if the so-called Achaean Sympoliteia or the Achaean Koinon had been dissolved at the time.

Demon had been there with some of his friends. The two young people met, by chance, at the festival that followed their participation in honoring the God Apollo. Chariclea had gone to celebrate this festival with her parents and her little sister Danae. They fell in love, and Chariclea thought of nothing but her good man. Eventually Demon, who did not come from a wealthy family, came to Patras, and asked Chariclea's father to allow him to marry her.

But her father refused, despite Demon's persistent efforts. At last, Demon decided, as he was malleable and robust, to try to make enough and quick money, so that he then could convince Chariclea's father that it was worth giving her to him,

E. M. L. Economou, N. C. Kyriazis, *Daily Life in Classical Athens*, Frontiers in Economic History, https://doi.org/10.1007/978-3-031-58541-8_7

since he would prove capable of providing her with a satisfactory and financially dignified life.

To achieve this, he dared something very dangerous: to become a mercenary in the Greek troops who were fighting at that time (343 BCE) in Egypt for its independence, under the military forces of Pharaoh Nektenabo II against the Persian Empire, under the Great King Artaxerxes III. There were Greek mercenary forces fighting for both sides, each in favor of the camp from which they were paid.

Chariclea was not an ordinary girl though.

When she learned that Demon was already in Egypt, she decided to risk everything, including her life, to be with him. By some trick she devised, she got money from her father's bank, and with the help of a friend of her father, Damocles, who knew her since she was a little girl and wanted to help her, with compensation of course, by paying him 100 drachmae in exchange, a non-negligible amount of money, she traveled with him from Corinth to Egypt in Naukratis with his merchant ship, which was carrying supplies to the Greek military forces in Egypt, to find Demon.

Unfortunately for her, it was too late, for the two forces, Egyptians and Persians, clashed fiercely at seaside Pelusium, on the eastern side of the Nile Delta. The Persians were victorious; Demon was probably killed or captured and enslaved. Chariclea searched for him with excessive persistence, patience, and anxiety, and to do so, she spent all her money, then was captured and raped by men of a Persian patrol, then escaped to Philistine Askhelon, where the inhabitants welcomed her since they were Philistines, originating from Crete of the Mycenaean period, and they had great love for the Greeks.

Finally, after many further adventures, Chariclea found herself in Athens being sold to Nicomedes as a slave by Phoenician merchants.

Nicomedes and Hegeso knew that Chariclea was Greek by birth, and had tried to induce her to speak; if she would provide them with further information, they may even make her an *apeleuthere* at some point, but she, not out of selfishness, but out of innate pride and need for a sense of dignity, even though she was a slave, but a slave with an unslaved mind and heart, she never wanted this secret of hers to be shared, for her own reasons. She characteristically replied, when asked about how she ended up in Egypt and the Philistia lands, that:

> this is something secret, that I have deep in my soul, and I will bear it in me, until I become dust and bones.

Chariclea filled her pitcher and returned to Nicomedes' *oikos*.

* * *

7.2 General Notes

The Battle of Pelusium between the Kingdom of Egypt and the Persian Empire took place in 343 BCE and ended in a decisive victory for the latter. Egypt then became a province of the Persian Empire. Both armies were supported by Greek *phalanx* type of mercenary troops.

There are solid genetic indications that the ancestors of the Philistines that had settled in this area were originating from the Aegean, Southern Europe, and the Mediterranean. A number of scientific research studies attribute the origin of the Philistines as Aegean-Pelasgian ("proto-Greeks"), as settlers in the wider area of (today's) Palestine from Crete after its destruction by the eruption of the Thera volcano around 1640 BCE. The archaeological findings rather argue that the region of Philistia was strongly relative to the Greek civilization as Stager (1988) and Sullivan (2018) explain, while Landau (2010) supports the Greek origin of the Philistines. However, today's remnants of Palestinians (another expression for Philistines) in this area are mostly of Arab origin.

7.3 The *Oikos* as a Dwelling Place

The basic social and economic unit that made up the city-state of the Athenians was the *oikos*, the household which was related to family activities. The *oikos* included all inanimate and animate things which were under the ownership of a couple, and the man had the main control over it. The house itself, the estates, any kind of property and money, the equipment that was used so that the *oikos* performs its entrepreneurial activities, the slaves, the clothes, and important belongings such as jewels and money, etc., all interrelatedly constituted the property of the *oikos* (Xenophon, *Oeconomicus*, 10.5–7).

Based on the latest scientific evidence, there is no doubt that from the Archaic period onward, in the wider Greek world there was a significant increase in wealth and, consequently, a rise in living standards and the population figures. Morris (2004) and Ober (2008, 85–86; 2011, 7; 2015a) found a great rise of population in metropolitan Greece and the colonies in the period 800–300 BCE, from 500,000 souls to 4 million. This subsequently affected residential construction. Between the eighth and fourth c. e.g. there was a dramatic rise in house size, from about 55 square meters to 230 for the average to wealthy family (Ault 2007).

Depending on the size and location, the price of the houses varied from 300 to 1200 drachmae. To make a deduction about the price value of real estate, as has already been mentioned, in the fourth century, the average daily wage of an unskilled laborer was 1.5 drachmae. The poorest ancient Greeks had houses with one, two, or three rooms. As Ault (*ibid.*, 262) argues, the houses of the wealthiest families were the only which had beautiful and elaborate mosaics, painted decorations, and elaborate peristyles. However, the average Athenian family at least had the

Image 7.1 View of the architectural layout of a part of a neighborhood in an ancient Greek polis. Source: Image created by painter Vasiliki Demopoulou

privilege of owning a house, which provided a number of important basic amenities such as spacious waterproof bedrooms and very often a bathroom (Image 7.1).

Regarding the residences of wealthy Athenians, from the second half of the fourth century, these were spacious and usually two-story buildings, as in other Greek city-states. Their size, based on archaeological findings, such as in Olynthus of Chalcidice, (shows that) gradually grew throughout the Classical period. Therefore, they were large buildings even by today's standards. For example, the average size of a house in today's Greece, both in the large cities and in the province, is about 80–110 square meters.

An important description of the arrangement and distribution of the rooms and spaces of an *oikos* of a well-to-do Athenian family, as well as the supplementary areas of production, the place where the slaves and servants also lived in and the place where domestic animals were grazing, is presented by Xenophon in *Oeconomicus*, in the dialogue he describes between Socrates and Ischomachos. Xenophon in *Memorabilia* (3.8.8–10) describes further the basic qualities a house should satisfy:

> When one means to have the right sort of house, must he contrive to make it as pleasant to live in and as useful as can be? . . . to have it cool in summer and warm in winter? . . . To put

> it shortly, the house in which the owner can find a pleasant retreat at all seasons and can store his belongings safely is presumably at once the pleasantest and the most beautiful. As for paintings and decorations, they rob one of more delights than they give.

As already mentioned, the Athenian *oikoi* (in plural) functioned not only as households but also as small or larger individual enterprises (in a modern sense) as agricultural production could also occur in a household (e.g., olive oil, fruit) either for their own consumption or for sale in the Agora with the aim of profit, which contributed to the overall income of the *oikos* and its ability to cover its operational costs.

In addition to the size of the houses, the quality of their construction and their interior decoration also improved. A house of a well-to-do Athenian of the Classical times covered an estimated area of 300–400 square meters and the usual structure was as follows: it had dormitories for the rest of the family members and for hospitality, a kitchen, a bath, a *gynaikonites*, and an *andron*, the room where men resided.

In the *gynaikonites* women could host their friends from other *oikoi*, for companionship. Of course, they also exchanged visits. The *andron* referred to rooms with beds, where the men held the symposia of the *oikos*. During symposia men could enjoy the company of *hetaerae* (courtesans) and food and drink. During the symposion, there were beds around the perimeter on a raised floor, in order for the invited guests (friends and colleagues) to relax. However, an *oikos* included additional dormitories for paid servants or slaves or both.

The furnishings of the *oikos* were relatively simple and functional. There were beds, known as *anaklindra*, which were used at symposia by moving them near the tables, as seats. There were various types of seats, similar to today's chairs and stools, beds, and of course tables, as well as cupboards. Greeks used pillows made of fabric or leather, as well as covers, towels, blankets, and "sheets," most of them made of wool. Some of them, as well as some clothes, were made in the *oikos*, made from the loom worked by the women of the *oikos*. This is dated to very early times, as we know from the Homeric Penelope. However, the furniture, at least in a rich and populous city-state like Athens, seems to have been supplied from the Agora, from the craftsmen of the time that produced and sold it. As in today's era, next to the large furniture workshops in the Athenian polis, there were also simple craftsmen-carpenters who made furniture with a place of work in a room in their *oikos*, and one or two servants as assistants.

Finally, Xenophon (*Ways and Means*, 3.12) mentions the construction of *pandocheia* (hotels) as one of the measures to attract merchants and *metics* to Athens. Hotels already existed, but those in Piraeus seem to have been of poor quality.

7.4 Individual and Collective Hygiene and Quality of Life

Regarding personal hygiene, Bresson (2007, 77) argues that the Greeks took particular care of their personal hygiene, as evidenced by written sources, vase paintings, and archaeological data. Baths (made of clay and rarely of stone or marble) are already known from the Minoan palaces of the Bronze Age period.

During the Classical period most medium to wealthy families' houses had a bathroom with a small bathtub with a seat, while those citizens or *metics* who could not afford to install bath at their *oikos* could attend public baths, known as *balaneia* (Demosthenes, *Against Conon*, 54.10). Gill (2008, 209–210) argues that by the mid-fifth century BCE the *balaneia* were well-established in Athens, in areas such as Kerameikos, as well as in many other places in mainland Greece and elsewhere, such as Olympia, Isthmia, Delphi, Nemea, Corinth, Delos, Epidaurus, Eleusis, Eretria, Messene and Olynthus, Syracuse (Sicily), etc. They were further expanded during the Hellenistic (322–31 BCE) and the Roman periods and can be found, among others, in Hellenistic Alexandria (Egypt) and elsewhere (Economou 2024, 284, 297). Therefore, before the famous baths of Rome, public baths existed in the Greek city-states, as described by authors such as Pseudo-Xenophon (*Constitution of the Athenians* 2.10).

Except *balaneia*, every citizen could alternatively enjoy, for a small fee, a comfortable bath of hot water in the public athletic facilities, known as *gymnasia* which were equipped with baths. These were multi-spaces with extensive sports facilities, where access was free to every citizen or *metic* to exercise himself regardless of income and social class. In Athens there were three public *gymnasia*, the Academy, the Lyceum, and the Cynosarges (Fisher 1998). This possibility of ordinary citizens to exercise sports "side by side with the aristocrats" demonstrates, according to Gutmann, Christesen (2012), and us in Kyriazis and Economou (2015a), the process of democratization of sports during the Classical Period.

With reference to public hygiene, which was related to the cleanliness of the streets, the neighborhood, and the city, from ancient sources and modern literature the existence of two important institutions is known that took care of this important task: the *ten astynomoi* and the *koprologoi*. The main duty of the *ten astynomoi*, five of which were active in the main city of Athens and the other five in the "twin city" of Piraeus, was, among others, to supervise the cleanliness of the city and to prevent areas of impurity by animals within the city. They were also responsible for removing any dead bodies in case they had died within the city limits (Aristotle, *Athenian Constitution*, 50.2).

The *ten astynomoi* had the right to intervene, both in public and private affairs, and could also impose fines, if necessary. This meant that the Athenian state considered cleanliness to be an important public good, and those citizens who were negligent or indifferent to this issue were considered to be harming not only their personal hygiene, but also that of their neighbors, as cohabitation with negligent individuals could damage the quality of life within the neighborhood, endangering public health through diseases (Economou et al. 2023). Also, the *ten astynomoi* were responsible for overseeing the non-encroachment of public space by any individual who might have the intention of building or digging in that public space for personal gain. In these cases, penalties were imposed on trespassers (Cox 2007, 771–772). Moreover, according to an inscription found (*IG*. 22 659), in 287/6 BCE, the *astynomoi* are seen cleaning the Temple of Aphrodite, anointing its altars, washing its seats, and tarring the roof of the temple, i.e., carrying out maintenance and cleaning work (Cox 2007, 770).

As for *the koprologoi*, the Athenian state had commissioned to private entrepreneurs the cleanliness of the city. The entrepreneur(s) who took on the project as contractors hired the so-called *koprologoi* from the private sector. The *koprologoi* were workers responsible for the cleanliness of public spaces, such as parks and groves. Essentially, the Athenian state provided this public good in collaboration with the private sector, which can be seen as a *public–private partnership (3P)* under a modern interpretation. Nowadays, *3P's* are very widespread (Besley and Ghatak 2017). The Athenian state authorities very often applied the *3P* system in various cases with an economic background, such as the building of warships through the *trierarchy* institution, the extraction of silver from the mines of Laurion for the production of coins,[1] the collection of taxes by specialized officials called *telonai*,[2] the use of state lands for cultivation to a private person, for a fee, etc. This demonstrates the confidence of the Athenian state in entrusting the implementation of a series of public services to the private sector on behalf of the state (Economou et al. 2023).

What is also worth to be mentioned is that the *koprologoi* were also able to make a profit by selling waste as fertilizer (Lindenlauf 2004; Ault 2007, 263). Bearing in mind modern economic theory, it would not be an exaggeration to argue that the institutions of *astynomoi* and *koprologoi* could be characterized as measures to deal with *negative externalities*.[3] This evidence overturns the completely wrong approach of Garland (2008, 133) who, without providing any kind of tangible evidence on the issue of the hygiene of the ancient Greeks, writes the following (*ibid*., p. 125):

> Facilities for the disposal of refuse were almost nonexistent. As a result, rubbish piled up in the streets in vast quantities, creating a terrible stench and constituting a serious health hazard, particularly in the summer months. Where houses were built close together, as in Athens and the Piraeus, the streets were ankle-deep in filth. Mosquitoes, rats, and flies were plentiful, carrying all manner of diseases and causing epidemics

We don't know how Garland even knows the point of the foot that the garbage reached, or how he knows that there were "armies of mice" moving freely throughout the city!

---

[1] We analyze this issue extensively in our recent works, Bitros et al. (2020), Economou and Kyriazis (2021a), Economou et al. (2021a, b), and Economou (2023), and in Chaps. 12 and 13 and elsewhere in this book.

[2] See Lyttkens (1994, 71; 2013). This practice is related to the internationally known concept of *tax farming*. This tax collection mechanism, which was probably first introduced in Ancient Greece, was later adopted by Rome and later, by states that followed, such as Russia from the end of the fifteenth century or the beginning of the sixteenth mainly for the collection of customs duties and taxes on salt and liquor, the USA in various forms during the nineteenth and twentieth centuries, etc.

[3] According to Baumol (1972) *negative externalities* are related to measures so as to neutralize the negative effects that a person's or a group of persons' actions have on the well-being of another person or society in general.

He does not mention the role of the *ten astynomoi*, the slaves who assisted them, and the *koprologoi*, etc. regarding the institutional mechanisms of keeping the city clean. Ancient sources as well as scientific research based on the findings of eminent historians do not reveal extensive and prolonged cases of mass infectious diseases in Athens, which could endanger a large part of its urban population, except for the special case of the Peloponnesian War, due to the "blockade" of Athens, in the second year of the war, in 430 BCE, and while the city was besieged for a long time by the Spartans, which led to the great plague that resulted in the loss of 1/4 to 1/3 of the city's population, which was 300,000.[4]

High-quality research such as that of Bresson (2007, 77) extols the system of personal hygiene of the Greeks, going so far as to argue that the common citizen of an ordinary Greek polis of the times would be able to give hygiene and cleanliness lessons to King Louis XV of France and his court (seventeenth century AD).

7.5 Water Supply System

Related to the above is the question of the water supply of Athens and the other Greek city-states. Water is a basic element of our lives, while modern medicine claims that the frequent use of clean water can improve our health, our physical condition, and even our appearance.

The Athenians considered *ydor* (water) of capital importance to the physical health and well-being of the citizens. For this reason, since the area of Athens was not sufficiently supplied with water from rivers, lakes, springs, and even artificial wells, as testified by Plutarch (*Solon*, 23.5), from the beginning of the sixth century, they had taken the following measure against water shortage periods:

> Since the country was not supplied with water by ever-flowing rivers, or lakes, or copious springs, but most of the inhabitants used wells which had been dug, he made a law that where there was a public well within a 'hippikon,' a distance of four furlongs, that should be used, but where the distance was greater than this, people must try to get water of their own; if, however, after digging to a depth of ten fathoms[5] on their own land, they could not get water, then they might take it from a neighbor's well, filling a five gallon jar twice a day; for he thought it his duty to aid the needy, not to provision the idle.

The Greeks had already developed, from the time of Minoan Crete, great water supply systems. Such are still witnessed for the period 1900–1700 BCE in the Palace of Knossos but also in the Cycladic islands. In mainland Greece, during the Mycenaean period (1600–1100 BCE) large-scale waterworks were built, including

[4]According to Thucydides (*History*, 2.47–50) the plague also appeared in other regions of the Eastern Mediterranean and manifested itself twice, in 429 BCE and in the winter of 427/426. To face extraordinary situations such as those particular plagues, the Athenians could revert to funds provided by the *treasuries—temples of the Athena and the Other Gods* (Economou and Kyriazis 2021b).

[5]Approximately 18.3 m.

fenced sections (nowadays mostly known as *polder*), dams, and artificial reservoirs for flood retention. Houses, especially the luxurious ones of well-to-do families, had bathrooms and in some cases bathtubs. Koutsoyiannis et al. (2008) and Koutsoyiannis and Mamassis (2015) and the further references they cite are providing very interesting evidence on these issues. Water supply systems continued to develop in the period following the collapse of the Mycenaean world and as early as the sixth century BCE, the famous Tunnel of Eupalinos, a tunnel 1036 m long, had been built by the tyrant of the island of Samos near the Pythagoreion to serve as an aqueduct. It is undoubtedly proof of the high level of know-how that the Greeks had developed regarding the opening of tunnels and the construction of water supply networks.

The Athenian state established a two-stage water supply system based on both public and private wells. Firstly, it is known that the majority of the inhabitants were supplied with water from public aqueducts, while only the well-to-do had taps in the yard of their *oikos*. Secondly, archaeological evidence has identified more than 400 wells with a great variation in depth, ranging from 2.5 to 37 m, dating from the early Classical to the Roman period (Angelakis 2016). Thirdly what is also very important is that, according to Koutsoyiannis and Mamassis (2015) the first recorded water supply system of Athens was built during the time of the tyrant Peisistratus and his sons. This water supply system functioned through gutters that reached a depth of up to 14 m. The gutter network was built piecemeal, in various phases. This sounds reasonable as it was a very large program.

It is enough to consider how much time and effort is required when changes need to be made to the current water pipes due to age, which entails closing roads and entire urban complexes to traffic, etc. The same applies to the Athens Metro, which despite modern means of construction took 21 years (between 1992 and 2013) to complete its segmental construction (for Lines 2 and 3). Parts of the ancient pipes of this system were discovered in the opening works of the Metro, near the Syntagma Station as presented in Image 7.2. This image depicts a part of the Peisistratid water supply network, unearthed in Athens at the rapid transit station of Evangelismos, not far from the Kerameikos cemetery.

The existence of a public water supply system from the time of Peisistratus onward undoubtedly falls into the category of one of the public goods provided by the Athenian state to its citizens. As will be further analyzed below, such were, among others, the defense of the polis, policing and ensuring law and order, partly the provision of education and health care, etc. Related to this discussion is inscription *IG* I^3 49 which provides evidence regarding a decree that the Athenians voted in the Assembly, probably at about 434/3 BCE, concerning regulations about the Athenian water supply system.

In addition to wells and large aqueducts, according to the description of Aristotle (*Politics*, 7.1330b) the Athenians developed technology to store rainwater from roofs into underground tanks. It is also known that flood prevention projects were carried out both at the *deme's* level and on the initiative of the citizens themselves (Demosthenes, *Against Callicles*, 55.17, 55.20). Finally, alongside an underground water supply network of the city with clean water, there was also another network of

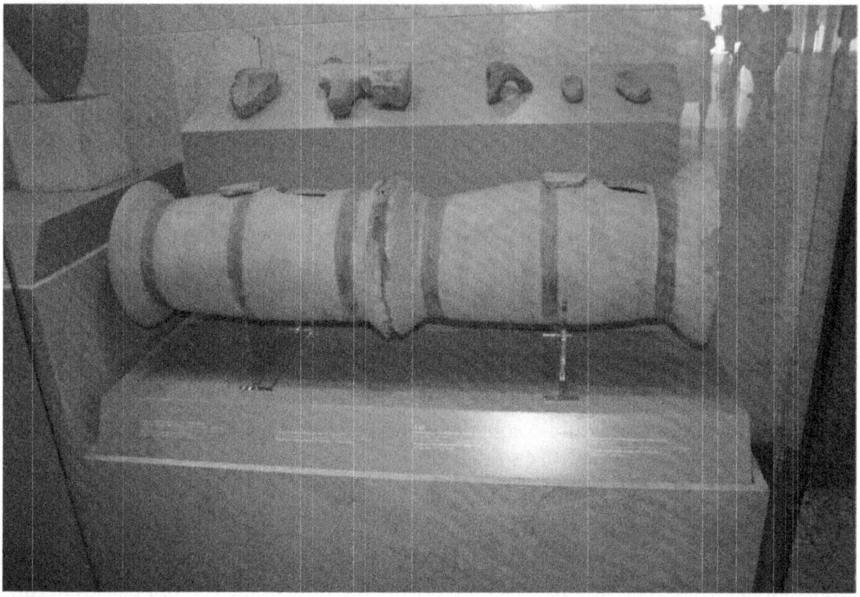

Image 7.2 Part of the water supply network of Classical Athens. Source: https://commons.wikimedia.org/wiki/Category:Ancient_Greek_terracotta_water_pipes#/media/File:1790_-_Athens_-_Finds_at_the_Evangelismos_Station_-_Photo_by_Giovanni_Dall'Orto,_Nov_12_2009.jpg

sewers, as is the case today, where sewage from the houses was extracted from city, in order to avoid infectious diseases, etc.

7.6 The Athenian Week and the Athenian Months

In Ancient Greece, the week began on Sunday, as it does now. The names of the days were as follows:

- Sunday: The ancient Greeks called it Hemera Heliou, *sun-day*, as it is called today in the international language in English, and in German, *Sontag*.
- Monday: The ancient Greeks called it Hemera Selenes, Selene Day, which in ancient Greek was also called *mene*, from which comes the English Monday (i.e., *Mo(o)n*-day in English) or Montag in German. The word "moon" derives from the word *mene* as well.
- Tuesday: The ancient Greeks called it Hemera Areos. It was dedicated to God Ares.
- Wednesday: The ancient Greeks called it Hemera Hermou, meaning Hermes Day.
- Thursday: The ancient Greeks called it Hemera Dios, Day of Zeus. Here there is also an indirect correlation with English and German. In English, in the word Thursday, the prefix *Thurs* is a paraphrase of Thor, god of thunder. But Zeus was

the god who unleashed thunder. Also, in German, in the word *Donnerstag*, *Donners* means thunder.

- Friday: The ancient Greeks called it Hemera Aphrodites, Day of Goddess Aphrodite [Venere in Italian—also Venerdi (Friday)].
- Saturday: The ancient Greeks called it Hemera Kronou, Day of Cronus, in Latin, Saturn, and in English Saturday, that is (*Satur(n)*-day).

The Athenian/Attic Calendar consisted of 12 months. The first Attic month began with the appearance of the new moon (*noumenia*) after the summer solstice and was known as Hekatombaion (mid-July–mid-August) in the modern calendar. It was given this name from the Hekatombaia, a festival held in honor of Apollo. The second Attic month (mid-August–mid-September) was called Metageitnion and derived its name from the *Metageitnia* festival in honor of Apollo.

The third month of the year (mid-September-mid-October) was called Boedromion and was named after the Boedromia festival which was also held in honor of Apollo. The fourth month (mid-October–mid-November) was called Pyanepsion, from the Pyanepsia festival which was also held in honor of Apollo. The fifth month (mid-November–mid-December) was called Maimakterion, from the Maimakteria festival held in honor of Zeus, who was considered to be the god of storms. The sixth month (mid-December–mid-January) was named Poseidon, from the Poseidea, a festival in honor of Poseidon. The seventh month (mid-January–mid-February) was called Gamelion, from the Gamelia festival, which was associated with the "sacred marriage" of Zeus and Hera. In this month most weddings took place in the Athenian polis because in that month Zeus married Hera according to mythological tradition.

The eighth month was Anthesterion (mid-February–mid-March). The month had taken its name from the Anthesteria, the festival held in honor of Dionysus. The next month (mid-March–mid-April) was called Elaphebolion, from the Elaphebolia festival, in honor of Artemis. The following month (mid-April–mid-May) was called Munichion after the Munichia festival and was also dedicated to the goddess Artemis. The 11th month (mid-May–mid-June) was called Thargelion from the Thargelia festival, in honor of Artemis and Apollo. Finally, the 12th month (mid-June mid-July), Skirophorion, derived its name from the Skirophoria festival in honor of the goddess Athena Skiras.

Other city-states had different months and a different measurement-name of the years. In Athens in 683/682 began the compilation of lists with the *eponymous archons*, because their year of power was characterized by their name. From 480 BCE up to 301, there is a complete list of names thanks to Diodorus Sicilus. We often have a nexus between the years of the Olympiad and the *eponymous archons*, e.g., "the second year of the 'X'th Olympiad when archon was 'Y.'" The first recorded was in 776 BCE with the first Olympiad held officially. This means that Olympic Games were taking place since earlier times, but their official recording started in 776 BCE.

7.7 Measuring Time

The day of the Greeks was divided into 12 h of light and 12 h of darkness, but not of equal duration. The daylight hours were longer in the summer, since the day was longer, and shorter in the winter, and vice versa for the night hours. Time was measured by sundials, which were used in Greece since (at least) the sixth century. Punctuality in the courts and the popular Assembly was timed with a *clepsydra* clock.

It is worth mentioning here an invention of Plato which, according to Aristotle's student, Aristoxenos, was called *nukterinon horologion* (night clock) and was essentially the first worldwide recorded alarm clock. It consisted of four ceramic containers, where from the upper container water flowed through an adjustable nozzle to the next container, and when it was full (e.g., after 5 h), it was rapidly emptied through the internally mounted axial siphon into the next closed container. The air contained in this container was then forced out under pressure through a tube, the end of which ended in a small container of water. The entrapped air was forced out by hissing from a syringe producing a sound effect that resembled the chirping of a bird. Aristotle had also invented a similar alarm clock.

It appears that technological progress was related to the evolution of the Greek society as a whole, from the Minoan to the Classical times, and was further developed in the Hellenistic and Roman times, even if with some interruptions in specific periods, such as the Dark Ages (after the collapse of the Mycenaean-palatial economies).[6] Thus, it is not impossible that by the time toward the end of Classical times which we are describing here, such systems of alarm and time-measuring were used more widely, not only being the privilege of their inventors or/and a few well-to-do citizens who could afford to buy them.

In two exceptional studies, Paipetis (2010) and Mayor (2018) discuss the technological achievements of the Greeks in pre-Classical times. Paipetis, in particular, discusses the technological advances of the Greeks as described by Homer who narrated the Trojan War, while Mayor describes ancient robotics and automata in times that even touch mythology. Lazos (1998), Acton (2014), and Sherwood et al. (2020) through their exceptional contributions provide persuasive evidence that, in actuality, significant technological breakthroughs took place during the Classical but mainly the Hellenistic period in Ancient Greece such as the Antikythera mechanism, the first analogic computer ever made, which could calculate astronomical phenomena.

[6]For some of these almost unknown, but great artifacts and technological achievements of the ancient Greeks, one can visit the Museum of the Ancient Greek Technology of Kostas Kotsanas situated in Athens. See details at: http://kotsanas.com/gb/exh.php?exhibit=0204003

7.8 The Achaean League

The Achaean League was shaped in two historical phases, the first between 389 and 338 (approximately), and the second between 280 and 146 BCE. In all probability was the most important case of an ancient Greek federal state, together with the cases of the Aetolian and Boeotian leagues (Economou 2020).

At its peak in 191 BCE, it reached 107 member city-states, all of which, except for the special case of Sparta, which remained a kingdom and was forced to join the league in that year, were democratic regimes (*ibid.*, 133). In 191, the remaining Laconian cities and regions of Messenia and Elis in Southern Peloponnesus were also incorporated into the Achaean League, completing the dream of the great visionaries and "Founding Fathers of the Achaean Constitution," Aratos, Lycortas, and Philopoemen for uniting Peloponnesus in South Greece, under a strong federal democratic scheme which could provide stability and security for its member-states.[7] Unfortunately, their dream proved to have been short-lived due to the defeat of the league by the mighty Romans in 146 BCE who then decided the dissolution of the Achaean federal structure.

The Achaean League, like all the other Greek federal states, known as *Koina*, developed very important state federal institutions, such as the right to the unlimited movement of people, goods and services throughout its territory, and the protection of the private property of its citizens as well as of merchants and foreigners who were active in any of its member-city-states. As was to be expected, the frequency of movement between people and goods to and from another city-state increased, and by introducing also a regime of parallel coinages to be circulated within the territories of these states, the Achaean League achieved an impressive rise of commercial activity and prosperity, as confirmed by historians who have carefully dealt with issues related to ancient Greek federalism.

Mackil and van Alfen (2006) have found that an important monetary practice of the Classical period that was further developed in the Hellenistic times was the appearance of "cooperative coinages." By this they mean the coordinated production of coins by more than one city-state (or between city-states that were members of a federal state such as the Achaean League), on a shared weight standard and usually with at least one common coin type, as a way to further extend their commercial cooperation with each other. By coordinated production we mean, an ancient type of monetary union were the member city-states decided to produce coins by the same standard with identical designs on both sides.

The Greeks of the times had understood that introducing a common type of currency, even if with some variations between the federal city-states, would lead to the rise of economic activity since it could make commercial transactions faster and less costly, as is the case with modern economic and/or monetary unions such as

[7]We extensively analyze the historical context, organization, institutional structure, and the philosophy of operation of the Achaean League in Economou (2020) and the citations we provide in ftn 28. See also Larsen (1968), Mackil (2013), and Beck and Funke (eds) (2015), among others.

the Eurozone. Under such a regime of ease of movement, Demon and Chariclea, whose turbulent relationship has been described in this fantastic Scene, met and loved with each other.

The Achaean League was a beacon of political and economic freedoms and could be seen as the forerunner of the modern large and powerful democratic federal states such as the USA, Germany, Switzerland, Canada, Australia, and India.

Chapter 8
The Athenian Agora and the Port of Piraeus

Abstract This chapter explains how the famous Athenian Agora (the Athenian marketplace) was organized. It explains that two key elements of its success have been the protection of consumers from abusive behavior and profiteering phenomena. The Agora operated, to a lesser or greater extent, on the (modern) logic, that prices are determined by the forces of demand and supply. Furthermore, the chapter describes the important infrastructure and the way of operation of the famous commercial port of Piraeus, which became the global transit center of the time, a global entrepôt.

8.1 A Merchant from Iberia in the Agora of Athens

Nicomedes arrived at the ever-bustling Agora.

Besides the shopkeepers and their customers who were wandering around the Agora, large or small groups of men were conversing, as the Athenians always liked, gesticulating, laughing, arguing, some chewing figs, walnuts, onions, bread, and cheese, sometimes halting, sometimes walking slowly. The Agora looked like a buzzing hive: laughter, voices by shopkeepers selling their wares. Various sounds covered the atmosphere: the clucking of hens and geese, the neighing of horses, the braying of donkeys, the barking of dogs, the grunting of pigs, all so familiar and common, that Nicomedes no longer noticed them.

He reached the point where his bank counter was located, in one of the streets of the Agora. There of course he found Ischomachos sitting in a chair next to the bank's bench. Nicomedes greeted him and asked him if there was any banking activity already made till that time.

- Not yet. But a merchant came, asked some information, and said he would pass by again.
- Foreigner? Greek; Where from?
- From a place I don't know. Emporion. He spoke Greek but with a somewhat strange accent.
- Emporion? Far indeed, from Iberia. It is a Greek colony, from Phokaia and Massalia, the well-informed Nicomedes explained to him.

E. M. L. Economou, N. C. Kyriazis, *Daily Life in Classical Athens*, Frontiers in Economic History, https://doi.org/10.1007/978-3-031-58541-8_8

– And what did he want? Nicomedes further asked.
– Currency exchange. Maybe to deposit also some currency in our bank. Or maybe to exchange currency for making some commercial deals here in Athens. Here is the man! He's coming. . .

The merchant, a middle-aged man, accompanied by what looked like a slave, arrived. They greeted each other and exchanged their names. Xenocrates, the merchant's name, had arrived in his ship with a cargo full of copper. Xenocrates, who was coming to Athens for the first time, also wanted to visit the city's monuments, the temples, the Agora, and the Pnyx, which were famous throughout the known world. Xenocrates wanted to sell the copper he was bringing and fill his ship for the return trip with goods that were in demand in Iberia, intended not only for the inhabitants of the small polis of his origin, Emporion, but also by non-Greek natives, Celts and Iberians.

– And what goods do they desire? Nicomedes asked with great interest.
– What they do not have: Goods of great value, some of luxury, for their chiefs, their wives, their homes: Gold jewelry. High quality metal utensils. Attic honey and wine. Dried figs. . . . I don't know what else...
– Decorated vases of high art? Painted? Fabrics? I will take you to a shop of an acquaintance of mine that has high quality fabrics. They come from far away, but in the Athenian Agora and Piraeus you find everything, without having to travel to their place of origin. If you wish, we could dine together at my *oikos* and talk about everything. And, of course, you can stay and sleep in my *oikos*. It would be a pleasure for me and my wife to host you as our guest.

Xenocrates accepted the proposal with satisfaction. First time in Athens and he didn't know anyone. Instead, he was informed from other merchants about Nicomedes and his bank. These merchants had already done business with him at an earlier time.

Nicomedes' reputation was that he was honest, helpful, and kept his agreements. Therefore, working with him limited the risks. Merchants operating in Athens at that time knew that the most essential element for a successful commercial transaction through a banking service was bank credit.

– Then, you can see the sights and when it gets dark, we can meet somewhere and then go to my *oikos*.
– That's what I'll do, replied Xenocrates.

Xenocrates sent his escort back to Piraeus to inform his crew where he would spend that night in Athens.

* * *

Image 8.1 Agora: The center of the city of Athens. Source: Uknnown creator

8.2 The Athenian Agora

The Agora of Athens was located between the Thission, the Acropolis (to the west), and the Areopagos. It was full of public buildings and arcades (although today's restored Stoa of Attalos is from the Hellenistic period). It was decorated with many statues, altars, and fountains. Among them, stood out the Prytaneion, the New and the Old Bouleuterion, known also as the Metroon (which was a temple dedicated to the mother of the gods, and a place where the records of the laws of the state were kept), the Heliaia court, the Poikile Stoa, and the Eleutherios Zeus Stoa (Image 8.1).

The galleries that served to protect the people from the sun and rain also were comprised by many shops and workshops, something like today's malls. The Poikile Stoa had become very famous throughout the Greek world for the epic representations of the famous artistic duo, Mikon of Athens and Polygnotos from Thasos who created them. That Stoa depicted various epic subjects such as the Battle of Marathon. It was a kind of open air museum, in all probability, being the first of such kind in recorded history, where Athenians and foreigners alike saw vivid depictions of Athenian history and art. In the northwest corner of the Agora was the altar of the 12 gods. It was the point where all the roads converged and the landmark (zero point) from which distance measurements for other parts of the city began. An excellent short guide regarding the excavations in the Agora (under the American School of Classical Studies at Athens), accompanied by wonderful descriptions and high-quality images, is provided by Camp (2003) (Image 8.2). Image 8.3 depicts a map of Athens during the 430s.

Image 8.2 Part of the ancient Agora of Athens. In the background is the Acropolis (For an important spatial illustration of the Agora of Athens, see also: http://www.thehistoryofancientgreece.com/2017/12/066-athenian-agora.html). Source: Image owned by the authors

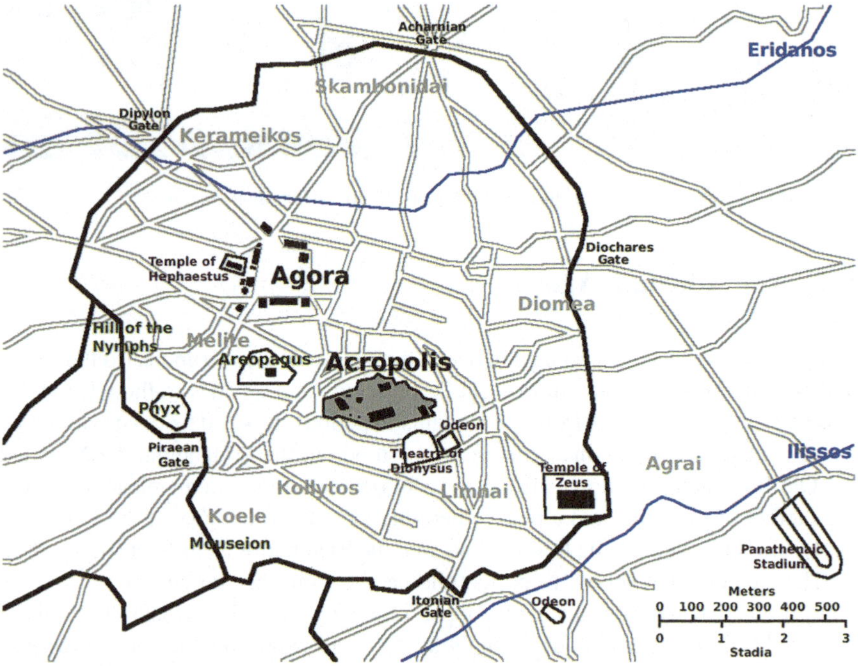

Image 8.3 Map of Ancient Athens c. 430 BCE. Source: https://commons.wikimedia.org/wiki/Category:Maps_of_ancient_Athens#/media/File:Map_ancient_athens.png

Images 8.3 and 8.4 depict a part of the city-state of Athens, including some of the most important buildings related to the political and social life of the polis, numbered from 1 to 20 in Table 8.1 [further explanations are provided by Camp (2003)].

One of the most important monuments for the functioning of the state was the Eponymous Heroes Monument, in front of the Heliaia court installations in the south of the Agora. It had been built in honor of the heroes who had given their names from

Image 8.4 The Agora of Athens. View from the Areopagos Hill

Table 8.1 Public buildings in the Athenian Agora (fifth century)

1. Square Peristyle	11. *Metroon/Old Bouleuterion*
2. The Athenian (state) mint known as *Argyrocopeion*	12. *(New) Bouleuterion*
3. Fountain House	13. Temple of Hephaestus (Theseion)
4. South Stoa (portico)	14. Temple of Apollo Patroos
5. Aiakeion	15. Stoa of Zeus
6. *Strategeion*	16. Altar of the Twelve Gods
7. Benches of Agora Hill	17. Royal Stoa (portico)
8. *Tholos/Prytaneion*	18. Temple of Aphrodite Urania
9. Boundary Marker	19. Stoa Poikile
10. Monument of the *Eponymous Heroes*	20. Former mistaken location of the Stoa Poikile

the ten *phylae* of Athens. It was established by Cleisthenes in 510–507 BCE. Its base served as a public notice board, such as conscription, notices of impending trials, agendas for public meetings (Assembly), proposed laws, etc.[1]

Merchants from around the Mediterranean and elsewhere could participate in the economic activities of the Athenian Agora. The unique atmosphere of the Agora is conveyed in a work by Athenaeus (*Deipnosophists*, 14.640b) which was based on an earlier lost work by the comedian Eubulus. This work gives a (not complete) list of items for sale: figs, grapes, turnips, pears, apples, roses, loquat, lamb tripe, liver and spice stuffing, honeycombs, chickpeas, cow's colostrum, curd, myrtle berries, lamb,

[1]For a reconstruction of the actual Eponymous Heroes monument as it was in ancient times, see https://uxdesign.cc/design-lessons-from-athenian-democracy-1da984424c1b and https://agora.ascsa.net/id/agora/image/2008.20.0028?q=references%3A%22Agora%3AMonument%3AEponymous%20Heroes%22&t=&v=icons&sort=rating%20desc%2C%20sort%20asc&s=2

hourglasses, ballot boxes, bells, law texts, law "books," indictments, properly prepared papers that could be used for summons, judges, court cases(!), witnesses (!), etc. In addition, there was a special area where slaves were traded (Garland 2008). Harris (2002, 88–99) provides a detailed long list of 170 professions practiced in Classical Athens.

There seem to have been concentrated markets for particular products such as the chicken market. There was a profession-craft of a maker of sacks and another of medicines (Demosthenes, *Against Olympiodorus*, 48.12), and even a processor and dyer of woolen garments. There was a trade market for timber and copper (Demosthenes, *Against Timotheus*, 49.35–36, 49.51). Pammenes from the *deme* of Erchia was a goldsmith and had a shop in the Agora (Demosthenes, *Against Meidias*, 21.22). Xenophon mentions people who were especially engaged in animal husbandry, baking, the production of cloth and the manufacture of tunics, etc. And he even describes Socrates's advice to a poor man to use the women of his household in the production of clothes so as to sell them and thus secure the necessary earnings for life (Xenophon, *Memorabilia*, 2.7.2, 2.7.6.).

Among other things, in the Athenian Agora there were also imported products such as shipping materials, timber, red ochre, dyes, resin, and perhaps some kind of tar for sealing, zinc, iron, and copper. Similarly, Aeschines (*Against Timarchus*, 1.97) mentions that Timarchus used skilled female slaves of his household to produce elegant fabrics from Amorgos which he sold in the Agora. Hermippus, a comedian writing in 420 BCE, provides us with an impressive list of exotic products that were sold in the Agora of Athens: Silphium (a plant for the preparation of medicine as well as a spice), ox, mackerel, and salted fish from the Hellespont, pork and cheeses from Syracuse, ship rigging and papyrus from Egypt, cypress wood from Crete, ivory from Libya, raisins and dried figs from Rhodes, pears and apples from Euboea, slaves from Phrygia, mercenaries from Arcadia, slaves with or without tattoos from Pagasai, acorns and almonds from Paphlagonia, wheat flour from Phoenicia, carpets and cushions from Carthage, etc.

Many services were also offered at Agora. There was a large extent of division of occupations in the economy. Some characteristic cases included barbershops and other small shops where Athenians were used to gather and chat (Lysias, *Against Pancleon*, 23.33). There were porters, slaves, *metics*, or even free men. The occupation of the hawker is also attested, which was probably poorly paid (Demosthenes, *Against Leochares*, 44.4). Self-employed women-farmers or weavers are also attested. Other occupations for women were those of women nursing babies, babysitters, sellers of ribbons in the Agora, etc. (Demosthenes, *Against Eubulides*, 57.35).

In the markets of Athens and the port of Piraeus any citizen or foreign traveler could find almost all the products of the known world as Piraeus had developed into the first historically recorded international trade and transit center, what nowadays is known as an entrepôt (Burke 1992, 204, 2010; Cohen 1992, 16, 141; van Alfen 2011, 13; Bresson 2016b; Harris and Lewis 2016).[2] This is also confirmed, among others, by Thucydides (*History*, 2.38) who argued that the naval power of Athens was based on both warships and merchant ships and writes that:

> We have this farther by the greatness of our city that all things from all parts of the earth are imported hither, whereby we no less familiarly enjoy the commodities of all other nations than our own.

The prices of goods and services were determined, more or less, according to what nowadays is characterized as market forces. For example, a tunic in 388 cost about 20 drachmae. The common workers in 329–328 BCE earned a salary of 1.5 drachmae per day and the skilled ones about twice that (Loomis 1998, 103, 111). There were even special markets found in specific areas. For example, the Plataeans had their own market where on a certain date each month they traded cheese (Lysias, *Against Pancleon*, 23.6–7).

Foreigners could also participate without limitations in the Athenian Agora. They could even borrow money from individuals and banks provided that they were obeying Athenian laws (Demosthenes, *For Phormio*, 34.1; *Against Lacritus*, 35.1). In the Agora there were also shops selling clothes and textiles and special goods for women (women's market). By today's standards some types of such clothes were not that cheap and due to this the women of the median *oikos* were actually making clothing by their own. Lands were also rented for cultivation for 1, 2, and 3 years (Lysias, *On the Olive Stump*, 7.5, 7.9–10). Hiring horses for war was also possible but if the animal was returned with injuries the owner was compensated with 12 *minae*, that is, 1200 drachmae, a large sum of money.[3] Animals such as horses were also hired for productive (work) purposes (Lysias, *On a Wound by Premeditation*, 4.1).

The nexus between the quality of a product and its market price is also corroborated even by an extreme incident related to the notorious noble Alcibiades who, in order to satisfy his vanity, paid 70 minas (7000 drachmae!), a huge amount of money so as to acquire a truly beautiful dog and take it with him in the Agora so as to impress the masses. Plutarch (*Alcibiades*, 9.1) narrates:

> Possessing a dog of wonder-ful size and beauty, which had cost him seventy minas, he had its tail cut off, and a beautiful tail it was, too. His comrades chid him for this, and declared that everybody was furious about the dog and abusive of its owner. But Alcibiades burst out laughing and said: 'That's just what I want; I want Athens to talk about this, that it may say nothing worse about me.'

---

[2] Another famous case of an entrepôt was Alexandria during the Hellenistic times. Modern entrepôts include, among others, Shanghai and Hong Kong in China, and Amsterdam and Rotterdam in the Netherlands.

[3] According to Aristotle (*Athenian Constitution*, 10.2), during Classical times, one *mina* (in sing.) known also as *mna*, was equal to 100 drachmae, while during the times of Solon, one *mina* equaled 70 drachmae.

There was even renting of houses (Demosthenes, *Against Nausimachus and Xenopeithes*), somewhat similar in logic to the current Airbnb practices. As today, groups of Athenians as well as foreigners had their favorite haunts, where they met and discussed, as we learn from a great court speech of Lysias (*On the Refusal of a Pension*, 24.20):

> For each of you is in the habit of paying a call at either a perfumer's or a barber's or a shoemaker's shop, or wherever he may chance to go, —in most cases, it is to the tradesmen who have set up nearest the marketplace, and in fewest, to those who are farthest from it...

There were also manufactured goods produced in a plethora of *ergasteria* (workshops) that employed quite a number of personnel, either slaves or free citizens. There were, for example, various *ergasteria* for the manufacture of shields, beds, etc. There were also large *ergasteria* that employed from 80 to 100 people, such as shipyards, armories, tanneries, cutlery shops, and shoe shops for campaign. The wealthy banker Pasion, for example, ran a shield factory employing 80–100 workers, being slaves. The fact that Pasion, who was one of the richest Athenians thanks to his successful banking activities, also kept a shield factory is another element of the many modern characteristics of the Athenian economy: the entrepreneurial activity of a citizen was not necessarily limited to a specific specialization (e.g., banking services), but due to the favorable institutional framework of the times, entrepreneurship could be extended in parallel to other areas as well.

Another possibility offered by the Athenian financial system, which is not very well known, is that it was allowed to rent the use and exploitation of an operating business (e.g., a bank, shield shop, etc.) through paying a rent to its owners (Demosthenes, *For Phormio*, 36.36–38; *Against Pantaenetus*, 37.4–6, 37.17, 37.29). However, things in this kind of deal were not always productive. Cases of presenting fake agreements and lease contracts have been recorded (Demosthenes, *Against Stephanus 1*, 45.1, 45.5, 45.29).

To sum up, there was a large unified network of economic-commercial and military cooperation that was created between Athens and its allied cities in the Aegean and the Eastern Mediterranean through the first and the second phase of the Athenian Alliance (known also as the Delian League). Figueira (1998, 52) who focused on the analysis of the monetary system of Athens raises the number of members of the Alliance to 316, a very high number, characterizing (like other major scholars) the Athens of the period as an "empire" of its time. The markets of Athens and the port of Piraeus were the most dynamic in this unified military and economic-commercial ecosystem known as the Athenian Alliance (Bresson 2014, 2016a, b; Economou 2023, 2024).

We believe that what Athens of the Classical period achieved resembles, to a lesser or greater extent, the international role of the USA on its allies, since the Cold War era to nowadays. The USA is the strongest country and democracy in the world, and in order to achieve this, in addition to the qualitatively superior features of its constitutional organization,[4] it further benefitted from a series of historical circumstances that have significantly favored it during WWI and WWII.[5]

8.3 Consumer Protection and Price Control

There were three important institutions that ensured the proper functioning of the Agora: the *ten epemeletai tou emporiou*, the *ten agoranomoi*, and the *ten metronomoi*. The first two groups had similar tasks: they supervised Agora's transactions on a sample basis, like a modern state agency entrusted to combat economic crimes, such as the US Center for Food Safety and Applied Nutrition nowadays.

As was already mentioned in Sect. 6.13, the *agoranomoi* were members of the Agoranomia service ("market police"). The office of the Athenian Agoranomia was placed in the so-called Stoa of Zeus. Perhaps the fact that the agoranomic agency chose to be installed in this specific gallery also had a symbolic character: As Zeus was the god of order, this office aimed to maintain order in the market for goods and services.

Each seller of goods was required to have a special scale supplied by Agoranomia, with which he would weigh the goods, in front of his/her prospective buyers, for cases of fraud to be avoided. Seasonal vendors could rent rather than buy a special scale from Agoranomia, apparently to incur lower rental costs since they were not active in the Agora year-round. When an *agoranomos* was inexperienced or ignorant of a matter or proved guilty of theft he could be treated with some kind of extenuation (Demosthenes, *Against Timocrates*, 24.112). This concerned also the posts of *astynomoi* and the judges of the *demes*.

Agoranomoi when accessing the Agora on foot were aided by a (usually bulky) Scythian archer, of those charged with maintaining order in the Agora. This probably happened in order to protect them against any violence in the market, in the event that during the performance of their duties, any disgruntled merchants or consumers acted threateningly against them.

Finally, van Alfen (2011, 13, ftn 36) and Leese (2017, 49–50) refer to Athenaeus, *The Deipnosophists* (6.225c, PCG fr. 7) who provides the interesting information

[4]The US constitution was formulated by the "American Founding Fathers," such as Thomas Jefferson, John Adams, John Dickinson, and George Washington. It is known that in its composition, the "Fathers'" were significantly influenced by ancient Greek and Roman authors, such as Aristotle, Plutarch, Polybius, and Titus Livy and had extensively studied the political organization of Athens, Sparta, the Achaean League, Rome, etc. (see Richard (2009) and Economou (2020) on this).

[5]For example, it should be considered rather correct that if WWII did not take place, which exhausted, from many aspects the other Great Powers of the time, mainly, the British Empire and France, as well as the Soviet Union (in terms of economic and military power, infrastructure, human resources, loss of colonial possessions, and strategic points after WWII), perhaps the USA would not have become so fast a planetary superpower, with only rival (in awe of) the Soviet Union during the Cold War (1945–1990).

that fishmongers accepted heavier Aeginetan obols as payment for a sea bass and were giving lighter Athenian obols as change. This was of course a fraud act since the fishmongers were exploiting differences in foreign currency values since Aeginetan coinage of the same denomination was worth more than Athenian because it contained about 66% more silver in weight. One might say that this is also a primitive version of an arbitrage technique, to use a modern interpretation, introduced by the fishmongers, at the expense of their customers. We assume that the *agoranomoi* were aware of this practice of the fishmongers, and when such acts came to their notice, they fined them.

The *metronomoi*, for their part, also supervised the Agora and had as their primary responsibility that the measures and standards by which the sellers priced their goods were correct. Practically their purpose was to ensure that the quantity of goods (e.g., beans) for which consumers paid was correct; i.e., customers did not receive less product than what they paid for, due to possible fraud on the part of the sellers. This is how they fought against profiteering (Johnstone 2011, 54; McAuley 2013, 181; Bitros et al. 2020; Economou et al. 2021a, b).

Furthermore, the Athenians were opposed to any practice that caused a technical increase in prices. For example, they considered it illegal to spread rumors about shortages in grain imports with the aim of causing demand and prices to rise. For this reason they had established a special body of "wheat overseers," known as the *ten sitophylakes* (Lysias, *Against the Corn Dealers*, 22.8, 22.13–14, 22.16) to combat the craftiness and opportunism of the *sitopolai* (grain retailers). A key measure to prevent speculation was to prohibit the *sitopolai* from buying more than 50 *phormoi* ("baskets") of wheat each, so as not to build up private stocks and thus manage to manipulate market prices, to some extent, through these stocks.

Another relative body of elected civil servants, the *sitonai*, took care of the wholesale purchase and importation of sufficient quantities of wheat in the economy. For a time, there was a synergy between the two bodies in collecting taxes on wheat from the islands of Lemnos, Imbros, and Skyros. Illegalities detected by the members of this body could even attract the death penalty (*ibid.*, 22.17–21) because the proper functioning of the grain market was absolutely vital for ensuring normal living conditions of the Athenians, since Athens was not self-sufficient in cereals and had to rely on imports.

Due to the above reasons, the prices of grain, as well as some other vital products such as oil, coal, and timber, were subject to state control through specific laws which were voted with a view to ensure the smooth running of the polis market regulations (Bresson 2016b, 420–425). Price fluctuations of wheat depended on changes in supply, mainly an increase or decrease in imports (Demosthenes, *Against Dionysodorus*, 56. 8–10).

As a final comment, there is no doubt that the ancient Athenians instituted the above pivotal posts to ensure credibility and the solvency of their internationalized market, known as *emporion*, and of course, to secure the welfare of the citizen-consumers of Athens in the long run.

8.4 The Port of Piraeus

As already mentioned, Piraeus was the main entrepôt of the Mediterranean during the Classical times. A merchant could find all the products from the known world there. The economic prosperity of Athens in the fourth century BCE is largely due to this function of Piraeus. In line with Thucydides's (2.38) view reproduced above, the importance of the Piraeus port in the economic activity of Classical Athens is also confirmed by additional primary sources; another one is provided below by Isocrates (*Panegyricus*, 4.42) in which he proudly states that there was no good produced anywhere in the world that one could not find in Piraeus:

> Again, since the different populations[6] did not in any case possess a country that was self-sufficing, each lacking in some things and producing others in excess of their needs, and since they were greatly at a loss where they should dispose of their surplus and whence they should import what they lacked, in these difficulties also our city came to the rescue; for she established the Piraeus as a market in the center of Hellas—a market of such abundance that the articles which it is difficult to get, one here, one there, from the rest of the world, all these[7] it is easy to procure from Athens.

The Athenian state, recognizing the great prospects of public revenue from the port's commercial traffic, imposed the *pentecoste*, a customs duty of 2% on the value of goods imported and exported from the port of Piraeus. The collection of this kind of tax had been assigned by the state to the private sector under a publicprivate partnership agreement (*3P*), following an open tender procedure. These tax collectors were called *pentecostologoi* (Johnstone 2011, 55). Hansen (2006, 92) provides us with the following important information: that around 400 BCE Athens must have had a huge foreign trade. This is extracted from a passage in a speech by the orator Andocides where he states that in the year 402/1 he took over the contract for collecting the 2% *pentecoste* tax, in favor of the state. The proceeds to be paid to Andocides were 36 *talents*. Thus, the total import and export trade of Athens, including transit trade that year (which was one of the worst in the history of Athens regarding economic performance), was worth more than 1800 *talents*, equivalent to 11 million drachmae.

This information proves the very large volume of transactions and the robustness of the Athenian economy (even though that year there was rather an economic recession), although due to a lack of cliometric data,[8] we cannot make a clear assessment for specific economic figures, such as public revenue, or the overall turnover produced in the economy, what we nowadays characterize as GDP, etc.

---

[6] He means populations of different city-states and nations.

[7] The goods from the international markets of the times.

[8] Cliometric methodologies relate the use of econometric techniques and economic theory to economy history. According to Diebolt and Haupert (eds) (2019, v) cliometrics represent the quantitative projection of social sciences in the past. On the role of cliometrics to economic history, see analytically Diebolt and Haupert (eds) (2019) and Diebolt and Haupert (2016, 2020).

The bottom line is that the extroversion of the Athenian economy, and the creation of a single economic/commercial network between Athens and its allied city-states, proved extremely beneficial for its long-term economic growth (Ober 2015a; Bresson 2016a, b; Harris 2016; Woolmer 2016; O' Halloran 2018; Bitros et al. 2020; Economou et al. 2021a, b; and Economou (2024).

A number of both Athenian and non-Athenian merchants developed commercial activity and links even in distant regions, where through correspondence they gave directions to their partners there as to what commercial activities they should carry out there on behalf of their customers (Johnstone 2011, 22).

Piraeus of the fourth century, apart from being a busy port, was probably the first city in the world to be designed with an urban plan, a square layout, and a large central market. The plans of the port were made by the architect-urban planner Hippodamus from Miletus who separated and demarcated the public and sacred spaces (Aristotle, *Politics*, 2.167b18). According to the spatial design specifications, 327 *trireme* types of warships could be hosted, including their *neosoikoi* (shipsheds).

In the center of the larger port of Piraeus known as Kantharos was located also the Emporion, a market for goods from the international markets as well as the Deigma which, in essence, exhibited samples of goods for purchase. The ancient Athenians pioneered also here; through the Deigma they actually introduced what nowadays is known as international commercial expos such as those in Shanghai (China), Dubai (UAE), Yeosu (South Korea), etc., nowadays. Importers mainly presented their goods to the public (Demosthenes, *Against Lacritus*, 35.29).

There was also a special market in Makra Stoa for the importation and sale of grain. Its importance was so great that the oligarchs who ruled Athens in 411 included it in the adjacent war wall. In addition to the main commercial port, there were also two smaller ones, Munichia and Zea,[9] being mainly "military" ports. They were the anchorages of the Athenian *triremes*. There were also other smaller ports that brought in duty-free goods secretly by smuggling them to avoid customs duties (Demosthenes, *Against Lacritus*, 35.28). Image 8.5 provides a reproduction of the spatial structure of the port of Piraeus, and Table 8.2 explains various critical points of Image 8.5.

8.5 *Neosoikoi* and Philon's Arsenal

As already mentioned, *neosoikoi* were the shipsheds of the war *triremes*. It has been estimated that in all three ports of Piraeus 327 ships could be sheltered in *neosoikoi*, 82 in Munichia, 196 in Zea, and 94 in Kantharos. The floor of the *neosoikoi* was wooden, placed in a groove, smeared with grease, so that the boat's keel would slide easily on them. Each warship had a predetermined *neosoikos*. The crews of the ships

[9] In the past, the ships carrying the precious grain from the Black Sea were being docked at the port of Zea. At the time we are dealing with the port was the base of the war fleet of Athens.

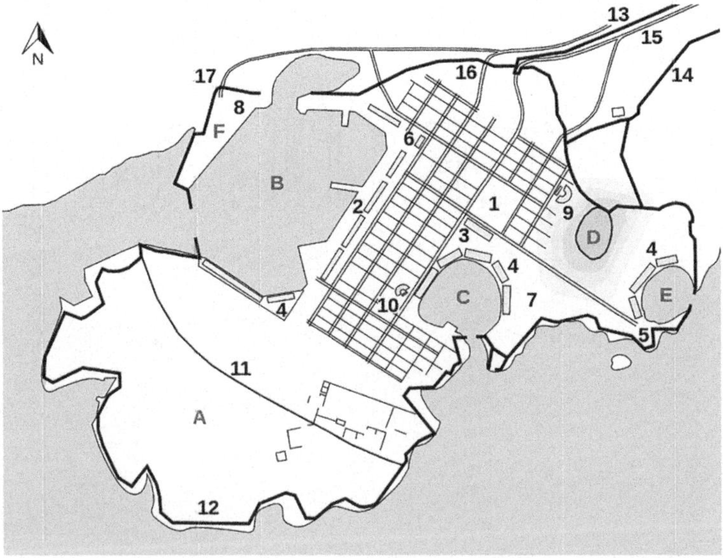

Image 8.5 A spatial illustration of the port of Ancient Piraeus. Source: https://commons.wikimedia.org/wiki/File:Plan_Piraeus.svg. Retrieved by: Tomisti

Table 8.2 Various critical points at the port of Ancient Piraeus

A. Akte Peninsula	B. Kantharos Harbor	C. Zea Harbor
D. Munichia Hill	E. Munichia Harbour	F. Eetioneia
1. Hippodameian Agora	2. Emporion	3. Philon's Arsenal
4. *Neosoikoi*	5. Temple of Artemis Munichia	6. Temple of Zeus Soter and Athena Soteira
7. Sanctuary of Asclepius	8. Sanctuary of Aphrodite Euploia	9. Older theatre
10. Theatre of Zea	11. Themistoclean Walls	12. Wall of Konon
13. Northern Long Wall	14. Southern Long Wall	15. Road from Athens to Piraeus
16. Main gate	17. Eetioneia Gate or Aphrodite Gate	

Source: https://commons.wikimedia.org/wiki/File:Plan_Piraeus.svg

would have to live near them. It wouldn't make sense for a *neosoikos* to have a mechanism to quickly launch the ship, in case of danger (e.g., a surprise attack), but require a long turn-up and manning time for the ship's crew!

An inscription from the fourth century discovered in 1881 in Piraeus refers to the construction of a magnificent building (124 by 17 m) for the storage of *trireme*

Image 8.6 *Neosoikoi* in Piraeus. Source: Image created by painter Vasiliki Demopoulou

equipment. It is known as Philon's Arsenal. Construction began in 346 based on plans by the architect Philon and was completed in 328. This, like most of the brilliant buildings of Piraeus, was destroyed by the Roman general Sulla in 86. It was a huge building, in which the movable parts of the warships were stored. When the ships were winterized, i.e., dragged into the *neosoikoi* where they remained for protection during the winter, their parts were removed and stored there. This naval warehouse housed sails, ropes, oars, ladders, awnings, and every kind of ship's equipment (warlike or not) so as not to be exposed to the winds and rains, when the ships were not in action, especially in winter when navigation was impossible. Any citizen could freely visit the arsenal, in order to see up close and verify the perfect condition and maintenance of the ships' items, but also as an indirect proof of the good management of public money. After all, Philon's Arsenal was built by charities from citizens (Images 8.6 and 8.7).

8.6 The Athenian *Long Walls*

Immediately after the end of the Greco-Persian Wars in 479 BCE the new fortification of Athens began to be built, following a suggestion by Themistocles, to deal with the possibility of a new invasion. The fortification of Piraeus that had begun in 493/492 BCE was completed.

Image 8.7 Performing maintenance of a *trireme* inside a *neosoikos*. Source: Image created by painter Vasiliki Demopoulou

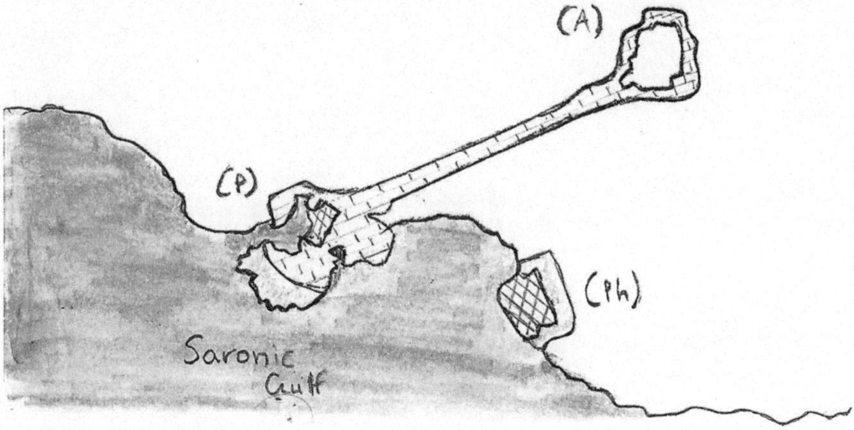

Image 8.8 The twin city-state of Athens and Piraeus through the Long Walls. (A): Athens, (P): Piraeus, (Ph): Phalerum. Source: Image created by painter Vasiliki Demopoulou

Image 8.8 presents the northern and southern walls that connected Athens with Piraeus as a “twin” and single city, as well as the walling of Athens and Piraeus. So, within a short period of time a 6.5-km-long wall was founded, which was named Themistoclean, after its initiator, and enclosed both the city-states of Athens and Piraeus as a coherent whole. It was 2.5 m wide and reached a height of 8 m. It should be considered as a huge project for the times. Its base was from stone and the rest was made of large bricks. Parts of the Themistoclean Wall are preserved to this day in various parts of the coast of Piraeus.

Chapter 9
Ancient Greek Hospitality, Food Habits, and Grain Supply

Abstract This chapter describes the element of hospitality, which is inherent to the Greeks, since ancient times, to nowadays. On a technical level, it describes the household utensils of an ancient kitchen and provides evidence regarding cooking, delicacies, and the usage of dairy products, vegetables, fruits, drinks, and spices, which were all part of the Athenian kitchen. It finally explains the vital importance of grain in feeding the Athenian population and what institutions had the Athenians established in order to ensure the fair disposition and distribution of grains to the society as a whole.

9.1 Meal to Honor a Stranger

After his morning cooperation with Xenocrates, Nicomedes handled some further transactions with his clients, then returned to his bank, and waited for Xenocrates, who arrived again there in early evening.

– How was your day; he asked him.
– Oh, very well. I went up to the Acropolis. I visited the temples there. Truly impressive, even more magnificent than the temples of the Sicilian city-states. The truth is that I would also like to visit the place where the famous Eleusinian Mysteries are held, but I don't know if my schedule will allow me to travel there. Have you traveled to Sicily?
– Yes. Rhegion, Catane, Messene, Leontinoi, Naxos, Syracuse, Kamarina, Gela, Akragas, Selinus, Panormos, Himera, when I was younger, answered Nicomedes.
– Then you know these temples. Next, I went to Kerameikos and visited the potters' workshops. I'm thinking of buying some for the return trip, as merchandise. Their painting is excellent, and the Celts and Iberians have learned about them and appreciated their art. On the way back, I went up to the Pnyx and I also passed by Dionysus's theater.
– So, you will be tired and hungry, smiled Nicomedes.
– That's true, replied Xenocrates.
– Fine, we're leaving. Let me close the bank first...

E. M. L. Economou, N. C. Kyriazis, *Daily Life in Classical Athens*, Frontiers in Economic History, https://doi.org/10.1007/978-3-031-58541-8_9

Nicomedes collected the bank book accounts and the money, and with Ischomachos and Xenocrates marched to his *oikos*.

Since the women in his *oikos* did not know that Nicomedes would come with a stranger, and Nicomedes did not know what the women had prepared for dinner, he took care and bought from the market stuffing with liver and spices and a honeycomb, which Ischomachos held.

They finally arrived at the *oikos*. They greeted first Hegeso and then Eriphyle and Chariclea.

They passed into the *andron*, and Nicomedes showed one of the couches to his guest. Xenocrates sat up, resting his elbow on a pillow. Ischomachos placed a small table beside each couch.

Chariclea tipped over a small basin and pitcher of water and the two men washed their hands and dried them with towels offered by Chariclea. Then Chariclea brought the food, porridge, bread with honey, olives, cheese and turnips, the liver with spices, and the honeycomb for dessert. It was accompanied by white wine from Mesogeia, which Nicomedes diluted with water in the *kylikes*.

Hegeso wanted, as a good hostess, to leave her mark regarding the satisfaction of the guest of her husband. And since they didn't have time to prepare a main meal, she thought she might add something that could be prepared quickly. She ordered Chariclea and Eriphyle to bring semolina, bulgur *feta*, a kind of cheese, and pomegranate with which they made a kind of salad. They also prepared *plakountes*, that is, small pies with dough, cheese, honey, sesame seeds, and spices. In the past Nicomedes had given not a few *symposia* but also meals to friends at the *andron*, and all of them had been perfectly pleased with the treatment Hegeso had reserved for them, and as before, she wished to continue this "tradition."

In addition to Chariclea, Eriphyle had now been "recruited" into the kitchen as "staff." After all, she had to gradually start learning the "art of cooking," like any daughter of a good Athenian family. How would she create her own family if she didn't know even the basics of cooking?

- What about the dough Eriphyle? Did you prepare it properly? Hegeso asked, almost imperatively.
- Yes mother, it is ready.
- Stay focused! Hegeso insisted.
- Come on now ma'am, don't stress her, Chariclea commented.

The salad and the *plakountes* tied harmoniously with the rest of the meals.

* * *

9.2 The Household Utensils of the Ancient Kitchen

For their meals, the Ancient Greeks used spoons and knives, as well as their fingers, which they later cleaned with a special dough or breadcrumbs. Forks were used in Ancient Greece, Egypt, and Rome, not for eating, but as cooking tools to remove meat from cauldrons or fire. Cooking utensils were usually glazed earthenware, although there were also metal ones. They were also using kettles (pots), deep pans with legs placed over the fire, and shallow pans, pots, and griddles (Image 9.1).

The dishes were served in small pieces, just like in Chinese cuisine. Some of the most basic utensils used by the ancient Greeks were the following:

Kakavion: Small metal kettle, which was placed on the fire to cook. It was a vessel for boiled foods and soups.

Lopas: Ceramic vessel, without handles, which also had a lid. It looked like a low kettle but was of larger dimensions. The diameter of the vessel was about 20 cm; it was deeper than the kettle and had two handles. There was a hole in the lid for the steam to come out.

Puraunos: Large vessel with length equal to 0.38 m, weighing 14 kg. It is estimated that its capacity was about 20 L. It consisted of an inner vessel, which fitted into a larger one. In the walls it bore two rows of holes, so that, when placed on the fire, air would circulate and the fire would be rekindled. It is the first ever recorded kind of a pressure cooker.

Tigani: They were very popular at the time. Their use goes back to the Mycenaean period. It was a wide and shallow vessel, with a long handle, so that the person

Image 9.1 Pots of various types. Source: Image created by Vasiliki Demopoulou

using it would not be burned by the fire. There were also ceramic pans, which cost less money.

Krater: Large vessel in which wine was mixed with water.

Kylix (in plural *kylikes*): Drinking vessels/types of glasses. They were mainly used at symposia and many times the hosts ordered them from the potters with specific decorations on them.

Amphora: Large vessel for storing wine, oil, and small fruits.

Hydria: Vessel for storing and transporting water.

Pelike: Storage vessel, variant of the *amphora*.

Pinakion: Type of dish.

9.3 Cooking, Delicacies, and Obesity

In the summer, meals were prepared outdoors over a wood fire or on a charcoal grill in the yard, like today's barbecues. In the winter, cooking was done inside the *oikos* on a portable brazier, which was also a source of heating. Smoke came out through chimneys (Tsakirgis 2007). In any case, the Athenians preferred charcoal to wood because it produced less smoke. Common cooking methods were boiling and baking, although various types of food were eaten raw.

From the end of the fifth century, the Greeks became interested in the haute cuisine of the East, especially the Persian Empire's cooking techniques. Greek mercenaries who were in the service of eastern monarchs (Babylonians, Lydians, Persians) as early as the seventh century BCE would have known the culinary habits (and culinary opulence) of the satrapic courts and would have probably spread some relative information when returning back to their cities, as tourists nowadays learn about the "ethnic" cuisines of the countries they visit. Cookbooks were written mainly in Sicily, excerpts of which survive in *The Deipnosophists*, written by Athenaeus, a Greek of Egypt in 200 AD.

The basic principle regarding food was that it should be consumed as much as is necessary to satisfy normal hunger, because gluttony was considered a vice. It was also unthinkable to eat alone; only those who had no friends had this sad privilege.

The *plakountes* mentioned in this Scene were small pies made of dough, cheese, honey, sesame, and spices. Greeks ate a pot meal of poultry quite regularly, while for ordinary citizens, *metics*, and slaves, roast meat was rarer, consumed mostly on feast days. They were about 60 feast days in Athens a year. In religious festivals, such as the Panathenaea, animal sacrifices (such as the *hecatombe*) were taking place. Sacrificial animals included, among others, bulls, cows, oxen, goats, and sheep. Their meat was shared among the people, while the gods had to be "satisfied" with the smell of the roasting meat! In less populated areas such as Arcadia, Laconia, Messenia, Aetolia, Thessaly, Epirus, Macedonia, Thrace, and many Greek colonies, hunting was also a source of meat. In densely populated Attica, by contrast, large wild animals such as deer and wild boar were extremely rare.

Fish were eaten either fresh or, more often, for reasons of preservation and ease of transport, dry or salted. Obviously, the consumption would be higher on the coast than in Asty. There was a great variety, such as tuna, mackerel, oxyrhynchus, mullet, carp, anchovies, sardines, and in general, all kinds of fish found in the Greek seas. Many of the above fish, such as the oxyrhynchus, were imported from the Black Sea region. Archestratus of Gela, a mid-fourth century poet and celebrated chef, provides us a recipe for cooking sardine, which survives in the *Deipnosophists*:

> Count all small fry as abomination, 42 except the Athenian; I mean gonos, which Ionians call foam; and accept it only when it is caught fresh in the sacred arm of Phalerum's beautiful bay. That which is found in ocean-washed Rhodes is good, if it be native. And if you desire to taste it, you should at the same time get at the market some nettles—sea-anemones crowned with leafy tentacles. Mixing them with it, bake it in a pan, after you have made a sauce of the fragrant tops of choice greens mixed in oil. (Athenaeus, *The Deipnosophists*, 285b)

A favorite delicacy of the Athenian rich were the eels. Those originating from Lake Copais in Boeotoia were perhaps the most famous. These could arrive fresh in a few hours from Copais, for example, by horse or mule, which could cover the distance, about 60 km from the southern shores of the lake, in possibly 5–6 h. Other areas famous for their eels were Sicyon, on the northern coast of the Peloponnese, the Arethusa spring, near Chalkis, and the Strymon River (Northern Greece). Due to the high demand for this kind of food, their price could become very high (could rise even as high as 5 days wages) especially when eels shortages appeared, either because of quantity shortages, or intentionally, caused by the fishmongers themselves: to cause artificial shortages in the market, and then, being benefited by the very high prices of eels, to profit at the expense of their customers. We guess that the *agoranomoi* were aware of these cunning tricks of the fishmongers and they tried to deter them by imposing fines on the latter.

Furthermore, the ancient Greeks consumed many types of herbs-plants, which also had therapeutic use, known to the doctors of antiquity, such as Hippocrates. After all, the mythical Centaurs, who lived in Pelion (like Achilles' teacher, Chiron), were supposed to be knowledgeable about the therapeutic use of plants.

As a final comment, it is worth mentioning that obesity was considered a sign of weakness and indicated lack of self-control as well as the absence of an almost sacred virtue: temperance. Some suggestions to remedy this were the obese should engage in hard work, having their lunch immediately afterward. In addition, they should drink a little wine diluted with water, take only one meal in 24 h, lie on a bed with a hard mattress, and go about naked at their home as much as possible.

9.4 Dairy Products, Vegetables, Fruits, Drinks, and Spices

Milk was mainly consumed by people in the countryside and less in the cities. The Ancient Greeks loved cheese. Cheese was produced from sheep's and goat's milk and there was a special place in the Agora for cheeses, many imported from Boeotia. Cheeses were divided into two categories: fresh or soft and mature. According to an account by Galen, the first were wrapped in dragon leaves (a leafy plant) in order to preserve them. The most common ones produced in Greece were *anthotyros* ("flowery cheese," made with milk from sheep or goats, sometimes in combination) and goat cheese. There was also pepper-crushed cheese (*koptos tyros*) as well as soft cheese from Sicily (*trophalis*). Today's well-known *feta* comes from these cheeses.

The main vegetables were cabbages, asparagus, carrots, radishes, cucumbers, pumpkins, celery, artichokes, onions, garlic, olives, and wild greens. There were also various legumes, beans, etc. The main fruits were grapes, figs, apples, and pears. There were also imported ones, such as dates, oranges, and citrus fruits in general, which according to the legend (Apples of the Hesperides) Heracles had imported from Spain. The Greeks also ate nuts, such as walnuts, almonds, hazelnuts, and chestnuts. Sugar was unknown, and honey was used as a sweetener. Honey was also used for mixing with liquids, such as some wines, while probably in the fourth century a "hallucinogenic" honey was introduced, which the *myrioi* (a body of 13,000 Greek mercenaries—700 of them being Spartans) had met on their way to Pontus (see in detail Xenophon, *Anabasis*). The bees of the area collected neurotoxic nectar from the poisonous rhododendron that abounded there, and the honey they produced had such properties. The *myrioi* called it "mad honey" (Mayor 2014, 147).

For cooking, the Greeks used oil, while butter, although it was known, was consumed in small quantities. The main alcoholic drink was wine, which was cultivated throughout the Greek world and sold everywhere. *Zythos* (beer), while it was known, for example, in Egypt, does not seem to have been widespread in the Greek world, like other "exotic" drinks, which some Greeks had tasted in their distant campaigns, or during their trade transactions outside Hellas. One of these was *kourmis*, made from fermented mare's milk, and it was (and still is) widespread among the steppe people (Eurasian nomads).

Finally, an interesting and inscrutable topic concerns what kinds of spices were used by the Athenians and the Ancient Greeks. Apparently, some, such as thyme, sage, and saffron, as well as many types of herbs, came from the Greek countryside. Other seasonings and spices used were dill, basil, mint, cardamom, coriander, capers, pine, and nuts. The question, however, is whether the Greeks already imported spices, such as pepper, cinnamon, cloves, etc. in the fourth century. Pepper was produced in tropical areas, as well as in India. The Persians, who held part of Western India, probably used pepper, and through them the Greeks. Other spices such as cinnamon and nutmeg were grown only on the islands of present-day Indonesia, Halmahera, Seram, Buru, Ambon, Ternate, Tidore, Aru Islands, Kai Islands, Lucipara Islands, and Benda, the origin of nutmeg. We do not know if there were any trade relations with such distant regions. But it is known that at a later time, Alexandria in Egypt during the Roman period became an entrepôt and an international spice trade center, receiving spices from India which were then promoted to Greece and Europe. Also, silphium was a spice that was used widespread in Ancient Greece and later in the Roman Empire.

9.5 The Athenian Grain Supply Institutions

Cereals provided 70% of the daily required calorie intake for the Athenians. There was also zea, which was an important cereal mentioned mainly in ancient texts. Athens, due to its large population for the time (in the fourth century probably over 300,000 souls), was not self-sufficient in food and especially grain. Thus, the Athenian authorities imported grain from the regions of today's Ukraine and South-West Russia, through the straits of the Hellespont and the Dardanelles, which they paid either with Athenian drachmae, sought after in the ancient world, or with exports of "industrial" products and services. For this reason, the geostrategic dominance of these straits was of vital importance for Athens.[1]

Due to the lack of self-sufficiency, following a proposal by the Athenian politician Aghyrrios, the Athenian Grain-Tax Law of 374/3 BCE was passed which required all ships with a cargo of grain from the islands of Lemnos, Imbros, and Skyros to unload in Piraeus compulsorily, and only then continue their journey perhaps with the remaining cargo. This grain was unloaded and stored in storehouses in the temple of Aiakos, and then distributed in the Agora by public officials (Stroud 1998).

The grain market was a special, separate market. The Athenian city-state had very significant shortages in domestic grain production and for this reason had to ensure the well-being and quality of life of its inhabitants through imports. For this reason, the Athenians did not allow the complete liberalization of the markets of grain, charcoal, and wood; thus, prices for these products were not shaped by the market mechanism, as applied for the rest of the products that were traded in the Athenian market (Bresson 2016b).

How important grains were for the prosperity of the city-state of Athens can be noticed also from the fact that when in 341/340 BCE the energetic and shrewd Macedonian King Philip II seized a fleet of 180–230 merchant ships carrying grain from the Black Sea, there was an alarm in Athens. Since the average capacity of a merchant ship was 3000 *medimnoi*, these ships could have contained at least 540,000 *medimnoi* (Moreno 2007, 207–208).[2] Due to Philip's act, panic reigned in Athens for a time, and the Athenian state's relations with the Kingdom of Macedon became more strained. Such an act caused a great financial damage that affected, at least to

[1]The strategic importance of the Hellespont and Bosporus straits is intertemporal and very well known and dates back to very distant times such as the (mythical) Argonautic Campaign and the Trojan War. The Crimean War of 1853–1856 and the Gallipoli campaign of 1915–1916 are a characteristic proof of this. Since the ancient times till nowadays it is known that the wider area of today's Ukraine was a large granary for the rest of Europe. Notice for example how much the price of cereal products in the EU today has risen because of the current Russo-Ukrainian War (since February 2022), which has caused significant production shortages (millions of tons) and has as a result the rise of inflation throughout the EU and the loss of purchasing capacity for European consumers.

[2]Moreno (2007) provides a detailed analysis regarding the food supply channels of democratic Athens of the times.

some degree, the economic aspect of the Athenians' military preparation before the Battle of Chaeronea in 338 BCE, which happened in less than 2 years after these events. Figueira (1986, 164) reveals that in less pressing (in terms of shortages) periods the Athenians, and more specifically, the *epimeletai tou emporiou*, in consultation with the grain merchants, provided greater flexibility in shaping of the prices of these specific goods, through the Agora, and this was done after discussions and negotiations with them.

There were two types of bread, *maza*, made from barley flour, and *artos*, a white type of bread made from wheat. Because barley was more abundant and cheap, *artos* was a luxury item and was mainly consumed by the wealthy. Despite this, in some cases it was distributed freely to the population, on certain festivals. Bread was usually eaten with honey, cheese, and olive oil, while it was cooked by making a kind of porridge, or broth, adding vegetables and meat.

Chapter 10
The Athenian Drachma and the Role of Money in the Economy

Abstract This chapter provides information on the various types and subdivisions of the Athenian currency of the times, the drachma series of coins. It explains why drachma became the international currency of the times, something like the "dollar" of the Classical times. Then it describes the Athenian monetary system, by arguing that money supply in the market was a combination of direct democracy procedures in the Assembly, but also the market forces themselves. This is why this chapter next describes the Athenian monetary regime in relation to later unconventional monetary regimes, such as the Scottish free banking regime and the digital currencies phenomenon. It then explains the famous Law of Nicophon, which was introduced with the purpose that only pure currency (unfraudulent coins) to be circulated in the economy. The chapter closes with the last subsection, which explains the related methods of assessing the purity of metal coins in Classical Greece.

10.1 In Nicomedes' *Andron*

After the meal, Nicomedes, Xenocrates, and Ischomachos remained in the *andron*. Chariclea turned on the lamps and candles, now that the sun had almost set.

At the same time, they started the discussion about the practical issues that concerned them:

– How much is the load of copper you brought? asked Nicomedes.
– Two hundred and fifty *medimnoi*.
– Have you found a buyer?
– Yes, there are quite a few interested in Piraeus.
– Absolutely natural. In Piraeus all the products of the earth are exchanged. And what are you thinking of taking on the return trip?
– I thought about what you suggested: Jewelry, maybe some amphorae and other vessels from the Kerameikos workshops. But also, those porphyry fabrics from Tyre. For ballast, instead of copper, maybe I should buy Attic marble. And should I put wine and honey in the amphorae?

E. M. L. Economou, N. C. Kyriazis, *Daily Life in Classical Athens*, Frontiers in Economic History, https://doi.org/10.1007/978-3-031-58541-8_10

- You could. For wine, I would suggest you not only Attic, but also Samian, Chiot and Rhodian. This will increase the variety of your products. How about some spices too? Do the Iberians and Celts know them? Do they like them;
- Ah, we call them barbarians, but after nearly three centuries of intercourse with us they have acquired quite a few Greek habits, at least the chiefs of the tribes and the aristocrats with their wives. They have started to have sophisticated tastes and preferences. I am sure they will appreciate such products. As do our wealthiest ones. Iberia is rich in minerals, so their kings, nobles and aristocrats can afford to buy luxury goods.
- Then I suggest the following: Start from Kerameikos tomorrow, buy as many amphorae and vases as you want. I will introduce you to a coachman with his cart to load them in Athens and bring them to Piraeus. Then I will take you to Pammenes' workshop. He is one of the best goldsmiths in Athens. Afterwards, we will go down to Piraeus together. We will visit Nicostratos' shop. He is a Sidonian, Phoenician *metic*. He has been living in Piraeus for many years and we gave him a Greek name, because we had difficulty pronouncing his real Phoenician name. Nicostratos imports and trades these porphyry cloths I told you about, as well as other types and colors of clothes.

Finally, I suggest visiting the shop of Artemis of Piraeus, which has perfumes, ribbons, tunics, and shoes for women, combs, brooches, belts, perfumes, and everything else that the well-to-do ladies like. I think you could also buy some perfumes. If you think there is a demand for spices in Iberia as well, then we can visit the shop of Philocles, partner of Nicostratos.

- What you are telling me sounds very tempting. There is only one small issue I further need to ask you about; I have only coins made in Emporion in my pouch, waiting for receiving Athenian currency from the sale of my copper in Attic drachmae.
- Don't worry at all. In Athens, thanks to the Nicophon's Law, all good quality coins are accepted, even if they are foreign, as long as they contain the right amount of silver, corresponding to the Athenian drachma. So, you don't need to change them. But if you need more. I trust you, and if you cannot sell the copper immediately, I could lend you money, pledging part of it, that will be a typical procedure, a kind of security of my money. Anyway, I look forward to our long-term cooperation.
- Very well Nicomedes! Thank you very much for all your help and kindness to assist me, which reached as far as to your *oikos*. But what is this Law of Nicophon?
- I will explain to you. Nicophon proposed a monetary measure, which after being passed in the Assembly became law. He wanted to facilitate the transactions of the foreign merchants who enter our polis, to stimulate the Athenian trade and economy, but also the revenues of the public treasury. As you know, there is the *pentecoste* for imports and exports from Piraeus, you will pay this as well, as every other foreigner who trades in Attica. The *pentecoste*, together with the income from the silver mines, represent the main public revenues of the polis.

Without them democracy would not work....In practice, Nicophon proposed, that all good quality (meaning not fake) copies of the Athenian drachma produced in mints from all over the world could circulate equally, alongside the Attica drachma. This further means that all foreign-made coins, such as, for example, the Corinthian or Aeginitan *staters* can also be freely circulated in the economy. Thus, foreign merchants need not to exchange their coins for Attic drachmae when trading at Athens, providing that the coins they bear with them are pure, not fraudulent.

- This is important for a trader to gain time when trading.
- Exactly! As you know, the Athenian drachma is regarded as the absolutely reliable, I emphasize this, the absolutely reliable coin in silver content, in international markets, which is also distinguished by a very high quality of craftmanship, which is carried out by excellent metalsmiths in the so-called Argyrocopeion, the Athenian silver mint. For these reasons and due to the mighty Athenian navy and the power of our state, our currency has become the most reliable international currency. I am sure that if you decide to return with Athenian drachmae to Emporion, they will be immediately snapped up.
- I didn't know, Xenocrates broke the silence. It sounds very good. But how can one, who has doubts about the quality of a coin he is about to receive in an exchange, be assured? Like maybe myself?
- Nikophon thought about it. He established the institution of *dokimastai* for this purpose. They are two slaves in the service of the state. You will find them at a central point of the Agora of Athens and Piraeus. Maybe you didn't notice them today. I'll show them to you tomorrow.
- And what the *dokimastai* do?
- Suppose you and I want to perform a commercial transaction. You want to buy from me and you propose to pay me with the currency of your polis. I do not know you, nor the quality of the currency from your polis, and I have some doubts about the purity of your coins. How can we proceed with this? We agree to apply to the *dokimastai.* On their bench you leave all your coins, and the *dokimastes* picks one or some at random, and test them on the spot to see if they are genuine, or fraudulent, so you're trying to cheat me.
- How do they test the coin?
- In various ways. Visual inspection, they check the designs and engravings of the coin, palpation, weighting, 'sound recording', even bitting, checking the authenticity of the seal of the coin, dropping liquid or acid, such as lydite on the coin where there is a change or not of its original color, intervention on the coin itself by making small incisions to determine whether the interior is pure silver or contains an alloy of silver mixed with other inferior metals, so the coin is of lesser content, that is, a fraudulent one. The *dokimastai* are so experienced that they know the designs of coins from almost every corner of the earth. This is how they realize whether the shape of a coin, and the letters or the seal of the city from which it comes from are official, or not. The weight indicates whether it is correct or underweight. Acids indicate the content of the precious metal. But there is also a safety valve that acts as a deterrent to fraud: if the coin turns out to be fake, then

all the coins the merchant bores with him are confiscated, then destroyed, and the silver that can be extracted from them is deposited in the so-called Temple of the Mother Goddess. As you can see, this is a serious disincentive for would-be fraudsters!

- I confess that Nicophon thought of it all.
- Correct! But if he hadn't done so, he wouldn't have convinced the Assembly to approve the relevant law!
- So, can I take Attic drachmae with me if I have any left over from my purchases?
- Freely. There is no limitation. Our drachmae are transacted everywhere as I told you. But you can also deposit a part in my bank if you wish.

They finished eating. Xenocrates thanked both Nicomedes and the women of his *oikos* and declared himself impressed with even this small sample of their cooking skills.

Hegeso felt nice with the words of Xenocrates. Because she performed her duty as a hostess well, and she pleased both her husband and his guest.

* * *

10.2 The Athenian *Drachma* and the Money Supply in the Economy

In the Agora of Athens there was the Argyrocopeion, a state institution which minted the coins with which the largest portion of transactions were carried out within the Athenian polis but also with states being members (or not) of the Athenian Alliance. The silver Athenian drachma, also known as *glauke* (owl), became the most important international currency of the Classical period in the Eastern Mediterranean, followed during the Hellenistic period by another internationally accepted Greek coin, the Macedonian *tetradrachm* of Alexander the Great and his successors, and then by the Roman *denarius*, followed by the Byzantine *solidus*, the Spanish *pesos*, the Dutch *leeuwendaalder*, the Austrian Maria Theresia *thalers*, the British pound, and today, the *dollar*.

The *glauke* is a nocturnal bird that has excellent vision even in the dark, where it can observe with great precision. It cannot be proven, but we surmise that the Athenians very intelligently decided to adopt the *glauke* to be engraved on their coins: they wanted to imply that whoever uses the coins as a means of transactions should do so with wisdom and insight, in the sense that he/she makes transactions based on careful and wise/rational choices. This is, of course, by extension, an unwritten intertemporal principle regarding the proper management of the wealth and financial resources of either a household or a business or the state itself.

The amount of coins that was issued each year by the Athenian Argyrocopeion was decided by the citizens' Assembly, after hearing in advance a series of experts on financial matters, such as Nicophon, who is known for the famous Nicophon's Law, of 375/4 BCE. Consequently, the amount of currency issued by the city-state authorities was decided by the citizens themselves, and not by unelected specialized authorities, as is currently the dominant international trend and practice with central banks, like those of the USA (Fed), the European Union (ECB), and the UK (Bank of England).

The Argyrocopeion had a directorate, i.e., people responsible for its daily operation, called *epistatai*. They probably served for a year and were accountable for their activities in both the Athenian Assembly and the Council. From several inscriptions found, such as *SEG* 21.667, dated before 356/5, as well as *PA* 6681 and *APF* 220, we even know the names of some *epistatai*, such as Anaphlestos, Doros, and Aemon, son of Theogeiton who belonged to the *deme* of Aphidnai, which belonged to the tribe of Aiantis. *Epistatai's* further duty was also to record and withdraw from the Agora old coins that had worn out. Remnants of the Argyrocopeion are located in the left handside of the Christian temple of Agioi Apostoloi which is inside the Athenian Agora.

Judging by the volume of silver coins produced each year and their excellent craftsmanship, it is rather certain that the Argyrocopeion was a relatively large production facility with highly experienced and skilled workers (slaves). In the presence of the 50 councilmen who served in each *prytany*, the *epistatai* weighed the silver that came for minting from the silver mines.

The majority of the lands that covered the silver mines belonged to the state which leased them, under a 3P logic, to privates who undertook the extraction process. At least 12% and, perhaps, as much as 20% of the Athenian wealthy elite (comprised of between 300 and 1200 people) were engaged in mining activities (Christesen 2003).

Thus, silver production was undertaken by private individuals, but the state also took a proportion of this silver bullion produced by the leases as taxes on revenue (van Alfen 2011, 16, ftn. 47). Aperghis (1998, 18–19) argues for a rate of 10% of the produced silver bullion as a whole, while Figueira (1998, 184–185) supports that, practically, 75–100 *talents* were minimum state income from all taxes that drew (even indirectly) from mine output, based on an estimated annual production from the mines of more than 700 *talents*. The amount of *talents* that the state withheld as taxes was significantly higher if we accept Bresson's (2019a) (convincing) arguments that during the mid-fifth century BCE, the Laurion silver mines increased their productivity to such an extent that they could extract silver bullion; even that was analogous to 1500 talents, an undeniably huge amount of currency. Van Alfen (2011, 19) adds that if the state wanted, it was in a favorable position to purchase even the remaining 90% or a part of it. Economou (2024, 207) argues that it is logical to support that state had this privilege, to purchase bullion in case of need in emergency such as financing a war effort.

On their part, those wealthy citizens who possessed silver and wished to strike it into coins at the Argyrocopeion could do it freely. The latter was receiving some commission to cut the silver to coins for these (mostly wealthy) citizens. Subsequently, these citizens could then use these new series of coins for their personal transactions, and essentially increased the overall amount of money circulation in the economy (van Alfen 2011), what is nowadays characterized as money supply increase in the market (Bitros et al. 2020, 24; Economou et al. 2021a; Economou 2024, 206–208).

So, it is very important to note that the **Athenian monetary policy was, in essence, shaped by a combination of decisions made in the Assembly and private initiative.**

We have estimated that the cost of minting by the state-owned Athenian Argyrocopeion yielded a 10% withholding on the value of the silver. Of this, 8% included the cost of cutting and the rest was related to costs which in the international literature nowadays are known as *seigniorage*.[1] But for small quantities, the cutting cost was only 5% and the total holding cost 7% (Kroll 2011, 236). This difference should be attributed to the fact that the Athenian state wanted to help small-quantity silver holders to make a satisfactory profit from the sale of their silver, in comparison to larger quantity silver bullion holders who could make profit more easily by selling at wholesale and at a discount of about 10%.

In this sense, any increase in the money supply was not carried out only by the official state authority, by decision in the Assembly of citizens under *direct democracy* principles, **but also by the market forces themselves**. It could be further increased through other factors, even "unorthodox" ones, such as war booty.

But what do the above constitute? That, in fact, the Athenian democratic regime was (probably) the first historically worldwide to implement in practice a monetary policy system that, to some extent, resembles a *free banking* monetary regime (Bitros et al. 2020; Bitros 2021). We elaborate on this issue in the next section.

The first recorded coins were minted in Lydia and some other Greek cities in Asia Minor sometime during the mid-seventh c. BCE. They were made of electrum, an alloy of gold and silver (see Image 10.1).[2] Then, in the same region, the first coins engraved on both sides. Kroll (2011) and Gabrielsen (2013, 346–347) argue that the first coins minted in mainland Greece were the Aegenitan ones, around 700 BCE, followed by those of Milos around 650, of Corinth around 600, and, a little later, of Euboea and Athens. Gradually, coins began to be minted by city-states in smaller value subdivisions to facilitate trade more efficiently. The principal mints were those of Aegina, Corinth, and Athens. The Athenian mint produced the so-called *Wappenmünzen* coins between 570 and 510 BCE. Image 10.2 presents such a kind of coin, a *didrachm* (two drachmae).

The rest of the Greek world soon followed, from Cyprus through Southern Italy and Sicily to Emporion in Spain, to Macedon and Thrace (Gabrielsen 2013, 347). According to Schaps (2008, 42–43, 47–48), from the sixth c. BCE and on, the

---

[1] The special issues that are raised in the explanations of this Scene are further analyzed in our recent works in Bitros et al. (2020), Economou and Kyriazis (2021a, b), Economou et al. (2021a, b), and Economou (2024). We remind the reader that *seigniorage* is the difference between the value of currency/money and the cost of producing it. It is essentially the profit earned by the government by providing liquidity.

[2] Bresson (2019b) offers an explanation of why electrum coins were firstly introduced in Western Asia during the Archaic period and not elsewhere.

Image 10.1 A Lydian electrum coin of 600 BCE. Source: https://www.wildwinds.com/coins/greece/lydia/sg3401.jpg. With the permission of Wildwinds.com

Image 10.2 An Athenian *didrachm*. Source: https://www.wildwinds.com/coins/greece/attica/athens/SNGCop_03.jpg. With the permission of Wildwinds.com

known Greek world had established a very broad monetary organization through the exchange of metal (mainly silver) coins. It is noteworthy that some 85 Greek city-states already struck coins since 550–475 BCE.

Image 10.3 shows the internationally accepted medium of exchange of the times, the Athenian *tetradrachm* (value of 4 drachmae). Archaeological research has brought to light a huge volume of such coins. Rhodes (1972, 97) and van Alfen (2011, 16–18) estimated that the total silver production in the Argyrocopeion could exceed 700 *talents* annually and reached even 1000 *talents* per year, that is, 6 million drachmae, a very large amount of money that practically corresponded to millions of coins per year. As already mentioned, Bresson (2019a) provides an even higher number: 1500 *talents* of silver coins per year, an undeniably huge sum of money. He has further estimated that between 540 and 450 BCE, a total of 16,197 *talents* were produced by the Athenian silver mint or, in other words, 97,182,000 drachmae, an enormous amount of money. Image 10.4 presents a *drachm* (one drachma) issued after 449 BCE. The coin depicts a helmeted head of Athena right on the obverse side and an owl standing on the reverse side.

Image 10.3 An Athenian *tetradrachm*. Source: http://www.wildwinds.com/coins/greece/attica/athens/sg2526.jpg. With the permission of Wildwinds.com

Image 10.4 An Athenian *drachma*. Source: http://www.wildwinds.com/coins/greece/attica/athens/SNGCop_043.jpg. With the permission of Wildwinds.com

Image 10.5 shows a subdivision of the drachma called the *obol*. A drachma equals 6 *obols*. The weight of the Athenian *tetradrachm* corresponded to 17.28 g. The *dekadrachm* (10 drachmae) corresponded to 43.20 g, the *didrachm* (two drachmae), also known as *stater*, to 8.64 g, the *drachm* in 4.32 g, and the *obol* 0.72 g.

There were *triobols* and *diobols* as well as subdivisions of the *obol*, such as the *tritartemorion* (¾ of an *obol*, 0.27 g), the *hemiobol* (half an *obol*, weighing 0.36 g—see Image 10.6), the *tetartemorion* (0.18 g, a quarter of an *obol*), and the *hemitetartemorion* (1/8 *obol*, 0.09 g, issued between 430 and 322 BCE—see Images 10.7 and 10.8) (Camp and Kroll 2001, 144–145; Kroll 2011, 246).

There were further subdivisions, introduced so as to successfully carry out transactions of lesser value, such as *chalkoi* and *kollyboi*. The *chalkoi* equaled 1/12 of the *obol* and the *kollyboi* were coins of even lesser value, made of copper. They were mainly produced by private mints (Figueira 1998). One *chalkos* was equal to two *kollyboi*.

Image 10.5 An Athenian *obol*. Source: http://www.wildwinds.com/coins/greece/attica/athens/SNGCop_053ff.jpg. With the permission of Wildwinds.com

Image 10.6 An Athenian *hemiobol*. Source: https://www.wildwinds.com/coins/greece/attica/athens/SNGCop_059.jpg. With the permission of Wildwinds.com

The reason why the minting of copper coins was mainly undertaken by the private sector while the state's involvement in minting such coins was relatively small is a very special issue that is beyond the scope of the analysis carried out here. In Bitros et al. (2020, 20), Economou and Kyriazis (2021a), Economou et al. (2021a, b), and Economou (2024) we provide an explanation on this, arguing that the seigniorage of these bronze coins was very small and therefore the Athenian state had no direct financial interest in their production.

As a general comment, the subdivisions of the Athenian currency suggest that they arose so as to meet the increasing needs of a complex and dynamically expanding economy with the volume of commercial transactions growing significantly between the fifth and the fourth century BCE. An economy with rudimentary institutions would probably not consider significant such a magnitude of monetary circulation. It is also worth noting that Table 10.1, which is based on Economou

Image 10.7 An Athenian *tritemorion*. Source: https://www.wildwinds.com/coins/greece/attica/athens/BMC_187.jpg. With the permission of Wildwinds.com

Image 10.8 An *hemitetartemorion*. Source: https://www.wildwinds.com/coins/greece/attica/athens/Mionnet_26.jpg. With the permission of Wildwinds.com

(2024, 203), shows that the weight of each of these subdivisions of coins is proportionally related to the value of the coins.

Finally, it is worth noting that although currencies of the ancient times had an intrinsic value (either of gold, silver, or bronze), there were also some fluctuations in their market value based on their overall demand. In particular, Kroll (2011, 236), who has extensively dealt with monetary circulation in Greek antiquity, argues that due to the high demand for Athenian drachmae, the currency showed revaluation trends that varied between 3% and 5% over the real value of coin.

Table 10.1 Athenian drachma and *obol* subdivisions

Subdivisions	Value	Weight (in grams)
Decadrachm	10 *drachmae*	43
Tetradrachm	4 *drachmae*	17.2
Didrachm	2 *drachmae*	8.6
Drachma	6 *obols*	4.3
Tetrobol	4 *obols*	2.85
Triobol (hemidrachm)	3 *obols*	2.15
Diobol	2 *obols*	1.43
Obol	4 *tetartemoria*	0.72
Tritartemorion	3 *tetartemoria*	0.54
Hemiobol	2 *tetartemoria*	0.36
Trihemitartemorion	1½ *tetartemoria*	0.27
Tetartemorion	¼ *obol*	0.18
Hemitartemorion	½ *tetartemorion*	0.09

Sources: Kleiner (1975), Camp and Kroll (2001, 144–145), Kroll (2011), Economou (2024)

10.3 Establishing Unconventional Monetary Regimes: The Athenian Monetary Model, the Scottish Free Banking Regime, and the Digital Currencies Nowadays

In the previous section, we referred on the Athenian monetary regime where money supply was determined by both the Athenian Assembly, that is, a state institution, and the market forces. On this, O' Halloran (2018, 132, ftn. 92) characteristically writes that:

> With no central bank or equivalent mechanism, and monetary supply effectively dictated by silver production, Athens could not be said to have had a monetary policy—**its money supply was effectively controlled by private mining entrepreneurs** (emphasis by the authors).

Van Alfen (2011, 12, 15) adds that the Athenians had established a policy of free-minting, that is, a policy of **open access to the mint for those private holders who possessed silver bullion**. He adds (*ibid*., p. 16):

> With free minting the motivation would simply be the polis's desire to reap profits from the conversion.[3] The question of free minting in Athens is important not only because of the substantial (putative) volume of privately held foreign silver entering Athens needing to be exchanged or converted, but even more so because a large proportion of the silver produced at the Laureion mines appears to have ended up in private hands...

Thus, what in actuality is described here is a regime of alternative channels of money supply that are related to private initiative. Such a system resembles, to some

[3] These profits could be achieved through seigniorage, as already mentioned in Sect. 10.2.

extent, the *free banking* regime, which was historically first implemented in Scotland in the years between 1695 and 1845 in successive phases of development as internationally renowned academics such as Selgin (1988) and White (1984) have demonstrated so far.

In accordance with the above, the eminent economist of the Austrian School of economic thought and philosopher of classical (economic) liberalism, Friedrich August von Hayek focused on this reasoning with his book entitled *The Denationalisation of Money* in 1976, where he argued that an ideal monetary system presupposes that governments should not exercise a monopoly on money issuing in a national economy (Hayek [1976], 1990).[4]

Instead, Hayek proposed that the money supply should take place through the market mechanism, itself, practically, with coins issued by private financial institutions: in other words, private banks. And this is because such a situation would create conditions for real and fruitful competition in a competitive money market.[5] Then, currencies that could manage to maintain a relatively stable value would ultimately prevail over currencies whose value would be characterized by continuous volatility. In practice, this would mean that the currency that would show the least volatility and would be characterized by the most stable value would drive the rest out of the market. This would have happened because of the self-regulation forces that would have been unleashed through the market.

To put it simply, consumers would gradually avoid currencies that would show a large volatility in their price because of the uncertainties that would arise from the fact that the purchasing power of the holders of these currencies could constantly change due to the change of the value of the coins they would hold. The result for Hayek was that this process of monetary competition would lead to a highly efficient monetary system where only currency of fixed value would prevail, and this would be the ideal scenario for a well-functioning economy.

This argument of Hayek's may resemble, to some extent, the logic of the famous Gresham's law. In 1588, Thomas Gresham, founder of the Royal Stock Exchange in London, being also an advisor to Queen Elizabeth the Great, sent her, on the occasion of her enthronement, a letter warning her that "bad money drives out the good money" because the former is kept in circulation, since its real value is lower than the nominal value, while the latter is withdrawn to be converted into precious metals.

Gresham warned his queen that after the devaluations of the coins in the reigns of Henry VIII and Edward VI: "all your worth of gold will leave the country," because if coins are circulating with different real value (one contains more silver or gold than the other) but with the same nominal value (say a gold pound), then citizens will

[4]Historically, the Austrian School appeared in the late nineteenth century with Carl Menger and his students Friedrich von Wieser and Bohm Wawerk. It continued through the twentieth century, with Ludwig von Mises and F. A. Hayek, up to modern philosophers such as Murray Rothbard and Israel Kirzner. Primarily, this school advocates the *self-regulation* of the markets.

[5]See also Friedman and Schwartz (1986) on this.

keep the "good," that is, pure in gold content coins at home, and they will use the "bad," that is, the fraudulent ones for their transactions. In the end, this process will lead to the disappearance of the good currency and only bad quality pounds would circulate in the economy, resulting in the devaluation of the currency and leading the overall economy into serious further troubles.

It seems that the Ancient Greeks, and more specifically the Athenians, had understood, to some extent at least, the core of the argument of Gresham's Law. This is captured very clearly in verse 718 of the work *Frogs* of Aristophanes where he strongly criticized the phenomenon of currency debasement because of the emergencies that caused the Peloponnesian War. He wrote:

> Many times, it seems to us the city has done the same thing with the best and the brightest of its citizens as with the old coinage and the new gold currency. For these, not counterfeit at all, but the finest it seems of all coins, and the only ones of the proper stamp, of resounding metal amongst Greeks and foreigners every-where, we never use, but the inferior bronze ones instead, minted just yesterday or the day before with the basest stamp.

A fundamental reason why the Athenians introduced the so-called Law of Nicophon of 375/374 BCE as will be further explained in the next section should be attributed to the problem of the forgery of currency, as analyzed above.

Another regime which currently tends to gradually replace the established form of fiat money, issued by Central Banks, is the current rising global trend regarding digital currencies. These are decentralized forms of money based on cryptography to secure digital transactions. Some of the most well known are Bitcoin, Ethereum, Litecoin, Ripple, Stellar, Dogecoin, Cardano, Monero, and Tether. The basic reasoning behind the creation, operation, and development of digital currencies is that they bypass transactions that take place through money issued by an official regulatory monetary authority under the control of a state, such as the Federal Reserve of the USA (Fed), or a group of states that cooperate with each other very closely, such as the Eurozone, where the role of issuing money for the members states is exclusively reserved for the European Central Bank (ECB).[6]

In fact, some researchers argue that there are good indications that in the future Bitcoin will be able to compete even with the dollar or gold as an international currency on a global scale (Ammous 2018). If this happens, the dollar will lose its "extravagant privilege," according to Eichengreen (2011), as an international currency. Very characteristically, on pages 3–4 Eichengreen writes:

> ...It costs only a few cents for the Bureau of Engraving and Printing to produce a $100 bill, but other countries have to pony up $100 of actual goods and services in order to obtain one. (That difference between what it costs the government to print the note and a foreigner to procure it is known as "seigniorage" after the right of the medieval lord, or seigneur, to coin money and keep for himself some of the precious metal from which it was made.) About $500 billion of U.S. currency circulates outside the United States, for which foreigners have had to provide the United States with $500 billion of actual goods and services...

[6]On various aspects on how digital currencies function in relation to financial affairs, see among others Dwyer (2015), Ammous (2018), Corbet et al. (2019), Kyriazis (2019, 2020), Kyriazis et al. (2020), Bitros (2021), and Papadamou et al. (2021).

Of course, this loss of the "extravagant privilege" of the dollar is something that the USA does not want to happen at all. However, at the time of writing, it must be noted that various countries who consist strong or emerging economies or (geopolitically) rising powers, or already existing strong powers, such as the BRICS countries, are trying to undermine the omnipotence of the dollar in the global monetary arena. This trend is sure to have been accelerated by the multifaceted negative side effects at the global level caused by the Russian invasion on Eastern Ukraine, from February 2022 to the present. For example, countries facing geopolitical risks in their relationship with the USA and Europe would seize the opportunity to switch out of the dollar system. In particular, in March 2023, Brazil and China agreed to use local currencies in their bilateral trade. Furthermore, at the Russia-China summit in March 2023, President Putin said that business transactions between Russia and countries in Asia, Africa, and Latin America would be done in RMB, that is, the official currency of China. On December 2022, China and Saudi Arabia conducted their first yuan transaction, following Saudi statements that they were looking to diversify away from the US dollar, etc.

As a final comment, there is no doubt that crypto-currencies have entered our lives. Mainly the followers of liberal economic thought consider digital currencies as a positive historical development since this monetary form can be seen as an emerging tool of economic freedom against the hegemonic role of the state (Milne 2017; Bitros 2021). However, whether digital currencies will ultimately survive (or not) in the future against established currencies issued by central banks, such as the dollar, is something only the future will tell.

In this section, we argued that a monetary regime where currency issuing was not only shaped by a state authority but also by the market forces themselves should be traced back to the practices applied in the economy of Athens of the Classical times. The analysis we performed to this point, in more general, is related to the current global discussion about decentralization of monetary decision making in relation to the money issuing privilege of the Central Banks.

10.4 The Law of Nicophon of 375/374 BCE

In order for the drachma to become the main international currency of the times, by circulating freely in the Mediterranean, like today's dollar, the introduction of Nicophon's Law was of paramount importance. This law was proposed for resolution in the Assembly by a financial expert known as Nicophon and was accepted in 375/374 BCE. It required, among other things, that all foreign imitations of the Athenian drachma entering the Athenian economy for the purposes of commercial transactions must have exactly the same content of silver as the Athenian drachma. This was achieved through the *dokimastai*, two public servants, one in Athens and one in the Piraeus, who each had a bench and special scales with which they undertook to check the coins of foreign merchants. If after a sample check these were found to be genuine imitations, they were returned to their owners, and this money could be traded in the market without any limitation. If they were not, they were confiscated and then cut and the amount of silver they included was dedicated to the Temple of the Goddess Mother, which like the other temples also acted as a treasurer of collecting money and property, which could then be loaned to the Athenian state/public if it they were in need, such as during an extraordinary event, such as a war.

It is also important to mention the fact that if after the inspection of the *dokimastai* there was a merchant (either Athenian or not) who still did not trust these coins "he would lose all the goods he sold that day" (Rhodes and Osborne 2003, 115; Psoma 2011, 33–35). Quite simply, his property would be confiscated, apparently as a punishment for not showing confidence as an Athenian in the state's statutory bodies that carried out the relevant inspection.

This element also shows that the philosophy of the institutions of the Athenian state was shaped in such a way so as to require from the citizens themselves trust in the institutions of the state, apparently with the ultimate goal to ensure social peace and trust between the local and foreign merchants, as a necessary precondition for ensuring long-term economic prosperity among the Athenian citizens. Ober (2008, 222–225) considers that the Law of Nicophon contributed significantly to *transactional cost* reduction, under Coase's (1960) logic, and ensured, with its provisions, trust between the trading parties.

The Law of Nicophon is related to some degree with the next conceptual step, which is if the Athenian system of monetary circulation was an "open system," meaning if even non-Athenian made currency was circulated or not in the Athenian economy. Eminent historian of money in Greek antiquity, T. Figueira (1998, 57) writes that while it is undoubtedly true that Attic coins mediated the vast majority of transactions occurring on Athenian territory, coins from Chios may have been legally usable in Attica and that Athenians, like so many other Greeks, occasionally used coins from Aegina. Van Alfen (2011, 13) adds that even small subdivisions of foreign coins could be circulated in the Athenian economy. He writes:

> Because Athens was a major international entrepot, other currencies flowed into the polis in the course of normal trade, but how well these other currencies were quarantined is open to question. While it might be expected that large denomination Kyzikene electrum (and Persian gold) coins would obtain (official?) currency in Athens (cf. Lysias XII.11), in part because of their tremendous value, lack of comparable Athenian denominations, and specialized use in Black Sea trade, comic references suggest that **foreign small silver change also circulated in the Athenian agora** (emphasis by the authors).

This was not a policy implemented only in Athens and its entrepôt Piraeus but, according to Figueira (1998, 266–294), it is possible that the Athenian Alliance member states had the right to pay their tributes to the Allied Fund in non-Athenian coins as well. This means that such a policy would be advantageous for a regime which permitted the use of parallel currencies within the Athenian Alliance.

Last but not least, Nicophon's Law in practice did not demand the mandatory inspection of all the foreign traders' currencies. The law served as a mechanism for **securing confidence and trust** between trade parties. In this sense, there was always the possibility (however weak) that counterfeit foreign currencies did circulate in the

Athenian economy. In such a case, both merchants could be mutually harmed. In Halkos et al. (2021) and Economou et al. (2021b) by introducing a game theory analysis we explain how and why both merchants could find themselves either losing or gaining from the operation of the market and the use or non-use of the *dokimastai* services. This interpretation, which mirrors that of Figueira (1998), is important since it supports that foreign coins could circulate in the Athenian *agora*, quite easily, if the two *dokimastai* were bypassed. Figueira (1998, 545) explicitly writes on this that:

> I emphasize that this legislation **did not forbid a seller to take such coins** in payment, but merely that he was not required to receive them as he would be required in the case of genuine Athenian coins, approved by the dokimastai

10.5 Methods of Assessing the Purity of Metal Coins in Classical Greece

To test the purity of a coin the *dokimastai* used a series of techniques which we sum up in Economou and Kyriazis (2021a) and Economou (2024, 219–221) based on the significant findings of Stroud (1974), Buttrey (1979, 1981), Figueira (1998), Tylecote (2002), Christesen (2003), and Ober (2008), among others. Counterfeited coins of the times are also known as plated coins, meaning coins, often counterfeits, made of bronze, copper, or iron and plated with a precious metal layer of silver, electrum, or gold. We have summarized these findings in Table 10.2.

To this point it is necessary to elaborate on the cupellation and touchstones techniques.

Regarding cupellation, this is a refining process in metallurgy where ores or alloyed metals are treated under very high temperatures. Through special techniques, *noble metals*, like gold and silver, are separated from *base metals*, like lead, copper, zinc, arsenic, antimony, or bismuth that might be present in the ore. The process is based on the principle that, unlike those metals, precious metals do not oxidize or react chemically; when they are heated at high temperatures, they remain apart while the others react, forming slags or other compounds (Craddock 1995).

According to Christesen (2003) and Ober (2008, 237), although it cannot be verified, it is possible that the *dokimastai* performed cupellation tests while not on duty at their tables. Ober argues that once a few examples from a series had been tested "in the lab," so to speak, the *dokimastai* would be able to deal efficiently with all coins from that series through visual inspection in their daily practice "at the table." Ober's claim is verified by Tylecote (2002), an expert on ancient metallurgy, who argues that the processing and melting of various types of metal, such as iron, was already known to the Ancient Greeks, at least from 900 BCE. Tylecote (pp. 57–61) explains in detail how coins from silver or other materials were made and adds that cupellation regarding silver ores from the Laurion mines was a common practice. Those mines were worked from very early times, even during the Mycenaean era, thus even before 1100 BCE (Tylecote 2002, 71). During the

Table 10.2 Methods of assessing the purity of metal coins in Classical Greece

Checking by sight	Examining a coin visually was the initial form of inspection and an important source of information critical to an experienced *dokimastes*, who could easily spot a coin with a slightly different figure of goddess Athena, not made from a die at the Athenian mint. In this case, he then proceeded to the next step of assaying the coin, palpation.
Palpation	The *dokimastai* had a lot of experience and simply feeling a coin in their fingers had become their second nature.
Sound diagnosis	Another method was to throw the coin onto a hard surface such as a bench. The *dokimastai* were familiar with the specific sounds indicating whether a coin was pure in content or counterfeit.
Checking by smell	For experienced currency users such as the *dokimastai*, smell was another determinant of a currency's purity. Bronze and silver have a distinct smell; a trained *dokimastes* could smell if there was bronze inside a counterfeit coin.
Using special scales	Special precision scales, sealed and certified by the city's official authorities, could be used by the *dokimastai* to determine whether or not the weight of a coin corresponded to the correct weight of a pure silver coin. These special scales were located in the Metroon.
Cupellation	The *dokimastai* could also perform cupellation techniques (see further below) when they were not on duty at their tables.
Test cuts	A method by which a *dokimastes* carefully inspected coins by making tiny cuts on the edge with a small chisel to diagnose if there was a plated core. Many surviving Athenian *drachmae* bear such cuts (see bottom left in Image 10.9).
Die differences	Another means for an experienced *dokimastes* to distinguish a pure Athenian *drachma* from a counterfeit was the size differences between the dies from which the coins were made. Athenian dies were smaller to dies introduced by other city-states and made a deeper impression in the flan, and Athenian flans were often more oblong.
Countermarked coins	A countermarked coin had some additional mark(s) or symbol(s) punched into it. Countermarking involved placing a tiny imprint on a coin with a small punch to verify its purity and/or validate it for acceptance.
Touchstones	According to authors such as Stroud (1974, ftn. 54), the *dokimastai* employed touchstone techniques (see below) to reveal if a silver coin was pure or counterfeit.

Source: Economou and Kyriazis (2021a) and Economou (2023)

Classical period, melting and cupellation practices became more advanced due to knowledge aggregated over the centuries. It is obvious that cupellation techniques made the *dokimastai* more experienced and capable of recognizing and separating authentic coins from the counterfeit ones.

Regarding touchstones, this is also related to the *argyramoiboi*, mentioned in Sect. 3.6. A touchstone is a small tablet of dark stone such as slate or lyddite, used for assaying precious metal alloys. It has a finely grained surface on which soft metals leave a visible trace. This stone has a very strange capacity. When a piece of gold or silver is rubbed on it, a trace of a specific color is engraved on its body. For example, if instead of pure gold, an alloy containing gold is rubbed on the stone, then the trace has a different color. The more gold or silver the alloy contains, the more intense is

Image 10.9 Athenian *tetradrachm* with multiple test cuts. Source: https://www.wildwinds.com/coins/greece/attica/athens/Kroll_08.jpg. With the permission of Wildwinds.com

the color of the trench. Sherwood et al. (2020, 189) write that according to Theophrastus, Aristotle's successor as head of the Peripatetic school, people suspicious of counterfeit money or jewelry commonly chose touch pieces of opaque, brown, red, or yellow quartz, chalcedony, or jasper of a lump of fine-grain schist called Lydian stone.

To determine variance, the *dokimastai* assembled proven metals for color comparison. Unlike assaying, which determined purity by weight and chemical makeup, the touchstone offered a suitable alternative for the on-the-spot examination of the authenticity of soft gold or silver coinage.

Chapter 11
The Financial Institutions of the Athenian Economy

Abstract This chapter describes the financial institutions of the Athenian economy, by focusing on banking services. It describes the types of banking and the lending policy that was applied at the times. It further describes the legal system through which protection of property and protection of commercial contracts were secured in the market.

11.1 Nicomedes: The Experienced Banker

Nicomedes spent part of the next day helping the merchant from distant Iberia to successfully proceed with his purchases. They had to pay a visit to various shops, in order to evaluate in detail prices and the quality of goods, asking for offers for better prices since Xenocrates would be buying wholesale and not retail. Due to this, Nicomedes finally arrived at his bank counter an hour and a half later than Ischomachos usually expected.

Ischomachos was at the time struggling to explain to two merchants, a Greek from Miletus in Asia Minor and his partner, a half Greek and half Pisidian,[1] some details about a problem they had with the loan the Greek had taken, but the Greek-Pisidian has also financially contributed on, a year ago. They had not paid the interest to Nicomedes' bank on time.

The Greek-Pisidian was telling Ischomachos a bunch of nonsense. Poor Ischomachos tried to explain to them the terms of the contract and why they were wrong, but in vain. The Greek-Pisidian persisted, and as he shouted more and more, he had himself become a spectacle in the rest of the stalls, as if he were a star of a comedy staged by Aristophanes, Hermippus, or Eupolis. He even threatened Ischomachos that if he did not give them a solution immediately, he would report him to Agoranomia and seek his fortune in the courts by putting Nicomedes to *dike emporike*. Ischomachos' temper, especially after this threat, was almost spent.

[1]Pisidia is a historical region of Asia Minor, in the present-day Antalya province of Turkey. It bordered the regions of Lycia, Caria, Lydia, Phrygia, and Pamphylia.

E. M. L. Economou, N. C. Kyriazis, *Daily Life in Classical Athens*, Frontiers in Economic History, https://doi.org/10.1007/978-3-031-58541-8_11

– You finally came! exclaimed Ischomachos when he saw Nicomedes.

The latter calmly explained to them that they were wrong and why. Perhaps not only the persuasiveness of Nicomedes but also his imposing figure was responsible for the fact that afterward the two merchants changed their attitude, and both left with compliments to Nicomedes, even telling him that they were happy for the extremely constructive cooperation that they had with him!

Ischomachos was not Greek; he came from distant Colchis, but having stayed so many years in Athens and serving near Nicomachos and Nicomedes, he was educated in the manners of the Greeks. Now that he had become an *apeleutheros metic*, he felt like a true Athenian. And as he was almost flushed in the countenance with nerves, especially after the Greek-Pisidian's threats, when the two merchants left the bank, though still seated on the bench, almost instinctively, he called out as if in despair:

– Alas Nicomedes! Finally, expel this Greek and the other, this 'half-barbarian' from being customers of yours!

Ischomachos spoke so naturally, as if he were vigorously defending the interests and ancestral customs of Athens against the barbarians from the east!

Nicomedes, turning his head slowly, looked at him, with a serious expression, which anyone who knew him well understood that this particular expression concealed also a tendency to sneer! Then, without saying anything, he briefly turned his face, looking slightly higher, toward the Acropolis, the pan-Hellenic architectural masterpiece of Pericles and Pheidias, this emblematic symbol of freedom and democracy. After a few moments, turning his look at him calmly, he answered him, in a very serious and imperative tone, and in a deep, manly, and commanding voice:

– Ischomachos, arise! Close the bank and let me treat you some delicious wine at a nearby winery to calm you down!
– Yes, but it is still not noon to close boss. . . .. answered Ischomachos with absolute naturalness.

In the same imposing and serious tone Nicomedes insisted:

– Close the bank! Now! answered Nicomedes, in an imperative tone.
– Okay boss, Ischomachos replied condescendingly and almost immediately, with a small dose of fear, and continued:
– I. . . .hm. . .I. . . . . .I want you to explain to me as we go, how you managed it again boss, within five minutes to persuade them, while I was trying in vain to explain myself to this half-barbarian, for half an hour!

* * *

11.2 Financial Institutions

As already analyzed, Athens had become the banking and financial center of the Mediterranean. The banks in Athens, which belonged to both Athenians and *metics*, followed, even if in a simplified form, many of the principal banking operations that are taking place today, varying from (mainly) deposits and loans, even to offshore services, which led to concealment of incomes, known as *aphaneis* transactions, such as today's tax havens (Cohen 1992, 8). Agreements could be oral, but usually, and apparently for large sums, written on papyrus, with seals and witnesses.

Demosthenes (*For Phormio*, 36.11) provides us with the following excellent and concise definition of what banking is, which comes not as a product of his own philosophical brainstorming, but apparently having realized the way banking actually functioned in the city-state of Athens at the times:

> ... the bank is a business yielding a hazardous revenue from money which belongs to others.

Therefore, through a modern translation, it is that kind of service that can bring income to one who exercises such a profession, that is, profits, which are characterized by high risk due to the uncertainty that always exists in the markets. And this money, which we risk for making profit, is not ours, but belongs to third parties. Demosthenes here provides with a perfect definition of the basic function of banking, which is *financial intermediation* and *financial credit.*

A commercial agreement for a bank loan for the purpose of maritime trade might include the following: the exact voyage of the ship and the ports of destination, the amount of the loan, the interest due, the period of its repayment, and the mortgage. The clauses for non-compliance with the agreement resulted in an increase in the cost of the loan, sometimes as far as paying double the amount of the loan, plus interest. Maritime loans were usually granted by mortgaging the ship or the goods with an interest rate of approximately 15% in normal cases. If the loan was not repaid on the agreed terms, the borrower, in addition to the fine, faced the possibility of imprisonment (Demosthenes, *Against Dionysodorus*, 56.3–7, 56.12, 56.29–30, 56.38, 56.45).

Interest-bearing loans with the presence of witnesses were guaranteed for repayment by law and could be paid in installments (Lysias, *On the Property of Eraton*, 17.2–3). A loan agreement and its specifications were signed in the presence of witnesses (Demosthenes, *Against Onetor*, 30.20–21; *For Phormio*, 36.28). If the agreement between two parties was breached, a trial would take place. If the lender (banker) was vindicated, the polis recorded the value of the borrower's assets; his property could be confiscated in order to repay the lender the principal amount of the loan plus the agreed interest. If the value of the borrower's assets was greater, while the borrower also owed debts to the polis, then the polis received the remaining amount, as long as it had claims from the borrower. Essentially, this is a seizure procedure against claims, and here is described a regulation of the priorities of the claimants which applies also nowadays as a practice.

A loan could be secured/pledged to slaves as well, since slaves were the property of their owner (Demosthenes, *Against Aphobus 1*, 27.24). After all, in the sixth century, loans were given to the Athenian citizens with themselves as collateral, who if they did not repay them fell into slavery, a practice abolished by Solon with the *seisachtheia*. An Athenian could borrow even to cover funeral expenses! (Demosthenes, *Against Boeotus 2*, 40.25) or for renting and exploiting a mine, mainly the silver mines at Laurion—Thorikos (*ibid.*, 40.52).

What is very important from an economic standpoint and in terms of protecting the economic rights of citizens is that under the Athenian legal system, in case of default of a borrower, private individuals should be reimbursed first and then the state (Lysias, *On the Property of Eraton*, 17.4–7; *Against Aphobus 1 and 2*). Furthermore, the Athenians had introduced an institution of (what nowadays is known as) securities. Harris (1993) provides a description on how this institution functioned in Athens of the times. He writes:

> In real security, the borrower pledges some of his property, either movable or immovable, as security to the creditor. If the borrower defaults, the creditor has the right to seize the property pledged as security, and, if he wishes, to sell it for cash in lieu of repayment. During the Classical and Hellenistic periods, the Athenians used both personal and real security in their legal agreements. . . .

The Athenians had already realized and put into practice a basic doctrine for the proper functioning of their economy: (i) they established a proper institutional framework that protected property rights and commercial contracts and (ii) they introduced impartial courts to resolve any disputes. The protection of private property was considered a "natural law" which no one should abrogate (Demosthenes, *Against Aristocrates*, 23.61–62).

Trials, regarding commercial matters, judged by experienced Athenian judges, were called *dikai emporikai* (Cohen 1973, 158–198, 1992; Economou and Kyriazis 2017, 2019a, b). Relative to this, the Athenians also understood the importance of rapid administration of justice so that entrepreneurship was not hindered (Cohen 1973, 93). Within this framework *dikai emporikai* had to be finalized with a decision within a month. This is important in modern economic theory, since it can lead to **significant transactional cost reductions. Written agreements through contracts** were very powerful in the Athenian legal system and took precedence over laws and resolutions (Demosthenes, *Against Apatourius*, 33.15; Demosthenes, *Against Lacritus*, 35.34; Lysias, *Against Simon*, 3.22). There was a special legislative regime for commercial agreements, loans, financial cooperation, buying and selling, and renting, which were quite similar to today's commercial law (see also Demosthenes, *Against Lacritus*; *For Phormio*, 35.3–4, 36.3).

11.3 The Regime of Property Rights Protection

In modern economies, property rights protection is a cornerstone for the functioning of an economically advanced state and a necessary element for its economic development (see among others North (1981, 1990) and Hodgson (2015a, b)]. The key fact is that both Athenians and *metics* as well as foreign merchants had established a legal protection regime in cases of trespass on their property (Economou and Kyriazis 2017, 2019b). In general, the ancient Athenians supported individual property as it strengthened social cohesion and unity among them.

Many of the orators' forensic speeches that have survived describe cases that came before the Athenian courts for resolution, involving disputes as to the rightful owner of property. Such cases are analyzed for example in the following speeches of Lysias: (i) *On the Confiscation of the Property of the Brother of Nicias* (18.1–27) of 396 BCE, which concerns the confiscation or not by the state of the property of a rich man, Nicias; (ii) *On the Property of Aristophanes* (19.1–16) of 388/387, concerning the confiscation (or not) of Aristophanes's property; and (iii) *On the Refusal of a Pension* (24.1–27), possibly of 403, where Lysias defends a person with a physical disability who was accused of defrauding the state and medical authorities to receive reimbursement as a pension.

Confiscation of property was carried out very rarely and only when there were very serious reasons and criminal acts that had been already condemned by a court decision, such as acts of treason, misuse of public money, etc. (Bitros and Karayiannis 2013, 15–16, 26–27). There were laws that protected property and through courts punished violators (Demosthenes, *Against Pantaenetus*, 37.30). For example, it was considered to be illegal to break into any *oikos* because it was considered a trespass on private property (Demosthenes, *Against Evergus and Mnesibulus*, 47.81). In fact, it is known that every person had the right to protect his property from theft, even going as far as to kill the thief on the spot without being punished by the polis's laws (Demosthenes, *Against Aristocrates*, 23.61–62). In defense of private property there were also cases that reached the courts, for example, sabotage of production, exceeding excavation limits of an area, etc. (Demosthenes, *Against Pantaenetus*, 37.36–39).

A trial was held because someone had erected a wall on his property that diverted rainwater into a neighbor's property, damaging his stored farm production. That is why the sufferer demanded compensation from the one whose actions caused him harm (Demosthenes, *Against Callicles*, 55.5–6, 55.10–11, 55.20, 55.24). In fact, this case seems complicated because the plaintiff would have to prove with tangible arguments that the damage was really caused by his neighbor, something he himself could deny, etc. This proves the high level of specialization of justice in solving even highly complex cases, based on specific laws.

We mention below some additional relative cases: In case of business bankruptcy, the tangible assets of the owner(s) were sold to pay off the debts. Loan guarantees by third parties were only being required for 1 year so that long-term entrepreneurship not to be impeded (Demosthenes, *Against Apatourius*, 33.25–27). A suit by an individual against the public has been recorded. The individual claimed a property which was awarded to him as compensation under a court order (Lysias, *On the Property of Eraton*, 17.3–5). Therefore, here is also the case where a private individual could sue the public if he considered that he was harmed in one way or another. This fact constitutes yet another feature of the Athenian economic-legal system which is a modern practice, that is, the **citizen can turn legally even against the state itself**.

Regarding the confiscated properties, the judges had to be sparing with confiscations since these properties would no longer bring the same value as before (Lysias, *On the Confiscation of the Property of the Brother of Nicias*, 18.20–21). For this reason, it was recognized that by not confiscating property this may have functioned as a motive to an individual to undertake new entrepreneurial activities, but, this time, in a more prudent way (Lysias, *On the Property of Aristophanes*, 19.62). Lysias (*Defense Against a Charge of Taking Bribes*, 21.13–14) believed that confiscating property could deprive the city of resources because the confiscated property would turn not to be as productive as when it was the property of the person to whom it initially belonged and brought him wealth. Confiscated estates could be given to poor Athenians so as not to lose their productive potential (Lysias, *On the Olive Stump*, 7.4).

Joint property was also taking place legally. Demosthenes in his *On the Navy* (14.16) explicitly refers on "joint holders of estates." Archaeogical evidence through the inscription *IG* XII. 5.872 has revealed that on the island of Tenos in the third century BCE, the land register there made possible the partial ownership of a building. With near certainty, one can assume that such a regulation also existed in Classical Athens which, after all, was the pioneer regarding such innovative economic institutions.

11.4 Inherited Property and Testament

A testament included all assets, even a dowry, and could only be challenged if it could be proved in a court that the deceased was not mentally healthy when he wrote it, a practice that also applies nowadays (Demosthenes, *Against Aphobus 1*, 27.40–41; Demosthenes, *Against Stephanus 1*, 45.28). According to Demosthenes (*Against Stephanus* 2, 46.14, 46.16), it could be challenged if it could be proved that the one who wrote it was driven to do so, due to drinking a magic potion! For a testament to be valid, it had to be sealed with the testator's seal; however (as happens also nowadays) there were cases of forgery, which is why there were usually witnesses when a testament was prepared (Demosthenes, *Against Spudias*, 41.21–22; *Against Stephanus 1*, 45.8; *Against Stephanus* 2, 46.11; Against Macartatus, 43.4). The testator could leave trustees not only in the case of a minor son, but also if he considered his heirs incapable of managing his property efficiently, due to e.g. "depraved morals" such as propensity to waste, etc., as the banker Pasion did for his son (Demosthenes, *For Phormio*, 36.4–5). In case of complaint and trial, these trustees were accountable not only to the heirs, but also to the judges (Demosthenes, *Against Nausimachus and Xenopeithes*, 38.8–9).

Here one can notice another modern practice as well: The Athenians had also practiced as an institution what today is known as an executor of a will, that is a legal entity which has been assigned to be legally responsible for carrying out the instructions in the person's will and handling his/her estate. Someone's "estate" is everything he/she owns, including their money, property, and possessions.

11.5 Protection of Commercial Contracts

In order to secure his rights, the investor/shareholder-banker demands a written contract known as *syngraphe*, regarding the loan he offers, signed by both parties, the lender and the borrower (Economou 2024, 172).

For both modern economic theory and legal science and its manifestations related to the economy, the protection of commercial contracts has been highlighted as one of the most important institutional arrangements to make transactions reliable for all involved (North 1981; Hodgson 2003, 2015a). In fact, on this issue, which falls under contract theory, Oliver Hart (Harvard University) and Bengt Holstrom (MIT) received the Nobel Prize in Economics for 2016 for their work on contract theory. Hart and Bengt Holstrom (MIT) argued that the design of better contracts is shaping better institutions in society.

Demosthenes saves us a case of legal protection of a written commercial agreement (Demosthenes, *Against Aristogiton 1*, 25.69). He writes:

> Suppose then that A accused B of owing him money, and B denied it. If the registered terms of the loan were still to be read, or if the pillars which marked the mortgaged property were still standing, you would clearly regard as impudent the man who denied the transaction; but if it was shown that these proofs no longer existed, then you would regard the accuser as impudent. That is natural.........

The repayment of loans on the agreed terms also applied. For example, in the case of marine loans, the ship and the goods served as collateral, and in case the loan was not repaid, the asset(s) pledged as collateral in favor of the lender were seized. In Demosthenes (*Against Zenothemis*, 32.14), there is a crystal-clear description of terms of such a contract. In Sect. 12.3, we reproduce another case of a signed contract regarding the terms of leasing a mine to privates for exploitation, where important details regarding this particular mine are provided.

But why did the Athenians insist so much on written and detailed agreements? The obvious reason was that the Athenian society was rapidly expanding from a face-to-face society to a crowded one, with too many people involved in financial transactions, from various ethnicities. In such conditions, the trust in each other's personal commitment could not be naturally maintained since Athens was dynamically expanding as an international cosmopolitan city and had exceeded the limits of a small city-state where almost everyone knew each other in person and had confidence in each other's personal commitment. In the late fourth c. BCE Athens, most of those involved in the Agora were not necessarily having personal relationships with each other, as is also the case in modern economies and societies. This is the obvious reason that necessitated their insistence on written financial agreements.

Private property was also protected by international commercial and mutual agreements between two or more city-states, in the form of international commercial law. These international agreements were related to the institutions of *enktesis* (reciprocity of property rights protection between two city-states regarding their citizens), *symbola* (reciprocity of legal rights between merchants and in general between the citizens of the two city-states), *isopoliteia* (reciprocity of acknowledging political rights between two city-states regarding their citizens), *proxeny* (permanent ambassadors between two city-states to better serve the citizens of both of them in a reciprocal basis), and *asylia* (avoidance of collective reprisals in case individual citizens of one city-state harmed in any way some or all citizens of another city-state). All these interstate agreements were backed up by international treaties between city-states for promoting cooperation between each other. They were intensified during the Hellenistic period (Lyttkens 2013, 124; Mackil 2013; Woolmer 2016; Economou and Kyriazis 2019a; Economou 2020, 2024, 131, 133–135, 227).

For example, in maritime trade, in case of fraud or disagreement between partners, courts were responsible to resolve impartially any dispute between merchants **independently of their origin** (Demosthenes, *Against Zenothemis*, 32.9, 32.14). This means that multilateral cooperation had been developed between the Athenian courts and the courts of the city-states with which Athens had established flourishing trade relations. In practice, the Athenian and other courts in the allied cities should have incorporated **common judicial practices of administration of justice**, perhaps by even fully incorporating a single framework of laws of a supranational character, based on a package of institutions co-developed through the *enktesis*, *symbola*, *isopoliteia*, *proxeny*, and *asylia* agreements, as they were briefly described above. These agreements followed a common standard so as to ensure *isonomia*, impartiality, and fairness among those trading parties involved in international commercial activities.

In modern times, such practices of introducing a common set of institutions on economic, judicial, and other issues can be found in supranational entities such as the European Economic Community (1957–1991) and the European Union since 1992 onward. Pillar III of the Maastricht Treaty of 1992, significant for further European integration, was intended exactly for such a purpose: the cooperation and harmonization of law and judicial practices among the member states.

Having Athens as the epicenter and pioneer of financial developments and innovations, in practice a single economic-commercial, geopolitical, ideological, and cultural ecosystem was created in the Eastern Mediterranean (Bresson 2014, 2016a, b; Harris and Lewis 2016; O'Halloran 2018; Bitros et al. 2020; Economou 2024). Athens had essentially evolved into an informal "empire," among its allies. Athens of the times was the school and the pioneer of various institutional developments of all of Greece.

11.6 *Dikai Emporikai*

An interesting issue is the selection of judges who judged the *dikai emporikai*. It is known that the judges of Heliaia were ordinary Athenians who were chosen by lot. By contrast, *dikai emporikai* required experienced judges with special knowledge. Cohen (1973) provides convincing arguments for this issue.

Provision by law to adjudicate commercial cases through specialized judges also existed in earlier times: from the end of the fifth to the beginning of the fourth century BCE, there were the so-called *xenodikai* and *nautodikai*. Trials involving such cases had to be completed quickly, without delay, and sometime between 355 and 343/2 BCE the Athenian judicial system adopted the requirement that the proceedings of these trials be completed within a month, so as not to hinder commercial activity. As already mentioned, nowadays it is known that fast adjudication of commercial cases reduces transaction costs. This mentality of the Athenians can also be corroborated through the following primary sources (Demosthenes, *Against Apatourius*, 33.6, 33.10–11; *Against Spudias*, 41.5, 41.7, 41.11; *For Phormio*, 36.6–9, 36.31–33; Demosthenes, *Against Nicostratus*, 53.13; *Against Lacritus*, 35.10–11, 35.13, 35.20–22, 35.37, 35.41–42).

The decisions these judges made should be fair in order to encourage business operations. If a commercial dispute did not receive a fair resolution from an Athenian court, it discouraged entrepreneurship while increasing illegal acts of outlaws. If the lenders of a sum of money to an insolvent investor were not vindicated in court, other would-be investors would be discouraged from financing ventures, letting alone those willing to get involved with high-risk commercial activities (*Against Dionysodorus*, 56.48, 56.50). Consequently, those who judged these cases had to be distinguished by a high sense of duty, considerable experience, moral integrity, honesty, justice, and impartiality. That is why the Athenians, wisely perceiving these matters, elected the above officials by appointment instead of by lot. This is also verified by the following claim of Aeschines (*Against Ctesiphon*, 3.29) who supports:

> There are, fellow citizens, three classes of public officers. The first and most obvious class are all who **are appointed by lot or by election** (emphasis by the authors); the second class are those who administer some public business for more than thirty days, and the Commissioners of Public Works; but third it stands written in the law that if any others[2] receive presidencies of courts, they also shall "hold office on passing their scrutiny.[3]

Aeschines essentially informs us that the *archai* in the Athenian democracy were a specific group of officials, characterized by the following elements: First and foremost was the undertaking of an office either by lot or by *cheirotonia* (appointment through democratic voting). Here Aeschines clearly states that the adoption of the *cheirotonia* instead of the lottery procedure is related to the complexity of a

[2]Here Aeschines refers to public magistrates.

[3]During their tenure.

public service where specialization is highly required. A second feature was the submission of each candidate to the *dokimasia* procedure before taking office (Fröhlich 2013, 261). A third feature was the *logodosia* regarding their financial auditing at the end of their term. Finally, the fourth feature was the duration of the office, which had to exceed 30 days.

The reasoning that made public magistrates either appointed or being selected through lottery is also highlighted by Aristotle (*Politics*, 1317.b15) from whom we conclude that (i) the selection of any public office could be made by any citizen available, with the only exception being those posts which required special skills and technical knowledge, and (ii) the offices for which experience or some special abilities were not required, were assigned by lot.

To sum up, the fact that experienced judges were appointed, rather than being elected to handle complex commercial cases, is a serious indication that the Athenians completely understood the importance of ensuring equal opportunities in entrepreneurship as a necessary requirement for the prosperity of the polis, directly related to the efficient conduct of international and domestic (in the city-state level) trade.

11.7 Types of Banking

Every banker, either Athenian or *metic*, carried out his transactions in a certain place in the Agora, where only such services took place. There were specially housed benches for carrying out banking activities. Banks also operated in specific arcades and the port of Piraeus in a specific area known as the Emporion which, as was already referred above, was related to market for goods from the international markets.

Transactions in the banks took place from sunrise to sunset, which means that they provided services for many hours during the day. An advertising of the times retrieved by Theocritus (*Epigrams* 14) reveals that a specific bank could provide services 24 h a day upon request, what we nowadays could characterize as "Open 24 Banking Services," obviously with an orientation toward attracting customers from other competing Athenian bankers, who were not willing to provide this type of service.

> This bank here, for townspeople and foreigners alike, manages whatever money they wish to put in properly and honestly,[4] or to take out immediately.[5] One may find excuses, but the owner owner of this bank, Caicos, and night if asked, will count them.[6]

---

[4]That is, to make a deposit.

[5]To withdraw money.

[6]Here it implies that usually bankers refused to provide their services for specific hours such as at night, but the banker Caicos was willing to satisfy his potential clients even at night, obviously in

It is probable that from the word *pagkos* (from the verb *pignimi* meaning "bench") came the word "bank," which has prevailed internationally, meaning banking services institutions. The Athenians apparently thought of dedicating a special area in the Agora for financial transactions, realizing that their city had gradually developed into an "international financial center" of the times. Today's financial centers include areas such as the City of London, also known as the Square Mile, the Manhattan in New York, the Financial Hub at Frankfurt, or the International Finance Centre at Hong Kong. There was also a second concentration point exclusively for banking services, in Piraeus (Cohen 1992, 18). The Athenians, like modern policymakers and global investors, had realized that the introduction of a specific financial center into their polis would contribute to its further economic development. Some of the funds that were circulating in the Athenian Agora were coming from businessmen from other city-states, a situation that today is translated as foreign direct investments (FDI), which according to scholars such as Krugman et al. (2023) is a key driver of development in a globalized economy. In general, borrowers paid interest rates of 12–18% and, in special cases, up to 36%. The rich investors, either Athenian or foreigners, found bank lenders (banks) much more easily (Demosthenes, *Against Polycles*, 50.56).

Cohen (1992) in his monumental work, *Athenian Economy and Society: A Banking Perspective*, where he diligently dealt with the types of banking services, based on the existing sources, considers that in addition to the *pagkos* in the Agora, Athenian bankers used their houses to carry out banking services, and apparently also as a place to store and secure the remittances or valuables entrusted to them by their clients—depositors (Demosthenes, *Against Timotheus*, 49.22; *Against Callippus*, 52.8., 52.14).

The *trapeza* (bank) kept detailed data of deposits and loans (Demosthenes, *Against Callippus*, 52.6). In fact, in a fairly detailed manner, a banker recorded the amount of the loans, who requested them, the dates that the loans were signed and agreed upon, the amounts of money to be repaid, any guarantees, pledges, even objects such as glasses, household and other utensils, or mortgages given for the loan, and the purpose of the loans, e.g., timber transport costs (Demosthenes, *Against Timotheus*, 49.11, 49.8, 49.17, 49.22–23, 49.29, 49.60, 49.62).

Recording in the contract the type and purpose of the loan functioned as a guarantee for the banker-lender that his money would be used for the correct purpose, for example, investing in building a merchant ship, instead of being used promiscuously. If the latter was the case, the bank lender could sue the borrower for wasting his money, seeking for a reimbursement through the courts. This further means that **the demand for mentioning the purpose of the loan explicitly in the contract** functioned as a guarantee, to a great extent, that the money of the loan would be used wisely at the end of the day, complying with the purpose that was

---

order to make them his customers and distance them from other bankers—being competitors of him and his bank.

dealt ex ante between the lender and the borrower. This was necessary for establishing a healthy banking environment among those involved in it.

The bank also acted as a witness to a commercial agreement (Demosthenes, *Against Dionysodorus*, 56.15). The "book" where a banker held all his accounts with his customers could be consulted by both the borrower and the judges in case of legal dispute, as it recorded all the acts of lending and levies collection (Demosthenes, *Against Timotheus*, 49.5, 49.43–44). Gold objects could be also pledged to the bank against a loan (Demosthenes, *Against Nicostratus*, 53.9).

In particular, according to Cohen (1992), Athenian banking institutions provided, among others, the following services to their clients:

- Acceptance of deposits by opening bank accounts, against interest (loan interest).
- Opening bank safes against payment for the purpose of safekeeping.
- Making payments on behalf of their customers.
- Granting of loans in various business activities, including highly risky loans in shipping.
- Providing loans related to imports and exports for the traders who carried them out. In order for a borrower to get the money from the banker, the borrower's financial solvency was thoroughly checked in advance by the banker (Demosthenes, *Against Callippus*, 52.3–4).
- Opening branches in other city-states for further developing international trade.
- Providing guarantees to a number of important customers, essentially offering them trust in the loan they needed, such as in the case of a transaction for the purchase of goods from abroad.
- *Consumer credit* financing.[7]
- Exchange of Athenian coins for foreign ones and vice versa.
- Providing advice (consultancy) to traders on financial matters.

There can be no doubt that these types of financial services required institutional arrangements found only in advanced economies as we understand the term today. At this point, but also through the additional argumentation and bibliography we provide below, we believe that the erroneous image of the previous decades, mainly created by scholars such as M. Finley and Austin Vidal-Naquet, who argued that the ancient Greek economy was considered as having rudimentary structures, subject strictly to the context of serving broader political goals and religious and social imperatives, should be revisited.

To conclude, (to this point) we dwell on the following illuminating verse as referred by Demosthenes (*Against Dionysodorus*, 56.1–2) that describes the role of the entrepreneur and the ideal framework, to conduct a banking transaction:

> I am a sharer in this loan, men of the jury. We, who have engaged in the business of overseas trade and put our money in the hands of others, have come to know one thing very clearly:

[7] *Consumer credit* is personal debt taken on to purchase goods and services. Consumer debt can also include collateralized consumer loans like mortgage and car loans. See https://www.investopedia.com/terms/c/consumercredit.asp

> that in all respects the borrower has the best of us. He received the money in cash which was duly acknowledged,[8] and has left us on a scrap of paper which he bought for a couple of coppers,[9] his agreement to do the right thing. We on our part do not promise to give the money, we give it outright to the borrower. What, then, do we rely upon, and what security do we get when we risk our money? We rely upon you, men of the jury, and upon your laws, which ordain that all agreements into which a man voluntarily enters with another shall be valid. But in my opinion there is no use in your laws or in any contract, if the one who receives the money is not thoroughly upright in character, and does not either fear you or regard the rights of the one making the loan.

Demosthenes in the above very comprehensive while so important quote explains to us the very essence of banking: A key element for the successful conduct of financial/bank credit is **the lender's legal protection by law**. But this in itself is not enough: it is required that the traders are also imbued by moral principles, the most important element of which is the honesty of the traders. What Demosthenes describes here is "building trust" among those involved in banking, one might say, from a modern perspective. Demosthenes considers that the honesty of citizens under the principle of *eunomia* sets, in the context of *kalos kagathos* behavior, the ideal framework of entrepreneurial principles, based on moral standards so that the traders conduct (between each other) an honest transaction.

Therefore, it is not only the fear of punishment and social outcry that are the key elements that ensure trustworthiness between partners regarding the full implementation of the terms of a trade agreement, but also the issue of, in a sense, business ethics one might also add, again under a modern perspective. Therefore, lenders can at any time lend money to the borrower, but they do not do so unless first they have checked his financial solvency. Within this framework, business agreements were strong and the Athenians applied in practice the later-known Latin saying *Pacta sunt servanta* (agreements must be served).

11.8 Lending Policy

The goods used as collateral for maritime loans had to be worth twice the amount of the loan as a form of security for the lender and could be of any kind including amphorae, gold objects, etc. The loan had to be mortgaged over tangible assets of the borrower. These assets should have not already been mortgaged through another contract.

Athenians distinguished *phanera ousia*, i.e., assets that were visible, from *aphanes ousia*, mainly bank deposits, which in some cases, for both Athenians and foreigners, functioned as a wealth concealment (somewhat like offshore services) for the purpose of avoiding *liturgies*. The lender-banker had the right to check

[8] It means the absolutely reliable in silver content and nominal value Athenian currency.

[9] A very small, insignificant amount of value, the cost of which does not really burden the transaction, something like today's postage costs, one might say.

the value of the mortgaged asset, and if it was real estate, to place "boundaries" in the particular estate, that is, signs of the mortgage, that were visible to everyone. The placing of boundaries on lands in order to demarcate clear property rights is already witnessed from the Homeric period (Lyttkens 2006; Economou and Kyriazis 2017, 2019a).[10]

When taking out a loan, the amount of the loan and the interest rate which varied according to the type of loan and the risks of the trip were mentioned in detail. An interest rate of 16–17% was considered normal, but it could rise to 22% and 30% in special cases, while in very high-risk cases, such as marine loans to cover dangerous commercial sea voyages, it could even rise to 100% (Amemiya 2007, 87). The loan was repaid at the place and time that had been agreed upon and it might have been in another city-state. There was a penalty clause for non-payment on time or non-implementation of the terms.

The written agreement, which described the risks assumed by the lender, expired after the fulfillment of the agreement. Another important institutional arrangement is that the mortgage and loan could be sold by the first lender to another, like any asset. This is a practice that applies today, for example with the sale by banks of "red loans" (which means, with very high probability of default) to distress funds and shows how sophisticated the Athenian institutional system was (this probably applied for many other Greek city-states of the times too).

As a final comment, the Athenians who were involved in the financial sector of the times were fully aware that solvency regarding financial agreements promoted economic activity, and this entailed both their profits and the prosperity of the polis to rise.

[10]This is a reminiscent of the so-called *enclosure policies* that were implemented in the English rural system since the medieval times and later on.

Chapter 12
The Financial Aspects of the Silver Mining Operations

Abstract This chapter describes how the economic exploitation of the Athenian silver mines was taking place at Laurion. In particular, it describes an auction procedure at Laurion, next, the authorized institution which was responsible for the mines leases, the *poletai*, and finally, in detail the whole procedure of extracting silver by the mines. Silver mining was vital for the success of the Athenian economic model of organization, and for Athens's hegemony in the East Mediterranean.

12.1 Nicomedes Becomes a Winner at an Auction

Nicomedes had decided to diversify his entrepreneurial activities, investing his profits in other industries as well. The polis would auction off new areas in Laurion for silver and lead mining, as both metals were mixed and had to be separated after they were mined.

He came to the region of Thorikos at Laurion, where on the sides of a hill overlooking the sea was a large theater. He left his horse at an inn where he would spend the night and walked to the area where the new lots were to be auctioned. He found one of the managers of the mines, who showed him around the area.

Nicomedes recorded on a papyrus the numbers of the different plots, studying the terrain.

– Will you take part in the auction? the manager asked him.
– I am thinking about it, replied Nicomedes. Are many entrepreneurs interested?
– Several so far. As usual. But when it comes to new territory, what you will find is a matter of luck. Or the favor of the gods... What am I saying? and Tyche is a goddess. Have you sacrificed to the Goddess Tyche, the Goddess of fortune?
– I won't forget it, smiled Nicomedes. I will sacrifice to the goddess Tyche and Kerdoos Hermes, the 'profitable Hermes'. Are you from here? Your name?
– I am native of the place. Like silver! Antisthenes is my name.
– Nicomedes, from the Alopekis *deme*.
– Hi Nicomedes! What's your profession?

E. M. L. Economou, N. C. Kyriazis, *Daily Life in Classical Athens*, Frontiers in Economic History, https://doi.org/10.1007/978-3-031-58541-8_12

– Hi Antisthenes! Banking services and trade. I also have an estate in Mesogeia. If you want, I'll treat you wine and food after work.
– Very kind of yours. Why not? Where do you stay?
– At the inn of Menecles.
– Good choice. The best in the area.
– Fine. What do you think about, just after dark?
– I'll be there.

As it happened. They drank wine and ate freshly caught grilled bream and squid, along with good wine. Nicomedes narrated to him experiences from his travels, making sure that Menecles' cup was never empty. Then, he began to ask questions about his work, about the area, about other stakeholders, gathering and recording useful information in his mind. The next day he made his way back. He had decided to bid on a plot of land that looked the most promising.

On the day of the auction, he went to a certain point in the Agora, the place where the public auctions were held by the so-called *poletai*, in favor of the public.

Bidding began for each plot, with those interested making their bids and each plot going to the highest bidder. A clerk recorded the name of the bidder and the price for each lot, one copy for the record and one for the bidder to begin his activities at Laurion.

Nicomedes bid for the plot he had chosen, quite a high price because there were two other interested parties. But he had a good feeling, along with Menecles' information. After all, without taking some risk, he could not expect a significant profit; this was known to all the Athenians and foreign merchants, since there were not few who were engaged in such a business: The higher the financial risk-taking the higher is the possibility of making profits!

Then Nicomedes organized the whole procedure. He hired ten slaves from Menesthenes, an entrepreneur, at a drachma per day. Food and lodging expenses would weigh Nicomedes. Then he chose the *epistates*, the supervisor of mining, Philocles, a citizen of the Thorikos *deme*, from among the most experienced in the work, as Antisthenes had confided to him. The pay they agreed upon was five drachmae a day, quite high, but Nicomedes also knew that in this kind of endeavor efficiency required no saving. He needed one of the best, and for such a person you had to pay! He knew this from personal experience as well as from the works and theories of the famous philosopher Xenophon, many of which Nicomedes had read and understood in depth. Before starting the whole process, he dedicated two small bronze statues to Goddess Tyche and Kerdoos Hermes, respectively.

The work began, digging, followed by a feeling of anticipation. It seems that the tributes to the gods combined with Menecles' information were effective. Philocles, jubilant, announced to him that they had discovered a rich vein of silver!

That night they all celebrated the news together, Ischomachos, Nicomedes, and the slaves. He promised them a personal fee of three *obols* a day if they mined enough ore. He connected their working efficiency to a satisfying wage, a powerful incentive to work, as Nicomedes also knew.

The raw ore could be taken either to Argyrocopeion or to the nearby workshops, where the separation of lead and silver would take place.

Nicomedes received the silver bullion in the form of silver bars, which he transferred by carriage to Athens and secured them in a special premise in his *oikos*, where he held the turnover of his bank.

* * *

12.2 The Board of *Poletai*

Van Alfen (2011, 2) has identified a number of economic activities that the state leased to private individuals or consortia that could be seen as a primitive version of joint stock companies. The *board of poletai* was responsible for these leasing assignments. Provisions for the establishment of this board were already included with the reforms introduced by Cleisthenes; however, references to them date back to Solon's times. In Classical times, the *board of poletai* consisted of managers-civil servants, one from each of the ten Athenian tribes. They were elected for an annual term and were directly accountable to the Athenian Assembly for the decisions they made. They could be subjected to various checks regarding their decisions (Aristotle, *Athenian Constitution*, 7.3).

Although the relevant evidence is limited, according to Hansen (1991, 260) and Papazarkadas (2011, 53), the *ten poletai* were entrusted with the granting of leases of the so-called sacred lands. They could also sell confiscated lands in favor of the state, but the contracts for the sale of confiscated and sacred lands had to be ratified by the *nine archons* and, certainly, by the Athenian Council. Hansen (1991, 253) argues that there was a close cooperation between the *ten poletai* and the Council, and Rhodes (1972, 97) adds that the final supervision and approval of the granting of these leases or selling land property to private individuals was made by the Council.

One of the major duties of the *ten poletai* was the leases of the silver miners, including the monitoring of the proper implementation of the terms of the related contracts to private mining contractors. They also collected the dues from the leases as well as the taxes which the law imposed from the mining of silver, as well as all other public properties which the state leased through contracts to private contractors in general, under a 3P logic (Walbank 1983).

Hallof (1990) argued that the auctions conducted by the Council may not have been as open as commonly believed and that in fact the successful candidates were pre-selected. However, Papazarkadas (2011, 55), based on epigraphic evidence (*SEG* XXVIII 103 III-23-4, *IG* II2 1241 1 52-2, *IG* II2 2492 l.34-6), argues that Hallof's view is false given that (i) the leasing of land throughout Athens followed identical practices, (ii) auctions were a common practice, and (iii) when organizing auctions, the *board of poletai* followed **open and transparent** procedures for granting and monitoring the progress of the projects they granted to private contractors.

Aristotle (*Athenian Constitution*, 47.2) argues that the leases for the use of these lands were signed between the *board of poletai* and the contractor through contracts he characterized as *leleukomena grammateia.*

If silver was found in the particular land, it could be exploited for 3 years. The mine in that case was classified as *ergasimon* (a workable mine). After this period, the mine was considered as *anasaximon*, that is, a mine that could be re-auctioned for further exploitation for a 10-year lease period with the possible renewal option for another 10-year period. If the mine was abandoned or left for more than a year and then brought back into operation, it was reclassified as *palaion anasaximon* (a mine that once was *anasaximon*), with a 10-year lease period (Aristotle, *Ath. Const.*, 47.2; Aperghis 1998, 6–8, 13; Papazarkadas 2011, 59–60).

If the bidder failed to pay the annual concession fee to the state at the appointed time, he lost the right of use which could be granted to a new bidder willing to pay the money (Langdon 1994, 255). Furthermore, the bidder who failed to appear solvent was fined and had to pay twice the amount of the original concession contract as compensation, while, in general, failure to appear consistent could lead a person to be declared as *atimos* and sentenced to prison (Papazarkadas 2011, 64). This was of course a very harsh punishment and it implies that those who really wished to be engaged in such entrepreneurial activities should not do so blithely, because mismanagement could have a negative personal impact on themselves. This set of severe punishments also denotes how important was for the Athenians the proper and the efficient use of these lands, since their proper exploitation was also not linked only to profits for the individual contractors but also to revenues for the state, and, as a consequence, with the future well-being of society. Thus, choosing the most promising contractors could guarantee higher state revenues over time, and vice versa.

A difficult issue to be defined is where these auctions were taking place, and whether other public officials besides the *ten poletai* were present or not. We can argue with relative certainty that they probably took place somewhere in the Agora, considering Hallof (1990) and Langdon (1994, 256), who provide information about relative inscriptions found in the Agora. On this issue, Kyriazis (2009, 117) based on Andocides (*On the Mysteries*, 1.92–93) and Aristotle (Ath. Const., 47.4) provides the important information that the auctions were held in the Council under the direction of the *poletai* (sellers), of the *eponymous archon*. In our opinion, the fact of the presence of the polis' highest political figure during this procedure proves the importance that the Athenians attached to it.

Like the rest of the bodies of public officials, and especially those related to financial issues, the members of the *board of poletai* were subjected to a scrutiny of their actions upon completion of their (annual) duties in order for transparency to be ensured. The *board of poletai* was carrying out the following financial activities on behalf of the state:

- Lease of public estates and lands, such as the mining leases from Laurion
- Leases of sacred lands
- Collection of various fees and fines

- Leases from forests and meadows
- Confiscations from court decisions
- Collecting court fees
- Collecting part of the taxes paid by the allies
- Gathering together the *pentecoste* sums of money after its collection by the *pentecostologoi*
- Penalties and fines imposed from courts decisions
- Sales of real estate and plots of land
- Loot gathering (in case of warfare situations)

Kyriazis (2009, 117) adds that the rents of all the leases of the silver mines were paid to the *apodektai* (cashiers) in the Bouleuterion building. Obviously, there was a synergy between the *poletai* and the *apodektai* regarding the collection of these remittances in favor of (and on behalf of) the state.

12.3 Laurion Silver Mining and Quarries

The export and production of silver took place in given places and *demes* where ores had been discovered, especially in Laurion. The demand for silver was continuous and increasing and for this reason it is estimated that between 25,000 and 30,000 people, mostly slaves, worked there on a permanent basis (Acton 2014, 117). Citizens and *metics* could work also in the mines for a fee, but with large salary fluctuations. However, there must have been a continuous demand for providing such services.

The silver production created great wealth for the Athenian city-state and the entrepreneurs involved, such as Kallias and the general Nicias. The ownership of the silver mines belonged to the city-state, with a few exceptions. Crosby (1950, 192) mentions such an exception, where a mine which belonged to a private was leased to an individual, under a contract which included the following important information: the name of the lessee (or purchaser), the price, sometimes the name of the man who registers the mine, the name, place, and classification of the mine, and the boundaries on the four sides. The contract often included the name of the owner of the property in which the mine was situated. It could also mention specific marker points so as to better define the topographical demarcation of the property. As a proof, Crosby provides the following info based on an archaeological finding (Plate 93, *Hesperia*)

> At Thalinos, Thoutimides of Sounion registered from the stele of Euboulos, the ergasimon mine Artemisiakon in Nape (which is) in the property of which the boundaries are, at the north, the Artemisiakon mine which is being worked by ---, at the south, the gully which runs from Nape and the workshop of Epikrates, at the east, the property of Teleson and his house, at the west, a workshop, the lessee, Thoutimides son of Phanias of Sounion, (the price) 150 drachmai.

There is no doubt that here we are dealing with a detailed contract which provides analytical information regarding the exact location and the boundaries of the leased

Image 12.1 Interior view of silver mine at Thorikos at Laurion. Source: https://commons.wikimedia.org/wiki/Category:Mines_of_Laurion#/media/File:Mineing_Shaft_in_Throikos.jpg

mine. Johnstone (2011, 40) argues that the Athenians considered agreements through written contracts as very important since they had legal force in the courts. Protection of commercial contracts has been considered as a pivotal institutional arrangement for making transactions reliable for all parties involved.

Thus, in principle, the Athenian public, through the *ten poletai*, leased these holdings either to private individuals or to joint private contractors who had set up primitive versions of joint stock companies so as to exploit these plots. Thus, there was not a large concentration of silver mining in the hands of a few people, although there was some family continuity in these activities (Image 12.1).

It is more than certain that the working conditions of the slaves in the mines were very unhealthy, laborious, and dangerous. This is testified by Xenophon (*Memorabilia*, 3.6.12). Exploiting the mines was a complex task. Although it could become quite profitable it also involved substantial business risk. This is described by Plutarch (*Nicias* 4). The minting procedure included considerable overhead costs in addition to taxes and rents: private contractors or consortia had to provide the entire technical infrastructure for mining, such as the purchase (or lease) and upkeep of slaves, the digging tools, the mine support, lamps, and other materials as well as slaves. The processing of the metals was carried out by slaves who hammered the

Image 12.2 Ore washing site (below the arrow) near the theater at Thorikos, at the Laurion silver mines. Source: Image owned by the authors

rocks until they became gravel. The gravels were then thrown into a trough into which a quantity of water was poured carefully so that the light gravels would be carried away by the water, while the rocks with the silver remained at the bottom. At this phase, if the silver content was estimated to be over 30%, the rocks were sent to the furnace for smelting (Image 12.2).

Mining operations required large quantities of food, wine, and olive oil to support the workforce, as well as wood, charcoal, and tools (Economou 2024, 205–210). However, the investment's return, according to Christesen (2003, 52), was very high, possibly rising to 50%. To share the risks of this activity, entrepreneurs mostly citizens and less *metics* rented small tracts of land for mining in different areas. Although these entrepreneurs had some affinity with the relative *demes*, this was not considered a necessary prerequisite so as for an entrepreneur to be engaged in such activities.

So profitable was this business activity for the Athenian state that its continuation was a key state policy. Therefore, according to Osborne (1985, 111), mining-related business was excluded from the *antidosis* procedure[1] which as a practice was related to the possibility of property exchange between two parties.

Lastly, it should also be mentioned that mining of silver or gold for the manufacturing of coins did not take place only in Laurion in Attica, but in addition, in other places inside and outside Greece. Vaxevanopoulos et al. (2022) explain that, in the last 60 years, isotopic research has revealed some major ancient mining districts in today's mainland Greece, which except in Laurion included Euboea, the Cyclades island complex, and Northern Greece (Chalkidiki, Thasos, Rhodope, and Mt. Pangaeon). Outside today's Greece, areas with related ores were found in Asia Minor, Southern Iberia (Spain), and Britain.

[1]For *antidosis*, see the explanations in Sect. 13.7.

Regarding bronze, this is an alloy of copper and tin. Copper was relatively abundant and could be found in several regions, including Cyprus, Etruria, Brutium, and Elba in Italy, and mainland Greece itself, in areas such as the Cyclades islands. Mining and metalworking activities were prevalent in these areas. Tin, on the other hand, was not abundant in mainland Greece and had to be imported from regions such as Asia Minor (modern-day Turkey), Palestine, the Iberian Peninsula, and Britain in Cornwall. Trade networks allowed the Greeks to acquire it for the production of bronze.

As a general comment, the use of copper has a very long history in Ancient Greece, stretching back to the Bronze Age (3000–1100 BCE), perhaps even earlier. For example, Renfrew (1967) had thoroughly studied the metallurgical activities in the Cyclades since the Bronze Age, with important findings also involving copper.

Chapter 13
The *Liturgies*, the Financing of the Navy, and the Tax Regime in Classical Athens

Abstract This chapter explains the *liturgies*, a special type of taxation burdening the wealthy citizens and wealthy *metics*. The most important of them were *trierarchy* and *choregia*, the former related to the financing of the Athenian navy and the latter related to staging theatrical plays. It also describes the Athenian tax system and *antidosis*, a mechanism through which a citizen could deny undertaking a *liturgy*.

13.1 Nausinicus: The *Liturgist* and the *Trierarch*

After the auction was over, Nicomedes went to his bank, where he met Ischomachos, and after a while a new customer came, Nausinicus of Nausimachus, an acquaintance of Nicomedes who was also a well-to-do citizen.

After the formal greetings, Nausinicus explained what he needed. He had been chosen as a *trierarch* with four other citizens, and all together constituted a certain *synteleia*, out of the 240 *synteleiai* appointed annually.

He felt honored due to his selection, but he also needed some money immediately to cover the financial share of the *trierarchy*, which was the most expensive *liturgy*. He wanted, together with other two *synteleia* members, to get a temporary loan to cover their *trierarchy*. He wanted a loan secured by some of his properties, specifically some farms in Mesogeia. He discussed with Nicomedes the details and agreed on the amount of the loan, the interest rate, and its duration.

Nausinicus explained to Nicomedes that although he still retained an income, his shipping business was experiencing difficulties, and as he considered his wealth to have dwindled, he would have to be excluded from the list of 1200 wealthiest citizens who undertook to participate in the *symmories*.

– If I didn't love my motherland and live four decades ago, when my father proposed the law on the symmories, I would never have been able to take on the *trierarchy* entirely, or even jointly with someone else as *a syntrierarch*, Nicomedes. And based on my current income situation, I would be forced to denounce someone by asking for an *antidosis*.

E. M. L. Economou, N. C. Kyriazis, *Daily Life in Classical Athens*, Frontiers in Economic History, https://doi.org/10.1007/978-3-031-58541-8_13

- Calm down Nausinicus, I understand you. Let me just remind you that I also regularly pay my membership to both the *symmory* and the *syntely*. We live in turbulent times. It seems that now our country needs us more than ever before in recent years. Do not forget that the rumors that the Macedonians have undertaken a large-scale shipbuilding program to prepare a new fleet in order to challenge us at sea have now been confirmed. And, unfortunately, it seems that their efforts are already successful. So, think what is at stake: if we lose in a future naval engagement, I say if, then, since the Macedonian *phalanx* is the strongest war machine regarding land army, we risk becoming a satellite state of Macedonia, or if things go to extremes, fight again and suffer a new Chaeronea. Do we want this Nausinicus?
- Alas! Of course not, Nicomedes.
- Then let us look at the big picture Nausinicus: let us sacrifice personal wealth, for the common good, by investing in our defense, through the private initiative, as our forefathers have done since the time of the Naval Decree of Themistocles. And let us prepare properly for the worst, for if we are to secure peace, we must be properly prepared for war. Therefore, if we, the well-to-do, do not do our best, we Athenians together will lose everything. Let's invest money now, because as Demosthenes also said: we need money, for defense, because without it nothing of what needs to be done can be achieved.

Nausinicus added that after discussing with the *strategos of the trierarchy*, he and his colleagues in the *synteleia* decided that he should also take on the duties of *trierarch*. And it would be his first time. He had no experience in commanding a *trireme* at sea at all and he was very anxious.

- Great Nausinicus! The honor is even higher! Which *trireme* will you take over?
- The Aristonike, a very old ship around 25 years old.
- But with an excellent and very promising name, commented Nicomedes, so as to encourage him.
- It means, 'excellent victory'! Nausinicus, I will undertake to cover your expenses, of all three, with an extremely low interest rate loan. And since you haven't assumed *trierarchy* again, I'll take it upon myself to help you. Tomorrow morning, if you agree, we will go together to find the *strategos of the trierarchy*, Pantaleon. I know him personally, and I will ask him to help you with anything you need. Then we will go to Munichia to talk with the manager of the *neosoikoi* about the process of accepting Aristonike by you.
- Wonderful Nicomedes, thank you so much!

Indeed, the next day, Nicomedes and Nausinicus went down to the port of Munichia and met with the the *strategos of the trierarchy* and the previous *trierarch* that Nausinicus was about to replace in his duty. It was actually Nicomedes who inspected the *trireme* Aristonike that Nausinicus would take over. He kept a record with all the needs to make Aristonike operational for the next 8 months: Replacing some oars, ropes, sails, waterproofing, and painting. Total cost, 5000 drachmae.

They needed cash. So, he took from his bank some silver bars from those he had mined after the silver auction he participated some time ago; next, he went to the Argyrocopeion in the Agora of Athens, found the magistrate in charge, and told him that he needed a *talent* to be produced by these bars. He gave him the silver bars which the magistrate weighed and recorded.

The magistrate informed him about the cost, in drachmae, of the silver conversion to drachmae, which included a small profit for the Argyrocopeion. Nicomedes of course was already aware. The magistrate handed him a papyrus detailing the transaction, the weight of the silver bars Nicomedes had delivered, and the amount of drachmae he would receive. He further informed Nicomedes that the coins would be available in a week.

A week later Nicomedes went to the Argyrocopeion and received not exactly 6000 drachmae but with some reduction, due to the cost of minting the coins. Nicomedes then went to his bank, drew up on papyrus the agreement, gave it to Nausinicus to read, and then Nicomedes put down his name, and his signet from the ring he wore. So, did Nausinicus. They called as witnesses two nearby shopkeepers, the banker Xenopoithes and the shoemaker Nausinoos, who also put their signatures as guarantors on the loan agreement between the two parties. Then Nicomedes, with the two witnesses watching, disbursed the sum of the loan, 1200 drachmae, to Nausinicus, who took it, thanked him, and departed. Two out of the four extra members who belong to Nausinicus' *synteleia* similarly signed their contracts, and they also received the 1200 drachmae which were allotted to them by Nicomedes' bank.

* * *

13.2 The *Liturgies*

Liturgies constituted a kind of taxation of the richest Athenians and *metics*, about 300–1200 men in a total of 50,000 citizens and *metics* (including the family members for both groups) in the fifth century BCE and 30,000 in the fourth century, who undertook the financing of a series of state expenses, such as the maintenance of *trireme* warships, by their personal wealth (Christ 2006, 146). *Liturgies* were not continuous to those who usually undertook them, so that the *liturgist* (the performer of a *liturgy*) would not be financially exhausted. The reward for the contribution of the *liturgists* was the rise of their personal prestige and the recognition they enjoyed from the part of their fellow citizens (Kyriazis 2009, 112). Characteristically, Thucydides (6.31.3–4) writes that:

> The fleet had been elaborately equipped at great cost to the captains and the state; the treasury giving a drachma a day to each seaman, and providing empty ships, sixty men of war and forty transports, and manning these with the best crews obtainable; while the captains gave a bounty in addition to the pay from the treasury to the thranitae and crews generally, besides spending lavishly upon figure-heads and equipments, and one and all making the utmost exertions to enable their own ships to excel in beauty and fast sailing....

From this resulted not only a rivalry among themselves in their different departments, but an idea among the rest of the Hellenes that it was more a display of power and resources than an armament against an enemy.

The main *liturgies* concerned covering expenses for the organization of artistic events (*choregia*) and expenses for military purposes (*trierarchy*). According to Davies's (1967, 1981) estimates, the annual minimum number of *liturgies* amounted to 97, but when the year happened to include the Great Panathenaea, every 4 years (the most important festival in Athens, which included many festivities and sacrifices to the gods) the number of *liturgies* increased to 118.[1] Other types of less expensive *liturgies* were:

- *Hestiasis:* Provision of *syssitia* (common meals) to citizens and receptions at festive events
- *The gymnasiarchy*: Operating and maintenance costs of the three public *gymnasia* athletic facilities
- *Architheoria:* Expenses to cover the sending of *proxenoi* (consuls) to a series of events
- *Hippotrophia:* Taking on the responsibility of raising horses either for the army or for major celebrations and races

13.3 *Eisphora:* The Taxation of the Athenians

As a general rule, well-to-do Athenian citizens were subject to taxation on property, known as *eisphora* only in extreme or urgent circumstances (war, natural disasters, etc.). In very special cases where the lower-income classes of citizens were also taxed, they were taxed much lower than the rich citizens, meaning that the rich were burdened much more than the less favored citizens (Christ 2006, 146). Thus, *eisphora* taxation was not *proportional* but a highly *progressive* one falling on the rich (Kyriazis 2009, 118; Ober 2017).[2] However, as Hansen (1991, 112) writes, from 347/6 BCE onward, the *eisphora* became a permanent regular annual tax for well-to-do citizens, 10 *talents* a year, and the Assembly could always impose extra *eisphorai*. For an analytical presentation of how the *eisphora* was implemented, one can among others consult Fawcett (2016), as well as us, among others, in Bitros et al. (2020) and Economou (2024).

---

[1] See further Lyttkens (1994, 1997, 2010), Kyriazis (2009), and Economou and Kyriazis (2017, 2019a) for a thorough analysis regarding the institution of *liturgies*.

[2] A *proportional* tax is the tax that levies the same percentage tax to everyone regardless of income. *A progressive* tax involves a tax rate that increases as taxable income increases.

13.4 The *Symmories* and the *Synteleiai*

In 378–377 BCE, a period of war when Athens was preparing its new fleet against the Peloponnesians, under Nausinicus as an *eponymous archon*, an inventory of citizens' property was made and the rich were classified into "tax groups" called *symmories*, based on property and incomes criteria so that the members have to pay equal *eisphorai* for reasons of fiscal justice. If we interpret correctly two reports of Demosthenes (*Against Aphobus 1*, 27.7; *Against Aphobus 2*, 28.44), the members of each *symmory* pooled one-fifth of their property in a common fund.

In 358/7 or 357/6 BCE, a citizen named Periandros linked the system of the *symmories* to the *trierarchy* due to a series of inefficiencies that appeared in the *trierarchy* system, basically, the growing reluctance of the wealthy men to contribute time, effort, and money to the task. Due to this, a list of the 1200 richest citizens, known as the *synteleis* (joint contributors), was formed, who were liable for the *trierarchy*, and grouped into **20 *symmories* of 60 men each** (Gabrielsen 1994, 182). In each *symmory* there was the *hegemon* that gave its name to the *symmory*, the *deuteros* (second) and the *tritos* (third). There was also the *diagrapheus* who kept the *diagrammata* (tax lists) and the tax due and he wrote off those who paid their annual contribution. *Hegemon*, *deuteros*, and *tritos* were accountable to the *ten strategoi* since they were entrusted, among other duties, with the supervision of the *symmories*. *Metics* were also obliged to belong to *symmories* (*meticikai symmoriai*).

A further sub-category in this system was known as *synteleia*. Each *synteleia* included 5 out of the 1200 well-to-do citizens. Therefore, 240 *synteleiai* were created and each one had to support a *trireme*, so the *syntrierarchy* ("joint *trierarchy*") now involved five citizens liable per vessel instead of two, as applied in earlier times. This is also the case of Nausinicus, whom we describe in this Scene. Demosthenes (*On the Navy*, 14.16–23) made a proposal to increase the number of members to 2000. He argues (14.17):

> Then I propose to divide these into twenty boards, as at present, each containing sixty persons. Each of these boards I would subdivide into five groups of twelve men, always attaching to the wealthiest man those who are poorest, to keep the balance. That is how I propose to arrange these persons; you will understand why, when you have heard the whole of the arrangement.

With this plan, 6000 *talents* would be gathered and could subsidize 300 *triremes* ready for war (*ibid*., 18–19). The plan was beyond the financial means of Athens, both in terms of the number, 6000 *talents*, and in terms of manning 300 *triremes*, which would require 60,000 crews (when the total population of citizens was 40–50,000) and wage costs could require 24,000 *talents* a year! Apparently, for these reasons the proposal was not accepted.

But another modification proposed by Demosthenes did pass in 340, in which the wealthiest 300 men within the *trierarchic symmories* were put in charge of 1 or 2 warships each, with the remaining burden distributed more equally among the total of 1200 as well (Demosthenes, *On the Crown*, 18.102; Aeschines, *Against*

Ctesiphon, Hansen 1991, 114; Rutishauser 2019, 235). This latter reform appears to have lasted until Athens' defeat in the Lamian War of 323/2 (Gabrielsen 1994, 209).

13.5 The *Trierarchy*

The *trierarchy* was the most famous and expensive *liturgy*. We know several instances of *trierarchy* cost, such as 20 *mnae*, that is, 2000 drachmae (Demosthenes, *Against Meidias*, 21.80). On the other hand, the *trierarchy*, in addition to costs, also brought honor to the *trierarch*, who did not miss an opportunity to invoke it in politics and the courts. The polis itself honored the *liturgists* (Lysias, *On the Confiscation of the Property of the Brother of Nicias*, 18.7; *Against Eratosthenes*, 12.20). An Athenian proudly says (Lysias, *Defense Against a Charge of subverting the Democracy*, 25.12–13):

> .....I have equipped a warship five times, fought in four sea-battles, contributed to many war levies, and performed my other public services as amply as any citizen. But my purpose in spending more than was enjoined upon me by the city was to raise myself the higher in your opinion, so that if any misfortune should chance to befall me I might defend myself on better terms.

"Your" refers to the citizen-judges of Heliaia, and "any misfortune" refers to any charge against him. At the end of the *trierarchy*, the *trierarch* had to hand over the ship with all its supplies; otherwise a court was held by the *epimeletes of the triremes*, that is, the person who was in charge of the dockyards, where this particular *trireme* was anchored (Demosthenes, *Against Evergus and Mnesibulus*, 47.18–24). The *trierarch* had to pay maintenance costs of the *trierarchy*, for example, to replace lost material such as broken oars, etc.

In 362/361 BCE, due to the financial inability of many Athenians to bear the cost of *trierarchy*, the *syntrierarchy* was decided where two people performed *trierarch* duties every 6 months (Demosthenes, *Against Polycles,* 50.1, 50.39). Refusal on the part of a chosen person to undertake this obligation was punished (*ibid*., 57). However, in case the *syntrierarch* had not come to take charge of the ship wherever it was, the prior *trierarch* continued this duty (*ibid*., 32, 36, 41–42). The prior *trierarch* had to deliver the ship intact and ready for war to the other; if this was not done, then, a *dike epitrierarchematos* (trial on *syntrierarchy*) was taking place, which although had the character of a trial between privates, it also had a public impact since it distorted the polis' fighting ability. Such a trial is mentioned by Demosthenes (*ibid*., 1) in a text written in 358 BCE.

In 349 BCE at the suggestion of Demosthenes, a new law was accepted by the citizens' Assembly that defined that every wealthy person who possessed a property of 10 *talents* should undertake the operational cost of a *trireme*. A richer man must undertake a higher cost, but never more than covering the maintenance cost of three *triremes*. The less wealthy continued to contribute to the *synteleiai* system.

However, no one was obliged to serve as *trierarch* or *syntrierarch* for two consecutive years, but some, out of patriotic zeal, did so.

In case that for whatever reason the polis was unable to cover the running expenses of a *trireme*, the *trierarch* should try to cover them, in the best way he could, that is, undertook himself to equip the ship with the necessary supplies, hire a crew, pay them, and give them rations (Demosthenes, *Against Polycles*, 50.7–8, 50.23–26, 50.34; Demosthenes, *On the Trierarchic Crown*, 51.5). These sums of money would have to be returned to him by the polis, but it happened that the *trierarch* would give them away in order to receive more honorable treatment from the people of Athens, e.g., to receive an invitation to a meal at the Prytaneion (Demosthenes, *Against Polycles*, 50.10, 50.13). To meet these expenses, some pledged their property and took out loans (*ibid*., 50., 55–56), like the fictional person we described in this Scene, an extra sign, among other things, of how advanced and flexible the Athenian economy was.

A prudent *trierarch* who kept his ship ready for war and fully equipped at any time could receive an honorary *stephanos* (crown) after a proposal made by some citizens or even a single citizen, providing that such a proposal was accepted by the Assembly. On the other hand, if the *trierarchs* in charge did not set sail by the final date they risked imprisonment (Demosthenes, *On the Crown*, 51.4).

We hypothesize that with regard to *trireme* manning, the *trierarch* would choose his crew based on the *deme's* and clan's network he belonged to. Since he was not just the financier but also the captain of the ship, he would have a personal incentive for his *trireme* to be well-equipped, since his own survival on the battlefield depended on it! Alternatively, the *trierarch*, who was not necessarily an expert in sea affairs, could appoint someone to replace him or even request exemption from the obligation to assume the *trierarchy* for financial or personal reasons for 2 years, in contrast to the *liturgist* of a *choregia* who could request an exemption for only 1 year (Christ 2006, 158). However, it seems that the case of not taking up the task of commanding the *trireme* was not very common.

The *trierarch* kept detailed ship's accounts that recorded any expenditures made, the purpose of these expenses, and at what prices and in what currency (including the exchange difference) the goods and wages were paid, so that the next *trierarch* and the polis would have a clear picture when and if needed (Demosthenes, *Against Polycles*, 50.30). Thus, a prudent *trierarch* should be keeping records with crew lists and the sums of money he paid them, since all his actions were subject to review by the Athenian authorities.

Some Athenians had used the *trierarchy* as an opportunity to reap profits from piracy. They leased from a *trierarch* the ship in order to siphon revenue from piracy loot and then pay the *trierarch* and with the rest of money to make a profit. However, this was considered a very dishonorable act: one or a group of people to seek personal financial benefits from the undertaking of a *liturgy* (Gabrielsen 1994, 99–100; Günther and Hahn 2019). But the general image is that those who assumed *trierarchy* took care to maintain and repair their ships well, by making them fast and highly capable in naval battle (Thucydides, *History*, 6.31.1). A well-maintained *trireme* was also a sign of prestige for the *trierarchs*, and this was exploited by those who had special political ambitions (Christ 2006, 146).

Finally, Rutishauer (2019) provides convincing arguments regarding the dubious issue whether or not *metics* were also assigned with *trierarchies*. He characteristically writes that (*ibid*., 235–236):

> It was apparently fairly common for trierarchs to discharge their obligations by hiring metics or *xenoi*, using a procedure known as *misthosis*. The most famous example is when Meidias held a trierarchy in 348, but subcontracted the command to an Egyptian named Pamphilos, who is specifically called a metic by Demosthenes.[3] It appears that such substitutes took full command of trierarchs' vessels, and as such could be blamed for defeats, such as the one at Peparethos at the hands of Alexander of Pherai in 361/0. Though not necessarily popular with the demos, as the comments of Demosthenes imply, such hiring out of duties was apparently tolerated, as it broadened the pool of citizens willing (and able) to undertake trierarchies. Whether or not it was strictly 'illegal' is difficult to determine. It has been proposed that there would have been a fairly large number of skilled commanders willing to perform these substitutions, perhaps because of chances to acquire plunder, even if there were risks involved in such activity....

Transferring the trierarchy obligation to another one under contract is another element of the flexibility with which the Athenians satisfied their financial and national obligation toward their polis, in a way that could not harm any party.

13.6 The *Triremes*

As already mentioned, the *triremes* were kept in special shipsheds known as *neosoikoi*. When not in service they were towed ashore to be protected against rotting and their parts were stored in other buildings.

The large number of *triremes* mentioned for Athens in the second half of the fourth century is impressive (Image 13.1). We know various names of them. Most of them referred to the female as Aura ("breeze"), Amphitrite (the wife of Poseidon, the "God-ruler of the Seas"), Thetis, Aphrodite, Melitta ("bee"), Salamis, Eleutheria (freedom), Demokratia (democracy), and Nikeso ("victorious") (Strauss 2004, 147).[4]

---

[3]Demosthenes (*Against Polycles*, 50.52).

[4]It is perhaps worth mentioning that the habit of assigning female status to warships has been preserved throughout history and is another valuable element that has its origin and reference in Ancient Greece. For example, during the Battle of Trafalgar, in 1805, at the height of the British Empire's naval dominance around the world, the famous Admiral Horace Nelson, who defeated the French fleet of Napoleon the Great, was on board on his flagship, the HMS Victory, a ship to which a female character was attributed. A century and a half later, British sailors still felt their ships as feminine entities. Proof of this is the way veteran British sailors who are still alive today recount the Battle of the Danish Straits in 1941, between the British battleships HMS Hood and HMS Prince of Wales and the German warships, the battleship Bismarck and the heavy cruiser Prince Eugen. Veteran British sailors even today refer to HMS Hood as "she" as if she were a real woman!

Image 13.1 The *trireme* Olympias (bow side). Source: https://commons.wikimedia.org/wiki/File:Triere_Olympias_at_Paleon_Faliron_Museum.JPG. Permission: Public Domain

Figueira (2022) has estimated that during the Periclean period Attic shipyards built probably 10–20 *triremes* annually, while, simultaneously, drying out, refurbishing, and re-equipping existing *triremes* under the supervision of Athenian *trierarchs*. Acton (2014, 197) estimates that a *trireme's* lifespan was approximately 25 years.

During 322 BCE, in the naval battle of Amorgos between the Athenian and the Macedonian navy, Athens had built 360 *triremes* as well as larger ships, 55 *quadriremes*, and some 7 *quinqueremes*, a huge number of ships as a total. It is clear that Athens could only man a percentage of all these ships. In the largest naval battle of the Social War (357–355 BCE) at Sybota, the Athenian fleet deployed 130 *triremes*, with a total crew of 26,000. So, the large number of warships could only be justified under the logic that any losses could be quickly replaced, by ready-to-be-used ships as replacements, something like a *fleet in being* strategy.[5] They probably counted in the total available warships ceilings also some older vessels that

[5]In naval warfare, a *fleet in being* is a naval force that can influence the enemy's doctrine without even leaving port. If a fleet leaves port and faces the enemy, it might lose in battle and no longer influence the enemy's actions, but while it remains safely in port, the enemy is forced to continually deploy forces to guard against it. Thus, a *fleet in being* can be part of a *sea denial* doctrine, but not one of implementing *a sea dominance* strategy. This term was coined as a theoretical concept by Lord Admiral Arthur Herbert Torrington (1648–1716), fleet commander of the English naval forces in 1690 during the Nine Years' War (1688–1697). This strategy was abandoned after WWII due to the limitations it possessed after military disasters such as the Battle of Taranto (November 11–12, 1940) and the Pearl Harbor campaign (December 7, 1941).

Image 13.2 The astern side of the reconstructed Athenian *trireme* Olympias. Source: Image owned by the authors

would have been almost unfit for combat, just before their final withdrawal from service. Finally, there is also the case that the Athenians themselves provided deliberately exaggerated numbers for their fleet, as a further psychological deterrent against potential enemies (Image 13.2).

The *hoplites* aboard the *triremes* were called *epibatai* and *pezonautai* (marines). Many of them carried only a *hoplon* (shield) and helmet, and not the defensive breastplate and shins, so that if they fell into the sea they would not be dragged to the bottom by their weight. They could easily get rid of the shield and helmet, but not the breastplate which was fastened with straps.

The two lowest rows of oars on the *triremes* were very close to the surface of the sea, and therefore their openings were protected by leather covers to prevent water from entering. Rowers usually brought with them a padded leather cushion to sit more comfortably on the wooden benches. A *trireme* had a displacement of 50 tons and developed a maximum ramming speed of about 9 knots. It had a strength of 200 men and consisted of the following crew groups:[6]

Officers:

- *Trierarch*: The commander of the *trireme*, in charge of the crew and the logistical support of the ship
- *Kybernetes*: The person responsible for safe sailing. He was handling the rudder.

[6]For a detailed description of the structure and operation of a *trireme*, see Morrison and Coates (1986).

- *Keleustes:* The person responsible for training and directing the oarsmen.
- *Prorates:* Usually, he stood at the bow, reporting (to the two above officers) in case he observed something of importance.
- *Pentecontarchos:* The name is a remnant of the time of *the penteconters,*[7] but in the *triremes* he had the duties of secretary, treasurer, and caretaker, as well as being responsible for all types of supplies.
- *Naupegos:* He was in charge of the technical matters of the ship which included repairs and fixes when these were required.
- *Trieraules:* He used a flute and was responsible for the rhythm of rowing.

Other Staff:

- *Epibatai* (marines): 14 (10 *hoplites*—spearmen and 4 archers)
- Rowers (170): (62 *thranitai*, 54 *zugitai*, and 54 *thalamitai*)

For the highest officer in the navy, the Athenians used the term *strategos* while the Spartans used the word *nauarchos*. Accordingly, the flagship, the warship from which the movements of the fleet were directed, was called by the Athenians as the *strategis naus*. Only much later did the Athenians replace this term with the equivalent *nauarchis*, already used by the Spartans.

The phrase *adephagai triremes* (voracious *triremes*) had prevailed in Athenian society at the time as synonymous to excessive costs, as indeed was the cost of annual maintenance of a *trireme* by a wealthy *liturgist*. Regarding the *trierarchs* expenses, feeding the crew for a month required approximately half of a *talent*—3000 drachmae (Gabrielsen 1994, 122). Davies (1981) estimated the annual cost for *trierarchy* at between 4000 and 6000 drachmae (or 0.7–1 *talent*), which would approximate the lifetime income of a skilled worker.

Regarding the state expenses, it included paying the crew for 8 months' service by the state, as well as the initial shipbuilding (6000 drachmae). All this made the whole fleet life cycle extremely expensive. Indeed, if a *trireme* was in service for 8 months, then given the daily wage, about 1 drachma for 200 crew (Loomis 1998, 32–67), this would mean a total running cost of approximately 9 *talents* per year:

- 30 • 200 = 6.000 = 1 *talent* for paying wages for a month.
- 30 • 200 • 8 = 48.000 drachmae = 8 *talents* for a single *trireme's* annual service.

But it is somewhat unclear what the operating costs included, since the crew's wages, the most expensive element of a *trireme*, were paid by the public. If we assume that Athens kept for 1 year (peacetime) 60 *triremes* in operational readiness, then the annual cost of the fleet would be the very high sum of 540 *talents* or 3,240,000 drachmae! This cost could be exceeded in wartime, depending on the degree of the escalation of war, the need for additional use of naval units, and the criticality of the tactical/military situation, which shows why Athens at the end of the Social War was financially exhausted. If we accept the annual logistic support cost of

---

[7] The *penteconters* were the previous generation of *trireme* warships, with 50 oars, which left their historical mark in the pre-Classical period (Figueira 2011; van Wees 2013).

a *trireme* undertaken by a *trierarch* and combine this sum with state expenses on running a *trireme* (based on the Loomis's (1998) above estimation), the total annual cost may have been approximately 9 *talents* a year, a huge sum of money.

13.7 The *Antidosis* Procedure

Because *trierarchy* was an extremely costly *liturgy*, the Athenians, in order to ensure as much as possible a fair distribution of the economic burden to the well-to-do citizens, instituted the *antidosis* procedure.

For that purpose, they instituted that any citizen or *metic* who was assigned to undertake a *trierarchy* could renounce it by pointing someone else, denouncing him as richer, and therefore, theoretically, better able to carry it out. The supposed wealthier citizen either accepted to undertake the *liturgy* or had the right to renounce it. However, refusing to undertake, he was obliged to go to trial to prove that his property was less than that of the complainant.

A special court was appointed to resolve the case, which examined detailed lists of the assets of the two parties that they submitted to the court. During the trial process (it took place once a year) all the property of the two citizens was examined, such as estates, money, movable and immovable property, and even slaves, animals, etc. (Isocrates, *Antidosis*; Demosthenes, *Against Phaenippus*; Xenophon, *Oeconomicus*, 7.3; Gabrielsen 1994; Thorley 1996, 15, 43; Christ 2006; Ober 2008, 129–130; Lyttkens 2013, 112). Some scholars even doubt whether an actual exchange of property ever took place, although indisputable evidence about an *antidosis* case comes from Lysias (*On a Wound by Premeditation*, 4.1).

We assume that the *antidosis*, in addition to the beneficial consequences of revealing the real assets of taxpayers so that their taxation becomes as fair as possible, would also have a negative side effect: forcing an individual to enter into a process of possible exchange of his property (or even legal confrontation for this reason) could possibly create enmity and hatred between citizens, disrupting social cohesion and peace. However, as far as is known from the available ancient sources, there is no evidence of such a disruption of social relations due to *antidosis*.

Antidosis was therefore a way of indirectly revealing the real property status of wealthy citizens. When a citizen was obliged through the *antidosis* to exchange his property, and this was done on the basis of a court order, there was a social outcry and he was considered an *atimos* and a non-intact citizen.

Chapter 14
The Port of Piraeus, the Agora of Athens, and Their International Role in Commercial Affairs of the Times

Abstract This chapter deals with the variety of goods that foreign merchants could access at the Athenian market and the port of Piraeus (such as fabrics, pottery, and books). The fact that the port of Piraeus had become the international entrepôt of the Mediterranean made it possible for Athenian and foreign merchants to have direct access (through the ports of Piraeus and the Agora of Athens), to every product, from the well-known world of the time.

14.1 Xenocrates' Purchases from the Agora

Next morning, Nicomedes went with Xenocrates to Kerameikos, where the latter selected and bought some amphorae. Then they went to the shop of Pammenes, where Hegeso, accompanied by Chariclea, met them, and gave them her advice as to what jewels the women of the Iberians would like. Then Nicomedes hired a carriage for transferring the goods and themselves and they went down to Piraeus.

They arrived at the bustling port, with its fine promenade, and disembarked at the Hippodameian Agora. Nicomedes showed Xenocrates the bench of the *dokimastes* of Piraeus. Then, they went to the shop of Nicostratos, an acquaintance of Nicomedes. Nicostratos, after listening what they wanted, showed them the most beautiful fabrics, truly wonderful, both in color, especially that porphyr color, in different shades, and in patterns, from simple meanders to gold-embroidered flowers and dolphins.

Xenocrates eyed them carefully and took hold of them, having difficulty in choosing between such beautiful fabrics. Later, Nicostraros showed them still more rare and special fabrics, which according to various popular beliefs were woven by dragons in places unknown to most of the world.

Xenocrates touched them, as soft in texture as butterfly wings, so thin and yet so durable, and those in various patterns and colors. He asked the prices, extremely expensive; he did his calculations. Until then no one had imported such clothes into Iberia and he was sure he could sell them at double the price.

With Hegeso's help he made his choices. Hegeso took the opportunity to buy some clothes also for herself. Nicomedes sighed... As was her wont, she had chosen

E. M. L. Economou, N. C. Kyriazis, *Daily Life in Classical Athens*, Frontiers in Economic History, https://doi.org/10.1007/978-3-031-58541-8_14

among the most expensive fabrics.....but what he could do instead?.....He owed this to her. She was a good wife and excellent at managing their *oikos* when Nicomedes was absent, making sure spending was reasonable, never missing anything.

Nicostratos undertook to prepare the cloths, as they should be for the long journey, in special boxes of straw, tightly closed to protect them from the moisture of the sea on the journey. Delivery and payment would take place in 3 days, when Xenocrates' ship would be ready to sail.

They continued to Philocles' shop, which was next to Nicostratos'. Philocles showed them various spices, letting Xenocrates smell them, touch them, and explain their properties and uses, some for cooking, some for healing, some for both. Xenocrates placed his order. He also procured some papyri with poetical works for the more philosophic Iberians.

Lastly, he left for last Artemis' shop, the best for women's accessories. Artemis, with her two assistants, showed them combs of ivory and ebony, pins to fasten the robes, some of silver, some of gold, finely wrought and beautifully shaped, belts, various types of cloth, some with gold or silver decoration, ribbons for hair or clothing, and footwear according to the latest fashion styles. For the end she left the perfumes, an endless variety in elegant and beautifully decorated *aryballoi*, explaining again the origin of each one.

Xenocrates smelled them, enjoyed them, and finally, dizzy with so much fragrance and variety, he didn't know which to choose. Fortunately, Hegeso with her experience helped him and Xenocrates chose a variety of combs, pins, belts, shoes, and perfumes, agreeing on the prices, always with the mediation of Nicomedes who knew the real value of the products and wanted to protect Xenocrates from excessive prices.

They returned to Athens with Xenocrates being very satisfied.

- Nicomedes thank you! I am indebted to you! You helped me so much with all this...
- Don't mention it. My pleasure. Do you have everything you want?
- Yes, except for the marble and wine. I am thinking of loading marble for ballast. And some amphorae of wine, as you recommended, from Rhodes and Samos, for a supplement.

* * *

14.2 Pottery

The potters' workshops were located in the area of Kerameikos, on the extension of the Panathenaea road to the northwest. The continuation of the road led to Plato's Academy. There was the inner Kerameikos, within the walls of Themistocles and, after one passed the Dipylon gate, the outer Kerameikos. Attic pottery was famous as early as the sixth century and has been found from Iberia to present-day Ukraine and

Russia and the Caucasus, areas inhabited by Thracian and Scythian tribes. The Greeks had continuous trade relations with them.

14.3 Fabrics

The Athenians were not as conservative in their clothing as we think. Although they were not ostentatious, they did not neglect to care about their personal appearance. They had developed commercial transactions with many nations and city-states, coming into contact with new consumer habits and goods, for example, silk fabrics from the East. Regarding the porphyr fabrics, these were sought after and dyed by processing the shell *porphyra* from Phoenicia. Thus, we consider it reasonable that the merchants of porphyra cloths were Phoenician *metics*. Porphyr tunics were expensive and only the wealthy men or women could afford them. Alcibiades was known for wearing a porphyr robe and special shoes (Athenaeus, *The Deipnosophists*, 12.534c). From a passage of Aristophanes (*Wealth*, 980–983) we know the value of a *himation* (cloth), 20 drachmae, and shoes, 8 drachmae.

It is also known that the Phoenician merchants enjoyed a special privileged status as *metics*, because the Athenians, recognizing their importance, wanted to attract them. They were exempt from their special tax, the *metoikion*, and other obligations, possibly also from the obligation to serve in the army.

The goldsmith Pammenes that was referred in this Scene is a historical figure. Demosthenes (*Against Midias*, 21.22) provides us the following characteristic information regarding him:

> Pammenes, son of Pammenes, of Erchia, have a goldsmith's shop in the Agora, where I reside and carry on my business. When Demosthenes, for whom I am a witness, commissioned me to fashion a golden crown, and to make a gold-embroidered robe, that he might wear them at the procession in honor of Dionysus; and when I had completed them and had them ready by me, Meidias, who is being prosecuted by Demosthenes, broke into my premises by night, having also others with him, and tried to destroy the crown and the robe, and a part of them he injured, but was not able to destroy them completely, because I appeared and prevented him.

14.4 Books and Illiteracy

In Ancient Greece, books did not take the form known to us today, but rather were in the shape of rolls made out of papyrus. For papyrus (which gave its name to the words paper, papier, papel, etc.) the Greeks also used the word *biblos*. It was imported from Egypt. Books written on papyrus were already widespread in the late fifth century BCE. Athens, like Amsterdam in the seventeenth century AD, was the "heart" of the production and export of books throughout the Greek world. They were usually copied by slaves and were cheap. Socrates mentions that one could buy the works of Anaxagoras for a drachma at the most. The price of a book in the middle of the fifth century must not have been very high as Plato informs us (*Apology*, 26d) when explaining how Socrates acquired his education when he was young, in 430 BCE. This reference by Plato is also a response to some historians who claim that Socrates did not know how to read and write!

The demand for books is an indication that supports the view that the percentage of Athenians (and Greeks in general) who were able to read was high. The Athenians believed that in a literate society, democracy worked better, which is why laws, resolutions, etc. were written on stones in central places such as the Monument of the Eponymous Heroes for the agenda of the Assembly, etc., where everyone could see and read them. Therefore, the anecdote preserved by Plutarch (*Aristides*, 7–8) about the illiterate citizen who asked Aristides himself to write his name on a shell, for ostracism, probably shows that this was an exception to the rule. Of course, it is also a matter of interpretation, because those who argue that ancient Greek society as a whole had very primitive organizational structures, such as M. Finley and his supporters, would have every reason to interpret this incident as a sign of generalized illiteracy.

On the other hand, it has already been mentioned that in the markets of Athens and Piraeus a plethora of entrepreneurial activities was taking place, where a very large volume of buying and selling of products was taking place every day, non-stop, while services could even be offered at home, such as private *pedagogues* (teachers for educating children). It is also known that at least in these two organized markets in Athens and Piraeus, goods were exchanged through the mediation of money (drachmae, *obols*, *chalkoi*, *kollyboi*), and the mechanisms of supply and demand, even in a primitive form, operated normally.

Therefore, if a large part of the population was illiterate they could (i) not access the Agora for selling goods and services; (ii) access the Agora even if only for just buying goods and services, by risking the possibility of being fraud on a permanent basis; and (iii) not participate for practical reasons, in the proceedings of the Athenian Council, the Heliaia courts, or as a public official in any other public post, especially those that were related to economic matters. And it is known that every active citizen served in the public administration of the polis, at least once in his lifetime (Hansen 1991; Ober 2008).

So, would it be possible for someone who did not know how to read and write to be assigned with a duty in a public post that required reading and writing or participating in the economic transactions of the Agora?

Therefore, it is logical for one to believe that the very functioning of democracy made it imperative that the citizens, in principle, should know how to read and write, at least the basics; otherwise it would be almost impossible for them to participate in practice at the state's institutional bodies and undertake a public post. On the issue of the degree of illiteracy of the Athenians of the times, we get back in Sects. 20.2–20.4.

Chapter 15
Insurance Premium as an Institutional Mechanism of Promoting International Trade

Abstract In this chapter, the importance of insurance premium is analyzed as a mechanism of further promoting trade by providing a safeguard while performing international commercial transactions. This is an intertemporal institution that, in all likelihood, has its origins in Classical Greece and the Athenian state of the times, like the rest of the financial institutions already described in the previous chapters.

15.1 Nicomedes's Insurance Practices and Credit Sales

In the following days, Xenocrates completed the sale of his copper and finished with the last purchases of goods before his return trip to Emporion. He decided to deposit 300 drachmae in Nicomedes's bank.

Of course, over the years he had gained a lot of experience in buying and selling commodities for profit. Having suffered some bitter experiences in the past, he knew very well that his profession was characterized by high risk.

Ischomachos prepared the contract, Nicomedes and Xenocrates signed it, sealed it in the presence of witnesses, and Nicomedes gave him a copy of the agreement, keeping the second, to be stored in a special room at his *oikos*. He noticed that Xenocrates was very frowning and thoughtful.

– What is your concern, my dear partner? Nicomedes addressed him in a friendly way to make him feel more familiar, and continued:
– You can make your trip fearlessly and without worries. Your money is here, guaranteed, waiting for you at any time.
– Thank you very much Nicomedes. Everything is great, but, but. . .but. . .no. . .

Nicomedes realized that something serious was bothering Xenocrates. He decided to goad him into revealing what was going on.

– So Xenocrates, I have booked a meal for the three of us at Athenais, the best restaurant in Athens to celebrate our partnership. Because the demand in this restaurant is high, if we are late, we will lose our turn.

E. M. L. Economou, N. C. Kyriazis, *Daily Life in Classical Athens*, Frontiers in Economic History, https://doi.org/10.1007/978-3-031-58541-8_15

Xenocrates decided to speak to him. He was concerned with the issue of pirates, or any other unstable factor that might lead to the loss of the goods or even the ship itself, and he wished to "reduce the risk to a minimum" as he said to his sailors. So, he decided, after much hesitation, to ask Nicomedes if he would accept to insure his journey. He had some misgivings about requesting this because of the fear of risking the partnership he had already established with Nicomedes. Finally, albeit hesitantly, he addressed the request.

Nicomedes had liked and esteemed Xenocrates, perhaps also because he felt sympathy with a little compassion, for a middle-aged man from so far away, who was actually asking for his help and was in need.

Although there were many other bankers who specialized in insurance services, and Nicomedes could have referred him to one of them, to get rid of him, he decided to help him and after a while replied:

- So that's it! Take courage Xenocrates!

Xenocrates didn't quite understand and an expression of a mixture of wonder and anguish was painted on his face. He sweated on his face as well as on his hands.

Nicomedes encouraged Xenocrates, by promising him that he would undertake to insure his merchandise with a final destination to Emporion, and indeed at an interest rate, much lower than the average in the Agora.

Xenocrates recovered!

Nicomedes had also learned something else, all these years through his work: He knew that the main elements of success were *pistis* (trust) and fame. Nicomedes saw beyond ephemeral, short-term gains. He knew that if Xenocrates came back to Emporion, he would glorify the honesty and hospitality of him; therefore, when other merchants from his city would come to Athens, the logic would be to trust Nicomedes, who served their fellow citizens in the best way. Conversely, if Xenocrates was not pleased, he would spread bad news about Nicomedes's services. And bad news "spread like a noisy hive that wants to attack anyone who wants to destroy its nest," as Nicomedes used to say.

- Calm down Xenocrates, don't be afraid, Ischomachos intervened. Our polis is a pioneer in banking services and in general, in what I call 'commercial credit services'. If you also sign the insurance premium, you won't have to worry about anything later. We'll cover you.
- So it is, added Nicomedes. In order you to realize how far commercial credit and the protection of contracts has advanced in our polis, I will describe to you a transaction I made this morning, before I came here. My daughter Eriphyle has been driving me nuts for some days now and she wants me to buy her a very specific red veil from a dress shop in Piraeus, owned by a certain Artemis. She has literally swelled me up! So today, I couldn't take this anymore and decided to go buy it and gift it to her in a few days for her birthday. I will surprise her. Do you want to hear the rest? Nicomedes asked to see if they were interested with the story.
- Go on please, asked Xenocrates.

– The veil, because it was of very high quality and had prosthetics, stitched pictorial representations and various other things, cost me quite a lot, twenty drachmae!
– Twenty drachmae! For a veil! ... Your daughter is very spoiled boss, Ischomachos scoffed at Nicomedes.
– Don't interrupt me Ischomachos!... After hearing the price, I admit that I decided to leave, but then the owner of the shop suggested the following: to pay what I could at that moment, and because she trusted me as a respectable citizen of Athens, she proposed to sign a contract, that she was about to finance my purchase with a small interest. And that's really happened. I paid her 10 drachmae that I had with me at that moment, and she gave me a 'purchase loan' of 10 drachmae. So, we both won: I did my job, and she didn't lose the customer.
– How far ahead is your economy Nicomedes! Xenocrates admitted, and an expression of admiration came over his face.
– That's why I tell you, don't be afraid. You will also sign the insurance premium and, after this, you will be fully covered.
– Okay, so you've convinced me.
– Allow me, Xenocrates, to provide you with a lunch. Let's join Athenais, the most famous *kapeleion* of the Agora of Athens, which has a wide selection of food and above all, amazing wines, from Chios, Mende in the coastal Halkidiki, Corinth, Samos, Rhodes and Lesvos.
– I am very happy! replied Xenocrates.

It was the best development for him, because he would have the entire afternoon free to meet with the Phoenician captain and his ship's sailors for a final inspection of the goods he had purchased with the help of Nicomedes, before the return voyage to Emporion, through intermediate stops of course in various coastal cities.

– The contracts will be prepared for us by Ischomachos while we are having lunch, and then we will come to sign them.
– Nicomedes I am indebted to you for everything! I hope this is the beginning of a long series of commercial cooperation between the two of us.
– Brilliant! replied Nicomedes.

After the lunch and as soon as Xenocrates had taken from the hands of Ischomachos the second papyrus with the copy of the insurance premium, he addressed Nicomedes and said to him:

– After this development, I am full of joy!

After this, Nicomedes left the bench where his bank was housed in the Agora. Ischomachos would take the day's cash to Nicomedes' *oikos* as the latter trusted him. Nicomedes remained at the Agora so as to meet some friends, in order to socialize for various issues regarding the polis.

* * *

15.2 Insurance and Interest Rates

As has already become clear, the entrepreneurship of the Athenians was heavily relying on maritime trade. There were rich Athenians who lent their money in return for some interest rate. These sums of money were used by merchants or shipowners who traded goods. The lenders who lent their money, for interest, indirectly shared in the risks of the ship's loss and cargo's destruction (Demosthenes, *Against Dionysodorus*, 56.22, 56.32). Such a partnership was usually made under a written agreement, the terms of which were not imposed by the polis, but were voluntarily agreed upon by the parties, and the polis only offered judicial services in case parties were driven to serious disagreements.

Almost all maritime loans included insurance in favor of those carrying out the commercial activity, against interest. As already mentioned, borrowers generally paid interest rates of 12–18% and more rarely as high as 36%. But this did not apply to maritime loans. For these, the lenders charged a much higher interest rate, from 15 to 35% and, rarely, depending on the degree of risk of a trip up to 100%! (transportation of cargo with return of the ship or without return, etc.) The high cost of borrowing through a loan with interest rate was probably related to the high risk of these loans, for example, a voyage where the ship might suffer a pirate attack or encounter rough seas or catch a fire and get sunk with the risk of losing the cargo. Of course, the total cost of borrowing for maritime trade was made even higher due to the additional cost of insurance (Isocrates, *Trapeziticus*, 17.35).

15.3 Credit Sales

How developed the Athenian financial system was can also be seen from the fact that the Athenians, first in recorded history, implemented the commercial policy known internationally nowadays as *credit sales*, which means selling a product in which the buyer uses credit (he immediately gets the product but pays in the future). As Cohen (1992, 14) analyzes with various examples, the practice of credit sales was very widespread at the times. He explains that credit sales were freely possible, especially by taking into account that would recognize whatever arrangements private parties agreed upon. For example, Cohen (p. 14) refers to Lycurgus (*Against Leochares*, 1.23) where it is revealed that a seller of slaves with the name Amyntas sold a number of slaves to Timochares and the latter because he could pay in cash; he reverted to a banker with the name Lysicles, who financed his purchase, by lending him 3500 drachmae, but with a very high interest rate, 34%.

15.4 The *Kapeleia*

The imaginary *kapeleion* (tavern) called Athenais was located in the Agora. Some of them were near the Acropolis, like Athenais in our own story. The first examples of a Greek restaurant or tavern were discovered in the Ancient Agora of Athens during archaeological excavations conducted by the American School of Classical Studies at Athens (ASCSA) in the early 1970s. Large quantities of food utensils were found at the Agora, such as for roasting meat, fish, and chickens, revealing the specialties of the Classical Greek tavern menus, such as oysters, mussels, shells, and large fish. A nearby wine shop in the Athenian Agora, possibly in conjunction with the tavern, served local Attic wine, as well as a wide variety of wines imported from Chios, Mende (in Chalcidice), Corinth, Samos, and Lesbos.

In Athens, there were lots of neighborhood taverns which served their customers from the evening till late night hours. Various social groups accessed them without restrictions: workers and craftsmen tired from work, to enjoy a few hours of relaxation, shopkeepers from the Agora, owners of *ergasteria* (workshops) that were scattered in Athens and Piraeus, women, *metics*, and slaves. Important research on these had been carried out by Davidson (1997).

The idea of taverns spreads from Greece to Rome and throughout Europe. It would perhaps not be an exaggeration to argue that alongside the popular Assembly and the other public posts, as well as the theater and the Agora, taverns contributed significantly to a process of further social networking between the residents of the polis (citizens and non-citizens) and foreigners (merchants and non-merchants). Ancient Greek taverns acted as mechanisms of social networking, like today's taverns, bars, and pubs to countries like the USA, the UK, Ireland, France, Italy, etc.

Chapter 16
Ancient Greek Merchant Marine and International Commercial Routes

Abstract This chapter describes various technical parameters of the ancient Greek merchant ships. It also provides information related to the naval routes of the Greek commercial cities of the Mediterranean.

16.1 Xenocrates Prepares His Return Trip to Emporion

Before Xenocrates left for his inn, after the meal given in his honor by Nicomedes, he was still possessed by anxiety.

His concern came from the fact that he had to properly organize the return trip. The voyage was objectively fraught with danger: a rough sea could sink crew and cargo, or a raid by Phoenician or Carthaginian pirates was the most feared potential problem. Of course, Xenocrates would be taking a "calculated risk": after loading goods from Piraeus, the ship would also make a quick stop briefly at Corinth. The commercial center of Corinth was always known to compete with that of Athens and, as the historian Thucydides had explained, the economic-commercial competition of Athens with Corinth was a key reason that caused the genocide among the Greeks during the Peloponnesian War. Xenocrates wanted to visit briefly Corinth's market as well, and if he found a good deal on a product, he would buy it. Xenocrates's "golden rule," dictated by his previous 25 years of trade experience, was to seek to buy high-quality products, at the lowest possible prices (to save money). Ideally these products should have a high potential of profit from selling them to his customers, back at Emporion.

The ship, in which he was not the sole shareholder, since it was co-owned by three other Greek merchants from Emporion, with whom he had formed a joint stock company, after Corinth, would take an almost direct course to Sicily, with small stops for small purchases in the cities of Sybaris, Croton, and of course the famous Syracuse, as large city in population and a splendor "cosmopolis," as were Athens, Sparta, and Miletus. Their ship would finally reach Akragas. Then the ship would leave Sicily and move to the island of Corsis, or Cyrnos or Calliste as was also known, to the coastal city Alalie, which the Greek colonizers from Phocaea from Asia Minor had built about two centuries ago. Next, the ship would go south,

E. M. L. Economou, N. C. Kyriazis, *Daily Life in Classical Athens*, Frontiers in Economic History, https://doi.org/10.1007/978-3-031-58541-8_16

circumnavigate south of Corsis, and then climb up to find the city of Haiakeion, which legend said was founded by the legendary hero of the Trojan War, Aias of Telamon from Salamis. The penultimate stop would be the famous Massalia, being founded by Greek colonizers from Phocaea about two and a half centuries ago, which had developed into a large commercial center. There Xenocrates would make his final purchases before heading to his final destination, Emporion.

As to the rough sea, Xenocrates had taken his measures. He had hired an experienced captain, a Phoenician named Ahinadab, originally from Carthage. The able Phoenician captain brought them safely from Emporion to Athens with stops in between. As for a potential pirate attack, if it did happen, Nicomedes' insurance contract would do its job perfectly and Xenocrates would be compensated by Nicomedes's bank.

He met with Ahinadab and his sailors and discussed the technicalities of the return voyage. He had plenty of time to spare until night when he would look for Ambrosia's companion, a *hetaera*, after a long walk to the ports of Piraeus.

He made his way through the port of Kantharos, one of the three ports of Piraeus, the others being Kantharos, Zea, and Munichia, which hosted *neosoikoi*. On Kantharos there were 94 *neosoikoi*, on Zea 196, and on Munichia 82. There were of course also a large number of fishing boats and merchant ships. Xenocrates carefully observed the multitude of different types of ships as well as the majestic war *triremes*. When he arrived at Kantharos, passing all the *triremes*, one by one arrayed, he felt awe and a thrill that he could not explain, since he was not an Athenian. He felt the need to sing softly an old patriotic song from his hometown.

Then, when it was almost dark, he made his way back and finally sat down at a small seaside tavern overlooking the harbor of Kantharos, the sea, and the almost full moon. It was an early autumn, early night, and at that moment a cool breeze was blowing, which made the atmosphere very pleasant. He ordered a goblet of wine from Chios, for he liked the taste of it very much, as he remembered it from the feast of Nicomedes.

Drinking, he relaxed and reminisced about his many sea journeys and endeavors of the past.

He would then go to rest for an hour at an inn in Piraeus. He had stayed for three nights as a guest at Nicomedes' *oikos*, and then he took care to choose one of the inns near the port of Piraeus, so that he might at all times be near his ship which was moored in the port of Piraeus.

He was planning to stay in that inn with a female companion, such as those *hetaerae* he had seen, not far down the road from the inn.

He had seen a *hetaera*, tall, with curling auburn hair and expressive sparkling green eyes, who made a great impression on him and who he learned, apparently by accident, that her name was Ambrosia and that she came from Corinth.

He also wanted, a simple man, a merchant from afar, with human weaknesses, although on a moderate basis, to enjoy Ambrosia, just like the Olympian Gods, this night in Athens!

He believed that if he tasted Ambrosia and drank nectar that night, in the next 2 days he would be sufficiently refreshed for the journey back to Emporion, with stops in between.

* * *

16.2 Shipbuilding

Merchant ships of the period had a displacement from a few tons (like modern boats) to a few hundred. At the time of Nicomedes, a merchant ship of average carrying capacity weighed about 400 tons, while in the Hellenistic period ships' displacement reached up to 500 tons. The Greeks had developed ways to calculate the exact weight of each merchandise that was placed inside the ship. Cargo could be categorized into either heavy or light cargo.

A merchant ship could move either through its oars or through its sails. It could reach about 5 knots, considerably less than the 9 knots or so that a *trireme* could reach if it was moving, "at full speed." *Trireme* warships had a displacement of 50 tons. The largest known ship of the fourth century, built by Dionysius I of Syracuse, had a displacement of 2000 tons[1] as part of his major shipbuilding program against the Carthaginians. These warships were called *quinqueremes* and Dionysius started building them from 399 BCE. Moreover, it is also known that the largest merchant ship and "cruiser" of antiquity, the famous Syracusia designed by Archimedes, was built in Syracuse in 240 BCE.

Cargo ships were more curved in shape than warships and wider, while their wooden construction was thicker and more durable. According to Thucydides (2.91) these ships did not need to be towed ashore, as was happening with warships, but instead, they were tied up in the harbor or anchored in the bay.

For sailing they had a large square sail, while two rudders—oars at the stern—served as a steering wheel. The crew was much smaller in number than the warships. Several of them were called *olkades*, a word which derives from the verb *elko*, which means tow because they often needed to be towed by other ships. These ships carried both dry cargo (wheat, timber, and metals) and liquid (wine, oil, water). There were ships that carried only one product entirely. One such category was the so-called *sitagoga* ships which carried only wheat.

Another modern practice that the ancient Greeks introduced was what nowadays is known as *load lines*, that is, the calculation of the point up to which the ship was allowed to be loaded, because exceeding this created risk of inflow of water or even capsize (Image 16.1).

The life span of cargo ships seems to have been much higher than that of warships. Evidence for this is provided, as per example, through the famous Kyrenia ship wreckage. In November 1965, a 14 m long fourth-century BCE Greek merchant ship wreckage was found close to Keryneia (Kyrenia) in Cyprus. It is believed that the ship sailed in the Mediterranean during the lifetime of Alexander the Great and his successors and it sunk sometime after 294 BCE. Experts have found that the ship was used for around 80 years (which implies a long-term endurance of this type of ship in being exposed to the sea) and they assume that it was owned by a family of shipowners (*naukleroi*). They assume that its trading route was Samos—Kos—

[1] That is, as much as a large Fletcher or Kagero class destroyer of the Second World War, or a *ship of the line* of the third series (60–74 guns) of the seventeenth century AD.

Image 16.1 Representation of a type of a merchant ship of the Classical period. Source: Image created by Vasiliki Demopoulou

Rhodes—Cyprus, and probably no more than four sailors were needed for each journey. It carried more than 400 amphorae as a cargo.[2]

16.3 Greek Commercial Cities of the Mediterranean

Fictional Xenocrates' hometown, Emporion, corresponds in Catalan to Empúries and in Spanish to Ampurias. It was founded in 575 BCE, by Greek settlers from Phokaia and Massalia (Marseilles, in present-day France).

Sybaris and Croton are located in what is now Southern Italy. Sybaris was founded in 720 BCE by Greeks from Achaea and Troezen and became an important city-state of Magna Graecia in today's South Italy.

Croton (today's Crotone) was founded around 710 BCE from Achaeans (Peloponnese). From Croton was also the famous wrestler Milo, son of Diotimos, who was crowned in six Olympiads, five times in the men's category and once in the children's category. He also won the equally important Pythian contests seven times and many other important ones. His life was surrounded by stories that touched the realm of myth.

Catane (today's Catania) is located in Sicily. It was founded in 729 by Greek settlers, from the neighboring Greek colony of Naxos, which had also been founded

[2]https://www.hellenicaworld.com/Greece/Technology/en/Ships.html

Image 16.2 A replica of the mythical Argo, docked at the port of Volos, Greece. Source: Image owned by the authors

a little earlier. Today it is the second most populous city in Sicily, with the first being Palermo (ancient Greek Panormos).

Alalie (todays Aléria) is located in what is now Central-Eastern Corsica and is a part of France, in the Haute-Corse region. Haiakeion, on the other hand, is located in Central-Western Corsica, coinciding with the well-known city of Ajaccio. As mentioned in the Scene, Corsica in ancient times was named as Corsis, Cyrnos, or Calliste.

The famous Massalia, today's Marseille in the South of France, was an important hub port from ancient times to the present. It is the most important port city in France and the third most important (as a port) in Europe nowadays. It was founded by Greek Phokaians around 600 BCE, with the exact date of foundation being unknown. It was one of the cities that most enthusiastically welcomed the French Revolution in 1792, sending many soldiers to Paris.

The great ancient Greek merchant, explorer, and geographer Pytheas (380–310 BCE) who conducted the voyage to Ultima Thule (to find the mythical Hyperborea) started from Marseilles, passing the Gates of Heracles, today's Gibraltar, the Atlantic, reaching the Cassiterides Islands (meaning "tin islands," today's South England, from where the Minoans and the Mycenaeans brought tin to Greece according to the mythical tradition) reaching perhaps as far as the Baltic, and to today's Iceland (Image 16.2).

After all, seamanship and naval tradition went hand in hand with the developments that took place in the geographical areas where the Greek civilization had progressively flourished through the passage of time. For example, the Minoans during the 2000–1350 BCE period had emerged as perhaps the first ever maritime power in recorded history, since it ruled both the Aegean and the East Mediterranean seas, respectively.

Even if this situation, mostly known as the "Minoan thalassocracy," is doubted by some authors, what cannot be denied are the strong bonds of the Greeks with the sea culture from the very ancient times even to the present. As of 2020, Greece was the largest shipowner country in the world with a total deadweight tonnage of 364 million tons and 4901 Greek-owned vessels.

Chapter 17
High Cost Made Eternal Athenian Monuments as a Sign of Economic Power

Abstract This small chapter describes the last preparations for a long-distance return merchant trip to its original destination. It also describes some important monuments, which indirectly indicate the great economic power of the states that launched their construction, such as the Athena Parthenos on the Acropolis and the Temple of Olympian Zeus, in the center of Athens.

17.1 Return to Emporion, Under the Auspices of Goddess Athena and Zeus

Xenocrates woke up late that day. The sun was well up when he rose from his bed. But he excused himself as next morning, almost at dawn, he would set sail for the return voyage, and he thought he should invest his time in resting to have enough strength for the return. After all, he wasn't young anymore, and he should manage his time more rationally and cautiously every day.

He had a quick breakfast, which was served to him by a maid of the inn and went down to greet the sailors of his ship who all these days were staying in a nearby but poorer inn. They were already on the ship, performing some last checks, and teasing each other, waiting for their boss.

The fact that the time had indeed passed was also certified by the sundial that was located a little further down, near a fountain.

Xenocrates told them that he would go to the Agora of Athens for a while and return in the afternoon to meet them again.

He wanted to greet Nicomedes one last time, but he also wanted help for the last time.

He found both him and Ischomachos talking to a customer. Ischomachos was willing to help him since Nicomedes could not at that moment speak with him.

– Ischomachos, I would like, before I leave for Emporion, to pray for having a good trip. I will go again to the beautiful and famous Temple of Athena on the Acropolis, to worship her majestic golden ivory statue.
– This is a very well act, replied Ischomachos.

E. M. L. Economou, N. C. Kyriazis, *Daily Life in Classical Athens*, Frontiers in Economic History, https://doi.org/10.1007/978-3-031-58541-8_17

– I also wanted to go to Eleusis to pray at the Temple of Goddess Demeter, but, with the obligations that arose, I could not make it, Xenocrates muttered, in a manner that suggested regret.
– Come on my friend, I don't want to see you like this! Ischomachos replied. Why don't you stay a day or two more to go and worship them? It is an act that I believe every godly person should do.
– Ischomachos, you are not at all wrong. But if I do as you suggest, my goods will be delivered to the intermediate stops, finally Emporion, with a delay, which I definitely want to avoid, because I have promised deliveries on certain dates, and if I am not strict with this, I will appear inconsistent to my customers. So, I will go to worship at the Temple of the Olympian Zeus instead. Thus, I will have with me both the blessing of the father of the gods and the patroness of the city of Athens. So, I hope to have a good journey, even if I did not manage to go either to Eleusis or to Sounion, to worship Poseidon, the god of sailors.
– Everything will be fine Xenocrates, don't worry intervened Nicomedes, who had just finished his cooperation with his client. You will come back to us soon.
– I hope so Nicomedes, replied Xenocrates, with a sense of melancholy, and continued:
– Who knows, will I have a good trip?
– You will have an excellent trip! My insurance premium will also accompany you.
– Thank you Nicomedes, you make me feel better. So, farewell!
– See you again, said Nicomedes.

Ischomachos spontaneously responded: – Xenocrates, when you come back to us from Emporion, bring us some local delicacies so that I can get to know your cuisine.

– Nicomedes squinted at him, and then addressed Xenocrates in a low voice: This man has all his brains in food! Don't you see how fat he is? He is like a five-month pregnant!

Xenocrates laughed.

– I heard what you said boss! Better not answer you boss! Ischomachos responded.
– This is the best thing you should do! replied Nicomedes.

* * *

17.2 High Cost Made Eternal Athenian Monuments

The chryselephantine statue of Athena Parthenos on the Acropolis was a sculptural work of art made by the famous sculptor, painter, and architect, Pheidias, a friend of Pericles. It was the most recognizable cult statue of ancient Athens and one of the greatest achievements of a sculptor in the ancient times at a global level. It is noteworthy that the works of Pheidias were made under the so-called *golden ratio* perspective, a highly sophisticated mathematical rule expressed with a special number approximately equal to 1618 and the Greek letter φ. It appears many times in geometry, art, architecture, and other areas.

Mario Livio (2002), an Israeli-American astrophysicist in his book: *The Golden Ratio: The Story of Phi, the World's Most Astonishing Number*, writes the following on this:

> Some of the greatest mathematical minds of all ages, from Pythagoras and Euclid in ancient Greece, through the medieval Italian mathematician Leonardo of Pisa and the Renaissance astronomer Johannes Kepler, to present-day scientific figures such as Oxford physicist Roger Penrose, have spent endless hours over this simple ratio and its properties. ... Biologists, artists, musicians, historians, architects, psychologists, and even mystics have pondered and debated the basis of its ubiquity and appeal. In fact, it is probably fair to say that the Golden Ratio has inspired thinkers of all disciplines like no other number in the history of mathematics.

According to the testimonies of Pausanias in his *Description of Greece*, Athena Parthenos stood upright. She was about 12 m tall. The naked parts of the goddess's body were made of ivory, while her clothing was made of gold. She was dressed in a long tunic down to her feet. She wore sandals, which were decorated with reliefs depicting the battle of the Lapiths and Centaurs.

On her head she wore a helmet decorated with a sphinx and two griffins. She held a winged victory in one hand, and rested the other on her shield, holding a spear decorated with a dragon. On the shield there were reliefs depicting Amazonomachy on the inner side, the mythological battle between the ancient Greeks and the Amazons, and Gigantomachy, a representation of battles between the Olympian gods and Giants in antiquity.[1] At the base of the statue there was a relief depicting the birth of Pandora. The statue was depicted on coins, miniature statues, votive objects, and in representations on engraved ornaments. According to Andreades (1933, 234) the Parthenon cost 700 *talents* and the Chryselephantine Athena, 1000. Modern research estimates the final cost of the Parthenon temple to have been about 470 *talents* (Samons 1993, 137; Migeotte 2009, 108).

The enormous amount of gold that was needed to invest/dress this amazing statue of Goddess Athena gave rise to Pericles' enemies to accuse Pheidias of abuse, in the hope that by tarnishing this immortal work of him, they would also hurt Pericles politically. Pheidias proved his innocence because Pericles had advised him to make Athena's golden garment assembled. So, he was able to disassemble it and weigh it, after the charges against him. The weight of gold was found intact. But still Pheidias was accused of arrogance, because he had immortalized himself and Pericles by giving their form to two corresponding characters in the battle scene that decorated

[1] Snell (1982, 35) writes characteristically:

> For the Greeks, the Titanomachy and the battle against the giants remained symbols of the victory which their own world had won over a strange universe; along with the battles against the Amazons and Centaurs they continue to signalize the Greek conquest of everything barbarous, of all monstrosity and grossness.

Image 17.1 Temple of Olympian Zeus (Acropolis in the font). Source: Image owned by the authors

Athena's shield. Pheidias was finally arrested and sentenced. These events are narrated by Plutarch (*Pericles*, 31.2–5).[2]

The Temple of Olympian Zeus, or Olympieion, was an important ancient temple in the center of Athens. Although its construction began in the sixth century BCE, it was not completed until the time of the Roman Emperor Hadrian in the second century AD. It included 104 colossal columns. Designed by the architects Antistates, Callaeschrus, Antimachides, and Phormos, the Temple of Olympian Zeus was intended to be built of local limestone in the Doric style on a colossal platform measuring 41 m by 108 m (Image 17.1). It was to be flanked by a double colonnade of 8 columns across the front and back and 21 on the flanks, surrounding the cella. It was the largest temple in Greece during the Hellenistic and Roman times. Pausanias (1.18.6–9) describes the temple as it was in the second century BCE:

> Before the entrance to the sanctuary of Olympian Zeus—Hadrian the Roman emperor dedicated the temple and the statue, one worth seeing, which in size exceeds all other statues save the colossi at Rhodes and Rome, and is made of ivory and gold with an artistic skill which is remarkable when the size is taken into account—before the entrance, I say, stand statues of Hadrian, two of Thasian stone, two of Egyptian. Before the pillars stand bronze statues which the Athenians call 'colonies.' The whole circumference of the precincts is about four stades, and they are full of statues; for every city has dedicated a likeness of the

[2]One version of his death is that he died in prison. But Philochorus (*Atthis fragments*, 121]) provides us with a different story: He did not die in Athens, but in Elis where he was exiled. There he made the great statue of Zeus for the Eleans but was afterward put to death by them.

> emperor Hadrian, and the Athenians have surpassed them in dedicating, behind the temple, the remarkable colossus. Within the precincts are antiquities: a bronze Zeus, a temple of Cronus and Rhea and an enclosure of Earth surnamed Olympian. Here the floor opens to the width of a cubit, and they say that along this bed flowed off the water after the deluge that occurred in the time of Deucalion, and into it they cast every year wheat meal mixed with honey. . . .. There are also statues in Phrygian marble of Persians supporting a bronze tripod; both the figures and the tripod are worth seeing. The ancient sanctuary of Olympian Zeus the Athenians say was built by Deucalion, and they cite as evidence that Deucalion lived at Athens a grave which is not far from the present temple. Hadrian constructed other buildings also for the Athenians: a temple of Hera and Zeus Panellenios Common to all Greeks, a sanctuary common to all the gods, and, most famous of all, a hundred pillars of Phrygian marble. . .

To ensure that such works of high religious and cultural value would be manufactured in the optimal possible way, the Athenians had established a three-member committee to oversee their construction. One was in charge of finding the right workers and materials, another responsible for the architecture and engineering of the building, and the third for the artistic decoration of the monument.

It is worthy to be mentioned that an important event took place in the Temple of Olympian Zeus in July 13, 1993, when the famous composer, Vangelis, staged his choral symphony Mythodea, a magnificent music masterpiece, ordered by NASA for its mission in 2001 in Mars.[3]

It is worth mentioning also the view of Lucius Aemilius Paullus Macedonicus (c. 229–160 BCE) regarding the statue of Zeus when he visited it at Olympia (not the one in Athens, described above) (Image 17.2). Lucius was a Roman Republic general, who conquered Macedon in the Third Macedonian War (171–168). Polybius (30.10) narrates:

> Aemilius entered the sacred enclosure at Olympia and was struck with admiration at the statue of the god, remarking that, to his mind, Pheidias was the only artist who had represented the Zeus of Homer; and that, though he had had great expectations of Olympia, he found the reality far surpassed them.

It is beyond certain that such colossal projects imply a great technological specialization, accompanied by great fiscal costs that can only be undertaken by societies that, at least during the period of their construction, are characterized as wealthy, that is, having achieved economic growth as the Greek one of the times.[4] Only rich societies can afford building works such as the Hanging Gardens of Babylon, the Parthenon in Acropolis at Athens, the Statue of Zeus (Olympia), the

[3] See and hear this splendid symphony through the following link: https://www.youtube.com/watch?v=NSenxpUxvpU

[4] As a proof that economic growth had been achieved, throughout Greece at the times, see again the citations of ftn 8 in Sect. 2.6.

Image 17.2 The famous statue of Zeus in Olympia. Painting made by Quatremère de Quincy. Source: https://commons.wikimedia.org/wiki/File:Le_Jupiter_Olympien_ou_l%27art_de_la_sculpture_antique_1.jpg

Temple of Artemisia in Ephesus and the Mausoleum of Halicarnassus (both in today's western Turkey), the Colossus of Rhodes, the Pharos (Lighthouse) of Alexandria (today's Egypt), the Colosseum (Rome), the Hagia Sophia (Constantinople), the Taj Mahal (India), the Eiffel Tower (France), the Neuschwanstein Castle (Bavaria), and the Statue of Liberty (USA).

Chapter 18
Managing the Athenian State Finances

Abstract This chapter explains the basic logic behind the fiscal expansionary programs (of Keynesian inspiration—one might say, under a modern perspective) that were introduced by the Athenian politicians Eubulus and Lycurgus between 350–s320s BCE that proved very successful and led to the impressive recovery of the Athenian economy of the times, after the recession that followed the Social War of 357–355 BCE. It further explains how the Athenian public finances were determined, based on a sophisticated package of institutions, which, in the end, secured their success.

18.1 A Symposion with Lycurgus for the Welfare of Society and the Polis

Lycurgus was constantly elected, because of his merit and knowledge, to one of the most important state posts, that of the *epimeletes tis koines prosodou* who supervised all the state's *tamiai*.[1] The one who served this post was selected by an appointment instead of being elected since the post required special skills.

Nicomedes planned for days to seek out and speak to Lycurgus. He left Ischomachos at the bank and walked to the building that housed Lycurgus' office to meet him. He found him working as usual with the help of his assistants in overseeing the management of the polis's finances. He asked him when he would like to hold a symposion in his honor, and they agreed on a certain evening.

Lycurgus wanted to talk to prominent citizens to develop his plan for the economic recovery of the polis, and the symposion in the Nicomedes *oikos's* was a good opportunity to prepare them. They discussed and agreed on the guest list.

He arrived in the evening at the ninth hour. Nicomedes received his guests, Lycurgus and seven other prominent Athenians, friends, and business partners.

[1]Treasurers in the treasury-temples of Athena and the Other Gods, as well as every other treasury of the polis. See further in Sect. 18.7.

E. M. L. Economou, N. C. Kyriazis, *Daily Life in Classical Athens*, Frontiers in Economic History, https://doi.org/10.1007/978-3-031-58541-8_18

Chariclea had prepared the couches and small tables in the *andron*, and Nicomedes called them to take their seats.

Nicomedes began the symposion with the formal invocation of the *agathodaemon*, and the *syndaitymones*, the symposion colleagues, drank from the *kylikes* few drops of wine. Then three *spondai*[2] followed: to Olympian Zeus and the other Gods and Goddesses, to the Athenian heroes and again to Zeus, now as Zeus Soter,[3] while they also sang a short hymn to the gods. Then they rolled dice to determine the *symposiarch*.[4] Fortune chose Lycurgus himself, and Nicomedes commented:

– May, *tyche,*[5] Lycurgus, be kind to all your works!
– Our works, my friends, replied Lycurgus.

Lycurgus undertook the main task of the *symposiarch*, mixing the wine with water in the *krater*, then pouring it into the cooler to keep it cool. Ischomachos poured a quantity from the cooler to an *oenochoe*[6] and served the guests on their *kylikes*, while he also placed an *hydria*[7] on one of the tables.

Chariclea brought the first dish, grilled eel from lake Copais with olive oil and thyme. Nicomedes did not like eel, but he had preferred it as a first course, as it was considered very fine, and he knew that his friends liked it. They ate it with bread, drinking wine, praising both.

The orator Demades asked:

– I don't think I've ever tasted such a wine. Where is it from?
– It is a new wine, from Thera,[8] replied Nicomedes.
– Its special taste is due to the volcanic soil of the island.

Chariclea brought the second dish, prepared by the women of the *oikos*, according to a recipe of Hegeso: roast pork, spread with honey, chestnuts, apples, raisins, and dried figs, quenched with red wine accompanied by mushrooms and chives. The smell was pleasant and the taste equally so. Aeschines, the orator, who appreciated good food, said:

– Nicomedes, please pass my congratulations to your wife. It is exquisite!
– Thank you Aeschines. I will do it. But now I think we should give the floor to Lycurgus, to develop his plans for us.
– Thank you Nicomedes. My friends, I want to unfold to you my plans for the recovery of our city and its economy. I will need your comments, and then, if you

---

[2] Libations.

[3] Zeus Savior.

[4] The "master" of the symposion.

[5] Fortune.

[6] Wine jug.

[7] Pitcher.

[8] Santorine.

agree, help me "prepare" in advance the opinion of the Athenians, before I bring the proposal to a vote in the popular Assembly.

– We listen to you carefully, said general Phocion, the oldest of the company.
– I want to continue the period of peace in Athens, so that our polis fully recovers from the last war and the disaster of Chaeronea. We need a long period of peace to improve our economy, to make Athens strong as before. I wish to propose that the Assembly adopts a program like that of my predecessor Eubulus, after the war with the allies. As you know, he restored the economy, raising the public revenues from a low of 120 *talents* at the end of the war to 400. I want to surpass him.

Lycurgus tasted some wine.

– And how will you achieve this? asked the banker Apollodorus.
– And how will you convince the Athenians? added Polycles.
– The two are connected, continued Lycurgus. My plan will succeed if I convince the majority of the citizens. I need the vote of the *thetes* of course, they are the most numerous. You must have thought why *thetes* are so warmongering.
– Of course, said Aeschines, with the cynicism that distinguished him. Out of patriotism and interest. Self-interest, when it wears the cloak of love for the motherland, is powerful.
– And why is it in their interest to be pro-war? inquired the goldsmith Pammenes, who had not followed the reasoning of Aeschines.
– Who rows the ships? he was helped by Aeschines.
– The *thetes*, replied Pammenes.
– And they get paid for it. Pretty good. So, they make a living. With relatively small risk due to the superiority of our navy, Aeschines continued.
– That's right, agreed Phocion. Throughout the war against the Allies, our naval losses were relatively small. Smaller than the losses of our army.
– And in the recent war with the Macedonians, at the 3 years of the war at sea, we practically had no losses, since the Macedonians did not have a significant navy, and they did not confront us at sea.
– Unlike our thousand dead *hoplites* in Chaeronea, Nicomedes added. But let's let Lycurgus continue.
– I want to continue my policy, with a compromise, among the citizens of the polis, which will be in everyone's interest. Peace, which will relieve the rich from the excessive burdens of the *trierarchies*, the middle-class soldiers, the *hoplites*, from the perils of war on land, and will satisfy the *thetes* by providing them with an alternative source of employment and income.

I will increase the *theorica* and *ecclesiastica*. But this is not enough: we will begin a great program of public works: to dress the Theater of Dionysus in marble. To repair the temples on the Acropolis and the public buildings in the market. To improve the sewage system in Athens and Piraeus. To improve the road network to Eleusis, Mesogeia, Marathon, Sounion, Rhamnous, Phyle, and Eleutherai. To build inns for foreign merchants arriving at Piraeus, as Xenophon suggested. To repair the forts on the northern border. Such public works would provide employment and wages to the *thetes* for many years, replacing the wages they would have received as oarsmen on the *triremes*.

Lycurgus fell silent, drank some wine before continuing. Apollodorus caught up to him before he continued:

- And the funding?
- The funding of course!, replied Lycurgus. As Demosthenes says, we need money, lots of money, without it nothing can be done. I may disagree with Demosthenes on a lot of issues, but I totally agree on the last one: Money!

He paused, while Polycles poured wine into his *kylix* from the *oenochoe*.

- Peace will increase public revenues. Without war and uncertainty, trade in Piraeus will increase, and so will *pentecoste* revenues. The second source of public revenues will be of course the taxes the state receives from the exploitation of the Laurion's silver mines. The third source will be you my friends, and the richest Athenians, if you agree. I will defend my policy, the *eisphora* at a certain height, to be made permanent, for you the richest 1200 Athenians who participate in the *symmories*. And do not think that I am taking advantage of you: it is to your advantage: even if you pay a levy of 100, 200, even 300 drachmae a year, that is, to say the maximum of 1500 in a 5 years period, it is much less than the expenses of a *trierarchy*. Is'nt that so? How much did you spend on *trierarchies* Nicomedes, Apollodorus, Polycles?
- I spent 5000 drachmae 2 years ago in the military operation at Byzantium replied Nicomedes.
- Me too, about as much, Apollodorus agreed.

Polycles nodded his head in agreement.

- In peacetime, *trierarchies* are limited. I do not think we need more than 20, at most 30 *triremes* every year, to patrol the Aegean against pirates and to keep the seas and communications open and free, a service of Athens for all merchants, regardless of their place of origin. If I calculate 200 drachmae average *eisphora* for the 1200 rich Athenians, I collect 240,000 drachmae, 40 *talents*. Calculating to give one drachmae a day for the 4 days of the theatrical contests, I pay 120,000 drachmae for almost all the Athenian citizens, that is, my 1 year's *eisphora* covers 2 years' *theorica*.
- You want to make *theorica* the "glue of democracy," said Demades half-jokingly-half-seriously.
- Exactly! The *theorica*, the *ecclesiasticon* and the wages from the public works. But all this is not lost. As citizens will spend for them, economic activity will be stimulated.
- -And how much revenue do you expect to collect in total? asked the practical Aeschines.
- Lycurgus was silent for a moment before answering.

– -Over a thousand *talents* a year at the end of a decade, if I manage to keep my schedule that long.

Everyone fell silent and amazed listening to the extremely ambitious number.

– Athens had this income only during the years of Pericles! Demades noted.
– Along with the contributions of the allies, Nicomedes added.
– Exactly my friends. My ambition is to reach Pericles. And without the contributions of allies. Only from our own effort. Will you continue to support my program?

They were silent for a while, calculating. Nicomedes answered first.

– I will support you Lycurgus. You're right. The program you propose is to the interest of all of us. Of the polis, and of all classes. I would say, a strategy where there is no loser, a strategy where everyone wins. The results from your program are becoming more and more visible.
– A strategy that forges *homonoia*, Demades added.
– I also agree. I prefer the certainty of paying 200 drachmae a year to the uncertainty of war and the burden of the *trierarchy*, said Apollodorus.

Pammenes and Philocles nodded approvingly, drinking wine in confirmation.

– And what about Demosthenes? asked Aeschines, keeping his mind always on his great rival.
– I think he will agree. Now he is weakened, after the destruction of Chaeronea. His attempt to unite all the southern Greeks and the Boeotians against Philip failed. Demosthenes is a patriot and intelligent. He realizes that we need peace to become strong again, and that at this stage we cannot provoke the Macedonians, the mightiest state at the times, replied Lycurgus.
– And will the Macedonians respect the peace? commented Polycles.
– They will respect it. Anyway, a large part of their army is in Asia and has already achieved great victories over the Persian Empire. And now they are marching on further, deep inside the Asian lands. They have no interest in not accepting our peace proposal policy. The conference of Corinth offered them, obligatorily, the leadership of all Greeks in the campaign against the Persians. Isocrates' dream for a Pan-Hellenic union against the Persians came true through the Kingdom of Macedon. The campaign is good for the Greek cities, if it stops the wars between us. We have been fighting for so many decades for the hegemony of Greece, Athens, Sparta, Thebes, and the result is that in the end we all lost. Let us fight all the Greeks under the Macedonian leadership united against the Persians, as we did against Xerxes, replied Lycurgus.
– I met King Philip, added Aeschines. He may have destroyed Olynthus but he did this so as to consolidate his hegemony in the north. Olynthus rivaled him. He wanted to be seen as the leader of the Greeks. Of course, he knew that he could not destroy the "school of Hellas," Athens. It would be a fatal blow to his reputation.
– And it would be no easy task. As long as Athens controls the sea, its long walls make it impregnable. The Macedonians showed their superiority, in land battles,

and in sieges of mainland cities such as Olynthus. But against cities that have an open sea behind them, such as Byzantium and Perinthus, they failed. Athens is infinitely stronger than Perinthus and Byzantium. Over 20,000 Athenians and *metic hoplites* and light armor troops are capable of holding off any Macedonian army, wearing it out in a long, costly, and bloody siege, Phocion said, and added.

- Antipater, the regent of the Macedonian throne in the place of Alexander knows how to calculate and assess every different situation, added Aeschines.
- Good, Lycurgus spoke again. Since we agree, let's move on. Talk to your friends, acquaintances, and fellow-citizens. When we have properly prepared public opinion, I will defend my policy, our policy, in the Ecclesia, taking your support for granted.
- And now, since we've covered the important stuff, let's relax and have fun, said Nicomedes.

He clapped his hands and called three *aulitris* pipers, one playing flutes, one with a harp, and one with a guitar. The pipers sat on stools placed by Ischomachos in the center of the *andron*, sang and played music. The symposion ended with a triple *paean*[9] to God Apollo and a hymn to health:

> Health, more revered than the blessed gods, may I live with you all the rest of my life and may you be a merciful housemate of mine.

* * *

18.2 Nicomedes's Symposion

In this Scene we presented an imaginary symposion, with real persons, except Nicomedes. Apollodorus and Polycles are known from works of Demosthenes. Aeschines and Demades are the well-known orators, Phocion was a well-known orator and general, who among other things won an important victory in Euboea during the Social War and was famous for his honesty and integrity of character. Pammenes was a well-known goldsmith. The most famous symposion's presentation that survived to us is the one narrated by Plato. Here, we present a "political" symposion, set around 334 BCE when Lycurgus introduced his own program of rebuilding Athens.

18.3 The *Theorica*

Regarding the *theorica*, Hansen (1976, 1999) provides a detailed analysis. They were probably introduced by Pericles. The Athenians had understood the importance of the theater as *paideia* for the citizens and had established this institution,

[9] A song or lyric poem expressing triumph or thanksgiving.

payments to the poorest citizens (2 *obols*) to be able to attend the theatrical performances, as a compensation for the loss of income from abstaining from their work to attend them.

It was forbidden for anyone to receive a *theoricon* from two different *demes* and in such a case a person was punished since such an act was theft of public money (Demosthenes, *Against Leochares*, 44.38–39). According to Plato (*Gorgias*, 515e), the *theorica* were introduced as an institution by Pericles.

One of the most important positive results of *theorica* was the education of individuals in matters of social behavior and ethics. In this way, even poor Athenians were able to attend up to 48 plays a year (three tetralogies for 4 days a year) of which 36 were tragedies and 12 satiric dramas.

Theorica, in parallel to the participation of the citizens in the workings of the Assembly, the Council, the courts, and the rest of the public posts were a further means to educate citizens on the morals of the polis and prepare them accordingly so as to exhibit the proper behavior in their everyday affairs (Aeschines, *Against Ctesiphon*, 3.246). Indirectly, theatrical performances educated citizens, teaching them mythology, for example, Trojan and Theban cycles, Aeschylus, *Persians*, ethics such as Sophocles, *Antigone,* etc. and political satire (the comedies of Aristophanes), etc. So, the citizens were indirectly educated through these works, in the proper manners of the city (Kyriazis and Economou 2015b).[10] Therefore, *theorica* were an important aspect of the social life of the Athenians.

With these additional stimuli, one can speak of "lifelong learning" procedures regarding the city's administration and social coexistence. The specialized speeches of citizens-"politicians" were open to all ordinary citizens through the *ecclesiastica* in the Assembly. Every citizen could attend the Assembly gatherings and benefit himself (in terms of education) by experts' speeches such as Cleisthenes, Isagoras, Themistocles, Aristides, Ephialtes, Pericles, Cimon, Nicias, Alcibiades, Eubulus, Lycurgus Demosthenes, Aeschines and Phocion, etc. on a variety of issues, from economics to politics and also international relations.

18.4 Lycurgus: The Honest and Able *Epimeletes/Tamias Tes Koines Prosodou*

Lycurgus came from the distinguished Athenian family of Eteoboutadai and was the son of Lycophron. He first devoted himself to the study of philosophy in the school of Plato, but later became a student of Isocrates.

He entered political life at a relatively young age. During the period 350 – 340 BCE he came into contact with the anti-Macedonian political faction in Athens, whose leader was Demosthenes.

[10]For the pivotal meaning of the concept of *paideia*, which is much broader than the concept of accumulation of practical knowledge, see Sects. 20.2 and 20.3 below.

Lycurgus was the scion of an old Athenian family; he followed the principles that characterized the ancient Athenians: adherence to religion and the gods of the polis, austerity in private life, and a relentlessly firm attitude toward those who by their behavior and actions betrayed the polis or violated the established morals and political institutions. Lycurgus led an ascetic life, and from this he derived the right to appear frequently as the persecutor of all deviation. For many years he was a kind of "informal punisher" of any illegal or immoral acts he spotted throughout the polis.

Lycurgus was a man of unyielding severity in cases of corruption. That is why he had no qualms about recommending the death penalty for those who defaulted on their duty to the polis. He hated the mean and the incompetent. Immediately after the Battle of Chaeronea he demanded, through trial, the death sentence of the general Lysicles, because, according to him, his attitude during the battle was not the proper one and undermined the outcome of the battle against the Athenians. Lysicles was condemned to death. Many times, Lycurgus appeared as a public accuser against various public officials who had harmed the interests of the polis. His conscientiousness in the exercise of his duties contributed to the increase of the public revenue to 1200 *talents* in 322 BCE. For the financial offices of Eubulus and Lycurgus a detailed historical analysis is provided by Lewis (1997, 212–230). His activity and his interest in increasing the security and prestige of Athens made his fellow-citizens honor him so much that when in 335 BCE Alexander the Great demanded his surrender along with nine other leaders of the anti-Macedonian faction, they refused to surrender him.

Lycurgus was continuously elected an *epimeletes/tamias tes koines prosodou* for 12 years, from 336 to 324 BCE. The term of office in this position was 4 years. Therefore, Lycurgus was elected three consecutive times between this period, after being replaced by a staunch enemy of him, Menaechmus. The holders of this critical post for the well-being of the state of Athens were elected by vote and not by lottery, because the position required special skills. The holder of this office had under his supervision the proper management of all state and non-state treasuries of Athens (see further below). He had freedom of movement as to where he would allocate public money. He was assisted in his duties by a body of civil servants called the *poristai*.

Continuing the extensive public works in favor of the polis, Lycurgus contributed to the creation of a new drainage system in Piraeus, with a new series of prominent monuments such as the theater of Dionysus under the Acropolis as well as to the spatial expansion of the assembly area on the Pnyx. He also built, among others, a famous public clock (of an hourglass type) and the Lyceum, which consisted of extensive sports facilities, as well as the Telesterion at Eleusis, one of the greatest cult centers of the ancient world. Also, a new Panathenaic stadium to host a multitude of sporting activities was made while the road network to Eleusis and Oropos was improved. Agora was beautified with new temples, and with new building facilities. Courts were also housed in new building facilities. For the defense of the city a new series of *neosoikoi* were built. The shipyard was enlarged and a new naval arsenal was created at Piraeus. The city walls were strengthened and a moat was dug in front of them. Also, the institution of *ephebeia*, that is, the military duty and training of young Athenians between 18–19 years of age, was introduced (Hansen 1991; Ober 2008, 68–69; Kyriazis 2009; Burke 2010, 407, 413). These extensive infrastructure projects, which offered guaranteed work to a large part of low-income citizens, from a modern economic interpretation, can be characterized as expansionary fiscal policy of Keynesian inspiration.

Fifteen of his forensic speeches were preserved in antiquity. Two of them he uttered himself in court, to defend himself in trials of accountability (*euthyna*). The speech of Lycurgus, *Against Leocrates* has been preserved where in verses 3–4 he states the following important:

> . . .For the things which in the main uphold our democracy and preserve the city's prosperity are three in number: first the system of law, second the vote of the jury, and third the method of prosecution by which the crimes are handed over to them.

Lycurgus was a very important statesman and among the honors bestowed upon him is that, at the suggestion of the orator Stratocles, during Anaxecrates' tenure as an *eponymous archon* in 307/6, it was decided to erect a bronze statue in his honor at Kerameikos. Also, the Athenians, to honor him, had decided that he and his eldest son could receive all the privileges of the Prytaneion, whenever they wanted and at public expense.

18.5 The *Hellenotamiai* and the Allied Fund

Although through the above analysis it was explained how advanced the framework of banking services in Athens of the times was, there was nevertheless no provision for the state to borrow money from the private sector (Kyriazis 2009, 123). However, there was another possibility: the state, in case of need, could borrow money from the so-called *tamia or treasury-temples*, which were as follows:

- The *ten hellenotamiai* of Allied Fund.
- The *Demosion* Fund.
- The *treasury-temples of Athena and the Other Gods* (TTAGs).
- The *Theoricon* treasury.
- The *Stratiotikon* treasury.

The Allied Fund was created in 478 BCE and was concerned with the collection of the taxes from the member city-states of the Athenian Alliance with the purpose to subsidize the defense doctrine of the Alliance, against the Persian threat. The logic of the alliance permits us to characterize it something like the "NATO of the ancient times." The financial managers of the fund were called *hellenotamiai* and were all Athenians.

In 454 the Fund, which at first was settled in Delos, was decided to be transferred to Athens. The duties of the *hellenotamiai* included supervising the proper collection and use of the remittances of this fund, drawing up tax rolls of the allied states, and disposing of the alliance's money in case of war. For that purpose, the *hellenotamiai* accompanied the generals on their campaigns, in order to cover the necessary war expenses.

This institution was maintained until the end of 404, as then the First Athenian Alliance was abolished due to the defeat of Athens. The remittances that the Allied Fund received from the allied city-states were known as *aparchai*. It is confirmed that 1/60th of the *aparchai* was transferred to the treasury-temple of Athena (Samons 2000, 70–83). The Allied Fund, situated in a chamber at the Opisthodomos at Parthenon (see below), after covering the annual military expenditures of Athens, then transferred any remaining annual surpluses it had to the treasury-temples of Athena and the Other Gods which were also situated in an adjacent chamber at the Opisthodomos (Economou 2024, 177–191). To ensure the prestige of this institution, it was decided that in case of corruption and embezzlement of money by *hellenotamiai*, the penalties would be the highest one; to drink the hemlock (a poison that caused death).

18.6 The *Demosion* Fund

The second fund was the Demosion which collected fines, rents, and remittances from the leasing of public properties to private individuals and was mainly the fund that collected significant revenue from the Laurion mines. The *board of poletai* was responsible for collecting these remittances on behalf of the Demosion. It was therefore the fund through which the Athenian public met a large part of its public expenditure, such as administrative costs of government, salaries of civil servants and judges, and covering the costs of the *trierarchy* (Andreades 1933; Samons 2000, 55–69; Economou 2024, 177–179).

18.7 The *Treasury-Temples of Athena and the Other Gods*

The third body that could provide loans to the state when in need was the *treasury-temples of Athena and the Other Gods* (TTAGs) which functioned as a credit bank in favor of the state to deal with emergency needs that arose either in peaceful or in extreme conditions such as a war period. At first there were separate treasuries, the treasury-temple of Athena for the treasures of the Parthenon, which had been established before the establishment of democracy, and the treasury-temples of the Other Gods for the treasures of the other temples throughout Attica. They were united in 406/5, separated in 384, and finally reunited in 346. However, there is also the opinion that the treasuries always kept separate accounts and revenues, and all these were merged into one in 406/5. Treasuries also existed in remote temples such as those of Nemesis at Rhamnous, Artemis at Brauron, etc.

The senior administrators and managers of the treasury-temples of Athena and the Other Gods were also called *tamiai*, as was the manager of each separate treasury, before they were all united into one. Apart from the financial resources that the temples collected from citizens' donations, but also from the *aparchai* that were transferred to the *treasury-temple of Athena*, the treasuries of these temples also collected sums of money in favor of the public, such as payment of fines, rental of public properties that belonged to the state in its jurisdiction, and even from private donations. Part of this money was used for the maintenance and repair of public buildings (Samons 2000; Bitros et al. 2020; Economou 2024, 180–184).

The temple of Athena during the period 433–427 BCE was lending money to the state at 6% interest. However, Blamire (2001) and Rhodes (2005, 93) report that the state paid 6% interest till 427 BCE, but only 1.2% from 426 and later on. The state borrowed at low interest from these funds in cases of emergency, such as war, disasters, etc. This meant that the state had to return the money to the funds at some point in the future. These interest rates were "real," in the sense that they were accompanied by low inflationary influence, because, in general, the inflation faced by the Athenian as well as the rest of the ancient Greek economy from the fifth century onward was not particularly high, due to the change in *relative prices* of the products prevailing in Agora.[11]

Regarding the collection of the monetary sums of these treasury-temples, Marcaccini (2015, 515–516) argues that in the fifth century, with the expansion of Athens' naval power, the Athena's treasury wealth increased significantly and the role of its treasurers was particularly important because they managed this great reserve of wealth, which was essential to the well-functioning of the polis and for implementing the defense dogma of the Athenian Alliance in practice. From 434/3 the Parthenon on the Acropolis contained many valuable objects, as we see from the findings at the Acropolis, mostly at Parthenon and the Opisthodomos (Image 18.1).

The Hekatompedon is the oldest important building on the Acropolis 100 feet long, a name known from an inscription referring to the layout of the sanctuary. This temple was perhaps dedicated to the warrior status of the goddess, Athena Parthenos, the bulwark of the city. The Opisthodomos was the back space, in ancient Greek temples in general, with an entrance from the outside of the building. The Opisthodomos at Parthenon held the position of an important treasury of the city-state, so it was guarded with railings. Also, this area was guarded day and night to avoid robbery of valuable objects and remittances of great value. It is known that the money deposited to Opisthodomos was loaned to the Athenian state. In particular, Marcaccini (2015, 515, ftn. 4) based on inscriptions referring to the Kallias Decree (*IG* I3 52A, lines 15–16; B, lines 24–25) argues that on the right side of

[11] We elaborate on this topic in Bitros et al. (2020, 148–152) and Economou (2024, 228–229). A *relative price* is the price of a commodity such as a good or service in terms of another; i.e., the ratio of two prices. Due to space limitations, readers can further consult Krugman et al. (2023) among others on this. We believe that the view that in the fifth century, the Athenian economy faced high levels of inflation is questionable, at least to some degree, seen through the lenses of the *relative prices* logic.

Image 18.1 The Opisthodomos of the temple of Athena at the Parthenon in Acropolis. Source: Image owned by the authors

Opisthodomos the remittances pertaining to the Temple of Athena treasury were collected in a chamber, while on the left were gathered the remittances of the Other Gods in another chamber. These remittances, by both chambers, as a total were very important.

Thucydides (*Histories*, 2.13.3–6) informs us that in the first year of the Peloponnesian War in 431, the Athenians immediately collected, for that year the non-inconsiderable sum of 600 *talents*, that is, essentially, 3.6 million drachmae. He also informs us that in 431 there were still at Opisthodomos another 6000 *talents* available for use, out of the 9700 that had been collected there before, and 3700 were already used for the building of the Acropolis and for the military operations at Potidaia. Thucydides goes on to state that in case of extreme need (as was the case) the Athenians could also melt down Athena's gold ornaments because the statue contained 40 *talents* worth of pure gold and could practically be converted into coinage. But as soon as the sociopolitical situation was normalized, they would have to return, the entire amount of gold.

It is not clear if Opisthodomos was a separate building from the Parthenon or its western terrace, but what is for sure is that **it housed three kinds of treasuries in three separate chambers; those of: (i) the treasury-temple of Athena (ii) the treasury-temples of Athena and the Other Gods (iii) the Allied Fund.** As already mentioned, the chambers of (i) and (ii) although being separate in principle, were under a common management since 346 (Economou 2024, 182–188).

Our general conclusion is that the TTAGs functioned as funding mechanisms for the Athenian state in emergency situations (see also Economou and Kyriazis (2021b)). But there was a strict framework for the use of these financial resources. The treasury-temples **did not "offer" but lent this money to the Athenian state, which, in times of better fiscal performance and periods of peace, had to repay to them (Bitros et al.** 2020**; Economou** 2024, **182–184)**. The operation of the TTAGs in general was not done arbitrarily: their treasures-managers were also subject to strict control in order to ensure the proper administration and management of these large sums of money in favor of the well-being of the Athenians.

18.8 The *Theoricon* and the *Stratiotikon* Funds

The Theoricon Fund had been instituted after the Social War (Rhodes 1972, 105). It collected the money for *theorica*, which, as mentioned, concerned the staging of theatrical performances in the city of Athens. This fund collected whatever remittances were left over to the Athenian state through the Demosion fund, in case it achieved annual public surpluses.

After 373 BCE, the Athenian Assembly instituted also the *tamias ton stratiotikon* (treasurer of the Military Fund) who was responsible for the military expenditure of the state (Aristotle, *Athenian Constitution*, 47.2). And from 348, following the proposal of a citizen in the Assembly, Apollodorus, it was decided that in case of annual surpluses in the state budget from the Demosion Fund, these surpluses should be channeled to the Stratiotikon Fund, and no longer to that of the Theoricon.

This change of priority shows the pivotal relationship between economy and war in the perception of the Athenian citizens but also the utmost importance the Athenians attached to the funding of national defense.

The responsibilities of the Theoricon and Stratiotikon treasuries being considered crucial are also acknowledged by Aristotle who, as already mentioned, maintains that all public officials engaged in public administration were appointed by lot, except some specialties such as the treasurers of the Stratiotikon and the Theoricon Funds. These treasurers were appointed by the Assembly and took office from the period beginning with the Great Panathenaea until the next, that is, a 4-year service (Aristotle, *Athenian Constitution*, 43.1).

After the unfortunate for Athens Social War and the undertaking of the city's financial management by Eubulus and Lycurgus, surplus money through the public revenues was channeled to the Theoricon Fund, while after the persistent efforts of Demosthenes, it was redirected to the Stratiotikon Fund by 339/338 BCE (Rhodes 1972, 105). Demosthenes, who was one of the most ardent opponents of strengthening of the Macedonian power under Philip II believed that all surplus money should be used for military campaigns and not for domestic public works or festivals.

Eubulus, on the other hand, was against costly military campaigns, and after the Social War he and his followers wanted to restrain the *demos* from further war adventures and convince it that peace would have beneficial effects in the long run, which indeed it had (Economou and Kyriazis 2016b). In the following years, after the defeat at Chaeronea, the influence of Demosthenes was limited and Lycurgus, being the *epimeletes tes koines prosodou*, continued his great public works, by not abolishing at all, the expenditure of Stratiotikon Fund (Economou 2024, 260–262).

Finally, Marcaccini (2015, 530) adds as a general comment, that all funds were obliged to prepare the so-called *logoi* which were detailed annual reports that explained how the treasuries–temples at Athens managed the public money. Undoubtedly, it was something like today's Annual Reports, of state and private bodies, organizations or firms at national or international level.

18.9 An Ancient *Social Contract*

The fictional symposion we have described in this Scene is based on real facts and we believe that it echoes the general philosophy that underpinned the economic recovery program of the city-state of Athens, as inspired and implemented by Eubulus and Lycurgus. Based on the fictional story we developed in this scene we believe that Lycurgus offered actually a "contract" to his fellow-citizens that promised them long-term economic prosperity (pacifist strategy) instead of any doubtful geopolitical benefits that could be gained due to war strategy.

According to Gough (1936, 2–3), a social contract, under the logic of eminent seventeenth–eighteenth century theorists such as Hugo Grotius, Thomas Hobbes, Samuel von Pufendorf, John Locke, Jean-Jacques Rousseau, and Immanuel Kant:

> ..., purports to define the terms on which that society is to be governed: the people have made a contract with their ruler which determines their relations with him. They promise him obedience, while he promises his protection and good government. While he keeps his part of the bargain, they must keep theirs, but if he misgoverns the contract is broken and allegiance is at an end.

At the beginning of the 4th c. BCE, Athens, defeated in the Peloponnesian War, aspired to reconstitute the Athenian Alliance in order to increase its geopolitical status. After Sparta's defeats at Leuctra (371) and Mantineia (362) by the Thebans, it appeared that this second Athenian Alliance would be successful. However, the sudden geopolitical eclipse of Sparta made the usefulness of the new alliance less necessary in terms of protecting Athens' allies, as they wanted to be freed from the large financial burden as an exchange of the military protection provided to them by the Athenians.

Due to the negative outcome of the Social War there was the erosion of the economic dynamics, the agricultural and commercial class and the exhaustion of the well-to-do Athenians through excessive taxation in the form of *liturgies*. Public revenues fell to 130 *talents* per year mainly due to the dysfunction of trade owing to the war (Kroll 2011, 237; Arvanitidis and Kyriazis 2013; Economou and Kyriazis 2016b). Subsequently, Eubulus (354–339) as in charge of the Theoricon treasurer and Lycurgus (338–322 BC) as *epimeletes tes koines prosodou* took over the management of economic policy, conducting important public works programs. Essentially, in economic terms, they replaced the public good of defense with public infrastructure projects (Economou and Kyriazis 2016b). The fiscal expansionary policies of both Eubulus and Lycurgus were completely successful. They secured 16 years of permanent jobs in construction, a lasting peace (the longest period of peace in Classical Athens) and prosperity and exceeded their goal: Athens' revenue reached 1200 *talents*, a spectacular achievement.

It may even be a lasting historical record. Is there any other state investment plan that has achieved an increase to the state's public revenue by 850% in just 33 years? Andreades (1933, 373, 377) and van Wees (2013, 1) argue that Lycurgus is said to have invested 18,650 *talents* over 12 years (336–324 BCE) on state's infrastructure, adding that no modern European state has exceeded such a financial performance before the UK during the Industrial Revolution made a quantum leap to another level.

The ultimate goal of the fiscal programs of Eubulus and Lycurgus was to achieve, a "win-win" scenario. The plan of Solon of 594 BCE, of Pericles with the great works of the fifth century, as well as of Eubulus and Lycurgus of the period 355–322 BCE described here, can also be seen in terms of Game Theory, as a *positive sum game*, according to which the desires and aspirations (in economic and non-economic terms) of all parties/social groups are satisfied, in this case, the rich, the middle-income, and low-income Athenians exceed the losses in the long-term.

Before the proposals of Eubulus and Lycurgus were about to be discussed in the citizens' Assembly, there was a great preparation of the public opinion, through social networks, part of which were the symposia. In this Scene, we emphasized on the very cautious preparation of Lycurgus's arguments regarding their costing (revenues-expenditures), something on which Kallet-Marx (1993), Samons (2000), and Ober (2015b) agree that is true, which further shows the superiority of the Athenian democracy over many of the modern ones in this regard.

The saying of Demades about *theorica* as the "glue of democracy" which is referred by Plutarch (*Ethics*, 1016b) is related, at least to some degree, with the logic of implementing a social contract into practice. Because, this "glue" creates *homonoia* as the highest goal for a society. That is why even today we notice the existence of such a logic, as shown, for example, by the naming of central squares, e.g., *Place de la Concorde in Paris*. In Kyriazis et al. (2014), Kyriazis and Economou (2015a), and Economou and Kyriazis (2019a) we connect this notion of Demades to the institutional changes on the economic structure and military organization that took place in Athens before and during the Classical times, which proved critical for the politico-economic regime change (democracy) that followed.

Achieving a social contract in practice was also related to the moral and social elements of the *kalos kagathos* citizen; the virtuous, the patriot, the moral, etc. These values had to necessarily constitute the personality of every new Athenian citizen. Such conditions do not apply in modern democracies, where the right of citizenship is granted indiscriminately to all who have simply reached the required age. We know that this position of ours is likely to raise strong objections, however by setting strict conditions on the question of citizenship, the Athenians, and the citizens of the other democratic city-states and federal states[12] of Greek antiquity, at least tried to ensure that the right to make decisions will be given only to "high-quality citizens," i.e. to *kaloi kagathoi* citizens, surrounded by the moral codes of conduct we described above. For the Athenians, it was necessary to create a common social code of values that would be based on trust, respect, and *homonoia* among them.

On the other hand, the candidate-citizen himself had the inalienable right of personal choice. In Plato's *Criton*, it is described that every Athenian male (over the age of 18), before becoming a citizen of Athens, had to accept a set of institutional provisions of a moral and political nature before officially becoming a citizen, which he could reject if he did not agree. In this case, he had to leave Athens and was given the opportunity to relocate to an Athenian *cleruchy*.[13] In the *Republic* (2.359a) Plato adds that laws should be seen as mutual covenants among the people in an organized community such as a polis, and 'justice:

> is a mean or compromise, between the best of all, which is to do injustice and not be punished, and the worst of all, which is to suffer injustice without the power of retaliation; and justice, being at a middle point between the two, is tolerated not as a good, but as the lesser evil, and honoured by reason of the inability of men to do injustice....

J. de Romilly (1994) considers that such a practice demonstrates the terms of acceptance or non-acceptance of a "contract." We consider that the value framework referred to by de Romilly fits the concept of the Social Contract, as formulated by the European Enlightenment philosophers.

[12] Op, cit., Chap. 1, ftn 28 and Chap. 7 ftn. 7.

[13] During the period between the Greco-Persian and Peloponnesian wars, known as the *pentekontaeteia*, the Athenians had established outside Attica and throughout the rest of Greece a respectable number of new communities called *cleruchies* (sing., *cleruchy*). Essentially, they were colonies in territories occupied by the Athenians for this purpose. A *cleruch* was considered an Athenian citizen who was allowed to settle in a colony of Athens, without losing citizenship and political rights in his birthplace.

Chapter 19
The Mentality of the Greek Way of War, the Battle of Chaeronea, and the Rise of Macedon

Abstract This chapter further describes the structure of the Athenian navy and how land army, the so-called *hoplite phalanx*, was organized. It describes the logic behind the phalanx land army organization and then narrates, in brief, the Battle of Chaeronea, which was a pivotal battle, with which the Macedonians prevailed over the Southern Greeks, establishing a new order of things in Southern Greece. The defeat at Chaeronea was a milestone, because it was combined with the gradual decline of Athens and the rise of Macedon in the Greek and global affairs of the times.

19.1 Nicomedes: A *Trierarch* in the Navy and an Infantry Officer at Chaeronea

Nicomedes, after the symposion with Lycurgus, remembered his participation in the war with the Macedonians in the Battle of Chaeronea, as well as his *trierarchy* a bit later.

Seven years ago, the Athenians had declared war on Macedonia, prompted by the fiery words of Demosthenes but also because Philip II had reached the Hellespont straits, and if he managed to control them, he would threaten Athens's vital grain supply. The Athenians had strengthened the fleet that would take part in the operations to repel the Macedonian threat by commissioning new *trierarchies*.

Three years ago, when Nicomedes was assigned with the undertaking a *trierarchy*, his first concern was to assemble the crew, 170 oarsmen, 10 *hoplites*, 4 archers, 8 sailors, and 8 officers, along with himself. As was the established practice, he selected oarsmen and the rest of the crew from men of his *deme* whom he knew and who knew him, and some others from his own tribe. Their wages were paid from the public treasury, but a good *trierarch* was always willing, to incur additional expenses if necessary, or to pay some advances of wages.

With some of the officers he chose he had served together during his father's two *trierarchies* many years ago. Nicomedes remembered that was the youngest officer in a *trireme* under his father's *trierarchy*, 25 years ago, which took part in the Naval Battle at Sybota, during the Social War.

E. M. L. Economou, N. C. Kyriazis, *Daily Life in Classical Athens*, Frontiers in Economic History, https://doi.org/10.1007/978-3-031-58541-8_19

Together with the *kybernetes* and the *keleustes* who had been selected to participate on his *trierarchy*, they went down to Munichia and supervised the available *triremes* to the *neosoikoi*. They chose the best available and launched it into the water. Then they collected the necessary provisions, masts, oars, anchors, ropes, and everything else needed for the 8 months' service. All the supplies were recorded and Nicomedes signed for their receipt. Finally, before departing on patrol duties, Nicomedes took care of the crew's rations, including nuts, cheeses, salted meat and fish, with which he would be resupplied at various stations.

Nicomedes also remembered the events of the Battle of Chaeronea.

Nicomedes served there as a land officer. He was in the front row of the *phalanx*. He remembered the unbearable heat, the profuse sweat, the dry bitter mouth. He also remembered the clash of two *phalanxes*, as the pikes from the long Macedonian spears, known as *sarissas* clattered against the great round shields of the Athenians, a sound like a thousand brass knockers slamming at once at gates, crawling over them and squeak. To these sounds were quickly added the shouts of the *hoplites*, their heavy breaths, all together like one issuing from a dragon's throat, the groans of the wounded, and the thud of bodies collapsing to the ground.

For a while the two *phalanxes* were immobilized, like two rams who, having entangled their horns, try violently and stubbornly to push the other back. The dust from the thousands of clatters rose to the sky, like smoke, making the warriors cough. Nicomedes, like the other Athenians, had no way of measuring the time that passed... Sweat, tension, and fatigue were those things that he felt at that particular battle moments. At some point, however, he felt an imperceptible movement forward. The first line of the Athenian *phalanx* was gaining ground, the others were following. The Macedonians were retreating, slowly and in a coordinated way.

A few steps forward...., a few more.... The Athenian *phalanx* was gaining ground....

Nicomedes understood, like the other *hoplites* near him, that something wrong was going on, when in his ears, among the other clatters of the battle, he heard the trampling and whining of horses. Cavalry... Which cavalry? At a moment he managed to look back toward the last eighth row of the *phalanx*. His soul was filled with terror! Behind, on their backs, came the Macedonian cavalry. Where was theirs?

The last two ranks reversed to face the Macedonian cavalrymen. Macedonian horsemen's spears crashed into Athenian shields, some found faces and necks. Athenians *hoplites* fell dead and wounded; some Macedonian horsemen struck by Athenian spears. The Athenian *phalanx* stopped. Frontally, the Macedonians who had previously retreated now attacked again. Light Macedonian *peltasts* hurled their javelins and slingshots at the Athenians, adding new sounds, like hail on tiled roofs, to the din of battle...

The Athenian *phalanx*, encircled in Haemon's gorge on the slope of Thourion, lost its cohesion....

Nicomedes did not know who broke first, but he could see the lines weakening, wilting, Athenians falling dead and wounded and others, in utter shame, throwing away their shields and panicked trying to seek salvation by abandoning the battlefield...

The rest of the battle was a blur in Nicomedes's mind, perhaps because his mind did not want to remember unpleasant, images of shame and destruction....

The defeat was heavy: 1000 Athenians had been killed, 2000 became Macedonian prisoners of war. He also remembered the panic in Athens when the fugitives arrived with the news of the disaster. However, the Athenians grit their teeth to make rough repairs in the city's walls, where necessary. When Philip's scouts approached the walls a few days later, they saw Athens ready for war and determined.

Philip behaved magnanimously.

- I don't want to attack the most brilliant city of Greece. The works of your ancestors are your best guard. These protect you.
- These, but also the walls and weapons of those living behind them. And our invincible "wooden walls" replied the Athenians ambassadors, among them Demades, who went to meet Philip at his invitation, reminding him of the oracle of Delphi before the Persian invasion. Philip released the Athenian captives without ransom, earning the Athenians' gratitude and participation in the congress of all the Greek city-states he convened in Corinth under the leadership of Macedonia.

These were all remembered by Nicomedes who actively supported Lycurgus. And his son Nicandros, now serving his military duty, the *ephebeia*, should not be found in a new Chaeronea in the future...

* * *

19.2 The *Hoplite Phalanx*

For the Ancient Greeks, war was a natural "order" of things and peace the exception. It is enough to consider that Athens between the Greco-Persian Wars and the Battle of Chaeronea (period 490–338 BCE) fought on average every 2 out of 3 years, while it did not manage to achieve a period of peace longer than 10 years in this period of time. Almost all adult Athenians (with the exception of only the disabled) would have participated in military operations on land and sea, thus war had become an important element of social life.

Depending on their income dynamics, the Athenians were subject to different conscription obligations. Wealthy Athenians became *trierarchs* and senior officers in *triremes* or, alternatively, *hippeis* (cavalrymen) in the land army. The Athenian cavalry consisted of about 1000 cavalrymen, commanded by two *hipparchs*, each of whom had under his command horsemen from 5 Athenian tribes. Each tribe had its own commander, subordinate to the *hipparch*, called *ilarchos*. Citizens of average income became *hoplites* in the *phalanx* or *pezonautai* (marines) in the *triremes*, while low-income Athenians, *thetes* and *metics* became oarsmen in *triremes* or lightly armed soldiers, e.g., archers. The main ground fighting force was the *hoplite phalanx*, the most capable type of land army of the times.[1] There were variations regarding the numerical size of an *hoplite phalanx*, but during the Later Classical period, that is, the time we focus on this book, a *phalanx* was comprised by approximately 4000 *hoplites*. *Metics* were also obliged to serve in the Athenian armed forces, but their exact commitment and participation was left to the discretion of the polis's leaders. For example, they could either be used or not in the fleet (Thucydides, 3.16) or as *hoplites* at Megara in 431 (ibid., 2.31) or as light-armed troops in the Delion campaign.

An important parameter of success during the conflict with an opposing *phalanx* was the effective application of *othismos* (push). If the rear ranks did not exert much forward push, the *hoplites* in the front ranks would not have much force to break the enemy line, but the opposite would probably be the case. The decisive element was the correct coordination and gait between the *hoplites*, so that the *phalanx* would move in the best cohesion it could, in combination with the coordinated push that the rear rows gave to the front ones. When the warring *phalanxes* finally engaged to one another, they looked like two large rams intended to crush each other (Kyriazis 2012).

The *hoplite* way of warfare did not stand still but evolved. During the battles of Leuctra (371) and Mantineia (362) the Theban type of *phalanx* was lined up 50 ranks deep, as the great Theban general Epameinondas was inspired and implemented a new type of *hoplite* warfare, the *oblique phalanx* with which he defeated the almost invincible until then Spartan *phalanx*. The *phalanx* was further developed by the Macedonians, through the introduction of the long spear known as *sarissa*, and thanks to this the *phalanx* became the undisputed Greek war machine. The Macedonian type of *phalanx* was surpassed only by the Roman legion at a later time (Images 19.1 and 19.2).

Also, in the fourth century, the use of various new types of weapons was introduced. Catapults throwing stones first had been in the battlefields since the end of the fourth c., by the Macedonian army of Philip II, but in the fourth century crossbows were widespread, influencing the defense technique as well. The walls were now equipped with numerous towers, which had large openings for the crossbows, turning them into "artillery platforms." Such towers are preserved in the Athenian fortress of Eleutherai and the restored walls of ancient Messene (Image 19.3).

Another dimension of the *hoplite* way of war that derives from the Archaic times is that those citizens who had joined the *hoplite phalanx* had to finance their armament such as a shield, a spear, etc., at their own expense. Already since the time of the Dark Ages (from the twelfth century BCE onward) the free-peasants had an increasing percentage of agricultural surplus at their disposal. Consequently,

[1]For the way of battle between two *phalanxes*, as well as between a *phalanx* and another military unit such as cavalry unit, see among others Cartledge (1977), Hanson (1994), Krentz (1985, 2002), and Economou and Kyriazis (2019a).

Image 19.1 *Hoplite phalanxes* clashing with each other. Chigi vase. Source: https://commons.wikimedia.org/wiki/File:Detail_from_the_Chigi-vase.jpg

Image 19.2 An *hoplite* citizen-soldier. Source: https://upload.wikimedia.org/wikipedia/commons/1/1b/Illustrerad_Verldshistoria_band_I_Ill_094.jpg

Image 19.3 One of the authors in the Aigosthena fortress (including towers). Source: Image owned by the authors

according to Hanson (1994, 1999), the gradual emergence of a "middle class" of free-peasants enabled them to finance their military equipment by themselves in order to participate in the defense of their city through *hoplite phalanxes* (Christ 2006; Kyriazis 2012; Lyttkens 2013, 37; Arvanitidis and Kyriazis 2013; Kyriazis, and Paparrigopoulos 2014; Economou and Kyriazis 2019a). Cartledge (1977, 23) writes that the very creation of the *phalanx* in the Archaic times presupposed the existence of a wider circle than a handful of aristocrats who could bear the cost of arms and other expenses of *hoplite* warfare. In fact, the Greek *hoplites* were according to Pritchard (2013, 176) "heavily armed infantry," implying specialized and potentially expensive weaponry that could be covered only by the medium-income owners of the agrarian lands of Attica.

It is certain that the ancient Greeks were very early aware of the economic dimension involved in the parameter of war: without a strong economy it is not possible to have strong armed forces over time. Athenian sea power in the East Mediterranean during the fifth and almost the entire fourth centuries was directly related to the Athenian economy's might, through which large fleets at high operating costs could be financed.[2] Spartans managed to prevail and defeat Athens in the Peloponnesian War (431–404 BC) only when they managed to temporarily "extend their power" at sea benefiting from Persian financial aid, but above all, finding in the

[2]The Athenian state provided also a ration that covered the land army soldiers' needs, established between 477–441 (Loomis 1988, 24, 34, 36).

personality of Lysander a very capable admiral, equal in value to the best Athenian admirals.

V. D. Hanson (1994), in his masterpiece *The Western Way of War* highlights the economic dimension of the Greek way of war (*hoplite phalanx*) and directly relates it to the question of the financial strength of the *hoplites*, who were relatively medium-income citizens who could finance themselves their individual armament such as a shield, a spear, etc. (see also Lommis (1988, 58–59) and Kyriazis (2012), among others). Hanson (1994, 4) adds that:

> The Greek manner of fighting must be explained as an evolving idea, a perception in the minds of small farmers that their ancestral land should remain at all cost inviolate – *apothetos* – not to be trodden over by any other than themselves, land whose integrity all citizens of the polis were willing to fight over on an moment's notice.

The nexus between economics and war can be seen through various passages of the ancient Greek literature. For example, Thucydides (1.83.2–3) reproduces the view of the Spartan king Archidamus II, who states that:

> The Athenians have allies as numerous as our own, and allies that pay tribute, and **war is a matter not so much of arms as of money, which makes arms of use** (emphasis by the authors). And this is more than ever true in a struggle between a continental and a maritime power.[3] First, then, let us provide money, and not allow ourselves to be carried away by the talk of our allies before we have done so…

In passage 2.13, Thucydides quotes a section from Pericles's *Funeral Speech* where the latter argued among other things that the Athenians should be confident of their victory in the conflict with the Spartans (during the Peloponnesian War) because the state apart from other revenue had an annual income of six hundred *talents* only from the tribute it received from the allies, as well as had gathered an additional 6000 *talents* in silver coins. The 6600 *talents* mentioned by Thucydides through the mouth of Pericles corresponded to a very large amount of money. Therefore, in this quote, Pericles emphasizes the dimension of economic power as a key parameter in determining the outcome of any potential confrontation.

Arisptophanes, in his *Wealth* (184–190), understands the nexus between economy and war by arguing that:

> 'Cario: In war, it's the flag under which you serve that victory favours.
>
> Plutus: What! I can do so many things by myself and unaided?
>
> Chremylus: And many others besides; wherefore men are never tired of your gifts. They get weary of all else, – of love …

Under the same logic Demosthenes, (*Olynthiac 1*, 1.20.7) warned the Athenians to prepare properly to face the militarily powerful Macedonia arguing that:

> Only money we must have, and without money nothing can be done that ought to be done.

[3] This is related to the classical dichotomy between *Heartland* versus *Rimland* and continental versus maritime power as defined in the seminal works of the geostrategists A.T. Mahan and H. Mackinder, etc.

Plato (*Phaedo*, 66c) had also understood the nexus between economic potential and military power, noting that:

> For all wars arise for the sake of gaining money, and we are compelled to gain money.

Furthermore, Aristophanes in his theatrical play *Wealth* provides various passages where he indirectly explains the nexus between economic and military power, while in *Lysistrata* the Spartan female fictional character Lampito asserts that the Athenians will never cease wanting to fight (173–144) "while they have *triremes* prepared to sail and silver." That's why Kallet (2007, 75) argues correctly that the Laurion silver mines were the catalyst of the Athenian naval power.

There is no doubt that the perceptions of the above philosophers are global intertemporal axioms, which modern scholars also highlight, among others, very thoroughly, through seminal works such as those of Knorr (1956), Cline (1977), Gilpin (1981), Kennedy (1989), and Copeland (2014).[4]

19.3 The *Ephebeia* and the Oath of the Athenian *Ephebes*

Young male Athenians of 18–19 years of age, known as *ephebes*, went through the institution of *ephebeia* (Aristotle, *Athenian Constitution*, 42.1–5). It was a 2-year, state-funded program, which focused on the military training of *ephebes* and coincided with their 2-year mandatory military service. Their training included hunting, controlling aggression, patrolling the city's walls, guarding the border fortresses and in general becoming efficient in the arts of warfare and surviving under extreme conditions. The idea behind *ephebeia* was that, if the state was ever threatened, its men would have the necessary skills and the character to defend it. And since according to Aristotle (*Athenian Constitution*, 53.4) all eligible citizens of ages 18 through 59 should bear arms, an *ephebe* could be drafted at any time, grouped by age based on permanent rosters displayed in the *agora* (Christ 2006, 52).

The Athenian *demos* probably created the *ephebeia* after Alexander's destruction of Thebes in September 335 BCE because they needed a standing army to defend Attica. *Ephebeia's* project cost was subsidized. At the end of his service, the *ephebe* was reincorporated back into society as a man and a citizen. Thus, during his 18–19 years of age, a young male was performing his military service to the city-state, and then, by giving the Oath of the Athenian Ephebes/Hoplites he became, at the age of 20, a citizen of the state, enfranchised with voting rights. The *ephebes* were trained in arms in their *demes* by appointed (again not elected) tutors and teachers. The oath was given in the temple of Agraulos (Aristotle, *Athenian Constitution*, 42.3; Aeschines, *On the Embassy*, 2.167–188). It was found in an inscription

[4] See also some of our own, among others, Kyriazis et al. (2018), Economou and Kyriazis (2019a), and Economou (2020) as well as the references that are provided therein.

at Acharnai in 1932. The oath, reproduced below, is an important indication of what Athenian education was for:

> I will not bring dishonor an my sacred arms nor will I abandon my comrade wherever I shall be stationed. I will defend the rights of gods and men and will not leave my country smaller, when I die, but greater and better, so far as I am able by myself and with the help of all. I will respect the rulers of the time duly and the existing ordinances duly and all others which may be established in the future. And if anyone seeks to destroy the ordinances I will oppose him so far as I am able by myself and with the help of all. I will honor the cults of my fathers. Witnesses to this shall be the gods Agraulus, Hestia, Enyo, Enyalius, Ares, Athena the Warrior, Zeus, Thallo, Auxo, Hegemone, Heracles, and the boundaries of my native land, wheat, barley, vines, olive-trees, fig-trees.... (Lycurgus, *Against Leocrates*, 77)

This oath's concept was related to things that young people had been trained to believe and do from an early age, that is, they had learned to have a developed altruism toward others, to observe and respect the state institutions and to obey the polis's laws. Also, they had been trained to honor the deeds of their great ancestors, that were bequeathed to them, and to respect the gods.

The consciousness of a glorious historical continuity, as well as the principle to respect the beliefs of their fellow-citizens, was what they learned not only from books but also from the plays they watched in the theater. The oath to the gods meant that if they did not keep what they promised, the gods would turn their backs on them.

Therefore, the goal of their education, stemming from this oath, was to achieve cohesion with each other, to defend their motherland, their values and ethical codes, as well as their property, welfare, freedom, and democracy.

After the completion of their military service-training, young Athenians earned the right to be proclaimed as citizens, with election rights (in the Assembly) after they had previously sworn by pronouncing the Oath of the Athenian Hoplites. The right to be elected in the Athenian Council and the rest of state posts was acquired after reaching the age of 30 (Aristotle, *Athenian Constitution*, 31.1). Based on Xenophon *Memorabilia* (1.2.35., 3.6.1.) it can be understood that the dual status of electing and being elected meant the acquisition of full political rights for citizens.

Aristotle (*Politics*, 3.1275a) informs us that the right of citizenship to every young Athenian was not a self-evident process after reaching the natural age of 20, as is the case in modern democracies. In the ancient Greek city-states, the condition of a previous honest life was a prerequisite of citizenship. There has always been the case for a citizen's rights to be revoked, if his general behavior toward the state, his parents, his fellow-citizens and his attitude toward respect to gods, the polis, and the motherland was not considered appropriate and due to this, he was examined by the authorities in advance, if he potentially harmed society as a whole at some time in the past.

19.4 The Battle of Chaeronea

The Battle of Chaeronea was fought in 338 BCE, near the city of Chaeronea in Boeotia, between the Kingdom of Macedon under Philip II and an alliance of city-states led by Athens and Thebes. The battle's result was a decisive victory for the Macedonians against the South Greeks. 35,000 infantry of the alliance of the Southern Greeks collided against 30,000 infantry and 2000 cavalry of the Macedonians. The battle took place on August 2, 338 BCE. During the battle king Philip executed a well-prepared plan in order to break the allied lines. In the left wing of his army he placed a *phalanx* formation together with *hetairoi*, the elite cavalry of the Macedonian army under his son, Alexander. In the center of the formation he placed the *phalanx* of the *sarissa* spears' bearers, while the right horn, according to the military customs of the Greeks, was honorably occupied by himself with his *hypaspistes*, an elite unit, facing the Athenians. The center was commanded by Antipater. The Macedonian cavalry was placed just behind the infantry, since there was no room to be deployed on the flanks, as was customary in more extended fields.

The Athenians on their part, with generals Lysicles and Charis covered themselves the left side of the allied army, toward Chaeronea, having the other allies in the center and the Boeotians with the Sacred Band of Thebes on the right. Thus, the Athenians were placed on the left side of the formation with Philip himself facing them directly, while in the center and the right were placed forces from the Boeotian federal state under Theban general Theagenes in command, as well as other allies; Corinthians, Sicyonians, Achaeans, etc. The Boeotian forces included the 300 best fighting men of Thebes who made up the so-called Sacred Band of Thebes.

Philip initially implemented a stratagem: a planned retreat of his flank toward the Athenians, driving them forward, creating a gap with the allied center. Into this breach the Macedonian–Thessalian cavalry entered, and despite the strong opposition of the allied forces, they gradually started to collapse. The allied center escaped with few losses, because the Macedonians turned against the two sides, Athenians and Boeotians, who suffered the heaviest casualties. The Sacred Band of Thebes fell to one. Philip then gave express orders not to pursue the enemy in order to avoid a general massacre of the southern Greeks. The losses of the allied coalition amounted to at least 1000 Athenians and the Sacred Band of Thebes, while it is certain that some losses would have been suffered by the other forces as well. For the losses of the Macedonians, there are no clear figures, however due to the intensity of the battle there must have been several dead and many more wounded. Shortly after these events, Philip skillfully called a Pan-Hellenic congress at Corinth where he convinced all the Greeks (except the Spartans) to unite under the leadership of Macedon, and then, to launch a counter-attack campaign against the Persian Empire (Fuller 2001) (Image 19.4).

The determination of the Athenians to defend their walls and their maritime empire was one of the reasons for Philip's magnanimity. The Battle of Chaeronea effectively marks the beginning of Macedonian dominance in the political affairs of

Image 19.4 *Tetradrachm* depicting Alexander the Great. Kallatis mint, issued in 250–225 BCE. Source: https://www.wildwinds.com/coins/greece/macedonia/kings/alexander_III/BlackSeaHoard_038.jpg. With the permission of Wildwinds.com

southern Greece for nearly a century and a half. For the life and deeds of the kings Philip II and Alexander the Great the reader can read the great works of Nicholas GL Hammond *Philip of Macedon* (1994) and *The Genius of Alexander the Great* (1997).

Chapter 20
Taking Crucial Decisions in the Athenian Assembly and the Pivotal Role of *Paideia*

Abstract This chapter describes a stormy debate in the Athenian citizen's Assembly, about continuing (or not) a new round of war with the powerful Macedonia. It presents, in a figurative way, the basic political dilemma that the Athenians were called to vote on, through *direct democratic* procedures: peace or war. Furthermore, it indirectly relates this discussion to issues of education, both as a process of acquiring knowledge and as a process of shaping the moral character of citizens, the so-called *paideia*, something on which the Athenians invested a lot in their relationships with each other.

20.1 A Special Day at the Assembly

After recalling the events of Chaeronea, Nicomedes also remembered an important incident that unfolded in the Assembly when, together with 49 other citizens from his tribe, he was elected an *epistates* of his *prytany*, for the first time in his life. It was a stormy Assembly on the future of the polis.

It was shortly after the events of Chaeronea and the Pan-Hellenic congress at Corinth. While all of Greece, under the leadership of Macedonia, with the exception of Sparta, was preparing for war with Persia, the shocking news arrived of the assassination of Philip II by one of his bodyguards, Pausanias. It took place during a procession for the wedding of King Alexander of Molossis, with Philip's and Olympias' daughter, Cleopatra. Philip's bodyguards were quick to kill Pausanias, very convenient for many, because then the real instigator of the assassination would never be known.

In Athens the news resembled a situation, as if someone had disturbed with a branch a wasp's nest. Emotions were mixed and opinions divided. For sure, a general emotion of relief was spread throughout the polis, because the shadow of Macedonia, which used to spread menacingly over Southern Greece, seemed to have disappeared, so suddenly, like the morning fog that is scattered by a strong sun.

But Nicomedes, like Lycurgus, Phocion and their friends, was worried. With Philip, and after the conference of Corinth, they knew what to expect, more or less, while now perhaps a new period of uncertainty and effervescence was beginning.

E. M. L. Economou, N. C. Kyriazis, *Daily Life in Classical Athens*, Frontiers in Economic History, https://doi.org/10.1007/978-3-031-58541-8_20

Lycurgus, who was definitely not a pro-Macedonian, believed however that the Athenians had to avoid new war adventures that would make their economy collapse and this would terminate his economic recovery program that he had just passed through the popular Assembly. He was worried about those reckless Athenians who had influence in public life such as Demosthenes and Hypereides, who probably thought that the death of Philip would weaken the Macedonians and would once again offer the opportunity for Athens to take over the hegemony of Greece, which was more like an illusional desire.

The heir to the throne, now king Alexander III, was a question mark. Very young and inexperienced, yet brave as he had proved at Chaeronea. He had received an excellent education, thanks to his teacher Aristotle, a student of Plato, from Stageira in Chalkidiki, who was among the greatest philosophers that had been active in the polis of Athens some time ago.

Ambassadors arrived from Thebes. That month, the tribe of Nicomedes held the *prytany*, and prepared the agenda of the Assembly, which at that particular time, the only issue to be discussed and decided was: continue the peace treaty or declare a new war with the Macedonians.

The Assembly began with the Thebans taking the floor first: They announced that they had driven the Macedonian garrison from the Acropolis of Thebes, Kadmeia, and that they were ready to fight the Macedonians again.

The Thebans, probably underestimating Alexander's strategic genius, and considering that they were dealing with an inexperienced young king, saw the moment as an opportunity to drive the Macedonians out of Southern Greece. Alexander would be busy for some time in the north of his kingdom, because his northern neighbors, Illyrians, Triballians, Getae, and Thracians had revolted and all together invaded Macedonia.

Perhaps, if the gods favored them, Alexander would be killed fighting against them, like many Macedonians kings in the past. Anarchy would then prevail in Macedonia, until a new capable king would be found between Philip's successors and the Macedonian factions.

Boeotian embassies had already gone to the Peloponnesian cities, Argos, Elis, Arcadia, and Corinth, and even Sparta, and the Aetolian League, to formulate a new anti-Macedonian alliance. Athens had to participate as well. They thought that with Athens, victory was certain. The time had come to get rid of the Macedonians once and for all, as with the Persians a century and a half ago!

These were the arguments of the Theban ambassadors, who also represented most of the Boeotian cities.

Then, when they had finished, Nicomedes, who had been drawn as *epistates of the prytaneis* that day so as to direct the debate in the Assembly, spoke the familiar words:

– *Tis agoreuein bouletai?*[1]

[1]Who wants to speak?

Demosthenes asked to speak, this was approved by Nicomedes, who offered him the floor, and turned the *clepsydra* to time him.

As the Athenians expected, Demosthenes delivered another fiery anti-Macedonian speech. Hypereides took the floor second, who surpassed Demosthenes in anti-Macedonian anger:

– How long Athenians will we tolerate being led by barbarians, who neither knew nor understood democracy, and all they know is to arrange the succession of the throne with blood and murders? Philip died murdered. Now, Olympias and Alexander killed all possible claimants to the throne: Philip's son, still an infant, by his last wife, Cleopatra, Cleopatra herself, Attalus' father, and many others. These are customs and habits not of Greeks, but of Orientals, Persians, and Medes. It seems that everything Aristotle taught him was lost. The barbarian always remains a barbarian. So, shall we accept them as our leaders and guides? To accept barbarians and murderers, we, the lovers of democracy and freedom?

Then the most prudent took the floor, Phocion, Demades, and Aeschines, recalling that, just 3 years before the Athenians had crowned Philip II and cheered Alexander when, as Philip's representative, he had spoken here at the Pnyx.

– So short is your memory Athenians? So easily do you now call a barbarian someone who we accepted to speak at Pnyx? Since when do we accept barbarians to speak to us in the Assembly? I don't think there is anyone who will speak in the Assembly, not being prejudiced, but speaking seriously and with sobriety, to dispute that the Macedonians are also Greeks by blood, like us, of the same race. And after we accepted him to speak to us, we accepted that he is Greek. Did you forget the 1000 dead of Chaeronea? Do you want more? Have you forgotten the magnanimity of Philip in returning us the 2000 captives without ransom? And what is the benefit of a new war? What will we gain? We are free in any case. Do you see any Macedonian garrison on the Acropolis? Will our trade and economy flourish after another war, with an uncertain outcome? What will we gain from a new war? Hegemony of Greece? We know what happened during the Peloponnesian and Social wars in similar efforts we made, not in the distant past. If we fight, we risk losing everything: prosperity, democracy, and freedom, for chimerical gains. Let us not sacrifice everything for illusions and deceptive dreams, the Demosthenes's chimeras! Prudence, Athenians! Do not be drawn into the abyss and destruction.

The crowd calmed down. Lycurgus, talking calmly now, commented:

– I see, my friends, that in Athens there is still respect for the laws. So, let us decide as we always do in our democracy, voting, not with shouts and threats, but with a rational thinking backed up by logical arguments.

Lycurgus's opinion prevailed. The Athenians chose peace, they refused the proposal of the Boeotians. Lycurgus probably thus saved Athens, for Alexander, acting with lightning speed, returned from Northern Greece in 14 days and found himself in front of Thebes, besieging them, before reinforcements from other Greek cities arrived. Alexander sent ambassadors to Thebes with compromise proposals, which the Thebans, not having a Lycurgus among them, foolishly rejected.

Ignorant even in tactics, the Thebans instead of waiting in the safety of their walls for allied reinforcements went out and fought a tactical battle with the Macedonians. They were defeated and in retreating to the city they did not have time to close the gates. The Macedonians entered, and there followed a terrible slaughter of men, women, children, chiefly, mainly by the sworn enemies of the Thebans who had formerly suffered from them, Plataeans, Orchomenians, Thespians, and Phocians. Some estimates put the dead at 5000 and the rescued at 10,000, sold into slavery.

* * *

20.2 The Ethical Dimension of the Athenian *Paideia*

In this Scene, we presented a particularly tense and stormy Assembly meeting due to special events. While the speeches are hypothetical, the facts are real, as are the main arguments on both sides.

The participation of Athenian citizens in the daily administration of their polis was part of their daily life, in contrast to the citizens of today's indirect-representative democracies, who exercise political "duties-rights" by voting in elections at rare intervals, or in also sparse referendums, except in countries that apply, at least to some extent, institutions of *direct democracy* and *referendums*, like in Switzerland and some American states such as California.[2]

We chose to briefly mention again, in this Scene the issue of *paideia*, this time having to do with the education of the young Alexander, son of Philip II, by Aristotle. *Paideia* is the most valuable thing for a man, emphasized by Isocrates (*To Demonicus*, 1.33). Lucian, in *Anacharsis* (20–23) in the second century AD uses a fictional dialogue of Solon with Anacharsis and describes how from a young age until adulthood the Athenians were taught the useful things for their lives and for the functioning of their polis. Children and youth were to be taught norms of social behavior so that they would retain these teachings into their old age (Euripides, *Suppliants*, 910–915). That is, *paideia* was concerned with the necessary knowledge and practices in various phases of individuals' coming of age (Demosthenes, *Funeral Speech*, 60.16). *Paideia* had various contents, such as justice, prudence, piety, and wisdom (Plato, *Protagoras*, 325A, 328D, 330B). Plato, through the mouth of Socrates, argues that knowledge and wisdom are better than pleasure. At the same time, the Athenians had realized that achieving a sense of generalized morality for society could only happen through *paideia*. As Isocrates informs us (*Antidosis*, 15.181–192), the exercise of body and mind were intended to teach the young through the knowledge they received. Another goal was to learn not to be unfair:

[2]For a detailed analysis of modern state institutions of *direct democracy*, see again the references in ftn 18 in Chap. 1.

> ...I maintain that everyone does everything which he does for the sake of pleasure or gain or honor; (*ibid.*, 217 and Isocrates, *Panathenaicus*, 17.30–32)

The main feature of the entire education system of the Athenians was that it did not focus only on the provision of technical knowledge, but great importance was further attached to the moral education of the students, so that they would then become useful members of society, and thus ensure its future prosperity. In this way, the education system constituted by the Athenians was twofold; on the one hand was related to the part of learning technical skills, while on the other hand, shaping their moral character accordingly, through *paideia* (Jaeger 1939/1967; Bitros and Karayiannis 2008, 2010; Kyriazis and Economou 2015b). Therefore, a key belief of the Athenians was that the proper *paideia* creates virtue and this can lead to the ideal state governance (Plato, *Protagoras*, 318–320). In other words, they believed that **without the proper qualitative and multidimensional education, there is no good democracy.** In accordance with this, in an important paper, Lipset (1959) emphasized the role of education and economic growth in promoting political development in general and democracy in particular.

For these reasons, the essential goals of *paideia* in Athens aimed at four improvements of the individual: moral, behavioral, economic, and acquiring skills.

The first consisted of the following sub-principles: respect to the gods, obedience to the laws (Sophocles, *Antigone*, 365–370, 660–675; Isocrates, *Areopagiticus*, 7.41; Plato, *Laws*, 659D-E, 797B), respect for elders and care of parents (Isocrates, *Areopagiticus*, 7.49). This included gymnastics, which for the Athenians, as for all Greeks, was a way of life. The teaching in the *palaestrae* (private athletic facilities) of various sports that started from an early age had the aim, on the one hand, to improve the physical condition of the individual so that he would later become a capable soldier and, on the other hand, to teach him *eu agonizesthai* ("fair game") (Plato, *Republic*, 410c; Humphreys 1974, 91).

The second goal consisted of teaching good manners of social behavior and living (Isocrates, *To Demonicus*, 4). The good manners taught were aimed to values such as prudence (Euripides, *Hippolytus*, 915–920), *aeschine* (shame), reward (Euripides, *Heracleidae*, 200–202), and the pursuit of glory, applauded by society (Euripides, *Andromache*, 317–325).

The third goal consisted of training for some productive or commercial occupation, so as laxity to be avoided among the young people, including those originating from the wealthiest families (Isocrates, *Areopagiticus*, 7.44–45, 7.55). A social norm, not of the privileged aristocracy, but of the citizens whose parents were engaged in agriculture, crafts and trade, was the continuation of the profession of their parents or, instead, learning a new one. Usually youths learned arts and trades from their fathers or from friends or others who practiced a similar art (Plato, *Protagoras*, 328; Aeschines, *Agaisnt Timarchus*, 1.40). They were also trained not to indulge in luxurious living and to willingly undertake public expenses, such as *liturgies* (Isocrates, *Areopagiticus*, 7.24).

The fourth goal concerned "basic" education that is: maths, writing and reading, music, as well as higher education, that is rhetoric art, philosophy, geometry, etc.

(Demosthenes, *Erotic Essay*, 61.37, 61.40, 61.44). The latter was a privilege only of high-income families who could afford to pay private tutors for that purpose.

According to the archeological findings (inscriptions and votives, honorary plaques) that are available from the sixth century (520–510 BCE), most Athenians knew how to write and read.

20.3 The *Paideia* of the Athenians as an Educational Process

As for *paideia* as an educational process, which falls under the last two of the four categories mentioned in 19.2, it was basically private. However, for specific social groups, the Athenian state covered the costs of children's basic—"elementary" education, as public expenditure.[3]

Aeschines (*Against Timarchus*, 1.8) presented the legal and customary framework that the Athenians had adopted for private education; the law originally defined the behavior of teachers who earned their living from this profession and who should have good manners and conduct (ibid., 1.9). Education at *didaskaleia* ("elementary schools") fell under the two following rules: children should arrive and leave school at a specified time a day, and there should be a given number of students of the appropriate age. The *didaskaleia* and the *palaestrae* should not open before the sun rises and close after the sunset because "there is a suspicion in desolation and darkness." There was a public authority that supervised the above principles in schools and monitored the behavior of the teachers and *pedagogues* (ibid., 1.10). And all this because:

> .... The lawgiver believed that it is the boy who has been well brought up that will be a useful citizen when he becomes a man. But when a boy's natural disposition is subjected at the very outset to vicious training, the product of such wrong nurture will be, as he believed, a citizen like this man Timarchus.[4]' (*ibid.*, 1.11)

From the above, it is easy to conclude that the educational system of the Athenians was basically humanitarian and aimed at strengthening the functioning of an open but creative society and economy. And as we read from Thucydides (2.43), every young Athenian learned that in every act he should be guided by philanthropy and always be willing to give his best to the city.

---

[3]For an analytical view of the Athenian educational system, Pritchard (2003) is a very good source.

[4]Timarchus was accused by Aeschines of behaving in a way detrimental to society. The case was brought about in 346–345 BCE. This speech provides evidence of a number of actions which, according to Aeschines, would cause a citizen to lose the right of addressing the Assembly. Aeschines accused Timarchus due to two kinds of non-socially acceptable acts: prostituting himself and spoiling his inheritance. Along with these two accusations, Timarchus was further prosecuted on trial, for charges of bribery, sycophancy, embezzlement, and perjury.

In principle, the majority of the Athenian families tried to provide the best education for their male children. Between the ages of 6–14, (in principle) all Athenian children received basic level education from private tutors. They were distinguished among (i) the *grammatists* who taught them writing, reading, maths and the great poets such as Homer and Hesiod, (ii) the *kitharistae* who taught their students how to play the seven-stringed lyre as well as the works of lyric poets, and finally, (iii) the *paidotribae* who were responsible for the physical training of the youth, teaching them sports such as high jumping, discus throwing, wrestling, and even the martial art of *pankration* (see further in Chap. 24). Literature, music, and painting were sometimes added to the lessons (Aristotle, *Politics*, 8.1337a.).

An equally important, but not well-known element is that, contrary to what is widely believed, the Athenian state provided also partially public elementary level education to children of specific social groups. Beaumont (2012, 135) writes that from the fifth c. onward the Athenian public undertook the payment of the teachers' salary (first grade between 6–14 years old) in cases of children who lost their parents in a war operation of the polis, children of poor families, and children of the *thetes*. From the last point, three main issues arise.

Firstly, that the Athenian state is, if not the first, at least one of the first historically recorded states that implemented an educational system in practice. On a purely technical level, the state entrusted the elementary education of the children of specific social groups to private teachers for a monetary fee at public expense. Essentially, the Athenian state provided this segment of the population with public education through a process of contracting/leasing to private individuals (the teachers) to provide services for the public, another successful *3P* paradigm as those mentioned already in previous sections.

Secondly, if the costs for children's education indeed included also those of the *thetes'* kids, then it would be no exaggeration to argue that the Athenian state provided public elementary level education to a large proportion of students, since the low-income *thetes* constituted the largest section of the population. Consequently, a very large portion of children would receive subsidized primary education from the state, probably exceeding 50% of the students of the Athenian state.

By contrast, between the ages of 15–18, the Athenian youth received a higher level of education from philosophers, who, of course, demanded a much larger wage, and for this reason the education was essentially directed only to the well-to-do Athenians. This means that the children of the low-income families did not have access to the secondary level educational system, and according to Xenophon (*Constitution of the Lacedaimonians*, 2), this was an unacceptable situation regarding the Athenian educational system.

Thirdly, between the years 19–20 the young Athenian *ephebes* carried out their military service, which included the basic training of the *hoplite*, sentries on the Long Walls, or in other border fortresses of Attica.

As Aristotle testifies (*Athenian Constitution*, 42.2–4) the *ephebes'* fathers elected three citizens from each tribe over 40 years of age (30 in all) of recognized moral value, considered as suitable to undertake the supervision of the *ephebes*. These tutors were known as *sophronistes* and *kosmetes*. Each *deme* elected the worthiest *sophronistes* and *kosmetes* so as to properly undertake the education of the *ephebes* because these positions required a high degree of expertise, ethical background, integrity of character, and sense of duty. *Sophronistai* and *kosmetai* were not drawn, but elected, like the generals and treasurers (Loomis 1988, 24–25). Apparently, here too, the Athenians understood that this specific post required special qualifications, therefore could not be filled by lottery.

As has already mentioned, another indirect form of *paideia* was provided to the Athenian citizens, at an indirect level, through their participation in meetings of the Assembly, the attendance of the theatrical performances and their participation in the courts and in the public administration. The education of the Athenians was further supported by poetry and plays (Aristophanes, *Frogs*, 1009–1010, 1030–1035, 1050–1055; Lycurgus, *Against Leocrates*, 100, 102). The tragedians with their poetry taught morals, virtue, etc. and could shape accordingly the behavior of the citizens (Plato, *Protagoras*, 325E-326A).

In Economou and Kyriazis (2019a, 62–63), we have calculated that an Athenian citizen, reaching his thirtieth year of age, would have received a cumulative 1600 h of "education" in all subjects, such as foreign and economic policy by attending even only half of the meetings of the Assembly each year, 20 of them. If we exclude the theatrical performances, it reached 1900 h of "education," and together with the participation and experience they further gained as judges and their participation in public administration would exceed 2000. A modern 4-year university study program gathers approximately 1800 h of specialized (and not general, like in the case of the Athenians) teaching.

20.4 Aristophanes on the Education of the Youth

Aristophanes (*Clouds*, 960–980) extols the education that young people used to receive in earlier times; being imbued by values such as justice and prudence, respect for others and especially elders, industriousness, moderation in the consumption of goods, avoiding illegalities at the cost of immediate punishment, and not to be promiscuous and effeminate. This education had resulted in a high level of generalized morality among individuals, which was not the case in his time. He criticized various facts, such as when young people, who consisted the future of the polis, were given bad role models such as focusing mainly on how to feed themselves better and with less effort and not to follow the laws of the city (ibid., 1037–1040).

Therefore, criticizing the quality of education of his time, he suggested that young people should not abandon the training of the body with the view to learn sophistry-rhetoric arts because the only utility that is provided by these rhetorical skills is to learn how to distort the truth in the courts (ibid., 873–876) and because of this young people should not pay money to sophists to be taught by them. Also mocking the pursuits of Socrates, he accused the philosophers of dealing with abstract concepts and meaningless things for life, in contrast to the real everyday issues and problems of citizens (ibid., 220–225). That is why he recommended that teachers of young people should deal with the real concerns and issues of everyday life (ibid., 230–235).

But why do we have this sharp attack of Aristophanes against philosophical pursuits and knowledge?

An obvious answer is that this knowledge, since it required a significant expense so as to pay the rhetors, would be acquired only by the children of a few families with the possible result that they would form a political elite that would progressively rule the city. This would have as a result the *direct democracy* that all the Athenians had struggled hard for[5] through the reforms of Cleisthenes, Ephialtes, and Pericles, to degenerate into an "elitistic" type of democracy where only the few and the (financially) privileged could afford to participate.

Another problem was that by leading all mentally skillful minds of the young Athenians toward philosophy, the Athenians would leave open the potential for entrepreneurial activities to be undertaken by foreigners and thus the city would lose resources and creativity.

[5]By this, we mean the power struggle between the aristocratic elites in Classical Athens that finally led to the intervention of a Spartan military unit in favour of the pro-oligarchic group under Isagoras, which was finally overthrown by Cleisthenes and his faction, who succeeded in overthrowing Isagoras due to the decisive intervention of the Athenian demos in favour of Cleisthenes, who then he established in Athens a direct participatory democracy—open to all free male citizens (see Economou and Kyriazis 2019a, 2019b, 2019c, 12–42 and 53–60). On the other hand, some other scholars argue that in reality Cleisthenes had prepared the movement of the *demos* behind the scenes, therefore it is not correct to speak of an "Athenian Revolution" but of behind-the-scenes actions of aristocratic circles that succeeded in mobilizing the Athenian *demos*, which led finally to the emergence of the democratic culture.

Chapter 21
Slave Trading in the Athenian Market

Abstract This brief chapter describes how buying and selling of slaves was taking place at the Athenian Agora and what informal "strategies" were followed by the Athenian citizens in order to secure slaves that would be "highly efficient" (in terms of labor performance, etc.) at the lowest possible cost. It also describes the fortification system of Athens, that, in a wider sense, should be seen as part of the overall public expenditure of the Athenian state, for the purpose of providing (what would nowadays be called as) the public good of defense.

21.1 Melanippe: An Amazonian, Given as Gift for Chariclea and Nicandros

– We need to discuss a matter, Hegeso informed Nicomedes, with a peremptory and decisive voice.

Nicomedes stretched his ears. When his wife was assuming such a tone, he knew that the topic of discussion was serious and that he could not avoid it.

– About Chariclea and our lad, Nicandros, continued. And about our *oikos*.
– I am all ears, he replied to her.
– Chariclea is getting old.... She... is not like she was a few years ago. She needs an assistant... I think it's time to get her an assistant. Let's buy a female slave. After all, it's the right moment. Prices have dropped. After Alexander's wars with the barbarians, all the Greek cities have been filled with slaves.

Hegeso was a smart wife and when she proposed something for her *oikos*, she had prepared it well beforehand.

And how do you know all this? he asked her.

– Don't I live in Athens too? I am also asking often Ischomachos for market prices, and, you know, sometimes, I decide to go for shopping with Chariclea at the Agora myself instead of remaining all day at the *gynaikonites*. I can also tell you the prices: Female slaves from Thrace, in good health and below 30 years of age, cost around 200 to 220 drachmae. Female slaves from Illyria, up to 20 years old,

E. M. L. Economou, N. C. Kyriazis, *Daily Life in Classical Athens*, Frontiers in Economic History, https://doi.org/10.1007/978-3-031-58541-8_21

depending on their health and beauty, from 150 to 300. A Syrian costs 240 drachmae, while boys from 70–100.

- And I thought I was the banker, joked Nicomedes.
- I am a banker's wife. I learned more and more about the proper management of the *oikos*. You taught me well and I think I manage our *oikos* well when you are absent. Without wasting money, but also without missing anything. Isn't this the right way of thinking?
- Really. You are a good wife and an exemplary manager of the *oikos*. I have no complaints.
- There is one more thing: Nicandros will return in 3 months from the fortress in Rhamnous, having completed his military training. It is good that he has a young slave woman in the *oikos* for a love partner. He is a young man, and instead of wasting his money and ours on whores, a young female slave would have been a much better option. Don't you agree?
- I have a wise wife, said Nicomedes, you're right.
- Wise as the wise Diotima of Socrates, as your teacher Plato used to say, smiled Hegeso. So, when are we going to arrange it? Can I come too?
- You should come. You will tell us what you think.
- When?
- Since it has to be done, and the moment is right, let's do it tomorrow. I can leave my seat to Ischomachos in the bank. The slave market is close anyway.
- Nice! Tomorrow then. We will come with Chariclea to pick you up from the bank, and then select Nicandros' gift.

Indeed, the other morning, Hegeso and Chariclea took Nicomedes from the bank and marched to the place in the Agora where the slaves were sold. The market was full of barbarian slaves, the spoils of Alexander's campaigns in the North and East, who had also arrived in the Agora of Athens. There were slaves of all ages and sexes, of different tribes, such as Illyrians, Thracians, Gaete, who lived above Thrace, Dacians, who bordered on the Gaete, though they dwelt somewhat further north, and Scythians.

Nicomedes spoke to one of the merchants he knew and explained what they wanted.

- I have everything you need, the merchant told them.

He instructed his assistants, who brought five girls from a stall, lined them up so that Nicomedes and Hegeso could choose. Nicomedes let the two women examine them.

- My husband, which do you prefer? Hegeso asked him.
- Difficult choice. They all look sturdy to me, and beautiful if you exclude the stink and the rags they wear. Maybe that blonde with the blue eyes? The tallest. How old should she be?
- Sixteen. And she is virgin, replied the merchant.
- Do you agree Hegeso? asked Nicomedes.
- I agree. It would be my choice too.

– Nice. What price are you asking for? asked the merchant.
– You chose the best one. The most beautiful and strong. A real Amazon. Did you notice her tattoo? The deer on her right arm? He showed it to them. How about 400 drachmae? Friendly price because I know you and you have helped me in the past.
– If this is a friendly price, I imagine what the hostile price would have been, laughed Nicomedes and they began to negotiate.

They ended up at three hundred.

Nicomedes went to the bank and took the three hundred drachmae. He returned, paid the merchant, signed the book of purchase and sale, he then greeted and the transaction was finished. Then, Chariclea took the girl by the hand, and asked the merchant to say the following to her:

– Don't be afraid, my dear. You are in good hands. I know, it's hard at first. That's how I also felt when I was brought up to your age. But I got used to it.... Life in Athens is good. You will like it much more than your home country...
– What shall we call her? asked Nicomedes.
– Since she is an Amazon, how about Melanippe? Hegeso replied.
– Her name is related to black colour, but she's blonde! countered Nicomedes.
– That's exactly why! Sometimes you make me think you have no sense of humor, no matter how many comedies of Aristophanes you have seen and read, Hegeso teased him.
– Well then, Nicomedes accepted his defeat. Melanippe....Anyway....

They reached home. The girl looked hesitantly, admiringly, impressed by the spacious two-story mansion, the fine furniture, the beautiful mosaic on the *andron*. She could not even imagine such dwellings when she lived with her tribe, in tents or simple huts made of bricks, wood and straw.....

Chariclea prepared her for taking a bath and have clean clothes. Then they performed Melanippe's initiation ceremony, thus making her a member of the *oikos*.

– Well, fine with this, said Nicomedes to Hegeso. Shall we tell Nicandros?
– No. We will make a surprise to him.

* * *

21.2 The Fortifications of Attica

Regarding military service, as already mentioned, young men served 2 years (18–19 years) in the armed forces of Athens, the second usually as guards in the border fortresses of Attica, Phyle, Aigosthena, Eleutherai, Oenoe, Rhamnous, Sounion, etc. On the organization and importance of this Attic fortress system in the effective defense of Attica as a whole Ober (1985) provides a thorough analysis.

The fortress of Eleutherai had been built at a strategic position for control of the narrow pass leading from Boeotia to Attica. Its construction took place between 370 and 360 BCE. The fortress follows the line of the hilltop, enclosing an area of 300 x 100 meters, with circuit walls 860 meters in length. The fortress contained towers, 6 of them still standing along the northern edge of the site, preserved to the height of 4 to 6 meters, with openings for *ballistrae* (a type of big crossbow), which helps dating the fortress at the fourth century.

21.3 The Amazons

Based on myths, some believe that the Amazons mainly came from the Scythian race that lived in parts of today's Ukraine and South West Russia. But Amazons came from other areas as well, such as from Asia Minor, the Black Sea, and from areas in Thrace and the Aegean islands. They were particularly popular in Ancient Greece, as can be seen from the multitude of paintings on vases, temple friezes, sarcophagi, etc. Thus, it seems that the mythical Amazons were not mythical at all; there were female warriors of nomadic peoples of the steppe but also originating from elsewhere. Dozens of tombs of women have been discovered buried with their weapons and horses (Mayor 2014).

These women did tattooing as can be seen from the paintings on vases, but also from the analysis of skin on skeletons which in some cases have been preserved. The most popular motifs were deer as seen, for example, on a vase painted by Pistoxenos, of 460 BCE, preserved in the Archaeological Museum of Athens. Many myths connected the Greeks to Amazons. For example, Heracles ninth labor was the retrieval of the girdle of Hippolyta, queen of the Amazons. Another famous scene portrayed is that of Achilles's victorious battle against Penthesilea, the beautiful Amazonian queen during the Trojan war. Penthesilea was the daughter of Ares and Otrera and the sister of Hippolyta, Antiope, and Melanippe. By the latter's name we inspired in the Scene. The joke of Hegeso is that Melanippe in Greek means "Dark Horse," while, in our fictional story, the girl is blonde.

Amazonomachy is also seen as the rise of feminism in Greek culture. In Quintus Smyrnaeus's *The Fall of Troy*, Penthesilea, was quoted at Troy, saying:

> Not in strength are we inferior to men; the same our eyes, our limbs the same; one common light we see, one air we breathe; nor different is the food we eat. What then denied to us hath heaven on man bestowed?

Chapter 22
The Athenian Symposia

Abstract This chapter explains the way *symposia* were held in Athens (and Ancient Greece in general). A symposion (*symposium*) was a part of a banquet that took place after the meal, when drinking for pleasure, accompanied by music, dancing, recitals, or conversation. In the symposia *hetaerae* (courtesans) could also take part, so as to please the attendees, through singing, dancing, participating in a philosophical discussion, and even, by providing the attendees sexual services.

22.1 A Symposion for Nicandros and his Friends

Nicandros completed his two-year military service, as part of the *ephebeia*, like all young Athenians. He had served successively in the Eleutherai fortress, in the borough of Oenoe which guarded the main road from Boeotia to Attica, and then in the fortress of Rhamnous, opposite Eretria, where higher up, there was the Temple of Nemesis. His proud parents dedicated him the *hestia* room[1] of the *oikos* one night to celebrate with his friends.

Nicomedes said to Nicandros:

– You fulfilled your military duty to the polis. Always carry the shield and spear with honor, like all our ancestors.

Nicandros invited five friends from those who had served together. They reclined in pairs on the couches after approaching the tables. Nicandros's mother had cooked in a clay pot in the *oikos*'s oven a piglet smeared with honey and oil, sesame and thyme, with mushrooms, chives, and vegetables. The *kylikes* were filled with wine from the estate of Nicomedes in Mesogeia. They were served on plates with spoons, cutting the meat with knives, ate it with his friends praising the dish, discussing their experiences in the service, teasing each other good-naturedly. They dipped bread in the sauce. The dinner ended with pies filled with walnuts, almonds, and chestnuts, spread with honey.

[1] The "hearth" room.

E. M. L. Economou, N. C. Kyriazis, *Daily Life in Classical Athens*, Frontiers in Economic History, https://doi.org/10.1007/978-3-031-58541-8_22

The symposion-fellows were playing a game known as *kottabos*, twirling the wine *kylikes* around the forefinger without spilling the wine.

When they had finished eating, Nicandros announced:

– My friends, I have a surprise for you!

Without waiting to answer their questions, he got up, opened the door and stepped aside.

Women came in, three young courtesans in short tunics that showed the legs up to the thighs, as was the Spartan attire, and behind them two more women, an older and a young one.

– My friends, Neaera, her daughter Phano and her musicians. They will entertain us with dance and song.

Nicandros's friends left exclamations of excitement!

Neaera together with Phryne were probably the most famous courtesans of Athens at that time, a worthy successor to Aspasia, as some said either jealously or admiringly; only that in their times there was not a Pericles to marry her. Other citizens had a negative view for Aspasia, being accused of having had an unsettled life due to being herself an *hetaera* at her previous life, as they accused her, without of course this having been proven with absolute certainty.

Neaera had become even more famous not long ago when she was accused, by Demosthenes and other accusers, that she and her daughter had usurped the status of Athenian citizen, while they were foreigners. The trial had aroused interest, but in the end the two women had been acquitted.

Nicandros looked at Neaera and Phano in succession. Neaera retained the mature beauty of a woman who had lived and known the world, and what time took (her) away, with a few wrinkles around the eyes, was replaced by her experience and technique, emphasizing the contours of the eyes, lips with cosmetics, and spreading a light fragrance of myrrh, brought from the East. She wore a white light tunic, cinched at the waist with a thin leather belt, with silver ornaments, a net to hold her black hair which shone in the firelight from the hearth and lamps, a gold necklace in the shape of plane leaves on the neck and a gold ring in the shape of a dolphin on the right middle finger. Nicandros assumed that she would have bought all of these from famous shops for women's goods in the Agora or that she received some of them as gifts from her fans.

Phano, estimated to be in her early twenties, was a very beautiful young woman, with blonde hair, like Homer's beautiful Helen, that looked like it had been sprinkled with gold. Thin nose, somewhat turned up at the tip, which gave her an air of cute insolence, well-shaped lips that beckoned you to kiss them, pearly teeth, arched eyebrows like the arches of well-built bridges, harmonious and symmetrical facial lines resting on a high, slender neck like swan. Her large blue-green eyes looked like those of Athena's statue in the Parthenon.

She wore a deep blue tunic at the color of the open sea that contrasted with her golden hair, which were held back above her ears with two small ivory combs. She wore no other jewelry, for her beauty was such that no human adornment was needed further. Nature had generously endowed her. Her body, under a tunic, was firm, with beautiful curves, her chest defiantly pushing the fabric as if she wanted to break free, her slim waist accentuated by a narrow belt, high legs, her hips were nice, and the thighs and calves were very fit due to dancing.

The three young courtesans that accompanied Neaera and Phano were also chosen for their beauty, but none could match Phano.

– Neaera, it is a pleasure to have you with us, said Nicandros, offering her a *kylix* of wine. Thank you and we hear you.

Neaera nodded, sat down on a stool brought to her by a servant, readied her harp, put her fingers to the strings, tried them, tightened them as they should be, and began to sing in a deep melodious voice, set to music poems of Mimnermus, Anacreon, and Sappho; Mimnermus for his beloved aulitris Phano synonymous with her daughter, Sappho for the girls of her school and marriage, and Anacreon for the ironic and happy verses that praised life such as:

> Let the enemy now rejoice my beautiful shield that I threw away to be swift for flight. I, without it, enjoy the beautiful life better.

and Sappho's like:

> Raise high the roof beam, carpenters. Like Ares comes the bridegroom, taller far than a tall man.[2]

They listened intently as her voice, always beautiful and clear, changing with the words of each song while her fingers traveled swiftly and artfully across the strings of the harp, scattering beautiful accompanying melodies.

* * *

22.2 General Notes

The outcome of Neaera's trial is unfortunately not known. We make the hypothesis that she was probably acquitted because it was probable that the Heliaia judges would have been moved by Neaera's tears, impressed by Phano's youthful beauty and convinced by the defense written by an experienced orator. On the contrary, Kapparis (1999, 42) suggests that despite the weak case for his position, Apollodorus may have been able to convince the jurors to his side by playing on their prejudices and fears.

Ancient statues were painted, as evidenced by the few traces of paint that have been preserved on some.

[2]This passage is reproduced here from Sappho's fragment LP 111.

22.3 Symposia and Music

At the symposia, the *aulitrides* played music (harp, flute, lyre), and the *orchestrides* danced and sang. According to a law, they were forbidden to charge more than 2 drachmae a night, as a protection against squandering the property of youths prone to extravagance and amusement (Aristotle, *Athenian Constitution*, 50.2). The *hetaerae* on their part provided amorous services and participation in philosophical discussions.

The word *mousike* (music) from the well-known *mousai* (muse—who, according to mythology lived in mount Parnassos) indicated all the arts, song, dance, and also philosophical discussion. Also, other modern words like harmony and orchestra have Greek roots. Professional musicians (in today's sense of the word) have existed since the time of Homer, probably originating even from earlier times, as well as *aoidoi* who were professional performers who recited epics and then lyric poems to the accompaniment of the lyre. In the Panathenaea, recitation competitions were held. The lyre resembled today's guitar. It usually had seven strings, while one variant, the *barbitos*, had five. Later, lyres were also made of wood. Another string instrument that was very common was the harp with many strings, possibly 15.

The most popular wind instrument was the *aulos* (from which the *aulitrides* got their name). Its sound probably resembled that of today's oboe. It consisted of a hollow tube of wood, brass (bronze), bone, or reed and had holes for finger-use, with a reed mouthpiece. The chorus in tragedies danced to the accompaniment of a flute. Spartans entered the battle with the escort of *auloi* that helped the proper pace of the *phalanx*. Another musical instrument was the *syrinx*, many pipes joined together, an invention attributed to mythical god Panas and a favorite instrument of the shepherds. There was also the *salpinx*, a long and thin organ that ended in a bell-shaped opening. It was used in ceremonies and in battle.

Many types of percussion instruments were known, such as *kymbala*, *tympana* (drums), *krotala* ("castanets"), and *seistra*. They were used mainly in individual cults, and possibly in battle. The *triremes* also used musical instruments, mainly flutes and perhaps some kind of percussion to assist the rhythm of rowing. Although approximately 46 musical scores have survived, mostly fragmentary, and despite the work of experts, we do not know how ancient Greek music sounded, although relative simulations have been made from time to time. Some of the oldest treatises on music come from this period, like Antiphon's of Taranto, which has been saved by Plutarch, in his about 50 pages long *On Music*, part of his *Moralia*.

22.4 Neaera: The Turbulent Life of a *Hetaera*

Neaera was one of the most famous *hetaerae* of antiquity. She had been abandoned as an unwanted child, picked up by slave traders and sold, along with six other girls, to Nicareta, who owned a brothel in Corinth. The latter was so famous for her prostitutes hence the verb *korinthiazein*, as a synonym for adultery, had prevailed. Finally, Nicareta sold Neaera for 3000 drachmae, a large sum, to two men, one Corinthian and one from Leukas to exploit her as a slave together. When the two men decided to create family and get married, they proposed to Neaera either to go to a brothel or to pay herself the amount of money they paid for her purchase, with a discount of 1000 drachmae.

Essentially, they gave her the opportunity to buy her freedom, to become an *apeleuthere* (freed woman), but in the end the amount was covered by Phrynion, who bought her and took her with him to Athens. They attended symposia, but Phrynion did not "manage" to be her only lover. In fact, Neaera abandoned him, took her personal belongings and two maids, and returned to prostitution. The Athenian statesman Stephanos was interested in her and her children and presented her as his wife. Over the years she developed a 30-year relationship with Stephanos. Around 340 BCE, Neaera was accused by Apollodorus, an enemy of Stephanos, in Demosthenes' famous speech, *Against Neaera*, of their illicit marriage. She was accused of with *a graphe xenias* (representing herself as a citizen when in fact she was not). According to Apollodorus and Theomnestos, Neaera, although not a citizen of Athens, usurped the citizen rights of Athens. She tried also to cheat the Athenian authorities by trying to recognize as legitimate citizens her two sons and her daughter, Phano, who was also a *hetaera*. Fisher (1993) argues that in fact these two sons were not Neaera's but of Stephanos, by an Athenian woman.

There were political motives behind this trial. Stephanos was a follower of Eubulus, a rival of Demosthenes, and had succeeded in condemning Apollodorus, accusing him of having proposed some illegal resolution. So Apollodorus and Theomnestos, seeking revenge and having nothing else to accuse Stephanos of, sued Neaera who was associated with him.

22.5 The Illegal Accommodation of Non-Athenians within Athens

Neaera was accused in court of not being an Athenian, and therefore the marital relationship she had developed with a citizen, Stephanos, entailed serious legal consequences for both of them. In particular, according to the law, if an Athenian citizen had as his wife a foreigner, who had concealed her identity and did not permanently reside in the city as a *metic*, she could suffer a *graphe*, i.e. a public complaint by a citizen before the *thesmothetai* and, if the complaint was judged and proved the fraud, the foreigner would be most severely punished: she would be sold as a slave, her property would be confiscated, and one-third of her property would be transferred to the one who made the *graphe*, while her husband would be sentenced to a heavy fine of a thousand drachmae (Demosthenes, *Against Neaera*, 59.16).

This proves that although Athens was a cosmopolitan polis, tolerant to the symbiosis of the native inhabitants with non-Athenians, *metics* and foreigners who resided temporarily, mainly for trade, as well as slaves, it was also considered imperative for the state authorities to know who, how many, and for what purpose foreigners were staying (temporarily) in Athens, as any modern state that respects itself must do, otherwise this is a fraud against its legitimate citizens.

Therefore, the Athenian state was very strict in cases where residents who illegally resided in its territory were also attempting to deceive the state's supervisory bodies.

Chapter 23
The Sexual Life of the Ancient Greeks

Abstract This chapter describes a famous *hetaera* pleasing a symposion's attendees by dancing and offering sexual pleasures, to the one, in whose honor the symposion took place. More general, the chapter reveals various aspects of the sexual life of the Athenians, such as the sex life of men and women, the sexual principles and habits, and the issues of prostitution, paid courtesans' services, homosexuality, and pederasty.

23.1 Phano's Dance and an Unforgettable Night for Nicandros

When Neaera ended singing, the young fellows of Nicandros applauded and congratulated her.

It was Phano's turn, to dance. The three *aulitrides* prepared their musical instruments, single, double flute and guitar, while Neaera left the harp and placed a small drum in front of her.

The music started and Phano stepped out into the empty space between the couches and began to dance.

The men's eyes were captivated by her movements. They even forgot to drink now.

The rhythm of the music changed, sometimes it became slow, dreamy, mesmerizing, sometimes it became intense and fast, like heartbeats after a great effort, sometimes challenging, swaying like reeds on a riverbank shaken by the wind, or a sea surface that lightly ripples due to the wind.

Phano's body was flexible and lithe, as if her bones were made of strands of wicker that bend without breaking. She followed or rather dictated the different rhythms of the melody, with her hands sometimes rhythmically "beating" the wind, sometimes looking like weapons in mortal combat, and sometimes embracing and caressing the body of a beloved lover.

Sometimes her body would turn quickly, she would jump lightly, she would lower herself forward, letting half of her breast be seen between its opening, sometimes she would kneel, always rhythmically, bending backward, with her

E. M. L. Economou, N. C. Kyriazis, *Daily Life in Classical Athens*, Frontiers in Economic History, https://doi.org/10.1007/978-3-031-58541-8_23

waist raised and her head at the back resting on the floor, like a bridge, with her hair spread down, like water lilies on the surface of a lake, before she bounced upright again, shaking them as if to scatter whatever earthly they had on them, so that only the reflections remained, which seemed like rays of the sun.

A little sweat appeared on her forehead, glistening in the lamplight.

When the dance ended with a bow from Phano, the enraptured guests erupted in cheers and applause.

The evening ended and the guests rose from their couches. Some would agree to finish the night in their own homes with one of the *aulitrides*.

Nicandros had agreed with Neaera to spend the rest of the night with Phano.

He greeted Neaera and took Phano by the hand. They went up to the first floor of the *oikos*, where Nicandros's room was located.

He opened the room, let her in, and placed the lamp on a small table in a corner of the room.

Nicandros sat up on the bed.

In one swift movement, Phano undressed, standing still for a moment while the dim light of the lamp eerily illuminating her body, white as Pentelikon marble. The way she stood motionless in the semi-darkness, she looked like a statue of a goddess in a sculptor's workshop, before filled in with colors.

Her body was so beautiful, with perfect analogies, that Praxiteles the famous sculptor or Apelles the famous painter could use her as a model for a statue of Aphrodite.

Phano let him admire her, turning on her axis, so that he could see her from every side, knowing the allure she held in men.

Then, without hurrying, she lay down next to him, hugged him and her lips met his in a sweet kiss. It seemed to him that they had the taste of cherry, strawberry! Nicandros caressed and cupped her breasts in his palms, sought her nipples on his lips, looking like the nipples of a grape... Phano sighed...

His hands wandered over her body, like explorers setting foot on new land and discovering its allures. Phano, skilled in the art of love, taught by her mother, responded with her own caresses, making his lust grow wild, becoming a dashing conqueror, like an army invading a conquered city and plundering its riches....

They completed the libation to Aphrodite and Eros.

Nicomedes' gift to his son had cost him a small fortune, but it was worth it. It would be a beautiful and sweet memory, for his whole life.

* * *

23.2 Sex Life of Men and Women

Another dividing point between men and women in Athenian society was the difference in sexual appetites and opportunities.

Since then, the opinion has been established that man is more of a polygamous being than woman. Paradox in terms of physical potential, since it is known that the sexual availability or potential of the woman is much greater than the man's.

Marriages between Athenian men and women were more "focused" than today. With the aim of strengthening the blood kinship to bring together as many members as possible, marriage with one's sister's daughter was also allowed (Demosthenes, *Against Neaera*, 59.22). This liberality in marriage was a means to keep the property (with the institution of dowry) within family boundaries and in this way, to forge a stronger bond between its members, for the sake of protecting one another, but also because they knew who the relatives of the bride were. For this purpose, they extended intermarriage to various *demes* (Osborne 1985, 13–15) with the aim of creating an invisible kinship network of scattered individuals who would be united by marriage vows.

The Athenians were in favor of maintaining monogamy and especially those who had children considering this as the main link between man and woman (Demosthenes, *Against Boeotus 1*, 39.29). The separation of the man from his wife—on his own initiative, without a significant reason—was not something he should be proud of. On the contrary, it was considered as a sign of unstable character and was socially stigmatized (Demosthenes, *Against Neaera*, 59.63). On the other hand, the man could divorce his wife if she had unethical or not the proper social behavior, that is, she succumbed to *moicheia* (adultery). What is important in terms of property rights protection is that in this case, the man had to return the dowry or, if he had wasted it, pay her alimony (ibid., 52) unless the woman herself had left the *oikos* by her own will (Demosthenes, *Against Onetor*, 30.8). But there was also the case that, if the husband did not behave appropriately, according to the social standard, her father would divorce her and give her to someone else (Demosthenes, *Against Spudias*).

In addition to these, the man from his deathbed could dispose of his wife and daughters to whoever he wanted by providing the appropriate dowry. This was especially the case when the wife of the deceased had no siblings (Demosthenes, *Against Stephanus 2*, 46.20; *Against Aphobus 1*, 27.5–7). If she had siblings, they undertook the obligation to marry her off to another man if they could, that is, if she was still young and beautiful and had a dowry. The justification for this status was, of course, determined in favor of various male interests: "I give her to the person whom I think will protect and treat her best" (Demosthenes, *For Phormio*, 36.31–32).

23.3 Sexual Principles and Habits

Without taking a Freudian approach to the subject of love, we must admit that it was dominant in Athenian life. Discussions about sexual relations, their limits and social "oughts" must have been frequent in Classical Athens as in modern times. Things don't seem to have changed much since then. Licht (2000) in his more than 500-page book *Sexual Life In Ancient Greece* describes all the forms of amorous intercourse and autoeroticism that he found in the writings and archeological findings of the ancient Greeks. It is not the purpose here to describe what these were, but to give some dimensions of the socially acceptable or unacceptable ways of sexual relations among the ancient Greeks by focusing on the Athenians.

According to various, mainly English, historians and prose writers since the nineteenth century, the homosexuality of the ancient Greeks has been brought up as well as other sexual situations such as pederasty. They did this by relying on some scattered passages of writings and depictions on vases and even some works that were essentially about love and friendship between very specific people (for example, Plato, *Symposion*; Demosthenes, *Erotic Essay*, etc.).

When it comes to texts, a reader's easy inferences change depending on which words or meanings he/she conjures up in his/her mind; what he/she thinks the writer wants to say. That is, a word or expression of admiration can easily turn into a sexual implication or target. On the other hand, regarding the vase paintings or statuettes with sexual content on which propagandists of the universality of the sexual perversions of the ancient Greeks rest, this argument can easily be countered: if some people want to be sexually entertained, like in Plato's *Symposion* case they will prefer an environment with scenes that stimulate the senses and bring merriment. **They will not gather in an environment surrounded by serious books to have fun**.

Furthermore, if at some point in the present a nuclear bomb fells on a certain city and life disappears while some of the buildings still remained intact, and an archeologist of the future would discover in almost every of the remaining buildings sexually perverted DVD-Rs or books with police content where the thief was achieving his goal etc., then he would conclude that everyone in this town had the same sexual preferences or that they were all thieves because those would be the tangible findings he/she could prove, by generalizing, regarding their behavior as a whole. It is well-known that the forms of entertainment that attract people are determined by what society has stigmatized either as unacceptable or normal/acceptable. It is therefore rather rash to draw general conclusions from such sources that homosexuality or *pedophilia* were acceptable situations in Ancient Greece.

What were the sex lives of people at the center rather than the fringes of a well-to-do parts of Athenian society, like the case of Plato's *Symposion*?

Quite often, in newspapers, or the TV news, or through the Internet sites, in all the languages around the world there are times that all of us will definitely read about some crime or illegality that was based on sexual causes.

The feelings of ownership, jealousy, fraud, the feelings of contempt felt by a cheated lover, regardless of gender or legal, social, or political status, are the causes that lead a person, who has an affair with another person, either to abandon him/her or to punish him/her in various ways (even illegal ones). This social pathology from ancient times to our days leads to ruptures of social cohesion.

The Athenians, living in an environment of individual freedom for citizens, established mechanisms to normalize the social relations of individuals taking also into account issues of sexual behavior. One of them was to convince women that family honor rested on their sexual fidelity. Again, and again Aristophanes, (*Ecclesiazusae*, 520, 1008; *Thesmophoriazusae*, 410–420, 510–520) satirizes this pursuit of men who do not want their wives to leave the *oikos*, as well as of those men whose wives were suspected of being adulteresses and the children were not theirs.

In case the husband accidentally caught his wife with a free citizen to have a sexual affair, the cheated man had a fundamental individual right to defend his honor and interest. His honor had two components: self-esteem and social esteem. By the act of sexual cheating, not only did the cheated husband lose confidence in his sexual and leadership abilities and the confidence on himself was shattered, but in addition his social environment after this would treat him with derision for what happened (Lysias, *On the Murder of Eratosthenes*, 1.4, 1.10).

Perhaps because many men had also sexual affairs with women other than their wives, they believed that women could be easily sexually seduced. This illusory view of men seems to have been true in Athens too. For example, Euripides (*Electra*, 1035–1040) through the mouth of Clytemnestra confessed that women are foolish too and want to imitate men in sexual relations. A man believed that he had the right to severely punish his wife's sexual fraud because if not, he thought, that he would lose the control of his *oikos*, and he could not be sure that the children he had with her were truly his. These reasons will be invoked in courts or elsewhere even today by someone who punished the adulterer.

But what happened in Classical Athens in cases where the woman's lover was caught on the spot by the cheated husband? The latter had the right even to kill him and not be punished! On the other hand, adultery even with a man's concubine could be punished to the same degree (Lysias, *On the Murder of Eratosthenes*, 1.30–31). This was the highest penalty and its magnitude was perhaps related to the fact that, as explained above, the woman's marital infidelity was considered to have significant negative impacts on the man's psychological and social health. Alternatively, the cheated husband could impose some physical punishments on the adulterer (burning of hair, etc.) without being punished by the law which Aristophanes mockingly mentions (*Clouds*, 180–185). But in addition to this punishment, the law allowed the cheated husband to reconcile with his wife's lover for some money (Lysias, *On the Murder of Eratosthenes*, 1.25–26). In fact, this way of monetary compensation could be taken as advantage by someone who had a wife who was giving in to this kind of life, so as to earn money. Such a case usually related to a courtesan, where a citizen had presented her as his wife, as Stephanos did with Neaera (Demosthenes, *Against Neaera*, 59.41, 59.65, 59.71). But such acts only brought social disrepute to the one who did them. When someone thought another man was planning or had already seduced his mistress or his wife, such cases could result the offended person to apply to court against the other man (Lysias, *Against Simon*).

On the other hand, adulteresses paid a high price for their behavior because not only could they no longer participate in public ceremonies and sacrifices (social ostracism) but they were also expelled from the man's *oikos* (familial estrangement) (Demosthenes, *Against Neaera*, 59.85–87). The Athenians believed that such drastic social acts and norms would discourage the adultery of Athenian women. Perhaps this was a product of the man's jealousy, or his inability to verify the authenticity of his children. This was also related to the contempt he would receive from those around him if he had an immoral wife, a social norm that men through the ages managed to impose over women as a social standard. On the other hand, it was not considered to be adultery of a man to associate with a *hetaera* or a prostitute (ibid., 67). A man's choice to associate with other women was considered acceptable because of his nature or due to his military life or because it was a sign of his masculinity, as it still happens today although it is not clearly acknowledged.

The men had the condescension of the society they had created for their heterosexual relationships as long as they did not relate to married Athenian women. An unmarried woman's virginity was guarded by her family as a sign of high ethical record of the family as a whole. The manifestation of the sexuality of young or more mature men could therefore be channeled—apart from their legal wife—only to other available women such as prostitutes and courtesans. Slaves under the law of property were bound to be also sexually available to their owner. This easy sexual outlet for the Athenian men does not seem to have caused them emotional or other problems with the offspring they would have.

23.4 Prostitution

For those, male or female, who were engaged in prostitution, Athenian society had established a special tax, the *pornikon telos* (prostitution tax), for these services, which brought 15 *talents* to the Athenian annual public revenue of the state budget (Aeschines, *Against Timarchus*, 1.119–124; Hansen 1991, 261). The prices for their services were two drachmae (about as much as a day's wage at the time) for "high-quality" prostitutes (such as today's call girls) and 3 *obols* (half a drachma) for simple ones, while well-known courtesans such as Phryne, Neaera, Aspasia (if indeed she was an *hetaera* before she was associated with Pericles) received ten drachmae and upwards. Excessive amounts are also mentioned, even *talents*! But these are texts by comedians, etc. who exaggerate on purpose (Loomis 1998, 184–185).

Things in the field of prostitution do not seem to have changed much from then until now. As now, so then, the price of such a profession depended proportionally on the following characteristics, age, beauty, nationality, and recognition. The younger, prettier, or Athenian women in origin were held in higher esteem than the others who were slaves or *apeleutherae*, that is, freed-women (Demosthenes, *Against Neaera*, 59.19). During the Classical period, the majority of prostitutes were of barbarian origin and worked in specific areas where the practice of this profession was allowed near the port of Piraeus and the Kerameikos of Athens. The institutionalization of specific venues for this activity was arranged by Solon, as a measure of a city's hygiene but also to limit adultery. This is again an intertemporal practice.

The association of citizens with prostitutes seems to have been quite a widespread phenomenon in Athens (Aristophanes, *Wealth*, 149–155). It was not condemned by the law, but of course it was not amenable to social approval either! From *Against*

Neaera's description we know how the prostitution ring worked—not much different from today's trafficking. Athenians assessed the result rather than the act of prostitution itself, claiming that if a prostitute did not cause them special financial burdens, then there was no problem.

The critique on those who were associated with prostitutes perhaps can be justified in that it was considered reprehensible behavior because the properties of men could be wasted on extravagance instead of being spent on constructive projects, such as taking on the financial burdens of their *deme*. The social perception had passed through the male population that many of those who were associated with harlots and courtesans had a rakish and profligate life and were socially condemned as cohabiting with some woman of loose morals (Demosthenes, *Against Neaera*, 59.30, 59.33, 59,108). These were considered despicable for a citizen by society as a whole and also by the judges who might be hearing a case involving such people.

From the ancient texts we are additionally informed that rarely an Athenian citizen or youth practiced the profession of prostitution, which was absolutely socially reprehensible (Aeschines, *Against Timarchus*, 1.40). Most prostitutes (either female or male) were former slaves or foreigners (Demosthenes, *Against Androtion*, 22.61; Lysias, *Against Simon*, 322–324).

If there was a relationship with prostitutes and proved to be costly, this was considered reprehensible and was loathed (Demosthenes, *Against Neaera*, 59.22–24). This was the case when a man had a permanent harlot as a concubine for his service, clearly inferior in rights to a legitimate wife. Concubines usually had no dowry but could agree with the man some financial benefits for themselves or recognition of their children (Demosthenes, *Against Boeotus* 2, 40.20). The last act was not accepted by the Athenians in principle, because they thought that if prostitutes and *hetaerae* were raised socially, family life morals could be relaxed (Demosthenes, *Against Neaera*, 59.113). In general, however, the Athenians had a legal provision that considered the promotion of prostitution, as a transactional relationship between individuals (Aristotle, *Nicomachean Ethics*, 1131a5–1131a10).

23.5 The *Hetaerae*

Hetaerae also aimed to be sexually desirable to men. The case of Neaera which we described in the previous Scene is well-known. Usually an *apeleuthere* (freed) woman—promoter bought slave girls from other Greek city-states at an early age and trained them for the profession of prostitution (Demosthenes, *Against Neaera*, 59.50). Then she exploited them herself or sold them to other promoters who exploited them by bringing them to Athens. These girls became high traffic prostitutes or were bought for a period of time by individuals for their exclusivity and then resold to others. That is, her master not only enjoyed her charms but also got money.

Neaera had been bought by two men together who had agreed to divide the days she would be with each other. A buyer, as expected, also lied to such kind of girls about the beautiful future that awaits them in Athens: he could even promise to make their children legitimate citizens (ibid., 18–21, 26, 29–30, 38–39, 46–47). The attitude of the Athenians toward women is summed up in a very macho way by Demosthenes (*Against Neaera*, 59.122):

> For this is what living with a woman as one's wife means—to have children by her and to introduce the sons to the members of the clan and of the deme, and to betroth the daughters to husbands as one's own. Mistresses we keep for the sake of pleasure, concubines for the daily care of our persons, but wives to bear us legitimate children and to be faithful guardians of our households.

However, even if this description is clear evidence of exploitation against women, it should be considered as important, in terms of social mobility, that a *hetaera* could at least collect a sum of money from her work and buy her freedom (one thousand drachmae in the case of Neaera) from her owner (ibid., 30).

The *hetaerae*, however, did not simply offer sexual services, but were among the most cultured women of the times, who could obviously entertain their clients with "quality" art (song, dance) but also of high-quality level discussions in symposia, like Aspasia. They socialized mainly with artists, philosophers, politicians, poets and in general, the social and intellectual elite of their times, so to speak, whom they inspired, but also influenced, at least to some extent, since *hetaerae* were participating, to some degree, in important polis's lives.

The *hetaerae* were something similar to the Japanese geishas, or French courtesans of the sixteenth–seventeenth centuries. The profession was also practiced by male and female slaves, *metics* (such as Aspasia, the Milesian) and citizens (such as Neaera, who was accused of not being). Other famous courtesans of the late Classical period were Phryne, Lais from Corinth and Pankaste, from Larissa in Thessaly, a very pretty *hetaera* which for some time became the mistress of Alexander the Great when he was very young, etc.

23.6 Homosexuality

If from the above we noticed that men in Athens enjoyed a lot of freedom in heterosexual love, as long as one did not "steal" the other's wife while at the same time women seemed available under the imposition of the power of the father or money, on the subject of homosexuality and pedophilia things were not so condescending.

As expected in any society, a percentage of men or women prefer homosexual love and preferably with the young and beautiful. So, happened in Athens of the times. We have references in written sources that tried to idealize such a love. On the other hand, the widespread social acceptance of such sexual preferences not only did not seem to exist, but instead a strict legal framework had been established to prevent it. It seems that the "I don't care as long as my son isn't involved" attitude worked even then.

Much evidence of the Athenians' homosexual preference over heterosexual preference has been preserved that if this were really the case, then the Athenians could not even manage to be multiplied in population. Why were these preserved?

Let's say a completely extreme and catastrophic scenario happens: A world war takes place, which develops into a thermonuclear one. If all the modern Greeks are killed but by chance some of their personal files, computers, television series that give a clear impetus to homosexuality are saved, and after a thousand years, let's say, radioactivity disappears and other people come to inhabit this country, they will definitely conclude, if they don't investigate anything else, that most of today's Greeks were homosexuals. By this we mean that most references in ancient texts that imply or describe homosexual tendencies are not connected to the general tendency and sexual principles and preferences of society, but to a portion of the ruling and intellectual elite of Athens, as for example described in Plato's *Symposion*.

Food for such a trend in the bibliography in the recent years was provided by written references in favor of homosexuality by some ancient authors. For example, Plato (*Symposion*, 178–179, 182, 191–192, 209, 222) refers to the potential sexual love between men "who fight side by side" although he mixes up this kind of behavior with friendship for one another. Aeschines (*Against Timarchus*, 1.138–141) considers that the ancestors of the Athenians did not turn against the pure love that an elder could exhibit for a child or youth, with a view to provide him advice for a good future life, bringing as an example the relationship of Harmodius and Aristogeiton, or of Achilles and Patroclus. But he focuses on the acceptance of their relationship on the development of some deep friendship and not on the sexual act.

But even if such a sexual relationship could develop between a man and a child or youth, this does not imply a generalized social trend but specific behavior between specific individuals, and any generalization, created by interpreting the ancient sources in a special way, is arbitrary or is made on purpose.

We can observe how the large mass of Athenian citizens dealt with the issue from cases that reached the courts. At first, the citizen who had homosexual tendencies (regardless of whether they were active or passive) tried to hide this from his social environment. He was secretly trying to meet his lover so that his preference would not be known to the general public (Lysias, *Against Simon*, 3.11–12). He thought that if he was found out, he would become a laughing stock and feel ashamed (ibid., 3.3–4, 3.9). In the event that a citizen openly showed his homosexual preferences and sought to relate to young non-Athenians, he was considered a social disgrace and this was a reason for being considered as an unworthy of a man (ibid., 3.4–5, 3.7). The publicizing of one's relative acts or behavior counted as one's shame (ibid., 3.30). In the event that neither became known to the public, there was no shame, although there might be a crisis of conscience. Covering the lover's living expenses again was something that the Athenians hid as much as they could because this was also related to social disgrace. By no means was this something an Athenian would like to display (ibid., 22). Those who had bisexual preferences and practiced incest were also loathed (Lysias, *Against Alcibiades 1*, 14.41–43).

There were laws punishing homosexuals and those who were prostituting themselves for money or who seduced children for money. In fact, a homosexual who prostituted himself could not be elected as *archon* or a polis's ambassador, or hold any other office in the polis, because he was considered as *atimos* (Aeschines, *Against Timarchus*, 1.19–21). The slur against homosexuals who offered sexual services for money is strong in the works of Aristophanes (for example, *Wealth*, 149–159) who in this way seeks to ridicule the moral decline of his time due to the disorientation and laxity in the *paideia* of the young (Aristophanes, *Clouds*, 980–1005).

In addition to all this, Plato who was inspired to guide his fellow-citizens to a correct way of social life and government by creating a normative utopian society that could in his view be applicable through good laws emphasizes that homosexuality should not be permissible by the state (*Laws*, 636D, 836C, 837, 840D, 841D). Xenophon through the mouth of Socrates turns, in principle, against homosexuality that fell to his notice at that times (Xenophon, *Memorabilia*, 2.1.2.30) extolling the pure friendship that springs up between two men as was that of Achilles and Patroclus and other well-known friendly relationships of heroes of antiquity (Xenophon, *Symposion*, 8.28–32). And in Demosthenes (*Erotic Essay*, 61.4–7), we read that the sexual love between men was considered as abominable and the right one was love between their souls which developed into a proper friendship.

Therefore, if some pictorial representations with homosexual elements survive, this was not a result of approval or proof of a corresponding generalized sexual behavior. On the contrary: they painted and discussed homosexuality laughing or criticizing it, by displacing it as a non-generally accepted behavior of the polis.

23.7 Pederasty

There was a law that strictly punished pederasty with death or a heavy fine, or if the guardian of a child delivered the kid to pederasts, especially for money (Aeschines, *Against Timarchus*, 1.13–16). Pederasts were also characterized as perverts.

The Athenians as a society had taken their measures against pederasts. Not only was the law prohibiting the visit of unworthy men to private schools, but also the operating hours of schools were fixed so that the teaching procedures did not end after sunset, for the darkness might conceal "evil disturbances and deeds." As the law required:

> The teachers of the boys shall open the school-rooms not earlier than sunrise, and they shall close them before sunset. No person who is older than the boys shall be permitted to enter the room while they are there, unless he be a son of the teacher, a brother, or a daughter's husband. **If any one enter in violation of this prohibition, he shall be punished with death** (emphasis by the authors). The superintendents of the gymnasia shall under no conditions allow any one who has reached the age of manhood to enter the contests of Hermes together with the boys. A gymnasiarch who does permit this and fails to keep such a person out of the gymnasium, shall be liable to the penalties prescribed for the seduction of free-born youth. Every choregus who is appointed by the people shall be more than forty years of age. (Aeschines, *Against Timarchus*, 1.12)

Aeschines, relying on procedural arguments, on these laws and the operating principles of the Athenian system of social life, supported the above views despite the fact that, as he himself confesses, he had expressed homosexual preferences in the past. But he emphasizes that he did this out of pure love and not based on money (Aeschines, *Against Timarchus*, 1.136–137). He was forced to admit this since the judges apparently knew about his past and could significantly weaken his defense against his opponent. Pederasty, for the Athenians was viewed as behavior to be criticized and be condemned, rather than something they would want for their children or siblings to adopt.

Taken the above into account, there is no need to "put old wine in a new barrel" because it will be spoiled. It is therefore not easy to place the sexual life preferences of the ancient Athenians in the context of our own beliefs and social values. It would be better to see them as they would probably be, act and feel themselves.

Chapter 24
The Athenian Welfare State and the Provision of Health Services

Abstract This chapter describes various aspects of sporting activities in Classical Athens. Athletic events were strongly related to the Greek way of life and ethos. It also analyzes Athens as the first historically recorded welfare state who provided financial compensation for various social groups such as orphans and wives who lost their parents in a war operation for the polis. The chapter also describes the provision of health services which were separate into two groups: (i) *private provision of health services* (ii) *public provision of health services*.

24.1 Young Nicandros Recovering After a Tough Fight at the *Palaestra*

Nicandros, uttering a cry of pain, heaved himself up on the couch in his room.

- Chariclea, Eriphyle, Melanippe, please stop! you hurt me! Slow down with the bandage!
- Slow down, you're hurting him! Hegeso shouted with an expression of anguish shaped on her face....
- Normally your head should pain, said Nicomedes. Who told you to go fight in the *palaestra*, with this Aristophon who is a candidate for our polis's Olympic champion in the *pankration* fight?
- He challenged me father!
- Oh, really? And what did he tell you, son?
- He knows that I am a friend of our polis's Olympian winner in *pankration*, Dioxippos, and since in the past Dioxippos has deprived him of honors and trophies in great Athenian and Pan-Hellenic athletic contests, such as the Panathenaea and Nemea, he follows the tactic: the friend of my enemy is my enemy too! He saw me with Melanippe when we had gone to the Agora to buy various provisions, and told me that Melanippe, who is slender and sexy, like an Amazon, if she were not a slave but free, would never want to be with me, while she would like to be with him.
- And so, what? Nicomedes commented.

E. M. L. Economou, N. C. Kyriazis, *Daily Life in Classical Athens*, Frontiers in Economic History, https://doi.org/10.1007/978-3-031-58541-8_24

– So, what? oh father! He insulted my manhood!
– Oh really? So Melanippe doesn't know your manhood?

Melanippe, who had in a short time managed to learn enough Greek, hearing this answer, understood it, blushed slightly, and feeling embarrassed, got up to go and fetch another bandage.

– I decided to redeem myself from this verbal disgrace that took place at the presence of many people in the Agora, by challenging him to a duel in a nearby arena.
– Oh, Zeus! What did you do my child! Hegeso replied in despair!
– Next time I will take revenge father, I was close to victory, but with a move I did not manage to avoid, he hit me in the side and knocked me down.
– There won't be a next time! replied Nicomedes in a stern tone. This will not happen again!
– Oh Gods! Oh, my child! I will tear out the hair of this Aristophon. Look how the side of my son bruised! Hegeso began to lose her temper....
– I'm going to call Diocles, the city doctor, to come and see you immediately! And then I'll go to Aristophon's mother and protest!
– Come on mother! He is not a child! Do you expect his mother to punish him? What about asking her beating him with the rod? Oh, come on mother!

He continued:

– Finally stop, you are all acting like mourning women at a funeral!
– For God's shake! Hegeso and Chariclea shouted at the same time.
– I am here too! commented Nicomedes.
– Oh, I didn't notice you! replied Nicandros in an ironic tone, and Nicomedes, annoyed, objected:
– Honor your father and your mother, child!
– Sins of parents chastise children, oh father!
– What is this again? What was my fault that you quarreled with Aristophon?
– It is your fault! That instead of teaching me *pankration* when I was younger, you sent me to all these philosophers whom you paid handsomely, filling my head with various theories about nature, philosophy, banking and commerce, and many other things, and now, you want me to come and help you at the bank. No, no, I won't come!
– Yes, yes, you will definitely come, Ischomachos has grown older and grown tired over the years. I also need a new competent partner...You must learn the practicalities of banking, to carry on my and your grandfather's business. Now, read this papyrus my son! It is the *Ways and Means* by the famous philosopher Xenophon. It will help you forget the pain and spent your recovering time in the bed, in a creative way!
– Father, read it to mother, at night, under the light of a lamp, so she can fall asleep more easily!

Eriphyle and Melanippe were ready to laugh at Nicandros' answer, but restrained themselves, lest they should be thought to offend Nicomedes.

– Nicomedes, call Diocles now! shouted Hegeso. Her voice betrayed the great anxiety she felt because of the situation.

Nicomedes made a move to exit the room of Nicandros so as to go to the doctor's office. Melanippe jumped up spontaneously:

– -Sir, shall I go?
– Go and quickly!

Melanippe had acclimatized very quickly to her new life in Athens. She liked it. She wished to be a part of the polis and be active in the social events of Nicomedes's *oikos*. She even secretly fell in love with Nicandros, but as a slave she didn't want to show it. She knew that any serious relationship between them could not arise because of the difference in social status, and she was under no illusions. However, she was also young, very beautiful, and the two of them had already shared a lot of nights together, and she herself seemed to care a lot for him, more than a female slave of the *oikos* who does her job well but also typically. She ran off to *deme's* local doctor's office, found the doctor attending to a patient, with three other patients waiting… She ran back and reported.

– This will take time, Nicomedes said seriously and got up to go out.
– Where are you going? asked Hegeso, all anxious, looking into his eyes very intently and expectantly.
– I am going to bring a private doctor, Philocrates, to examine Nicandros.

Philocrates was one of the most famous and sought-after doctors in Athens at that time. He even went as far as Kos, where he attended the famous Hippocrates's School to upgrade his knowledge and practical experiences in a multitude of medical cases. Of course, he usually served only the well-to-do families who could afford his high salary.

Philocrates came and examined Nicandros. He palpated very carefully all over his right side, which had presented something like a hematoma. He wanted to locate the points of pain. After this he prepared a treatment with various herbs and ointments and explained to the women how they should put the bandages on him.

– Do not worry my son. It's nothing serious. Your pains and hematoma are from the blow you received on the side. But, fortunately, it's not a breakage. You will not move suddenly, you will follow the treatment I will give you and I will come and watch your progress every other day.

Philocrates prepared to leave.

– What do I owe you Philocrates? Nicomedes asked him.
– Give what you want, Nicomedes. To you, I am always indebted. Years ago, you helped me with that loan when I really needed it to go to Kos and improve my medical knowledge.

Nicomedes gave a sum of eight drachmae to Philocrates, and he, before living, bowed to Hegeso and he also saluted with a nod the others. He finally urged Nicomedes that if they need any further assistance he would be at their disposal.

Nicomedes returned to Nicandros's room. The young man was very impressed by the famous doctor's behavior toward his father.

- Do you feel better son?
- Yes, father, I will finally come to the bank. Because I realized that physical strength is not everything. If I cannot defeat Aristophon in martial art, I can defeat him with other, more important weapons, spiritual ones.
- Yes, my son. You are absolutely right! And remember: in the end, the pen is mightier than the sword!

* * *

24.2 *Pankration*: An Ancient Mixed Martial Art

Wrestling, boxing, and *pankration* were Olympic contests, the *pankration* was introduced in 648 BCE. These, like most athletic contests, foot race, *hoplite* race, javelin throwing, etc., were directly related to the military training of citizens. The course of *hoplomachia* was already taught as a part of the *ephebeia* education in order to introduce young people to martial arts.

Pankration (*pan* + *kratos*, all power) was the toughest Olympic event, a combination of boxing and wrestling, but also included other techniques such as kicking, holds, joint-locks, and chokes on the ground, making it similar to modern mixed martial arts. Only gouging and biting were prohibited. Deaths of athletes in the Olympics are reported, who preferred to die in the fight rather than accept defeat. According to the research of master George Karavidas, creator of the ShotoKunthai karate system with roots in the ancient *pankration*, the depictions, mainly on vases, of *pankratiasts*, remind the stances, strikes, grips, and defenses of modern martial arts, such as karate, judo, kung fu, etc.[1] There were also *pankration* contests for *ephebes*.

Like modern sporting events, to ensure fair game and that rules are applied, the Greeks had introduced the so-called *hellanodikai*, literally meaning "judges of the Greeks," who were the judges of the Ancient Olympic Games. It was their sacred duty to maintain the standards of the games and to uphold the rules (Image 24.1).

In this Scene, we referred to the Athenian *pankration* champions Dioxippos and Aristophon. Dioxippos was crowned Olympian winner of *pankration* at the 111th Olympic Games (336 BCE), which roughly coincides with the period we are describing in this Scene, where he appears as an already known Olympian winner.

---

[1]The reader, if he/she so desires, can contact the revivalist of the *pankration*, Grand Master George Karavidas, through the link below: https://el-gr.facebook.com/gkaravidas73.

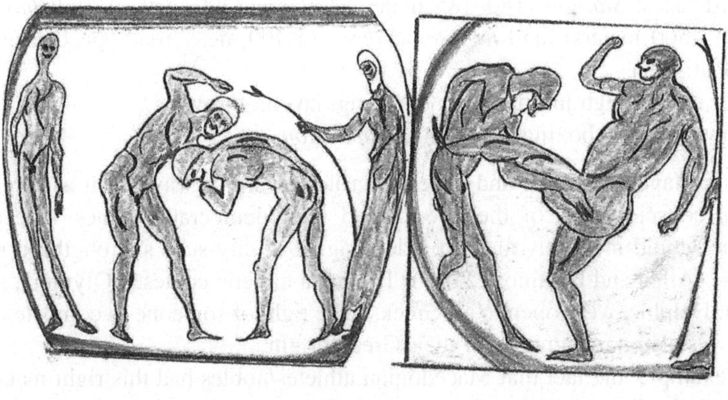

Image 24.1 Two *pankration* athletes fighting (under the watchful eye of two *hellanodikai*). Source: Image created by painter Vasiliki Demopoulou

Aristophon was crowned as Olympian winner in the *pankration* event at the 117th Olympic Games in 312 BCE. It is reported that the city-state of Athens erected a statue in his honor in Olympia. It is worth mentioning the shocking story of the Olympian *pankratiast* Arrhichion of Phigalia who was killed in 564 BCE. During the final fight, he received a very dangerous knock from his opponent. Summoning the last of his strength, Arrhichion managed to dislocate his opponent's foot forcing him to resign, while at the same times he passed away! He finally won even though he died.

Arrhichion chose death for victory, instead of living and being accompanied by the stigma of defeat!

Pausanias's (*Description of Greece*, 8.40.1.2) narrative is shocking on this:

> For when he was contending for the wild olive with the last remaining competitor, whoever he was, the latter got a grip first, and held Arrhachion,[2] hugging him with his legs, and at the same time he squeezed his neck with his hands. Arrhachion dislocated his opponent's toe, but expired owing to suffocation; but he who suffocated Arrhachion was forced to give in at the same time because of the pain in his toe. The Eleans crowned and proclaimed victor the corpse of Arrhachion.

24.3 The Olympian Truce

The Olympic games included the following sports:[3]

- Horse races (with subdivisions of races with 1, 2, 3, or even 4 horses).
- *Pentathlon* (mix of sports).

[2] Arrhichion was also spelled as Arrhachion, or Arrachion.

[3] See analytically Miller (2003a, 2003b, 2004), Philips and Pritchard (eds) (2003), and Pleket (2005).

- Speed races: *Stadion* (180–185 meters), *diaulos* (400 meters), *dolichos* (about 4200–4500 meters), and *hoplites dromos* (a 400-meter road speed race in full combat gear).
- Other sports: high jump, discus throwing, javelin throwing.
- "Heavy" sports: boxing, wrestling, *pankration.*

Sports played a special and beneficial role in various ways such as forging the national consciousness of the Greeks and their democratic values. The ancient Olympics could indirectly also provide a signal of city-state's strength, in relation to others (Allen and Lantinova 2013). The great athletic contests, Olympia, Nemea, Isthmia, Delphic, were open to all Greeks. The right of someone to compete in these games was also a recognition of their Greek origin.

For example, the fact that Macedonian athletes/nobles had this right makes self-evident their Greek origin. Sports competitions, along with religion, common language, common national origin, the amphictyonic councils along with institutions such as *asylia*, *isopoliteia*, *enktesis,* and *symbola* were the connecting links of the Greek nation, which transcended the separation of city-states and distinguished Greeks from non-Greeks—foreigners. The importance that the Greeks attached to these sports games can be seen from the fact that before the Olympic Games a truce was imposed on the military encounters, so that the athletes could attend them without obstacles. Also, another common feature of these games was that the ancients dated historical events based on them, starting with the first officially held ones, in 776 BCE. This means that athletic contests were held in Olympia and other places throughout mainland Greece even before 776, including a series of sports such as discus, archery, boxing, wrestling, and chariot races with 4 horses. Archeological evidence has verified such a claim (Lee 1988). The existence of sports is attested even from the period of the Trojan War, or even earlier, with events such as bull-leaping in Minoan Crete.

24.4 Sports in Athens

Sports were particularly popular in Ancient Greece, so there were *gymnasia* (or gymnasiums) in every Greek city-state. The word *gymnasium* comes from naked, since the athletes were either naked or lightly clothed. *Gymnasia* were supported by large structures containing spaces for each type of exercise as well as a stadium, *palaestra*, baths, etc. They usually had locker rooms and other facilities such as baths, an open space, and were usually located near rivers so that there was an abundance of water for athletes to cool and wash. Athletes used various instruments to clean themselves, including scrapers and an early type of oil-based soap.

Already from the sixth century BCE, Athens had three public *gymnasia*, the Academy, the Lyceum and the Cynosarges, all outside the city's walls. The first two institutions were accessed only by citizens and their children. By contrast, Cynosarges, located in the southern suburbs of the polis, was only accessed by the *nothoi* (illegitimate) children and those kids whose father or mother was not an Athenian by birth. It became also the place where the so-called Cynic philosophers were active (Athenaeus, *The Deipnosophists*, 6.234e; Demosthenes, *Against Aristocrates*, 23.213; Plutarch, *Themistocles*, 12). Aeschines (*Against Timarchus*, 1.138) informs us that slaves were forbidden by law to strip and exercise in *gymnasia*. Humphreys (1974, 90–91) explains that *gymnasia* were related to services offered to citizens but no source states that *metics* were excluded. He further provides evidence which however does not make it clear whether adults using the services of *gymnasia* were required to pay a small fee or no fee upon entry.

Gymnasia were, as they are today, also a place for social interaction. So, it is not surprising that Plato and Aristotle established their schools near *gymnasia* the Academy and Lyceum, respectively. In addition to the *gymnasia* there were many *palaestrae* where boys from the age of seven onward or athletes could practice for a fee. Boys could practice under the care of an experienced trainer, the *paidotribes*. Each of these athletic facilities owned and operated by private individuals (and not the public) was run by a *palaestrophylax* meaning 'who was the guardian or the director of a *palaestra*.

Wrestling and the other martial arts, boxing and *pankration*, were related also to the preparation of young people for war in the service of the motherland. Therefore, gymnastics for the Greeks was not just an exercise, but a way of life. *Palaestrae* were intended to improve the individual's physical condition, and this could help him become a good warrior and teach him the moral attitude toward victory, defeat, and fair play.

However, the Greeks also had further types of sports for entertainment, such as various ball games. A relative reference comes, for example, from the Odyssey where Nausicaa plays ball with her friends.

Could it be that the Greeks were the first to invent a type of football that is considered the "king of sports" nowadays? Indeed, there was a sport named *episkyros* where, according to the game, there were two teams, usually of 14 players separated by a line, as in today's football. Another two lines existed behind the two groups. The ball was placed on the center of the pitch and the team that got it first had to throw it over the opponent, who had to catch it as it moved and throw it back to the other. *Episkyros* was mainly played by men, but it was also practiced by women. The ball was made of pieces of leather, sewn together with animal entrails. Outside it was painted with bright colors. FIFA recognizes *episkyros* as one of the first forms of football.[4]

[4] See the related image in National Archaeological Museum in Athens and in https://www.fifa.com/about-fifa/who-we-are/the-game/. This image is derived from a marble grave stele, found in Piraeus, 400–375 BC. See item (NAMA) 873 of the National Archaeological Museum, Athens.

24.5 The Great Panathenaea and the Funding of Athletes

The Great Panathenaea were introduced in 566/5 BCE and were held every 4 years. The Pythia were instituted in 586 BCE, the Isthnia in 580 BCE and Nemea in 573 BCE and they took place every 2 years with the provision that they take place the year before or after the Olympic Games (but never in the same year). Other famous sports games were the annual Little Panathenaea, the Delphi games, Eleutheria in Larissa in honor of Zeus, Hyacinthia and Carneia held in Laconia and Sparta, respectively, in honor of Apollo, etc.[5]

The organization of the Panathenaic Games was undertaken by the so-called *athlothetai*. They were ten Athenian citizens, one from each tribe, who were elected by lot and charged with important tasks, such as they arranged the procession, and the musical, gymnastic, and equestrian games. Because of the importance of these duties their term of office was 4 years and for a month before the games they stayed in the Prytaneion together with the councilmen. Their food and expenses were covered by the polis (Miller 2004, 136). The ancient Athenians (as well as the Elians where the Olympic games, etc. were held) seem to have acquired in this way an important organizational culture of sports. In the Great Panathenaea, a series of sports were held that were not included in the Olympic games such as dance (*pyrrhichius*, etc.) and music competitions, *hoplomachia*, small boat races, torch relay, etc. (ibid., 141–144).

Furthermore, beyond the "olive branch" and personal prestige, victorious athletes received gifts and prizes for their performance (ibid., 129, 132). The prizes offered a very high compensation to the winners for any financial investment they had made by themselves so as to prepare accordingly for the games. Miller (ibid., 134) calculates in today's values, the amount of the first prize at 150,000 dollars. In the Panathenaic Games, further prizes were given, such as amphorae with oil, etc. There were also special categories of games for children. For example, the winner of the children's *stadion* race received about 1944 liters of oil, which Miller (2004, 135) estimated at about $10,000 in today's terms. These sums of money were very high and it is obvious that through them their holders could refinance their preparation costs to participate in the next major sporting events at a high level. Furthermore, winners in the music competition (with flute or guitar) at the Great Panathenaea received very high prizes. For example, the first winner received a gold crown worth 1000 drachmae and an additional 500 (silver) drachmae, the second 1200 drachmae, the third 600, the fourth 400 drachmae, and the fifth 300.

With Solon's reforms there was provision for Isthmia winners to receive 100 drachmae as prize and Olympic winners 500 drachmae (Pleket 1975, 2005; Kyle 1987: 29–31). Pleket (2005, 406–407) further argues that during the period 400–300 BCE, the sum of money for winning the Olympic Games increased to 3000–6000 drachmae, which was undoubtedly a significant advantage for the

[5]Philips and Pritchard (eds) (2003) provide a detailed analysis of the most important ancient sporting events. More generally one can consult Miller (2004).

winners, giving them extra incentive to prepare accordingly and win again in future events.

These state grants to the winners were offered through the costly *liturgies*. Therefore, the motivation for excellence and first place in sports competitions was high, probably in all Greek city-states as in some of them victory could bring great financial benefits to the winners. In Athens, Olympian winners could reside forever in the Prytaneion (thus covering board and lodging costs), receive honorary positions at public events, be exempt from tax obligations, and have their name associated with the recitation of poems, odes, and the creation of statues, to their credit (Miller 2004, 217–218; Allen and Lantinova 2013, 36). In addition, the winners could receive various other "gifts" from the state itself, including money or material goods, such as oil, worth a few hundred drachmae.

24.6 Sports and Prestige of Greek City-States

The sporting achievements of a city-state were indirectly considered to be a sign of political and military power and prestige, which other city-states had to take seriously into account. Therefore, the competition in the Olympics and other games was not only for an "olive branch," but also was related to a number of parallel important features.

For this reason, Olympian winners held a prominent position in society. Osborne (1993) argues that the giving of gifts and rewards to victorious athletes helped to create and foster a spirit of cohesion among both the athletes and the members of the society to which they belonged.[6] Cases where capable athletes competed representing not their city-state but another city were considered a public scandal and the athletes faced discredit, ostracism, and confiscation of their property.

As has already been mentioned, during the fifth century BCE, not only in Athens but also in other Greek cities, the training of young people was institutionalized in the public elementary schools of the basic 8-year education from 6 to 14 years of age.[7] The importance of gymnastics in the educational system in Classical Athens was considered as one of the main subjects of the youth, together with music and grammar etc.

The management of *gymnasia*, whose operation was subsidized by the *liturgies*, was entrusted to appointed aristocrats called *gymnasiarchai* (or *gymnasiarchs*) (Miller 2004, Chap. 12). Motivated by the potential of raising their personal prestige, *gymnasiarchai* sought out promising young athletes and undertook to subsidize and

[6]Even today, the acquisition of Olympic medals from an athlete's country creates a sense of pride in the citizens of this country.

[7]In contrast to Athens, the pedagogical system of Sparta through the *agoge* focused mainly on gymnastics and military training and can be characterized—compared to other Greek cities—as particularly arduous and harsh. For the *agoge* educational system, see Cartledge (1987).

Image 24.2 Ancient Greek women athletes exercising on various sports. Source: https://commons.wikimedia.org/wiki/File:Casale_Bikini_modified.jpg#/media/File:Armerina.jpg

cover their expenses related to sporting activities in order to increase their chances of victory in local or "international" sporting events such as the Olympic Games, where there were also special competitions for young athletes between 14–18 years old. Besides the *gymnasiarchai*, there were the *choregoi* (sponsors) who also financed cultural events with a sports background as a part of undertaking a *liturgy*. For example, the *choregia* for the preparation of the *pyrrhichius* dance competition cost the *choregos*, the non-inconsiderable sum of 800 drachmae (Miller 2004, 140).

24.7 Greek Women and Sports

Another important dimension of sports in Ancient Greece is women's active participation in sports events, something which is not well-known. Of course, their participation in athletic activities was less active than that of men, but it should not be considered negligible. Spears (1984) states that the participation of women in sports events was a pan-Hellenic phenomenon. It refers to the Heraea races, with the exclusive participation of women, which took place, like the (men's) Olympic games, in the area of ancient Olympia. A number of winners in women's athletic events are mentioned, such as Tryphossa, the first Greek woman to emerge victorious three times in the *stadion* (twice at the Pythia and once at the Isthmia Games) and Dionysia who won twice at Isthmia.

Image 24.2 presents a splendid mosaic depicting ancient Greek women playing various sports. The image is originated from Villa Romana del Casale, in Armerina, Sicily, in Italy, a magnificent example of a Roman country house of the late Imperial period (third-fourth c. AD), consisting of baths, a peristyle, and a basilica. The villa is particularly notable for its splendid series of mosaics, covering 3535 square meters, which are among the largest and the best of their kind. The Villa was declared to be UNESCO World Heritage site in 1997. Villa Romana del Casale was probably owned by a member of the Roman Senate or, possibly, Emperor Maximian (reigned from 286 to 305 AD). The room is referred to as the *Sala delle Dieci Ragazze* ("Room of the Ten Maidens"). Of the ten women depicted in the mosaic, nine wear what look like two-piece bathing suits. The girls are engaged in sports; the "bikinis" are clearly intended as sportswear, not swimwear. The women are engaged in a number of sporting acts, such as long jumping, throwing discus, running, and playing a form of handball.[8]

It is worth noting that women could also indirectly participate in the Olympic games and win laurels, prestige and prizes, as owners of chariots. The first recorded winner in this capacity was the Spartan[9] Cynisca, sister of King Agesilaus, in two consecutive Olympiads (396 and 392 BCE) as her chariot, presenting Sparta in the games, led by a male rider, won the famous *tethrippon* four-horse race (Pausanias, *Description of Greece*, 3.8.1–8.2; Miller 2004, 153 and Chap. 8 in his book, on women's sports activity).[10] To commemorate her achievements, Cynisca dedicated a set of bronze statues which depicted herself, her charioteer, her chariot, and her horses at the Temple of Zeus in Olympia. According to Pausanias, these statues were placed in a prominent location in the entrance way of the temple, next to the throne dedicated by Arimnestus, a king of Etruria. Along with the statues, Cynisca also celebrated her victories with an inscription, declaring that she was the only woman to win the wreath in the chariot events at the Olympic Games until then. The relative inscription (c. 390–380 BCE) in Olympia states:

> Kings of Sparta are my father and brothers.
> I, Cynisca, victorious with a chariot of swift-footed horses,
> have erected this statue. I declare myself the only woman in all Hellas to have won this crown.
> Apelleas son of Callicles made it.

This victory should be considered important because it highlights the concept of equality in two ways: firstly, a woman is indirectly declared as an Olympic champion (in male-dominated events) and secondly in terms of property rights: a woman

[8]Read further in: https://archaeostore.com/blog/girls-in-bikini-mosaic/.

[9]Spears (1984) states that sports in Sparta aimed to create tough and physically strong warriors as well as healthy and robust mothers. From this mentality we believe that two further values emerge as a result of sports: hard work and endurance (physical and mental).

[10]Chariot races known also as *harmatodromiai* were one of the most popular ancient Greek, Roman, and Byzantine sports. Chariot racing was adopted by many Greek states and their religious festivals. Horses and chariots were very costly. Only the wealthiest aristocrats could afford to subsidize such sports.

becomes the owner of the chariot under the same ownership regime that was in force for men. It is also worth noting that Cynisca's successes were not an isolated incident, but were followed by further Greek women's successes in subsequent Olympiads, such as Euryleonis, similarly from Sparta in 368 BCE, Bilistiche from Macedonia in 264 BCE, as well as Zeuxo, Encrateia, Hermione, Timareta, Theodota, and Cassia, etc. (Schaps 1979, 117; Spears 1984; Cartledge 1987, 29; Allen and Lantinova 2013, 34; Kyriazis and Economou 2015a, 446). However, according to Pausanias (*Description of Greece*, 3.8.1–3) none of these women gained greater recognition for their victories than Cynisca.

24.8 Athens: The First Historically Recorded Welfare State

Democracy in Athens gave birth to the welfare state. Having the destiny of their lives in their hands, the Athenian citizens took care to secure their quality of life as much as they could. With the exception of some historical cases, such as the Byzantine Empire, where social welfare policies were introduced regarding orphans and old-aged people (Gilleard 2003; Miller 2003a, 2003b), it took two and a half thousand years for modern states to re-engage, on a large scale, with the issue of provision of services under the auspices of a welfare state. It was not until the early 1940s that Lord Beveridge with his *Report on Social Insurance and Allied Service* in 1942 expressed in Great Britain the principles for the development of a system of social welfare and insurance for the poor and the infirmed people. It had to precede the slaughter of millions of people in World War II for the democratically advanced states to deal with the misery of their citizens. We can imagine how surprised Lord Beveridge would have been if, after writing his report, he had read Lysias's speech, *On the Refusal of a Pension*.

The Athenians had developed at least from the time of Peisistratus a pension system. Pericles extended the measure to those unable to work as a system of social welfare based on two key societal elements: on forging friendship and *homonoia* between fellow-citizens and on reducing economic inequality. If to the first element is added philanthropy and hospitality, both of which are high on the scale of social values, then it becomes clear why the Athenians pioneered in this matter as well. We should not miss the fact that even today there is an effort by the EU institutions to formulate principles and develop mechanisms to help the economically, socially, and physically weak. But what was this system of social welfare that the Athenians had implemented in practice?

In Sect. 20.3 it was stated that the Athenian public undertook the payment of the salary of teachers (elementary level education, between 6–14 years old) in cases of:

- Children who lost their parents in a war operation for the polis.
- The *demarchs* in each *deme* were required by law to provide any relief possible to the poor and orphans and to protect them from acts of injustice on the part of the rich (Demosthenes, *Against Macartatus*, 43.75).

- War orphans, after reaching adulthood, were exempted from taxes for another year (Lysias, *Against Diogeiton*, 32.24).
- The children of poor families in general. This may have included also the *thetes* social group, or a portion of them (very low-income citizens).

If the children of the *thetes* were indeed included in the state payments that covered the cost of educating children, since they constituted the most numerous group of citizens in the polis, it would not have been an exaggeration to argue that the Athenian state provided public education at an early stage to a large part of the population.

Aristotle (*Athenian Constitution*, 49.4) attests that there was indeed an institutional post of social welfare and solidarity known *tamias tois adynatois* through which the Athenian state offered opportunities for a better quality of life to those citizens who were unable to survive:

- due to individual physical handicaps they had from birth,
- due to various illnesses or because of war (for example, in case they were severely injured due to the war),
- because their work or the income they earned was not more than 3 *mnae* (known also as *minas*), that is 300 drachmae a year.

The ceiling of 300 drachmae also denotes something further: As the average daily wage was 1.5 drachmae during the third century, if we assume that the average Athenian worked about 300 days a year, he would therefore earn a total income of 450 drachmae. Therefore, the Athenian state essentially considered that those citizens who did not earn incomes corresponding to approximately **2/3 of the average daily and annual salary, should receive an allowance/assistance.**

This aid, amounting to one *obol* per day (Lysias, *On the Refusal of a Pension*, 24.26) was offered to them even if they could work but their work did not cover their livelihood under a specific set of income criteria. They were also entitled to this aid if they were old and had no financial resources (ibid., 4–8). Later this aid was increased to 2 *obols*.

Those who benefited from such remittances were often required to be examined by Councilmen on specified days, for verification that they met the criteria to continue receiving the aid. Every Athenian had the right to appear on this day in the Council and denounce that someone was wrongly receiving this aid. Then the Councilmen were investigating the complaint and the conditions relied on the applicant for the aid. In addition, the local *demes* undertook to bury their poor fellow-citizens in a proper and dignified manner. There was in every *deme* a cemetery available for all citizens (Demosthenes, *Against Macartatus*, 43.58, 43.79).

It is worth mentioning that Demosthenes was not a supporter of this type of public remittances. He suggested that the money given for allowances to the polis should have alternatively been given toward its further military preparation. He was mainly against the 2 *obols* that the Athenians received for *theorica* (Demosthenes, *On Organization*, 13.2–4, 13.6, 13.10).

24.9 Provision of Health Services

In Athens and other Greek city-states health care services were provided by a parallel system of three levels, so to speak: (i) private provision of health services (ii) public provision of health services (iii) Asclepieia. For the ways of determining the cost of providing health services in Ancient Greece, one can read Woodhead (1952) and Lyttkens (2011) and the references therein.

Private Provision of Health Services

In the first-tier, doctors offered their services privately and were paid exclusively by their patients. The majority of doctors worked on this basis. Some even became personal doctors of well-to-do citizens.

In this Scene, we referred to the imaginary doctor Philocrates, assuming that he was a famous doctor in Athens. Most likely, such a doctor would provide his services to well-to-do Athenians and receive a high salary. Payment was made after examination or treatment. More generally, the financial compensation of a doctor was determined by the reputation that accompanied him and by how high the demand was for the specific services he provided (Lyttkens 2011).

Regarding the salaries of these doctors, the Hippocratic principle, which stated that a doctor should charge his clients according to their earning potential, was generally applied and this meant that, in special cases, it would be ethically speaking right and perhaps necessary, due to special circumstances, medical services to be provided by doctors even for free.

Ancient sources are extremely scarce regarding the question of determining the price of medical services. It is estimated that the annual salary of a doctor started at about 500 drachmae in the Classical period, but in several cases, it rose significantly, especially during the following Hellenistic period (Woodhead 1952, 14).

Demes and Public Provision of Health Services

In the second level private doctors provided medical care to individual patients but were paid by the *demes* annually. The availability of medical services of this type was considered to be a fundamental obligation of the state and the citizens considered it as a right, that is, the *deme* should provide them with health services by hiring/leasing private doctors in favor of the public, another form of a *3P* practice.

According to Plato (*Gorgias*), an open competition was held by the *demes* for the purpose of hiring doctors and each candidate for public service had to exhibit his qualifications in the best possible way in order to be preferred over other candidate-doctors. Socrates, after pointing out the pitfalls that could arise regarding the subjectivity of this kind of selection process, argued that even a lawyer, using the proper persuasive words and argumentation could deceive the citizens, pretend to be a doctor, and be chosen in the place of a real public doctor! (Plato, *Gorgias*, 456b). Therefore, the vetting of candidates should be very cautious.

Doctors contacted by the public/state or the *demes* were required to attend public events such as sporting events, so that they could immediately treat athletes in case of accidents. They also undertook special duties during periods of military training and exercises.

Doctors, both public and private, were organized into something like a primitive version of Medieval and post-Medieval era European guilds, centered around the cult of Asclepius.

The Asclepieia

The third tier of providing medical services included the so-called *asclepieia*. These were large medical centers surrounded by a wide variety of facilities such as temples, baths, stadiums, *gymnasia*, libraries, theaters, etc., which were considered necessary for the process of healing wounds and restoring health to patients.

The *asclepieia* were owned and operated either by a single city-state or jointly by several city-states. Scattered throughout the ancient world, over 300 such centers operated. The largest and most famous were those of Athens, Trikke (today's Trikala), Corinth, Epidaurus, Pergamos, Knidos (Asia Minor), and the island of Kos. As argued by Christopoulou-Aletra et al. (2009), *asclepieia* were the first ever hospitals in the world to offer comprehensive health services to their patients. In the south slope of the Acropolis there is the sanctuary of Asclepius. The sanctuary functioned like an ancient hospital.

Hippocrates was the most famous of the teachers of the *asclepieion* and the medical school of Kos and he lived in the fifth century BCE. Hippocrates is still internationally recognized as the "Father of Medical Science" as he was the one who published the first and basic principles of this science. The so-called *Hippocratic Oath* is an internationally accepted declaration nowadays, regarding the obligations of doctors toward their science and patients and was given to the following gods: Apollo (doctor of the gods), Asclepios (doctor of men and gods and mythical son of Apollo), Hygeia and Panakeia (mythical daughters of Asclepios). We reproduce the oath below:

> I swear by Apollo the physician, and Asclepius, and Hygieia and Panacea and all the gods and goddesses as my witnesses, that, according to my ability and judgement, I will keep this Oath and this contract:
>
> To hold him who taught me this art equally dear to me as my parents, to be a partner in life with him, and to fulfill his needs when required; to look upon his offspring as equals to my own siblings, and to teach them this art, if they shall wish to learn it, without fee or contract; and that by the set rules, lectures, and every other mode of instruction, I will impart a knowledge of the art to my own sons, and those of my teachers, and to students bound by this contract and having sworn this Oath to the law of medicine, but to no others.

> I will use those dietary regimens which will benefit my patients according to my greatest ability and judgement, and I will do no harm or injustice to them.
>
> I will not give a lethal drug to anyone if I am asked, nor will I advise such a plan; and similarly, I will not give a woman a pessary to cause an abortion.
>
> In purity and according to divine law will I carry out my life and my art.
>
> I will not use the knife, even upon those suffering from stones, but I will leave this to those who are trained in this craft.
>
> Into whatever homes I go, I will enter them for the benefit of the sick, avoiding any voluntary act of impropriety or corruption, including the seduction of women or men, whether they are free men or slaves.
>
> Whatever I see or hear in the lives of my patients, whether in connection with my professional practice or not, which ought not to be spoken of outside, I will keep secret, as considering all such things to be private.
>
> So long as I maintain this Oath faithfully and without corruption, may it be granted to me to partake of life fully and the practice of my art, gaining the respect of all men for all time. However, should I transgress this Oath and violate it, may the opposite be my fate.

A few meters far from the ancient theater of Epidaurus is the Asclepieion of Epidaurus. For centuries people have been coming to this shrine to seek the help of the god-doctor for healing, Asclepius. From all parts of the then known world they came in every way, bringing with them precious vows, but above all, their prayers, to be heard by Asclepius. The Asclepieion, in addition to being a cradle of medicine where knowledge was combined with divine intervention in health, had buildings that were pioneers of their kind. A characteristic description that has been found states:

> Everyone who enters the sanctuary, which smells of incense, must be clean. But clean is considered only he who feeds his mind with pure thoughts.

Chapter 25
Religion and the Great Panathenaea

Abstract This chapter focuses on the role that religion played in the Athenian everyday life. It describes the famous Great Panathenaea festival, in Greek religion, an annual Athenian festival of great importance. It was eventually celebrated every fourth year with great splendor, probably in rivalry to the Olympic Games. It also analyzes the religious consciousness of the Athenians and the role of priests and priestesses in the related religious procedures in Athens.

25.1 Panathenaea: Participating in the Athenian Polis's Greatest Festival

The twenty-first of the month Hekatombaion arrived, shortly after the summer solstice, where the festival of Athena Polias, the Great Panathenaea, was celebrated by the entire polis. The circumstances at that year were favorable, because there was a peace period, so nothing distracted the attention and expectations of the Athenians from the celebration.

The whole city was in a state of rejoicing, a day when no one worked and everyone, citizens, *metics*, slaves, and those foreigners were found themselves for a short period of time in Athens, had poured into the streets and into the Agora through which the procession would pass. It was a colorful, noisy crowd, laughing, talking, hunkering down for seats for a better view, there were people munching on figs, raisins, turnips, onions, bread, cheeses. The Scythian archers were trying to keep the center of the streets clear for the celebration.

The procession started from the Dipylon and proceeded to the Agora, from where it would then ascend to the Acropolis with its final destination being the Parthenon. A group of young horsemen was advancingat the beginning of the procession, on their beautifully decorated horses, among them Nicandros, Nicomedes, and Hegeso had perched on the bank table of Nicomedes in the Agora to look over the heads of the crowd. Chariclea, Melannipe, and Ischomachos also went up to the table at some moments.

Behind the cavalry followed the two ranks of young men serving as *hoplites*, and then a body of oarsmen.

E. M. L. Economou, N. C. Kyriazis, *Daily Life in Classical Athens*, Frontiers in Economic History, https://doi.org/10.1007/978-3-031-58541-8_25

Beautiful young maidens with baskets of coarsely ground barley followed, which would sprinkle on the heads of the oxen to be sacrificed. Other girls followed with cushions-offerings for the invisible gods; the Athenians did not doubt that the Gods would honor them as always at the Panathenaea with their presence. Young people with jugs of water, old people with olive branches, the sacred tree of Athena, *metics* with discs with offerings upon them continued the procession, followed by the oxen that would be sacrificed at the altar, where their roasted meat would be distributed to all in the Dipylon area.

The highlight of the procession was a wooden ship on wheels, which was pulled by ropes and pushed. On its mast, instead of a sail, it had a woolen veil, which had been woven by properly chosen girls between 7 and 11 years of age, originating from noble Athenian families, assisted on this duty by some additional young but older Athenian virgins, also originating from noble families, who stayed on the Acropolis to weave it. These maidens, Eriphyle among them, were on board and greeting the cheering crowd.

As the ship reached the Propylaea, where the horsemen were lined up, Nicandros nodded and raised his hand to his sister, who smiled and nodded her hand to him as well.

Leosthenes, captain of the cavalry and commander of the fortress at Rhamnous when Nicandros was serving, noticed this and asked him:

- Who is she;
- My sister Eriphyle, answered Nicandros.
- I didn't know your sister is so beautiful! commented Leosthenes admiringly.

The ship reached the Parthenon. The girls descended, removed the veil from the mast, proceeded inside, holding it with care and respect. They came to the old wooden statue of Athena, made of olive wood, that, according to the tradition, had fallen from the sky when the city was first founded. They removed the old veil, placed the new one, at the apex of the ceremony.

In the afternoon, the contests of reciting Homer's rhapsodies, flute, harp, dance, followed, as well as athletic and equestrian competitions.

The winners won Panathenaic amphorae filled with oil, since the olive tree was Athena's gift to the city, with the inscription: "a prize from Athena."

* * *

25.2 The Religious Consciousness of the Athenians

Most Athenians were religious, some perhaps zealously religious, but religion did not guide politics from the mid-fifth BCE century onwards (Tridimas 2022). There were about 60 days of religious festivals a year, such as the Dionysia, and many were related to agricultural activities, culminating in the Panathenaea.

Unlike most religions of the time, Persian-Zoroastrianism, Egyptian, Israeli, there was no representative of the god on earth, in the sense that, for example, the Pharaoh was considered a living god, or the Persian Great King who was the representative of Ahura Mazda ("God of the sky") on earth, or the prophets of the Jews who were guides of kings and people, and exponents of the divine will. The *eponymous archon* of Athens had religious duties, but no involvement in the decisions of the Assembly. Also, while there were priests and priestesses in temples, there was no established priesthood with the defining importance it had in Persia or even more so in Egypt, where it was related to strong political power. Although priests and priestesses existed, it seems that they did not offer continuous religious services, like in today's churches.

Another special feature of the Greek religion is that there was no written dogma but only myths, traditions, and practices, unlike, for example, the Old and New Testaments, the Quran, or the Indian Vedas. In this way, the *demos*, through the Athenian political institutions, watchfully guarded its decision-making powers, preventing other actors, such as a priestly interest group, to challenge its authority (Tridimas 2022).

There were certain clans in Athens, such as the Eteoboutadai, many of whose members had exercised priestly duties. Greek religion favored democratic politics, because the *dodecatheon*, the Greek pantheon, functioned as a "parliament of the gods," where the gods discussed, disagreed, often quarreled with each other (for example, Hera to Zeus), took different positions, with goddesses having exactly the same rights as gods, something women would not achieve until the twentieth century in the modern era (Economou and Kyriazis 2019a). The Athenians punished acts of disrespect and sacrilege, because they believed (in the majority at least) that such acts caused a miasma in the city, as in the case of the mutilation of the heads of the god Hermes, throughout Athens, before the Sicilian Campaign, where Alcibiades was accused, rather unfairly. In the private sphere of the Athenian *oikos*, the *hestia* (fireplace) was dedicated to the Goddess Hestia, while Zeus was the protector of property, as Ktesios Zeus, "protector of possessions," of property, from which it can be seen how much importance the Athenians attached to the institution of property.

The Athenians were receptive and tolerant of foreign gods, sometimes adopting them, sometimes allowing foreigners to worship their own deities. Later, they went so far as to allow their own temples to be built, such as the temple of the Egyptian gods at Marathon (160 AD by Herodes Atticus).

Of course, in some cases, Athenians could perhaps be accused of not respecting the familiar gods, as in the case of Socrates who introduced "fiery demons." But we believe that it was an accusation intended to turn the most religious Athenian citizens and judges against him, in a trial that was mainly political in nature, because the real accusation (even if it was not true) was that with his teachings he was leading against democracy. The trial took place in 399, in the wake of the fall of the Thirty Tyrants in 403 BCE, who had executed over 1000 democratic Athenians. Socrates had been held responsible in one respect, for several important members of the Thirty Tyrants regime, such as Critias, who had been one of his pupils and possibly friends. But since the offenses during the tyrants were lapsed with the restoration of democracy—

through the first ever amnesty in world history, the only charge that could be raised against Socrates was essentially sacrilege.

25.3 The Athenian Priests and Priestesses

Priests and priestesses had to have no disfigurement or disability. They had no formal training regarding religious matters, and their duties were rather part-time. In Athens they were appointed by annual lotteries among all the citizens, that is, the priests did not constitute a special class or caste, such as the Brahmins in Hinduism. The Athenians believed that every citizen (with the exception of those who had been convicted for a crime) could cope with priestly duties, a view that Luther and Calvin would probably have applauded! Only the positions of priests of "old" gods, such as the patron Athena, were the privilege of certain generations (such as the Eteoboutadai) and were lifelong (Garland 2008). The priests received a modest fee but were entitled to select a piece of meat from the sacrifices, which was not an inconsiderable fee for poor citizens—priests. Their duties were ceremonial in the temples, but also administrative, given that, as we have already analyzed, most of the temples had their own property, and functioned also as treasuries throughout Attica, with the Parthenon for Athens being the most characteristic case of such. Thus, some priests, such as in Delos and Delphi, also undertook the duties of a banker—financial manager, just as in the Catholic churches in the Middle Ages. A well-known bank related to religion is the *Banco di Santo Spirito*, founded on December 1605, and being considered as first national bank in Europe, as the bank of the Papal States.

The most powerful priestess of them all in ancient Greece, the Oracle at Delphi, even foretold the future. They were normally chosen from among the aristocratic elite class since these offices conferred great prestige.

The priests did not function as "intermediators" between the people and the divine. The Greeks considered that this was the duty and business of each individual and did not need the mediation of an "expert," again as is the case, for example, with the Protestants (with the existence of pastors). Priests did not perform sacraments or ceremonies such as weddings, births (baptisms), or funerals.

A superstition prevalent among the Greeks was the contamination or miasma that could have a religious dimension or origin, as a divine punishment for human errors, such as the pestilence unleashed by Apollo on the Greeks at Troy, to punish Agamemnon for not returning Chrysiis to her father and priest. Causes of miasma were murder, sacrilegious acts (such as the mutilation of the heads of the god Hermes) but also natural phenomena, such as death. In all these cases purification ceremonies, some public, some private, were foreseen. The purifications included special means, such as salt water (often sea water) or fire, brimstone and blood, especially a pig's blood.

As with men, women were also entitled to hold ceremonial/religious posts. They were called *hiereiai* and held very important religious positions in society. They were leading various processions, such as litanies, they were responsible for guarding the treasures of the temples, lit the fire on the altars of the shrines, and preached the sacrifices. They were also responsible for following the regulations of the sanctuaries. In addition, they put their seal on the official documents of the temples. Many inscriptions that have been found testify the generosity of many priestesses as benefactors of their polis and its sanctuaries, since, in several cases, when they were financially capable, they themselves undertook the expense of building temples, or infrastructure or water tanks. The priestesses felt great pride regarding these constructions.

Inscriptions and tombstones reveal that priestesses were buried at public expense, with large processions and in impressive burial monuments, erected to their memory. A famous Athenian priestess was Chrysiis, who devoted her life to the worship of Athena Polias. Her countrymen considered her equal to the male priests.

There were also young priestesses, aged between 7–11 years, called *arrhephoroi*. The temple of Athena on the Acropolis housed two or four such priestesses. These were chosen each year to weave the *peplos* of Goddess Athena with which they covered the goddess's robe during the festival of the Panathenaea (Pausanias, *Description of Greece*, 1.27.3). They were chosen from well-to-do and respectable Athenian families. They lived in the Arrhephorion, a square building in the north-western part of the Acropolis. At the end of their term, they returned to their family. Aristophanes (*Lysistrata*, 1.1.663–673) provides the following information regarding them:

> Your own mother will not know you when you get back to the town. But first, my friends and allies, let us lay these garments down. And all ye fellow-citizens, hark to me while I tell. What will aid Athens well. Just as is right, for I have been a sharer in all the lavish splendor of the proud city. I bore the holy vessels. At seven, then I pounded barley at the age of ten and clad in yellow robes. Soon after this, I was Little Bear to Brauronian Artemis; then neckletted with figs, grown tall and pretty, I was a basket-bearer. And so it's obvious I should give you advice that I think good. The very best I can.

An inscription *IG* II^2 3488 in a statue dated a little before 103/2 BCE commemorates the service of Panarista[1] as *arrephoros*:

> Panarista daughter of Mantias of Marathon; her father and her mother, Theodote daughter of Dositheos [of Myrrhinoutta], and her brothers, Kleomenes and -, dedicated (a statue of her), when she had been *arrephoros* for Athena Polias [and Pandrosos].

[1]This is a very beautiful name. It is a composite word that derives from pan (everything) and *aristos* (perfect). Greek names were also denoting capacities. Thus, Panarista means, "she who does everything perfectly"!

Chapter 26
Marriage and Life Expectancy

Abstract This chapter describes a wedding ritual at Classical Athens. It also describes in brief various aspects of a couple's relation, such as the dowry, the divorce, and the case of abortion. It also connects this discussion to the issue of life expectancy of the Athenians.

26.1 Eriphyle's Marriage

Nicomedes was paid a visit by Leosthenes, as his son Nicandros had arranged.

Leosthenes proceeded straightforward to his request, to allow him to marry Eriphyle. Nicomedes (and Hegeso), who had discussed the issue in particular, although Eriphyle herself was not present, were not opposed. Leosthenes was of good family, a well-to-do, young man, of good appearance and good character, as Nicandros had informed them from his service under Rhamnous. He was in the right age for marriage, around 30.

They discussed various matters, chiefly the dowry of Eriphyle, which was considerable, commensurate with the fame and fortune of Nicomedes. They agreed and then discussed on the wedding day. Hegeso and Nicomedes announced the decision to their daughter, while her brother did not miss an opportunity to extol the qualifications of the bridegroom. Eriphyle had noticed him at the Panathenaea, as he was by her brother's side, and liked him, so she had no objection, as a daughter of a good Athenian family should.

The wedding day has arrived, in the month of Gamelion. The ceremony began with sacrifices to the gods of marriage, Zeus and Hera. Eriphyle cut a lock of her hair and dedicated it to Hera. She collected her childhood items, including her dolls, and dedicated them to Artemis.

Then she performed a ritual bath. Then followed the wedding symposion at the *oikos* of Nicomedes, attended by the friends of both families. Nicomedes had spared no expense because he wanted the symposion for his daughter's marriage to be splendid, with the best food. The symposion ended with small sweets of honey and dough, covered with sesame seeds. Eriphyle sat apart from the men, covered with a veil, with her mother and a *nympheutria*, an old woman friend of her mother, who

E. M. L. Economou, N. C. Kyriazis, *Daily Life in Classical Athens*, Frontiers in Economic History, https://doi.org/10.1007/978-3-031-58541-8_26

guided her through the marriage ceremony. Her heart was pounding; she was glaring at her husband, who was also looking at her. Whenever their eyes met, he smiled at her. Leosthenes drank sparingly, and although his friends urged him to drink, he did not want to get drunk, on the first night of his wedding. When the symposion was over, Leosthenes, taking Eriphyle by the hand, went out of the *oikos* of Nicomedes. The procession that would lead them to his own *oikos* was waiting outside. Leosthenes helped Eriphyle to go up the carriage, drawn by four white horses. Eriphyle sat in the middle with Leosthenes on the one side and the bridesmaid on the other side.

The procession began with torches accompanied by musicians with flutes and lyres singing wedding hymns.

When they arrived at the *oikos* of Leosthenes, the members of his *oikos* welcomed them by throwing them nuts and dried figs.

Leosthenes led Eriphyle to the bridal chamber, where she removed her veil while Leosthenes closed the door. From outside, family members chanted the *epithalamios hymn*.

* * *

26.2 The Wedding Ritual

Before the wedding, the engagement was taking place. The presence of the bride was not mandatory. There the dowry was agreed upon, which usually included cash, clothing, valuables and slaves, or land and amounted to at least one-tenth of the bride's father's wealth. Paintings on vases of wedding processions have survived, such as a red-figure *pyxis* (vessel for perfumes, balsam) depicting a chariot drawn by four horses, but more often, oxen or mules were used (Garland 2008).

On the first day of the wedding, the bride's father made the customary offerings to the gods, the bride offered her childhood's toys to the Goddess Artemis to symbolically show her severance from her past life, and the bride and groom bathed in water brought in a special vessel from a holy spring, Callirhoe.

When evening came, the bride accompanied by an escort went to the groom's *oikos*. In Athens it is true that customs changed from place to place, just like today. A carriage carried the newlyweds from *oikos* to *oikos*, followed on foot by a procession of relatives and friends, singing and holding candles and flowers. When they arrived at the groom's *oikos*, his father was standing at the entrance wearing a wreath, while the groom's mother, beside her husband, was holding a candle. On the second day, the wedding meal was held by the bride's father and the bride went to her new *oikos* in a carriage. On the third day, the bride received the wedding gifts at her new *oikos*. Weddings have always been dedicated to the Goddess Hera, the patroness of the institution of marriage.

The *epithalamios hymn*, first mentioned by Homer (*Iliad*, 18.478, 18.491–496) was a wedding hymn, sung either outside the bride's chamber or on her bridal march to the groom's *oikos*.

26.3 The Dowry

If a woman was left a widow, and this was highly probable to be expected in a city that was involved in many wars, the woman got her dowry back and her brothers (according to the law) married her off to whomever they chose by giving him the dowry of the widow. We do not know if this was done with the condescension of the bride (Demosthenes, *Against Boeotus* 2, 40.6–7, 40.19; *Against Onetor*, 30.15–16, 30.33–34). Even if she had no siblings, her close relatives were required by law to care about and marry their orphaned and poor relatives (Demosthenes, *Against Macartatus*, 43. 54).

The institution of the dowry was the primary qualification among the primary ones—apart from age, beauty, and descent—that would make a man consider marrying a particular woman (Demosthenes, *Against Aphobus 1*, 27.48; *Against Boeotus* 2, 40.27). The above accompanying characteristics of the prospective bride also led to a concentration and perpetuation of wealth between specific families, so that a class of people with at least a similar standard of living was formed. In other words, the slogan "wealth goes to wealth" was something that was verified by the pursuit of matrimonial relationships among the Athenians (Demosthenes, *Against Boeotus* 2, 40. 25).

Although the dowry was (in principle) a property of the bride, since it initially belonged to her father, in practice her husband managed it and reaped its financial returns. The wife's dowry after her death had to pass to her children (Demosthenes, *For Phormio*, 36.32) and could not be transferred to children who were born by another woman (Demosthenes, *Against Boeotus* 2, 40.14). This is another element that shows that the institution of marriage was essentially a way of defending individual property indirectly, and the ideal scenario was to be passed to close blood relatives.

The Athenians, with the above-mentioned way of family life that had more or less established, were essentially trying to achieve an increase in the well-being of the father first, then the mother and the rest of the other family members.

26.4 The Divorce

Both men and women had the right to seek divorce, especially in cases of adultery. In such a case a woman was usually represented in court by relatives, although she could appear in court herself. Hipparete, wife of Alcibiades, was so disgusted by her husband's illegal love affairs forced her to left the conjugal *oikos* and went to live with her brother. But when she filed suit against him in the courts, and appeared in person, Alcibiades seized her and dragged her back home through the marketplace without anyone daring to stop him or help her (Plutarch, *Alcibiades*, 8.2–5). We believe that Alcibiades' behavior was not that of the average Athenian. That is why Plutarch quotes it, as something worthy of mention that was not common. After a divorce procedure was finalized, then, the dowry was returned to the father of the bride.

26.5 The Abortion

Cases of abortions for unwanted pregnancies and unwanted babies are also reported. However, some of the babies who were abandoned were adopted by childless families. Those women who resorted to this measure were mainly unmarried, prostitutes, *hetaerae,* and slaves. Abortion should have been considered an extremely dangerous and painful procedure for the woman and presented a high risk of serious infections. The risk of contamination did not only concern the practical part of the process but was also condemned from a religious point of view as a cause of "contamination" of the *oikos*. Aristotle (*Politics*, 7.1335b. 24–26) accepted abortion only before the fetus gradually evolves as a baby in his mother's belly and he considered abortion to be a serious risk of disease and infection. The *Hippocratic Oath* contains a specific promise to refuse to perform abortions.

When pregnancy was not desired, they administered silphium for abortion, which they imported from Libya. Silphium was a species of fennel that was quite well-known in the Mediterranean countries for its abortifacient action but was not available in sufficient quantities. It even had contraceptive powers. They also used some plants as contraceptives. In abortion, however, it was administered in large quantities.

26.6 The Life Expectancy of the Athenians

The intertemporal nexus between economic well-being and life expectancy has been proven through a plethora of historical paradigms around the globe. The more satisfactory the economic situation and the diffusion of wealth and prosperity in a society, the higher the life expectancy becomes, due to the better living conditions caused by the possession and use of more and better-quality goods and services by the members of a society.

In relation to the degree of mortality, Bresson (2016a, 80) considers that there is no evidence that the average mortality in Ancient Greece was higher than the level observed in post-Medieval Europe. There is unfortunately an erroneous view, with international influence, which claims that the life expectancy of the ancient Greeks was very low.

What is true is that many Greek philosophers lived to ages comparable to today's, which indicates a high level of quality of life. For example, Isocrates died at the age of 98 after committing suicide due to an incurable disease. Sophocles died aged 91 and Euripides aged 74. Gorgias died at the age of 107. Plato lived 80 years and Socrates 71 until the moment he was forced to drink the hemlock. Aristophanes lived 60 years, a short life-span if one compares this age with the above.

The counterargument could be that the surviving references concern the higher intellectual elite of Athens, who demonstrably enjoyed better living conditions than the average Athenian; however, this does not necessarily mean that the life expectancy of the average Athenian was much lower than that of the elite. If we assume that the average well-to-do Athenian lived approximately 75 years of age, it would probably be wrong to assume that an ordinary citizen would live significantly less on average. Therefore, arbitrary estimates regarding the life expectancy during Greek antiquity should be treated very cautiously even if they have managed to prevail intellectually as a dominant dogma.

26.7 The Lamian War (323–322 BCE) and the *Strategos* Leosthenes

After the events described in Scene 19 (Chap. 20), political calm, peace, and economic growth prevailed in Athens for the next 7 years, thanks to the economic recovery program of Lycurgus who died in 323 BCE, the same year as Alexander the Great. The Athenians, having straightened their finances, without having Lycurgus to consult them with prudence (he was continuously elected as *epimeletes tois koines prosodou* until 326 BCE) and, with Demosthenes and Hypereides negatively influencing them, made one last attempt to play an important role in Greek affairs.

Thanks to the Persian gold that Alexander had mastered in Asia, the Macedonians built a powerful fleet and recruited experienced crews from the open market. But Persian gold was not the only reason. An important additional reason was that the Macedonian Empire of Alexander had incorporated areas with a great naval tradition, power, and infrastructure, such as the islands of the East Aegean, Cyprus, and Phoenicia, whose naval forces came under the Macedonian navy.

Athenian-Macedonian relations began to deteriorate again after Alexander's death for a number of reasons: (i) the desire of the Macedonians to wrest Samos from Athens by granting it its autonomy (ii) the refuge that Harpalus, a notorious embezzler of the Macedonian imperial treasury seeked in Athens. He transferred to Athens 700 *talents*, that was, a part of the money he misused, and it is more than certain that later this huge amount of money helped him to obtain the Athenian citizenship. The Athenians, like other city-states, were thinking of revolt in order to end the Macedonian influence on them.

In Athens, the anti-Macedonian faction was led by the general Leosthenes, whose proposals received great response thanks to the influence they exerted, among others through the very capable orator Hypereides. Under the leadership of Leosthenes, a significant coalition of military forces was formed to confront the Macedonians. Despite the initial military successes of Leosthenes, which were also due to the recruitment of eight thousand mercenaries, the Athenians and their allies lost the so-called Lamian War (323–322 BCE) to the Kingdom of Macedon after Leosthenes was killed besieging the Macedonian garrison in Lamia. The Athenians, recognizing the services of Leosthenes to their motherland, buried him with special honors while his Funeral Speech was delivered by Hypereides.

The final defeat of the Athenians took place at the Naval Battle of Amorgos (May or June 322 BCE), fought between the Macedonian navy under Cleitus the White and the Athenian navy under Euetion. Few details are known, but what is for sure is that it was a decisive Macedonian victory which signaled the end of Athenian thalassocracy and political independence. Democracy was suppressed but nevertheless revived in the third century.[1]

[1] A great historical narrative regarding Athens after the Classical period, till the period of the Roman general Antonius is provided by Habicht (1999).

Chapter 27
The Athenian *Choregos*

Abstract This chapter deals with the issue of *choregia*, an important *liturgy* undertaken by a rich citizen for the polis. A *choregos* was responsible for the recruitment, training, maintenance, and costuming of the members of a chorus at a festival. This chapter raises also the intertemporal and key issue of freedom of expression, which was a key element of the democratic ethos of the Athenian polis.

27.1 Nicomedes: The *Choregos*

Nicomedes was chosen as *choregos* for the plays to be performed that year at the Great Dionysia. It was a *liturgy* just as complex and only slightly less expensive than the *trierarchy*.

The *eponymous archon* commissioned him to stage one of the selected tragedies to be staged for that year. Nicomedes met the playwriter and they sat down to draw up the necessary budget for the play. Then, they chose the actors, the choreographers, the makers of costumes and masks that the actors would wear, as well as the musicians and the scenery makers.

When everything was settled, rehearsals began, under the watchful eye and strict instructions of the dramatist and often the silent presence of Nicomedes. When the chief actor had asked Nicomedes who he was and what business he had there, Nicomedes answered him:

– I am the money!

The actor replied:

– Then stay but be quiet. Money has no voice!

Nicomedes, as a banker, had a different opinion. He knew that money had in fact, a different, very eloquent and persuasive voice, like the gold coins of Philip before Chaeronea, which secured him allies and made certain orators make fiery speeches in his favor. However, he preferred to remain silent and not open a philosophical discussion with the actor.

E. M. L. Economou, N. C. Kyriazis, *Daily Life in Classical Athens*, Frontiers in Economic History, https://doi.org/10.1007/978-3-031-58541-8_27

As always in such cases of preparing a theatrical performance, problems kept arising, some smaller, some larger, but finally they managed to solve them, and when the day of the theatrical contests came, in the theater of Dionysus, glittering with the new marble linings of Lycurgus and suffocating by Athenian citizens, *metics*, and Greeks from almost every Greek city-state who had flocked to it, the play of Nicomedes triumphed and took the first prize, amid the cheers of the spectators, bringing glory to him as *choregos* as well as to the performers.

Together with the actors and the playwriter, the audience also praised Nicomedes as a sponsor. Hegeso and Eriphyle moved by the success of Nicomedes, filled with great joy, and kissed him on the cheek. Nicomedes's friends as well as other Athenians and *metics* congratulated him passionately. The play may have cost to Nicomedes a lot, but it was worth it: How many people would have the privilege in their lives to be cheered on, even just once, in the famous theater of Epidaurus?

* * *

27.2 The Tragedy, the Comedy and the Theaters

Roselli (2012) who has extensively studied various social aspects of the theatrical plays participation, provides valuable and convincing evidence, which proves (against long-standing contradictory views) that except citizens, *metics*, women but also *xenoi* (foreigners—in our case, as tourists and fine arts enthusiasts) could also attend theatrical performances.

Each dramatist had to submit three tragedies and one satyr drama, while the comedians only one work, to the *eponymous archon*. The *archon* would choose three tragedies and three comedies and distribute them to the *choregoi* who had been chosen (perhaps by lottery) for that year. Like today's Hollywood blockbusters, theatrical productions were expensive. It is estimated that 1500 people were employed to stage performances at the Great Dionysia of the fourth century. In Athens, Peisistratus promoted the Great Dionysia, a 4-day celebration in March, into a national festival to honor God Dionysus. This festivity attracted a large number of tourists, like the great modern festivals of Salzburg, Bayreuth, Verona, etc. Comedy was introduced into the Great Dionysia in 486 BCE and from 440 also to the Lenaea, the minor festival of Dionysus.

The Theater of Dionysus built on the south slope of the Acropolis hill, originally part of the sanctuary of Dionysus Eleuthereus. This theater had a capacity of 20,000 spectators and Epidaurus even more. Like all Greek theaters, at first it was earthen, but during the fourth century it was filled with stone or marble seats, like those of Epidaurus. The marble lining of the Theater of Dionysus was one of the works of Lycurgus's public program. Admission was free in the fourth century as performances were sponsored and did not depend on spectator payments. Such was the importance of the theatrical plays so as to educate society with moral values, that even prisoners were given temporary permission to attend them.

Image 27.1 View of the famous theater of Epidaurus, with the perfect acoustics. Source: Image owned by the authors

The prizes for the first three works were decided by a panel of ten judges. Each judge wrote his decision on a sign and the ten signs were placed in a *hydria*. The *eponymous archon* drew the five and based on these the three awards were given which conferred great prestige on the winners (Image 27.1).

The heyday of the Athenian theater is from the beginning of the fifth century until the beginning of the fourth century, when Euripides and Aristophanes died. Of course, we must add on this the comedies of Menander of the second half of the fourth century.

The production of fine arts in Ancient Greece shifts from century to century: the eighth-sixth are the centuries of epic and lyrical poetry, the fifth of theater and history (which continues uninterruptedly), the fourth of philosophy (which of course had begun in the fifth but peaks on the fourth and continues on the third with less important representatives) and rhetoric.

27.3 Freedom of Expression

The Athenians were demonstrative people who were not afraid to express their approval or disapproval. For example, we have a mass parade of *hoplites* so that the people could honor them openly (Lysias, *Against Agoratus*, 13.80) while they blew whistles and chased bad actors from the theaters (Demosthenes, *On the False Embassy*). They expelled and openly condemned those who practiced magic (Demosthenes, *Against Aristogiton 1*, 25.80), while they removed from their polis the so-called *miaroi* who had committed a crime (Antiphon, *On the Murder of Herodes*, 5.82). Their society, in other words, was almost entirely informed by word of mouth of the good or bad deeds of their fellow-citizens and applauded or condemned them openly. They especially stigmatized and strongly disapproved of certain behaviors and actions such as arrogance, envy, and ostentatious consumption.

Chapter 28
The Demosthenes Speech *on the Crown*

Abstract This chapter deals with the famous speech of Demosthenes *On the Crown*, delivered in 330 BCE, which is considered as a masterpiece of rhetoric art. The chapter revives this discussion, which was again indirectly connected with a permanent Athenian dilemma of the times; adopting a pacifist or war strategy against Macedon. It further explains how public interest was defended through the Athenian political institutions.

28.1 Nicomedes *on the Crown* of Demosthenes

The following year, when the *eponymous archon* was Aristophon, Nicomedes was selected by lot as a judge of Heliaia. He was among those who would trial Ctesiphon, but in an important trial that under the cloak of justice and legality covered political strife. Two years after the Athenian defeat at Chaeronea, Ctesiphon proposed Athens to honor Demosthenes for his services to the city by offering him the golden crown. This proposal became a political issue, and some years later, Aeschines prosecuted Ctesiphon on charges of legal irregularities.

Nicomedes felt uncomfortable. What was the point of this trial, which would simply rekindle old passions now that they finally, thanks to Lycurgus's policy, seemed to be calming down? What was the point of bringing up the old disputes, now that Athens was at peace, no one threatened her, and Alexander with the rest of the Greek army, had annihilated the once mighty Persian Empire, fulfilling the dream and exhortations of Isocrates, and not only?

He felt troubled, for he knew personally both the real competitors, Aeschines and Demosthenes.

He recognized that Demosthenes was a patriot, and that what he had done and proposed was for the good of the polis, and that if they had sooner listened to and followed his advice, before Philip became so powerful, if they had saved Olynthus, as they saved Byzantium and Perinthus, they might not have had to fight at Chaeronea. These were the big ifs... But he recognized that Demosthenes was pro-war and was drawn into extreme proposals without correctly calculating the military power potential of Athens and the possible consequences. Fortunately,

E. M. L. Economou, N. C. Kyriazis, *Daily Life in Classical Athens*, Frontiers in Economic History, https://doi.org/10.1007/978-3-031-58541-8_28

thanks to the prudence of Lycurgus and Phocion, the Athenians had not listened to him to ally with the Thebans to fight again against the Macedonians after Philip's death.

He also recognized that Aeschines's motives were predominantly focusing in favor of the interest of Athens but was very pro-Macedonian and he was also weighed down by the suspicion (which had of course not been proved) that he was bribed by Philip's gold coins and this made him so eloquent in favor of the Macedonians. Aeschines had supported the peace program of Lycurgus, who had restored the polis.

Nicomedes also remembered the emergency measures which the popular Assembly had decided after Chaeronea: conscription of all citizens up to the age of 60, the granting of amnesty to the exiles and their recall, and the restoration of the civil rights to those who had been deprived of them, for the whole city-state to fight with one mind for its freedom. These were suggested by Hypereides, who together with Lycurgus and Phocion had assumed the leadership of Athens until Demosthenes returned from Chaeronea.

Hypereides had gone even further, proposing to grant political rights and *isoteleia*, that is, equal tax regime to foreigners, *metics* and (even) slaves who would agree to fight for Athens as a compensation, and the Assembly accepted by voting his proposals.

The walls were repaired with everyone, young, old, middle-aged, women, children, *metics*, slaves working non-stop under the supervision of Demosthenes who had just returned. Citizens volunteered money and prepared the weapons that the *hoplites* kept in their homes, while the city's artisans and workshops prepared new and repaired old ones to be distributed to the citizens at the city's expense. Lycurgus had taken over as *epimeletes tois koines prosodou*, the management of the state finances. Kallias took over the new Stratiotikon fund and Demosthenes took over the Theoricon fund which was reconstituted this time, not any more for financing the theatrical performances but to support the financially weaker Athenians.

Philip seeing the strong fortifications of Athens discerned the determination of the Athenians and realized that he had no interest in straining his army in an ambiguous siege. He knew very well that as long as the sea was open, Athens had never fallen. When the danger faded away, the disturbance took another form in Athens. The measures proposed by Hypereides, so innovative, had shaken the economy. The prospect of freeing the slaves had alarmed a large portion of citizens who owned slaves. The resolution of Hypereides was annulled after being insulted by *graphe paranomon*. Athens began to find normalcy again.

Two years later, a councilman, Ctesiphon proposed a *probouleuma* to honor Demosthenes for his services with a golden crown at the Great Dionysia festival, at the opening of the theatrical games. Demosthenes' sworn enemy, Aeschines, immediately tried to annul Ctesiphon's proposal through a *graphe paranomon* procedure.

However, unforeseen events had led to the postponement of the trial: First, Philip's assassination a few months after Aeschines' lawsuit. Then, the facts before and after siege and destruction of Thebes, the new treaty of peace between Athens and Macedonia, with Alexander III, and the preparation of the campaign against the Persians. It seems that the case would be forgotten and that the political passions would calm down.

But here Nicomedes and the more moderate Athenians were wrong, for political hatreds might be half asleep, but they did not disappear and flared up again, as strongly as before.

So, the charge against Ctesiphon, that is, in effect, against Demosthenes, came to the court. The trial began before the Pythian Games, and since its subject concerned the whole polis, the whole day was dedicated to this trial. It began with Aeschines delivering the charge, as if giving a theatrical performance, sometimes raising his voice, sometimes lowering it to make the judges to pay attention, sometimes pacing, sometimes still as a statue, emphasizing some points with gestures.

Only the actor's mask was missing to distinguish him from the protagonist of a tragedy. Aeschines blamed Ctesiphon saying that his proposal to crown Demosthenes was illegal for three reasons.

Firstly, because he proposed to honor a man who held public office, as superintendent of fortifications and manager of the Theoricon fund, before he completed his duty and before he was accountable, as every other public magistrate, upon completion of his duty. Secondly, it was contrary to the formal law which forbade the awarding in the theater and prescribed that any awarding should be given in the Bouleuterion, or to the Pnyx. Thirdly, Ctesiphon's proposal contained false statements, for Demosthenes by his policy had harmed and not benefited the polis, so he was not entitled to the crown. But because it was approved and filed in the public records, it violated the law against filing false documents.

The politically experienced Nicomedes discerned in the third point the sophistry of Aeschines. He essentially presented Demosthenes as the corrupting spirit of Athens, responsible for all the recent calamities.

When he was over it was Ctesiphon's turn to plead, but essentially Demosthenes himself as a defense witness.

If Aeschines was a howling wolf, Demosthenes was a roaring lion. He began very calmly, just to contrast with Aeschines, not moving at all, like a statue, with a measured voice.

But his voice grew stronger as he recounted the events and what he had done so far:

> But all the cities were demoralized. The active politicians were venal and corrupted by the hope of money: the unofficial classes and the people in general were either blind to the future or ensnared by the listlessness and indolence of their daily life; in all the malady had gone so far that they expected the danger to descend anywhere but upon themselves, and even hoped to derive their security at will from the perils of others. In the result, of course, the excessive and inopportune apathy of the common people has been punished by the loss of their independence, while their leaders, who fancied they were selling everything except themselves, discover too late that their own liberty was the first thing they sold. . . ..[1]

---

[1] Demosthenes (*On the Crown*, 18.45–46).

Nicomedes could not help but admire Demosthenes, because he had turned the apology into an accusation, putting the Athenians to shame. Undaunted, he continued:

> They[2] did not use those pleas as excuses for deserting men who had sought their protection. For the sake of honor and glory they willingly encountered those perils, - a righteous and a noble resolve! For every man death is the goal of life, though he keep himself cloistered in his chamber; but it behoves the brave to set their hands to every noble enterprise, bearing before them the buckler of hope, and to endure gallantly whatever fate God may allot.[3]

Demosthenes added, among others, that:

> At home I never preferred the gratitude of the rich to the claims of the poor; in foreign affairs I never coveted the gifts and the friendship of Philip rather than the common interests of all Greece.[4]

And then he recalled the glorious past and the examples of patriotism of the Athenians:

> Who would not exult in the valor of those famous men who, rather than yield to a conqueror's behests, left city and country and made the war-galleys their home; who chose Themistocles, the man who gave them that counsel, as their commander, and stoned Cyrsilus to death for advising obedient submission? Aye, and his wife also was stoned by your wives. The Athenians of that day did not search for a statesman or a commander who should help them to a servile security: they did not ask to live, unless they could live as free men. Every man of them thought of himself as one born, not to his father and his mother alone, but to his country. What is the difference? The man who deems himself born only to his parents will wait for his natural and destined end; the son of his country is willing to die rather than see her enslaved, and will look upon those outrages and indignities, which a commonwealth in subjection is compelled to endure, as more dreadful than death itself.[5]

He did not omit, like Aeschines before, personal pinpoints against his opponent, reminding them of Aeschines's past as an actor, being a very bad one at that, making them laugh.

The afternoon had arrived and the Athenians, as if watching a theatrical performance, had not realized that the time had passed.

The time came for the vote, and Demosthenes, like Ctesiphon who was the accused, was acquitted.

Aeschines, unable to bear the shame of defeat, left Athens, went to the island of Rhodes, a rising naval power of the times, where he taught rhetoric until his death.

* * *

[2] Demosthenes refers to the "Men of worth" to this point.

[3] Demosthenes (*On the Crown*, 18.97).

[4] Demosthenes (*On the Crown*, 18.109).

[5] Demosthenes (*On the Crown*, 18.246–247).

28.2 General Notes

Demosthenes was chosen to deliver the Epitaph for the dead of Chaeronea in the month of Pyanepsion, October–November 338 BCE.

The radical measures proposed by Hypereides (granting amnesty to exiles and recalling them, restoring political rights to those who had been deprived of them, freeing slaves) are mentioned by Demosthenes (*Against Aristogiton 2*, 26.11).

28.3 The Defense of the Public Interest

The judicial system of Athens was characterized by many sophisticated features. The defendant received a written court summons that determined the day of the trial. Lawsuits were divided into public, involving the city-state as a whole, such as the one we have described, and private above, regarding individual disputes.

Already from the time of Solon there was a law that "anyone who wished" was free to appeal on the basis of a public lawsuit, known as *graphe*, as a defender of the public interest.

Here is another basic difference between ancient and modern conception of the defense of the public interest. In ancient Greece-Athens, any citizen could appeal against another, if he considered that a proposal of the latter was against the public interest for any reason.

In today's Greece and elsewhere by contrast, this is not applied as a concept, even if there is a suspicion of a violation of the Constitution. In order for an applicant's action to be accepted, he must relate to personal benefit or damage, that is, his personal legitimate interest from the violation of the Constitution.

Chapter 29
The Child as the New Member of the Family

Abstract This final chapter focuses on the duties of the young mother toward her children, as well as the ceremony regarding the toddler's birthday. This small chapter refers also on a very nice and rather moving description of motherhood as provided by Xenophon in his *Memorabilia*.

29.1 A Mature Couple Strolls in the Acropolis at Dusk

Nicomedes and Hegeso attended with great joy the meal provided to them by Leosthenes and Eriphyle to celebrate the birth of Nicomedes' grandson, of the same name.

After the meal, Hegeso asked Nicomedes, before returning to their *oikos* decided to go up to the Acropolis, to worship the statue of the Virgin Athena Pallas, patroness of the polis, and then, from there, to gaze at the Asty, the glorious polis, as far as Piraeus and even further, as far as the eye could see.

– We can also gaze from our *oikos*, Nicomedes said reluctantly….
– Nicomedes, lately, with your obligations at the bank, you have been alienated from me; you have almost become a different person. You don't pay attention to me like you used to; you don't pay attention to me at all! Hegeso shouted.
– Come on honey, feminine excesses as always!

Hegeso was irritated, and as she was a strong-will woman by nature, name and deed, she grabbed his hand saying imperatively:

– Let's go now!
– Okay Hegeso! But I warn you, that if you look at me like this as soon as we are inside the temple, you and Goddess Athena will blind me with your blinding gaze! And then I won't be able to sign any more bank contracts to live off my work.

Hegeso, being glib as always, answered immediately:

– Your son Nicandros will sign them from now on…

E. M. L. Economou, N. C. Kyriazis, *Daily Life in Classical Athens*, Frontiers in Economic History, https://doi.org/10.1007/978-3-031-58541-8_29

They went up to the Acropolis, worshiped the famous statue of the goddess, looked at the surrounding pediments of the temple, passed by the Erechtheion, gazed at Lycabettus hill, behind them, proud, majestic and mysterious, as if placed there to watch over Athens and the Acropolis eternally, and in the end, before descending from Acropolis, they stopped at the temple's borders for a last gaze, just before dusk.

- Fortunately we made it. . . .How nice it is. . . . Hegeso commented with an expression of reminiscence and nostalgia in her voice.
- Don't you agree honey?
- Leon, Nausinicus, Aristonicos, Nausinus, this man owes me only five hundred drachmae. . . . murmured Nicomedes.
- Nicomedes, where is your mind? Back to work?
- No, no my dear. My thoughts are always on you. . . .

Hegeso took his hand. They sat silent, looking at the dusk from the Sacred Rock of the Acropolis. . .

- Nicomedes, do you think our Eriphyle will be happy with Leosthenes?
- Yes, I think so. He loves her.
- How do you know;
- I think so. . .
- Will they be in love forever?
- How do you want me to know? Leave it all to the will of the Gods. . .
- Are we in love?
- Of course!
- Or are we just living in a symbiotic kind of relationship?
- What does this mean Hegeso? I didn't quite get it. Don't give me a hard time!

Nicomedes at the preceding dinner at the *oikos* of Leosthenes sat between Leosthenes and Nicandros, feeling joy between the two young men, who had the whole future before them but also the required skills and ability to make even more glorious the name of his family. And in a moment of euphoria, he drank a little more wine, the wine relaxed him enough, and now, after the pilgrimage to the Goddess' shrine, he did not want to tire his mind with Hegeso's philosophical quests about love and romance.

- What is love Nicomedes? asked him Hegeso, with a tone in her voice that testified persistence.

Not getting an answer, Hegeso squeezing his hand tighter, insisted:

- What is love Nicomedes?

Nicomedes understood that he would not easily get away with Hegeso's questions. Hegeso, when she wanted to achieve something, became very persistent. She looked like a general besieging a city wall with determination to storm it, at any cost. Fortunately, just in time, inspiration struck him! At some other symposion who attended a few days before, he had heard from a philosopher of Plato's Academy a fine interpretation of love and decided to tell it to her. He took a breath and as if reciting verses in the theater answered:

– Love is the salutation of the angels in the stars!

* * *

29.2 General Notes

The phrase: "Love is the salutation of the angels in the stars" belongs to the great French novelist, poet, and dramatist, Victor Hugo. We pulled it from his well-known work *Les Misérables* of 1862, from Chap. 4.

29.3 The Duties of the Young Mother Toward her Children

The first duty of a wife was to give her husband offspring, both for the continuation of the family, but also for maintaining and increasing the population of the city. Due to the high infant mortality, it is estimated that each married couple had 4–5 children so that at least two survived. According to today's data, 2.1 children per woman are needed to keep the population stable. Sweets were considered to be beneficial for a woman's fertility. Deaths in childbirth and abortions must have been common then. Births were taking place either in homes or in the countryside, with the help of an experienced maid. Doctors attended only in cases of complications.

Pregnant women were under the protection of the Goddess Eileithyia, her name meaning: "the one who comes." The birth was also linked with the religious element, so that the wrath of the Goddess Artemis to be appeased since Artemis was a virgin and strictly condemned sexual intercourse. This could be achieved with hymns and prayers before the birth and dedication of clothes to her temples after the birth.

This was followed by the naming ceremony of the child, which had the purpose of recognizing the infant by the father as his genuine child and welcoming him/her into his/her family. The ceremony of naming the baby took place in the presence of the family's dear friends and relatives and began with an animal sacrifice in honor of the goddess of childbirth Eileithyia. It was a very beautiful custom that began with the father running around the central hearth of the house, three times, holding the baby in his arms to dedicate it to the goddess Hestia (hearth), and guests showered them with flowers and fruits. The mother on her side contributed to the ritual by invoking the Three Charites (Graces). The Graces were the goddesses of charm, beauty, nature, human creativity, and fertility. As Charites are reported the following ones: Aglaia the Younger, Euphrosyne, and Thalia, but sometimes others are also mentioned, such as Auxo, Charis, Hegemone, Phaena, and Pasithea.

Relatives brought gifts which included amulets "against any evil eye." Finally, a symposion was provided for the relatives and friends of the family where sweets

Image 29.1 Ancient Greek baby feeder. Source: Image created by painter Vasiliki Demopoulou

were distributed to the guests and the various gifts for the child were placed next to the altar of the *oikos*.

Wealthy families secured the service of a nanny to nurse the babies, who were members of the family. Most were slaves, although poor free women could also be used for that purpose. The upbringing of infants in the first years of their lives was the responsibility of their mothers and servants. Xenophon (*Memorabilia*, 2.2.5) provides us with a very nice and rather moving description of motherhood:

> The man supports the woman who is to share with him the duty of parentage and provides for the expected children whatever he thinks will contribute to their benefit in life, and accumulates as much of it as he can. The woman conceives and bears her burden in travail, risking her life, and giving of her own food; and, with much labour, having endured to the end and brought forth her child, she rears and cares for it, although she has not received any good thing, and the babe neither recognises its benefactress nor can make its wants known to her: still she guesses what is good for it and what it likes, and seeks to supply these things, and rears it for a long season, enduring toil day and night, nothing knowing what return she will get. . .

Regarding ancient Greek toys, according to the prevailing view, young children played with toys that were made at home (Image 29.1).[1] Taking into account the delicacy of the construction of these toys we cannot rule out the possibility that toys were also sold by shops in the Agora, which were made by various carpenters, etc.

---

[1] See some Greek toys through the following links: https://commons.wikimedia.org/wiki/Category:Ancient_Greek_toys#/media/File:Small_terracotta_figurines,_Ancient_dolls,_AM_of_Corinth,_202927.jpg and https://commons.wikimedia.org/wiki/Category:Ancient_Greek_toys#/media/File:5014_-_Archaeological_Museum,_Athens_-_Dolls_-_Photo_by_Giovanni_Dall'Orto,_Nov_13_2009.jpg.

29.4 The Toddler's Birthday

The ancient Greeks celebrated the infant's birthday until he/she reached adulthood. For his/her birthday, they made honey pies in his/her honor, which they decorated with candles. They believed that the Goddess Artemis was the protector of children and thus would protect them from diseases and all evil. In honor of their child, the ancient Greeks prepared a cake with candles, as we do today, which was called *hamilos*. The candles symbolized the stars and the moon. This ceremony resembled a corresponding ceremony of honor to the goddess Artemis. The ancients then were extinguishing the candles because they believed that the smoke conveyed their wishes to the gods.

Chapter 30
Conclusions

Abstract This introductory chapter summarizes the core findings of our research. It concludes that the success of the Athenian system of governance should be attributed to a sophisticated package of economic and political institutions that were wisely implemented by the Athenians. This package included: (i) democratic governance (direct/participatory democracy) as a prerequisite for institutional change (ii) a market-oriented maritime economy based on advanced financial services (iii) the development, in practice, of advanced institutions regarding public administration (iv) the establishment of advanced auditing mechanisms of public magistrates that secured efficiency in public administration and the smooth functioning of the market (v) the rule of law which proved highly supportive of the commercial activity of the polis (vi) fast administration of justice (vii) an excellent blend of cooperation between the state and the private sector (viii) the provision of a series of public goods that increased the prosperity of the citizens (ix) establishing the optimal blend between elected and appointed public magistrates (x) establishing an effective system of *paideia* x) A religion that characterized by tolerance. We further argue that these institutions (that also function as values) have an intertemporal character that applies also for all modern advanced economies and democratic societies around the globe.

Historically, it has been proven that stable and durable democracies are linked to prosperous and growing economies that are characterized by advanced institutions (Acemoglu and Robinson 2013; Economou and Kyriazis 2019a). Throughout the book we attempted to show that the Athenian politico-economic system (presented in Fig. 30.1 in a general form) was characterized by such institutions considering its times.

It is essential to elaborate a bit more on two issues regarding Fig. 30.1. Firstly, that various institutions such as the Ecclesia of Demos and the Assembly had responsibilities in more than one aspect of the Athenian political-economic edifice. For example, the Ecclesia had not only political decision-making duties but also legislative and judicial ones, while the Council had not only governance duties (through the *prytaneis*), but also legislative and supervisory ones. It appears that this institutional settlement did not cause inconsistency and overlaps in the Athenian

E. M. L. Economou, N. C. Kyriazis, *Daily Life in Classical Athens*, Frontiers in Economic History, https://doi.org/10.1007/978-3-031-58541-8_30

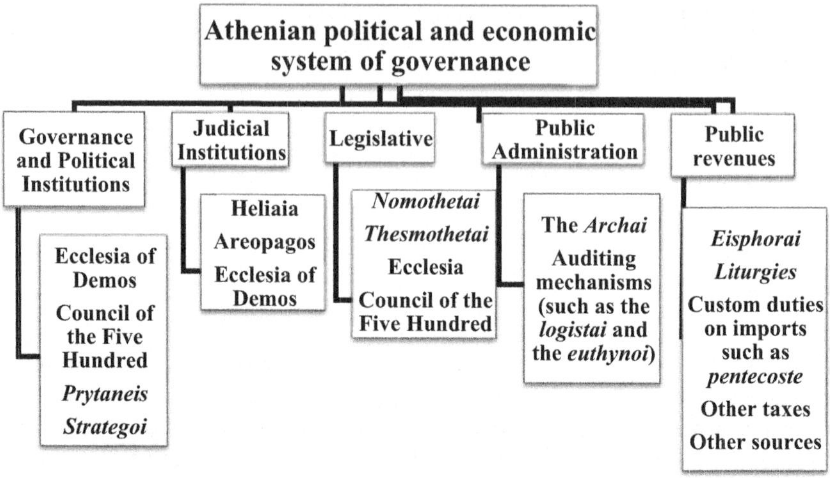

Fig. 30.1 The Athenian political and economic system of governance

system of public administration. On the contrary, it seems to have efficiently functioned, as far as we know, based on the available historical information.

Secondly, the Athenian state budget was determined by both public revenues and expenditures. Based on Economou (2024, 239–266), in Fig. 30.1 by "Other sources" we further mean public revenues which come from: renting public estates and lands, imposing various fees and fines, leasing state and sacred lands forests and meadows, etc., performing confiscations upon court decisions, performing sales of real estate. Public expenditures on their part were mainly covered by the payment of the *Archai*, as well as the military expenditures, the provision of public goods and services, etc.

Furthermore, all the available evidence that we have gathered in this book suggests that the Athenian market, the Agora, also functioned in a quite efficiently way. This happened through the introduction by the Athenians of the proper blend of market institutions as appeared in the following Fig. 30.2. For example, the *trapezitai* provided various types of loans such as bottomry loans, as analyzed in Sects. 11.7 and 11.8, as well as insurance services, mortgages, etc.

And there is no doubt that efficient institutions under a regime that safeguards qualitative democratic governance can ensure economic growth and prosperity in the long run. Eminent authors from different perspectives, such as Hayek (1960, 1973), Olson (1965, 1982, 1991, 1993), North and Thomas (1973), North (1981, 1990), Alesina and Perotti (1996), Rodrik (2000), Rodrik and Wacziarg (2005), North et al. (2009), Rothstein (2011), and Acemoglu and Robinson (2013), have provided convincing arguments regarding this perspective so far. Throughout this book, we testified the above notions by analyzing various aspects of the Athenian economic institutions. This further means that **the above values endure over time, therefore they have an intertemporal character**.

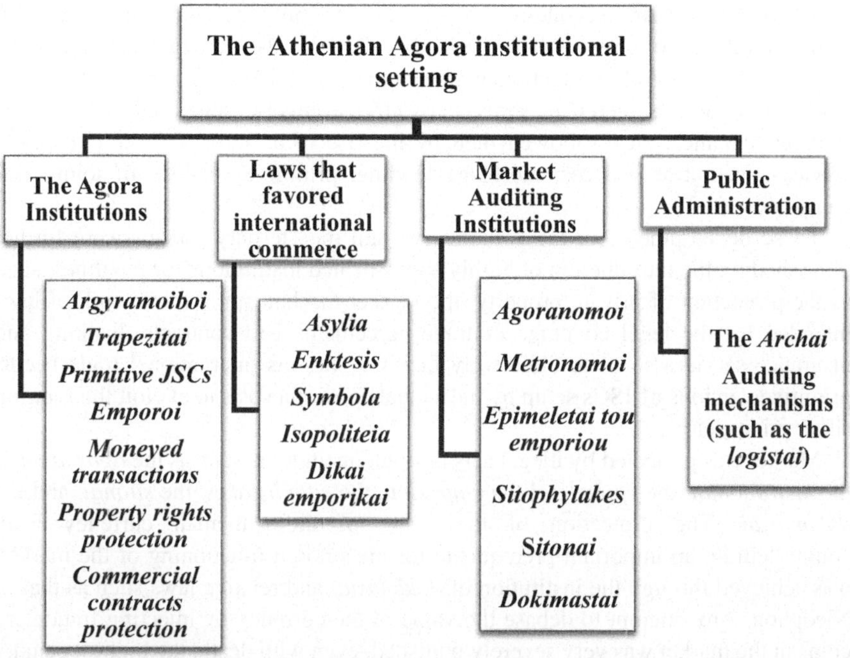

Fig. 30.2 The Athenian Agora institutional setting

In Georgiou et al. (2015), we have performed a literature review based on the findings of authors such as the above, and we argued that a state's economic growth is mostly determined by the stability of the political system. In Classical Athens, for almost two centuries there were only two short-lived coup d'états in 411 and 404 BCE. And despite the fact that there were many turbulent times during the Classical period for Athens, in general, democracy functioned well and the regime was relatively stable.

Athens faced a grave external threat, the second Persian Empire's invasion to Greece that took place in 480 BCE, but it managed to overcome it and survive. This proved that the Greeks in general and more specifically the Athenian society were receptive to new ideas and institutional innovations. This is of course directly related to the structure of the civic and political institutions as analyzed in Scenes 4 and 5.

In Sect. 6.2 it became obvious that the Persian invasion, that should be seen as a major external shock to the Athenian regime, forced the Athenians to quickly proceed on an impressive package of institutional reforms that, in a short period of time, laid the foundations for significant changes in the productive structures of the city-state, from a basically introverted agricultural-type economy to an extroverted one based on maritime trade, international commerce, and a plethora of sophisticated financial services that supported this turn.

The need to repel the mighty Persian army and fleet led the Athenian state to defend itself, through the construction of 200 warships (*triremes*) in two consecutive years, something that, in economic terms, means not only the significant increase of what in modern economies is characterized as GDP but also the gradual creation of a "secondary" sector of production which employed a large number of people in sub-sectors such as merchant ships, carpentry, ironwork, shipyards, dye houses, ship maintenance, etc.) followed then by the rise of a "tertiary" sector (banking services, insurance services, mortgage lending, primitive versions of joint-stock companies, etc.).

These developments in the "secondary" and the "tertiary" sector were further flourished by the introduction of highly sophisticated institutions for the times, such as the protection of private property, the market mechanism, a framework of laws intended for the legal coverage of trade agreements and contracts, banking and insurance services so as to effectively facilitate various international trade needs, primitive versions of JSCs setup by individual consortia so as to exploit the Laurion silver mines, etc.

Market was protected by illegal acts through institutions such as the *agoranomoi*, the *metronomoi,* the *epimeletai tou emporiou*, the *sitophylakes,* the *sitonai,* and the *dokimastai*. The protection of the value of the Athenian currency from counterfeiting, an important prerequisite for the smooth functioning of the market, was achieved through the institution of *dokimastai* and relative laws such as that of Nicophon. Any attempt to debase the value of the currency by injecting fraudulent coins in the market was very severely punished, even with death, the highest penalty of all, which denotes that the Athenians had understood the crucial role of securing the reliability of their currency within the boundaries of their city-state but also in the international markets. The Athenians understood that this was highly beneficial for the strength of their economy in the long run, which was directly related to their prosperity as a whole since it made the Athenian drachma something like the "dollar of the Classical times."

What is also true is that another important aspect regarding the success of the Athenian politico-economic model of governance is related to the establishment of efficient mechanisms of public administration. This is of course related to the strict conditions set by the Athenian state for a citizen before taking office as a public magistrate.

Becoming a public magistrate required integrity, honesty, altruism, and selfless interest so that efficient administration is achieved. We believe that modern democracies can be inspired by the Athenian model of governance regarding their electoral procedures in selecting public magistrates. The widespread political corruption phenomena that have been observed internationally in recent decades with increasing frequency constitute a socio-political degradation that could undermine the prestige and future of democratic ideals worldwide.

Thus, the qualitative elements that are related to the success of the Athenian politico-economic model of governance of the times are lie on the following 12 issues:

i. The democratic spirit of governance (*direct* / *participatory* democracy) as a prerequisite for institutional change.

ii. The nexus between institutional change and economic transformation toward a market-oriented maritime economy based on advanced financial services.
iii. The development, in practice, of advanced institutions regarding public administration.
iv. The establishment of advanced auditing mechanisms of public magistrates that secured efficiency in public administration.
v. The establishment of auditing mechanisms which ensured the smooth functioning of the market institutions and the private sector.
vi. The establishment of laws that proved highly supportive of the commercial activity of the polis.
vii. Fast litigation as a mechanism of increasing the volume of economic/commercial transactions in the market.
viii. An excellent blend of cooperation between the state and the private sector through *3P* projects, such as collecting taxes or exploiting the Laurion silver mines, or collecting garbage from the streets, or the *liturgies* as a whole, etc.
ix. Provision of a series of public goods that increased the prosperity of the citizens.
x. Establishing the optimal blend between elected and appointed public magistrates.
xi. Establishing an effective system of *paideia.*
xii. A religion that was characterized by tolerance.

Regarding (i), a number of theories have been developed on the emergence of democracy in Classical Greece. The main ones are:

- The competition between aristocratic groups during the Archaic period that finally led to democracy (after the interregnum of the tyrants).
- The geomorphology of the soil of Attica (and of Greece, in general) and the granting of property rights to free peasant-cultivators by the aristocratic elites.
- The growth of the Athenian population during the Archaic period, its impoverishment before the Solonian era and the demarcation of borders.
- The socioeconomic and socio-political reforms of Solon.
- The events of 508 BCE, the conflict between Cleisthenes and Isagoras and the spontaneous reaction—"revolution" of the Athenian people.
- The spirit of liberty and freedom in Greek religion.
- The existence of a "proto-democratic" spirit of values during the Homeric period and beyond.
- The gradual establishment of a regime for the protection of property rights during the Homeric period and beyond.
- The parameter of military organization and war through the *phalanx* formation, the *hoplite*s, and the *trireme* type of warship.
- The parameter of the democratic character of sports.

We have analyzed the above theories as a dynamic synthesis of situations and institutions that created the conditions for regime change, in our case, democracy, in

Kyriazis et al. (2014), Kyriazis and Economou (2015a), Economou and Kyriazis (2019a, 2022a, 2022b), and the references we provide therein.

We have found that a key reason for the rise of democracy in Classical Athens is related to the logic of such a regime itself, which encouraged innovation and change. This is also verified by evidence for modern economies as analyzed by authors such as Alesina and Perotti (1996), Rodrik (2000) and Rodrik and Wacziarg (2005) who among others have argued that democracy is associated with more stable political systems that provide benefits for higher education systems, institutions and paths of technological and economic change. Thucydides (1.70) mentions the view of the Corinthians who praise the innovative spirit of the Athenians which is emphatically exhibited in their discussions with the Spartans, but he also acknowledges that sometimes this spirit drives them to wrong or frivolous acts.

Herodotus (5.78.1) explained why an authoritarian ruler's choices can become disastrous for a nation by analyzing the notorious case of King Croesus of Lydia in Archaic times and his final defeat by the Persian Empire, which should be largely attributed to his personal wrong strategic decisions. In contrast to authoritarian rule of governance, democracy can lead to better outcomes. Herodotus persuasively writes:

> . . .the Athenians grew in power and proved, not in one respect only but in all, that **equality is a good thing** (emphasis by the authors). Evidence for this is the fact that while they were under tyrannical rulers, the Athenians were no better in war than any of their neighbors, yet once they got rid of their tyrants, they were by **far the best of all. This, then, shows that while they were oppressed, they were, as men working for a master, cowardly, but when they were freed, each one was eager to achieve for himself** (emphasis by the authors).

Based on the above passage and by making a more general elaboration and critique on Herodotus's work, Ober (2022) argues that a cooperative system of decision-making such as the Athenian one, imbued by the principles of equality and *isegoria*, limits the chances of making strategically wrong choices.

If we extend Herodotus's view, we can reach that of Acemoglu's and Robinson's (2013) who argue that citizens, if they have the ability to choose, prefer democracy because it is consistent with collective decision-making whereas under autocracy, there is a monopolization of power in the hands of a very few privileged people, and because of this, according to Olson (1991), autocracies can become predatory, since there is no one to control the autocrat.

Thus, essentially democracy is related to an environment that in principle (but not always in practice—unfortunately) promotes equal opportunities and in general reinforces the evolution of institutions of a society through an innovative spirit. According to Grossman and Helpman (1991) and Acemoglu and Robinson (2013), these two are strong prerequisites for achieving economic growth. Related to this is that the Athenians worshipped Goddess Athena, the patron and savior or Athens, also as *Ergane*, meaning the "industrious Athena" (Pausanias, *Description of Greece*, 24.3) since they believed that with their own individual efforts and industriousness as well as the help of the gods, they could achieve their goals in real life. It was a common belief in Athens and the rest of Hellas, the famous motto: *syn Athena and cheira kinei*, derived from the myths of Aesopus meaning that asking for the gods' help can be productive when you yourself have also already tried (hard) for something, otherwise you pray in vain. At least, under democracy, the Athenians knew that their struggles in life may lead to success and improve their social position in the polis both in private and collective terms.

Finally, in the Introduction we have already referred on various structural problems of modern *participatory* form of democracy (and economy) such as *asymmetrical or/and imperfect information*, as defined by Akerlof (1970), Rothschild and Stiglitz (1976), and Jovanovic (1982), and the *principal-agent problem* also known as the *agency problem* (Ross 1973). Usually, the principal-agent problem is accompanied by an asymmetrical distribution of information from which problems for the principal arise both before and after the conclusion of an agreement, a contract, etc.[1]

A politician nowadays who is elected but during his term proves to be untrustworthy to his voters and acts differently from their wishes does not face any consequences, except for the possibility of not being re-elected. In addition, a politician or a political body can possess "internal (asymmetric) information" about an issue. For example, a modern Finance Minister, through the nation's statistical office, has a complete access to information regarding the status of the nation's macroeconomic condition, in contrast to the median citizen or even other economic experts who have no access in such information, at least for a specific period of time. In this case, this particular Finance Minister can deceive citizens by providing false information, at least, for a period of time.

By contrast, in the Athenian regime, which was based on a *direct* form of democracy, such problems did not exist due to the political process and the institutions such as the citizen's Assembly, the Council, the Heliaia, the *Archai*, and the Agora, that all functioned together as a coherent network. **All citizens, if they so desired, could have sufficient, direct, and satisfactory level of real-time information about an issue that concerned them. Therefore, they could, at least theoretically, choose wisely**, when their opinion had to be expressed through voting in the Assembly or the Council and the other posts regarding public administration.

There were no political representatives; the citizens themselves were the masters of their vote. This means that the success of their democracy was based on what Arrow (1950, 339) characterized as "citizen's sovereignty," that is, they were able to shape their common future through the Assembly by taking, in principle, well-justified decisions regarding either law-making or approving or rejecting a policy, such as war or peace strategy against Sparta or Macedonia. This is also verified by Kallet-Marx (1993), Samons (2000), Ober (2015b), and us in Kyriazis and Economou (2015a) and Economou and Kyriazis (2019a, 2022a, 2022b).

Of course, one cannot argue that in Athens during the Classical Period everything was perfect. There have always been demagogues who aspired to gain the trust of the people by using various unfair means and techniques of manipulating the masses,

[1] In such cases, before the conclusion of an agreement, a situation that is known as *adverse selection* appears. After the conclusion of an agreement the well-known problem of *moral hazard* appears. These are the two basic components of the *information asymmetry* problem.

such as lies, misleading proposals, opportunism, flattery, and promises, seldom fulfilled, that did not correspond to reality at all, as happens also today, a situation that nowadays is characterized as populism. However, the influence of the demagogues could be restrained after a response from an honest politician who proposed or counter-proposed in the Assembly. Every citizen, independently of income capacity, had free access (of information) to the Assembly.

Globally nowadays, the role of promoting misinformation by a portion of political demagogues and various other opportunists is taken over by a bulk of "systemic" mass media controlled by corrupted media businessmen and political elites, who are using "prestigious and well-known" journalists, serving interests by propaganda, that is, they systematically and deliberately misinform citizens. This is summarized with the phrase "fake news," but the problem is not limited to this; it is also swelled by controlled blogs in various social media internet platforms, etc.

This discussion is obviously connected to the issue of "active participation and decision-making" procedures through the establishment, in practice, of a system of fast exchange of information on a plethora of social and civic matters among citizens themselves in practice, or what we characterize as "Athenian network governance" being inspired by the seminal research on networks by modern scholars such as Manville and Ober (2003) and Ober (2008), especially in the case of Classical Athens. Of course, in today's representative mass democracies, it is difficult to motivate citizens effectively to become informed, because according to Buchanan and Tullock (1962) and Achen and Bartels (2017, 187, 198, 199) the cost of becoming informed, in terms of time and effort devoted to this, outweighs the benefit of better information in decision-making.

We believe that this problem can be ameliorated with the implementation of direct democracy techniques in decision-making in practice, such as the *recall* procedure, the *citizens' initiatives*, *referenda,* and *e-democracy* techniques.

As far as the *recall* procedure is concerned, an elected representative (ranging from a simple municipal councilor, or a member of a school board, to the mayor, prefect, or member of Parliament, or even the governor of a State) can face a *recall* procedure. If it is considered by the citizens-voters that he/she has fallen short of their expectations, due to incompetence, corruption, etc., they can ask for a *recall* procedure, before the completion of his/her term of office. The process begins with the *initiative* of any citizen or group of citizens who undertake the collection of signatures. If the signatures reach the required threshold (usually 8% to 10% of those who voted in the previous elections), then a mandatory vote is taken, and if the candidate for *recall* receives a majority of votes, he is removed from office. This is dissuasive because it significantly reduces the immunity enjoyed by politicians (Economou and Kyriazis 2019a).

As far as binding referenda and *citizens' initiatives* are concerned, citizens undertake to collect a critical minimum number of signatures (usually 8–10% of those who voted in the previous elections) and can then request a referendum that is binding on the authority addressed (at the level of a municipality, a state, or at a federal or a national/regional level). Some federal states such as Switzerland or some US states and the state (*Länder*) of Bavaria in Germany provide this institutional arrangement to their citizens. In the EU, under Regulation (EC) No 211/2011 of the European Parliament and the Council of the European Union, of 16 February 2011, *citizens' initiatives* are to be accepted by the European Commission if each new proposal gathers at least 1 million signatures from at least 7 of the 27 EU Member States.[2] But the outcome is not binding. So, it is no wonder that no such initiative has ever taken place.

Referenda and citizens' initiatives are *bottom-up* processes. Citizens, as actors, legitimately introduce them to issues that concern them. However, it would be possible for the referenda to be provoked *from the top, down,* i.e. to take place through the decision of the government of the state itself or the municipality, etc. One such characteristic case was the July 5, 2015 referendum in modern Greece regarding the introduction (or not) of austerity measures by the government. Regardless whether the people's decision was right or not (see Economou et al. 2017) the government of the times did exact the opposite of the popular mandate! This outcome should be seen as an act exhibiting huge democratic deficit, because the government was not ethically legitimate to ignore the real essence of the vote and the will of the people, by interpreting it differently.

Regarding referenda, if they have a nationwide character, they should be binding for the government, with a penalty of dismissal if the government does not implement the decisions/outcomes. A government should also pledge not to interpret a referendum result as fits its interest. If it does, the Senate in states which have such a political institution should intervene constitutionally and force the government to obey the will of the people. The same applies for the President of the Republic in states like modern Greece, which is characterized by Parliamentary (not Presidential) type of Republic. In this case, this seems to be the best way to secure the implementation of the popular will. The same applies to referenda at a regional or municipality level, etc. as happens, for example, in Switzerland.

In Classical Athens, the Assembly was taking place about 40 times a year. In a broader sense, the Athenian democracy had instituted the statutory conduct of at least 40 referenda a year, a number inconceivable in the present-day situation. Important issues were not only discussed in the main Assemblies (*Kyriai Ecclesiai*) but could concern any regular meeting of the body.

Another qualitative difference of the superior characteristics of the ancient democracy relative to today's is that by discussing and voting separately on particular issues, the real preferences of the citizens-voters could be fully revealed, according to Samuelson's (1938, 1948) perspective. In Sect. 6.3, it was argued that the Athenian popular Assembly discussed important issues such as peace, war, alliances, sending ambassadors, welcoming foreign diplomats, economic policy, finance, and administrative bodies of the state. This means that by deciding as a whole (the Assembly of citizens) on each issue separately, such as economic policy, e.g., public works, or foreign policy, e.g., war or peace, citizens voted openly, and

---

[2] See http://ec.europa.eu/citizens-initiative/public/legislative-framework, as well as ec.europa.eu/citizens-initiative/files/guide-eci-el.pdf.

this could lead to a decisive solution of a problem even if the issues to be discussed were rather complex.

Regarding (ii) we believe (and hope) that in this book we described quite well how and why institutional change led to the Athenians' strategic move to "turn to the sea," which proved a wise choice, because it led to structural change and transformation of the economy that entailed to economic growth and prosperity in the long run. Modern research and distinguished authors such as Kuznets (1966) have confirmed that an innovative spirit that is linked with structural changes is directly related to economic growth. In addition, in his seminal work *Capitalism, Socialism and Democracy*, J. Schumpeter ([1942], 2013) argued, among others, that economic change revolves around innovation, entrepreneurial activities, and market power. Having in mind his theoretical concept known as *creative destruction*, he further wrote that:

> Capitalism . . . is by nature a form or method of economic change and not only never is but never can be stationary. . . . The fundamental impulse that sets and keeps the capitalist engine in motion comes from the new consumers' goods, the new methods of production or transportation, the new markets, the new forms of industrial organization that capitalist enterprise creates.

What is for sure is that the Athenian strategy to "turn to the sea" was accompanied by a dynamic sequence of developments and interaction of institutions that contributed to the creation of an economic structure, which could fairly be argued that had set the very beginnings of the capitalist production model of the sixteenth c. AD, at least in terms of its basic principles. The period we describe in the book, approximately 338–323 BCE is almost toward the end of the Classical Period, which means that the series of the economic/financial institutions we analytically described throughout the book had already become functionable and mature. We believe that our findings coincide with Ober's (2022, 38–39) view who characteristically writes that:

> The transformation of Athens, from 'the world of Tellus[3]' to 'the world of Themistocles and Pericles' - from a relatively simple and directly comprehensible traditional society in which rational choice-making was straight forward, to a complex and 'modern' society accessible only by organized, yet inevitably partial and indirect, knowledge - was in large part a product of three conjoined endogenous changes: the development of Athenian democracy, the growth of an Athenian maritime empire, and the burgeoning of an Athens-centered Mediterranean exchange economy.

Regarding (iii) in Sect. 6.14 we have analyzed the various *archai* that comprised the Athenian public administration. There was a highly developed and complex system of various state offices that needed to be effectively coordinated with each other so that the Athenian *dioikesis*, that was the management of the Athenian public administration, would function well, to the benefit of the citizens. In various sections of the book, the institutions of the Athenian state were analyzed, which ensured, admittedly quite satisfactorily, the smooth operation of the Public Administration. It

---

[3] An Athenian citizen of the Archaic period.

is not claimed here that in the case of the Athenian state "everything was perfect." What is certain, however, is that corruption phenomena were not widespread.

This leads us to (iv). It is well-known that in practice, efficient public administration is directly related to the issue of corruption. In an inspiring speech, European Ombudsman, Emily O′ Reilly speaking at an event in October 2020, to celebrate the 25th anniversary of the existence of the EU institutions, among others declared that:

> Transparency and openness are not abstract concepts. When they are lost or absent, the fabric of the social contract between those who govern and those who are governed is damaged, and the consequences are negative for both.'...' Democracy works on the basis of trust but also on a strong system of checks and balances. Citizens need to know that oversight bodies work independently and with the public interest as their only interest.'... 'The EU can and should show leadership through its strong championing of independent oversight and excellence in public administration.

In Athens of the times, in principle, the law-abiding "citizen-public official" had to be honest, virtuous, respect the customs and traditions, having fulfilled his military and tax obligations and be faithful to the gods and the state.

As has already been argued, the Athenian society was very strict in confirmed cases of corruption. Abusers of public money were severely punished. To prevent corruption, public officials were barred from leaving the city-state during their tenure, apparently to avoid the same situation that is observed in many societies today, embezzling public money and then escaping abroad to make it difficult for the perpetrators to be punished by the national prosecuting authorities or Interpol. In some cases, through the *euthyna* procedure, it was possible to confiscate even all the property of a public magistrate whose corruption had been proven, as a compensation for the damage that a state suffered due to the illegal acts of this particular corrupted public servant.

Another way to deal with the corruption in the Public Administration introduced by the Athenians was the lottery process which provided equal opportunities for all citizens to hold public office (such as auditing offices), so there were no foggy appointments and/or direct assignments as happens in many countries today. In our modern democratic societies, to make the process of selecting executives even more inviolable in terms of, for example, oversight bodies in the public administration, it would be possible to adopt the lottery process to man the related institutions, so as to suspend favoritism and other distortions.

Several institutional arrangements that effectively curbed corruption in the Athenian Public Administration were analyzed at appropriate points throughout the book. These were: the *dokimasia* and the *euthyna* which was performed by the ten-member boards of the *logistai*, the *synegoroi*, and *the euthynoi*. All of these were institutions for monitoring the public servant before, during, and upon the completion of his duties. Moreover, with the process of *eisangelia* and the similar procedure of *epicheirotonia* of public officials, any citizen had the opportunity in one of the key annual assembly gatherings, an *Ecclesia Kyria*, to accuse openly any public official of misperforming his duties. In this case the accuser was also obliged to provide the necessary evidence regarding his accusations so as to justify the request for a vote (of the Assembly) for the recall of the accused public magistrate. If the accusation was well-founded, the civil servant was obliged to undergo the *apocheirotonia* procedure, which meant that he was removed from office. If the charge was unfounded, the accuser was punished severely. In this way, it was ensured that the complaints were substantiated, otherwise the accuser would face legal consequences.

Therefore, the Athenian state was not a litigious society as has been wrongly supported by some authors, but a society that, to achieve the transparency of the state institutions, conditioned the role of the citizens themselves, as active supervisors in public life. In this sense, citizens as public prosecutors assisted in achieving transparency of the state under the logic of creating an environment of "generalized morality" in the society. Under such a perspective, through the Heliaia court, the state gave an active role to the citizens, to assist on the administration of justice.

Regarding (v), we have extensively referred on the role of sophisticated state institutions to ensure the smooth functioning of the market such as the *agoranomo*i, the *metronomoi*, the *epimeletai tou emporiou*, the *sitophylakes*, the *sitonai,* and the *dokimastai*.

Regarding (vi), economic and political activity was taking place under a regime which functioned based on the principles of rule of law, like every modern prosperous democratic regime. Citizens elected their own leaders, and their public officials were bounded by the law. In principle, the law should have been respected among the citizens of the state. Democracy could not exist without the rule of law, especially regarding the rule that dictates who should occupy public office based on the outcome of electoral procedures.

As concerns (vii), which is directly related to vi), an important element of the success of the Athenian political-economic model was were fast court decisions, a situation which is considered to be fundamental in modern civil and criminal procedures. The famous Enlightenment philosopher Baron de Montesquieu considered this as a prerequisite for an effective judicial system. Unfortunately, in many countries nowadays, the phenomenon of court cases becoming very time-consuming with continuous postponements taking place, etc. is observed. The message of the Athenian democracy is clear in this regard: justice should be provided immediately, so as distortions and injustices between parties as litigants, such as extortion and harassment of court officials, suspension of entrepreneurship, etc., to be avoided. The primary aim should be justice to be regarded as impartial in the conscience of all citizens.

Regarding (viii), as analyzed throughout the book, the Athenians encouraged private initiatives. For that purpose, they implemented in practice an extended series of institutional mechanisms, such as the granting of rights to exploit the silver mines in Laurion, or tax collection, or the implementation of the institution of *liturgies* (through the 1200 wealthiest Athenian families), or the cleanliness of the streets, etc., what is internationally considered as a *3P*. From its success in Athens in various aspects such as the exploitation of the silver mines, it seems that a harmonious relationship had been found between private initiative and the public interest. Such synergies further included rent of public property, collection of fines, leases of state and sacred lands, leases of Laurion mines, quarries and forests, meadows, confiscations by court decisions, levies, court fees, the *pentecoste*, real estate sales, etc. The Athenian state received a significant share of the profits from these leases.

As far as (ix) is concerned, the Athenian democratic regime provided various public goods such as defense, elementary level education (partially), health services through payments at a public or a *deme*'s level, such as paying doctors or redistributing remittances to infirm people through the *tamias tois adynatois*.

Concerning (x), some authors or thinkers in general consider that democracy's purest form and apex was achieved after the reforms of Ephialtes and Pericles because all posts became accessible to any citizen and this secured *isonomia* among the citizens. But this is not completely true. In reality, as argued in Sect. 6.12, most public offices were filled indeed by *klerotoi* (magistrates elected by lot) but some offices, which were of great importance and required advanced technical expertise, were filled by magistrates appointed by vote in the Assembly, known as *cheirotonoi*.

Did the Athenians limit to some degree the quality in their democracy by such a measure? The answer, at least for us, is negative.

Imagine, for example, that the post of a Finance Minister in any advanced and modern democracy of the Western word, or the post of the general who is in charge of the NORAD (North American Aerospace Defense Command), to protect the USA from any attack, including tactical or strategic nuclear missiles, or the post of the president of the European Commission, to be filled by common people. This, of course, could not be possible and practically would have been counterproductive. The same goes for Classical Athens. regarding very special posts which required expertise. Plato in his *Laws* (738d ff., 759b, 771e.) and Aristotle in *Politics* (1300a 19ff) have realized and explicitly referred on this. Plato (*Laws*, 759b) specifically writes that:

> …In establishing all these offices, we must make the appointments partly by election and partly by lot, 1 mingling democratic with non-democratic methods, to secure mutual friendliness, in every rural and urban district, so that all may be as unanimous as possible.….

Thus, the Athenians had understood that few but highly important posts, as mentioned in Chap. 6, that were related to the very existence of their state, such as the *ten stretegoi*, should be filled by experts, as also happens in modern advanced democracies, for example, the chairman of the Board of Governors of the Fed. But on the other hand, any other post was accessible by every male citizen. Thus, it seems that in this way the Athenians somehow found an efficient way of distributing harmoniously state posts between highly and/or less expert citizens.

Regarding (xi), the Athenians had shaped their system of *paideia* as an ongoing process of gaining knowledge. *Paideia* was seen as a process of continuous perfection of citizens so that, ideally, sometime in the future they would progressively reach the level of *kalos kagathos* citizen. For achieving this purpose, the Athenians' system of *paideia* was not based solely on the provision of the technical aspect of education from schools. It was further reinforced through the participation of citizens in the workings of the Assembly in the way we described in various cases throughout the book and through their further participation in various state posts. It was further enhanced through the high moral standards and role models that the theatrical plays of the times promoted, through immortal works such as those of Euripides, Aeschylus, and Sophocles. These plays were accessible by all citizens and *metics*, through the provision of the *theorica* payments, which should be seen as a public good provided by the state so as citizens to be "educated" by the best tragedians or comedians in various aspects of social life, through which the citizens could reach the *kalos kagathos* life mode, which was the ideal scenario and the ultimate goal of the polis.

In addition, through the *ephebeia*, which was a form of education related to military duty (but not only), Athenian *ephebes* were further educated by properly selected teachers with a recognized degree of expertise, ethical background, integrity of character and sense of duty, the *sophronistai* and *kosmetai*. The latter should inspire the young *ephebes* to acts that are related to *arête*, that is, acting with excellence and through virtuous acts in real life, as many Greek ethical philosophers of the times supported, such as Socrates, Plato or Plutarch in *Moralia,* and Aristotle in his *Eudemian* and *Nicomachean* Ethics, respectively.

As a final comment on this, the Agora itself could also be seen as a huge pool for gaining knowledge, an indirect form of education, since the Agora was basically the proper place for exchanging goods and services, but indirectly was also an unlimited pool of information and knowledge that was offered for free. In essence, one could also see the Athenian Agora, as well as the other Agorai of the Greek world of the times, as "markets of exchange of ideas" where access to information about various series of events related to the workings of the polis developments was provided free of charge.

Regarding (xii), as already mentioned, religion did not guide politics in Classical Greece. Religious positions carried some authority, and religious expertise could be turned to some political advantage, but was not particularly important (Osborne 2013, 280). We know about a priest of Asclepios raising an issue in the Athenian Assembly (*IG* ii^2 47), but this is the only example of priestly intervention at Classical Athens, based on the existing evidence, and it concerns a cult matter. In another case of the fifth c. BCE, epigraphic evidence (ML 73) has secured a case where an influential man, a "prophet" with the name Lampon intervened in an assembly debate but his intervention had a rather limited effect.

In the general perception of the Greeks, the Greek pantheon functioned as a "parliament of the gods," **where both gods and goddesses had equal rights**. Greek religion was receptive and tolerant to other dogmas as well. This is emphatically observed with the famous Areopagus sermon, which refers on Apostle Paul who found himself at Athens, at the Areopagus, as recounted in the *Bible* in Acts 17:16–34, where he began his speech in the following way:

> As I walked around and looked carefully at your objects of worship, I even found an altar with this inscription: (*To Agnosto Theo*) 'To Unknown God'. Therefore, what you worship in ignorance, this is I proclaim to you. . . .

If the Athenians (and the Greeks in general) were not tolerant, they would not have left him speak in that way.

Osborne (2013, 288) based on Pseudo-Xenophon's *Constitution of the Athenians* in verse 3.2 argues that the Athenians were annually running more festivals than everywhere else. These festivals were related to religious cults. He adds that these festivals had a highly participatory (thus democratic) character at both the *deme's* and the state's level and these festivals were open to all residents of Athens, either citizens, or *metics*, foreigners and slaves, without discrimination (ibid., 291). Thus, he concludes that although a causal relationship between democracy and religion cannot be determined, what cannot be denied is that every expression of religion at Classical Athens was an expression of a democratic community.

As a final comment, in a highly disputed but also influential book with the title *The End of History and The Last Man*, Fukuyama (1992) among others wrote that the free-market economy is the only appropriate economic and institutional framework where economic development and the moral argument for a good life and a good society can be achieved internationally. There is no doubt that at least the fundamental principles of such values were met by the Athenian state during Classical times, and especially, during their last part, on which this book focuses, where the economic institutions that functioned in practice had become more efficient and mature.

Thus, we believe that our book's value added is twofold. Firstly, from an economist's and a social historian's point of view, the book explains that the beginnings of market-oriented institutions and production patterns (even if of a primordial form) should be traced back to Athens in Classical times, which served as a precursor to capitalist-type economies from the time of Early Modern Europe onward. In an important contribution, De Vries and van der Woude (1997) have persuasively characterized the economy of the Dutch Republic (the United Provinces) of Early Modern Europe as "the first modern economy." This, more or less, also applies for England of the times. This also applies to the maritime empire of Venice during the Late Medieval period, as well as Genoa, Pisa, and Florence, where relative economic institutions started flourishing and then further expanded by the United Provinces and England. Lane's (1973) detailed work regarding Venice is indicative of this.

But we believe that our book motivates historians to look more carefully into the case of the Athenian paradigm, as well as the rest of the cases of Ancient Greece[4] and Rome in general. Important contributions by Scheidel et al. (2008), Temin (2013), and Verboven (2021) have proven that the ancient Roman economy like that of Ancient Greece was also much more advanced than was previously believed by *primitivist* historians.

Secondly, and in accordance with the above, one critique against such a kind of historical research, as the one that is performed here, is that we cannot be driven to

[4] Such as the federal democracies of the times, such as the Achaean and the Aetolian Leagues. See again the references of ftn. 28 in Chap. 1, such as Economou (2020).

conclusions unless we can have tangible statistical data so as to measure the economic performance of specific historical cases, such as Classical Athens, or the Achaean League or Rome, or Late Medieval Venice and Genoa. To remedy this, in the absence of cliometric data, a safe method to interpret the ancient economies of Greece and Rome, as well as other historical cases at later times, is through the lenses and the conceptual instruments that are offered to us through the New Institutional Economics (NIE) field of research.[5] Our book follows such an approach.

Thus, the 12 points that were raised in this Epilogue by us can be considered as preconditions that a state should follow so as to evolve and achieve growth and prosperity in the long run under decision-making through a democratic constitution.

Through our book we hope that we have convinced our readers that such values are actually characterized by an intertemporal character, and the proof of this is Athens during the Classical times, the case study we dealt in this book.

We believe (and hope) that the research odyssey we undertook with this book, where we tried to deal with many difficult and multidimensional issues that needed very cautious handling regarding their interpretation, has rewarded its readers by shedding light on the underexploited historical connection between the ancient Athenian economy and the establishment of nowadays moral values, institutional frameworks, and modern economic growth dynamics.

[5]See again the related discussion on this argument in the Introduction of this book.

Glossary

Ancient Greek Authors (Primary Sources—Perseus Library)

Aeschines Against Ctesiphon
Aeschines Against Timarchus
Aeschines On the Embassy
Aeschylus Persians
Andocides On the Mysteries
Antiphon On the Murder of Herodes
Aristophanes Acharnians
Aristophanes Clouds
Aristophanes Ecclesiazusae
Aristophanes Frogs
Aristophanes Knights
Aristophanes Lysistrata
Aristophanes Peace
Aristophanes Thesmophoriazusae
Aristophanes Wealth
Aristotle Athenian Constitution
Aristotle Eudemian Ethics
Aristotle Nicomachean Ethics
Aristotle Oeconomics
Aristotle Politics
Athenaeus The Deipnosophists
Deinarchus Against Philocles
Demosthenes Against Androtion
Demosthenes Against Apatourius
Demosthenes Against Aphobus 1
Demosthenes Against Aphobus 2
Demosthenes Against Aristocrates
Demosthenes Against Aristogiton 1

E. M. L. Economou, N. C. Kyriazis, *Daily Life in Classical Athens*, Frontiers in Economic History, https://doi.org/10.1007/978-3-031-58541-8

Demosthenes Against Aristogiton 2
Demosthenes Against Boeotus 1
Demosthenes Against Boeotus 2
Demosthenes Against Callicles
Demosthenes Against Callippus
Demosthenes Against Conon
Demosthenes Against Dionysodorus
Demosthenes Against Eubulides
Demosthenes Against Evergus and Mnesibulus
Demosthenes Against Lacritus
Demosthenes Against Leochares
Demosthenes Against Macartatus
Demosthenes Against Midias
Demosthenes Against Nausimachus and Xenopeithes
Demosthenes Against Neaera
Demosthenes Against Nicostratus
Demosthenes Against Olympiodorus
Demosthenes Against Onetor
Demosthenes Against Pantaenetus
Demosthenes Against Phaenippus
Demosthenes Against Polycles
Demosthenes Against Spudias
Demosthenes Against Stephanus 1
Demosthenes Against Stephanus 2
Demosthenes Against Theocrines
Demosthenes Against Timocrates
Demosthenes Against Timotheus
Demosthenes Against Zenothemis
Demosthenes Erotic Essay
Demosthenes For Phormio
Demosthenes Funeral Speech
Demosthenes Olynthiac 1
Demosthenes On Organization
Demosthenes On the Crown
Demosthenes On the False Embassy
Demosthenes On the Navy
Demosthenes On the Trierarchic Crown
Diogenes Laertius Lives of Eminent Philosophers
Euripides Andromache
Euripides Antigone
Euripides Electra
Euripides Heracleidae
Euripides Hippolytus
Euripides Ion

Euripides Suppliants
Herodotus Histories
Hesiod Ways and Means
Homer Iliad
Hyperides Against Athenogenes
Isaeus Apollodorus
Isaeus Ciron
Isocrates Antidosis
Isocrates Areopagiticus
Isocrates Panathenaicus
Isocrates Panegyricus
Isocrates Plataicus
Isocrates To Demonicus
Isocrates Trapeziticus
Lucian Anacharsis
Lycurgus Against Leocrates
Lysias Against Agoratus
Lysias Against Alcibiades 1
Lysias Against Diogeiton
Lysias Against Epicrates and his Fellow Envoys
Lysias Against Ergocles
Lysias Against Nicomachus
Lysias Against Pancleon
Lysias Against Philon
Lysias Against Simon
Lysias Against the Corn Dealers
Lysias Defence Against a Charge of Subverting the Democracy
Lysias Defence Against a Charge of Taking Bribes
Lysias For Callias
Lysias For Mantitheus
Lysias For Polystratus
Lysias On a Wound by Premeditation
Lysias On the Confiscation of the Property of the Brother of Nicias
Lysias On the Murder of Eratosthenes
Lysias On the Olive Stump
Lysias On the Property of Aristophanes
Lysias On the Property of Eraton
Lysias On the Refusal of a Pension
Pausanias Description of Greece
Plato Alcibiades 1
Plato Gorgias
Plato Laws
Plato Lysis
Plato Menexenus

Plato Phaedo
Plato Protagoras
Plato Republic
Plato Symposion
Pseudo-Xenophon Constitution of the Athenians
Plutarch Alcibiades
Plutarch Aristides
Plutach Moralia
Plutach Nicias
Plutarch Pericles
Plutarch Solon
Plutarch Themistocles
Sophocles Antigone
Theocritus Epigrams
Thucydides History
Xenophon Anabasis
Xenophon Hellenica
Xenophon Memorabilia
Xenophon Oeconomicus
Xenophon Symposion
Xenophon Ways and Means

Ancient Greek Terms

Adikia Unjust behavior.

Agathoi Virtuous.

Agora The political and economic center of the polis; a large open area where commercial transactions were taking place (pl. *agorai*).

Agoranomia 'Market police': A state service responsible to protect consumers for profiteering. The magistrates who undertook this task were called *agoranomoi* (sing. *agoranomos*).

Anasaximon A mine that could be re-auctioned for further exploitation.

Andron Men's apartment, especially dining room, in a medium to large *oikos*.

Antidosis A process where any Athenian who was charged with undertaking on a costly *liturgy*, such as *trierarchy*, could potentially avoid it by nominating a potentially richer man to perform it.

Aoidoi Professional performers who recited epics and then lyric poems to the accompaniment of the lyre (*aoidos* in sing.).

Aparchai The remittances that the Allied Fund received from the allied city-states of Athens.

Apeleutheroi Freed citizens (sing. *apeleutheros*). A freed woman was called *apeleuthere*.

Apocheirotonia Vote taken in the Assembly by a show of hands whereby a magistrate was temporarily suspended from office until the Heliaia court had heard the charge brought against him for misconduct in office.

Apodektai A group of public officials responsible for ensuring the collection of most of the state's annual revenues.

Archai The total number of public services and their staff.

Areopagos The 'Supreme Court' of the polis, functioned as the seat of the aristocratic political council during the Archaic period. During the Classical times its duties were restricted to adjudicate cases of deliberate homicide, wounding and religious matters.

Arete Virtue.

Argyramoibos Moneychangers (plural, *argyramoiboi*).

Argyrocopeion The Athenian silver mint. Its administrators-supervisors were known as the *ten epistatai tou argyrocopeiou* plus their secretary. Its staff consisted of slaves. The *epistatai* who collected public money from various sources, were elected for one year and were not chosen by lot.

Asclepieia Large medical care centers (sing. *asclepieion*).

Astynomoi Public magistrates responsible for maintaining order and cleaning of the polis.

Asylia Avoidance of collective reprisals in case individual citizens of one city-state harmed in any way some or all citizens of another city-state.

Athlothetai Magistrates who managed certain aspects of the Great Panathenaia. They were ten in number, chosen by lot. They stayed in office for four years. They arranged the procession, and the musical, gymnastic and equestrian games.

Atimos Dishonorable man.

Balaneia Greek public baths (*balaneion* in sing).

Banausos Vulgar and 'illiberal' work.

Boule The Athenian Council of the Five Hundred. The councilmen were called *bouleutai* (pl. *bouleutes*).

Bouleuterion The building where councilmen were housed and where their daily meetings were taking place.

Cheirotonia Appointment of a public magistrate (instead of being elected by lot).

Cheirotonoi Magistrates appointed by vote in the Assembly. Those appointed by lot were called *klerotoi*.

Choregia A *liturgy* or public service performed by a rich citizen for the polis. A *choregos* was responsible for the recruitment, training, maintenance, and costuming of *choreutae* (members of a chorus) of a theatrical play.

Clepsydra Water clock.

Cleruchy (pl. *cleruchiae*). A specialized type of colony established by Athens in which settlers, known as *cleruchs*, retained their Athenian citizenship.

Deigma A place where samples of goods for sale were on exhibit in the port of Piraeus.

Demarchs The Athenian 'mayors' in each of the 139 *demes* of Athens. The town hall in each *deme* was called *demarcheion*.

Deme Municipality (pl. *demes*). The urban *demes* of Athens were known as the *asty* area, as opposed to the inland (*mesogeia*) and coastal (*paralia*).

Demos The citizens of Athens.

Demosion A state fund which gathered and collected a large portion of the annual state's revenues.

Diagrammata Tax lists.

Didaskaleion 'Elementary school' in Classical Athens.

Dikai emporikai Trials for commercial - economic cases only. Such cases were heard by specialized and experienced judges.

Dioikesis The management of the Athenian public administration.

Dokimasia A process of evaluating one's candidacy for becoming a councilman. Rejection of a candidate was known as *apodokimasia*.

Dokimastai (in sing. dokimastes) Coin testers who had a bench in the *agora* of Athens and at the harbor of Piraeus and examined foreign currencies against fraudulence. They were under strict supervision by a body known as the *syllogeis* (collectors).

Douloi Slaves.

Drachma The Athenian currency unit (pl. drachmae).

Ecclesia (of the Demos) The popular Assembly of citizens. When a very important assembly was taking place, it was known as *Ecclesia Kyria*. Extra (irregular) assemblies taking place within the year were known as *Synkletoi* or *Ecclesiai Synkletoi*.

Ecclesiasticon State remuneration (half a drachma) to the citizens to motivate them to actively participate in workings of the Assembly (pl. *ecclesiastica*).

Enktesis The right of holding land property in Athens, in general, granted as a reward to foreigners.

Eisangelia A legal procedure where any citizen could accuse any office holder for not fulfilling correctly his task as a public magistrate or abusing his position, or acting against the public interest or against democracy, or being corrupted, etc.

Eisphora A tax on property raised at Athens in war-time only, paid both by wealthy citizens and *metics* (pl. *eisphorai*).

Ephebeia Military training and duty. The trainees (known as *ephebes*) were young 18-19 years of age.

Epibatai (marines) The 14 marines that manned a trireme.

Epiblema It was the shawl worn by women over the veil or tunic.

Epicleroi Athenian women controlled their husband's lot when he died till their male offspring became adults (sing. *epicleros*).

Epimeletai tou emporiou A group of magistrates responsible to oversee the warehouses of imported commodities in general, and of grains in particular, in the port of Piraeus. They also examined accusations of potential profiteering by the *sitemporoi* (merchants of grains) known also as *sitopolai* (sellers of grain).

Epimeletes epi ton hydaton and ton krenon A magistrate with the duty to supervise the distribution of water in the polis and the cleanliness of the springs.

Epimeletes tes koines prosodou, or tamias epi tes dioikeseos, or tamias ton koinon prosodon He was responsible for the overall supervision of the system of collecting and dispensing public revenues. He had to report to the Assembly of citizens regarding the proper management of state revenues.

Epistatai Administrators-supervisors of various state posts or construction projects by the state. An important post was the *epistatai tou argyrocopeiou* being the administrators-supervisors of the silver mint.

Epistates i) A 'chairman' of the *prytanic* council elected by them. ii) Caretaker of a *gymnasium*.

Ergasimon A workable mine.

Eunomia Good order.

Euthyna A special accountability procedure for every public magistrate. The board of those magistrates was known as the *euthynoi* (sing. *euthynos*).

Glauke Literally meaning 'owl', it was another name of the Athenian drachma (*glaukai* in pl.).

Grammateia Contracts.

Grammatists Elementary school teachers who taught their students writing, reading, maths and the great poets such as Homer and Hesiod. Other teachers were the *kitharistae* and the *paidotribae*.

Grammateus Secretary. There were various kinds of *grammateis* (secretaries) that were related to the functioning of the Athenian state.

Graphe paranomon A law provision where every citizen had the right to accuse a *boulomenos,* that is, a person who wished to propose a *psephisma* (decree) or managed to already pass a *psephisma* (accepted and voted by the Assembly), which according to the accuser, it contradicted with the existing laws of the state or, that it was accepted as a state law even though the correct legal procedures were not followed.

Gymnasia (e.g., *gymnasium*). Large public athletic facilities. Each was supervised by a magistrate called the *epistates*.

Gymnasiarchai Those citizens who were in charge of the running of *gymnasia*.

Gynaikonites Women's apartments in a house.

Heliaia The popular court of Athens during the Classical period. The court's members were called *heliastai*.

Hellenotamiai A group of ten public treasurers, being the chief financial officers of the Athenian Alliance. They were appointed by the Athenians (one from each tribe) to handle the financial contributions from the allied states.

Hegemon i) The chairman in a Heliaia court ii) A chief in charge of every *symmory* group.

Hellanodikai Judges of the Olympic Games who became well-known for enforcing fairness during the games.

Hestia The central hearth of an *oikos*.

Hetaera (pl. hetaerae) They were somewhat similar to the Japanese geishas, or French courtesans of the 16th-17th centuries.

Hippeis Cavalrymen.

Homonoia Concord.

Hoplites Heavy infantry citizen militia army (*hoplite*, in sing.).

Ilarchos Cavalry commander.

Isegoria Right to speak freely. Also, the right of every citizen to speak and make proposals in the Assembly.

Isonomia Equality before the law. It meant also equality of political rights for all Athenian citizens.

Isopoliteia A treaty of equal citizenship rights between states. It was initiated during the Classical period but was much more expanded during the Hellenistic period.

Isoteleia A status of equal taxation for everyone, either Athenian or a foreigner.

Kalos-kagathos The proper behavior for one, to be considered as a morally and physically attractive man (pl. *kaloi-kagathoi*).

Kallos A concept denoting natural beauty combined with mental virtues.

Kapeleia Restaurants/taverns (*kapeleion* in sing.).

Kleroterion Allotment machine for the selection of the *Heliaia* judges.

Klerotoi Elected by lot magistrates.

Klope Theft.

Kollyboi Very small value bronze coins (*kollybos* in sing.). Similar were the so-called *chalkoi* coins (sing., *chalkos*).

Koprologoi A body of private scavengers who acted as public sweepers. They were under the direct supervision of the *astynomoi*.

Kybernetes The person responsible for safe sailing. He was handling the rudder.

Kylikes (kylix in singular) The most common type of wine-drinking cup in Ancient Greece

Kyrios The head of the *oikos* who was responsible for his wife, children, and any unmarried female relatives. Also known as a woman's 'guardian'.

Liturgies A special type of taxation burdening the wealthy citizens and wealthy *metics*. It included *trierarchy*, *choregia*, *hestiasis*, *gymnasiarchy* and *hippotrophia*.

Liturgist The performer of a *liturgy*.

Logistai Literally meaning, the accountants, this 10-member group supervised any public magistrate of the state upon completion of his duty. They were also responsible to audit the magistrates of the treasury-temples. In their duties they were assisted by the *ten synegoroi* and the *ten euthynoi*.

Logodosia, also known as logoi Detailed reports provided by public magistrates to the Council and the *logistai* upon completion of their duties regarding the proper management of public money.

Logoi Detailed annual reports issued by the treasuries–temples at Athens.

Medimnos A container that functioned as a unit of measurement mainly for agricultural products such as corn (pl. *medimnoi*).

Metics Alien residents of Athens. They relocated in Athens for work purposes (sing. *metic*).

Metoikion A personal tax on *metics* (alien residents), both paid by men and women. It was also known as *xenikon*.
Metronomoi Magistrates whose duty was to check if sellers invoiced their goods by using the correct weights and measures in the market.
Metroon A temple dedicated to the goddess-mother, being also the building where the archives of the written laws of the state were stored. It was also known as *nomophylakion*.
Mina (also known as *mna*). An amount of money equal to 100 drachmae.
Misthosis A common practice for *trierarchs* to hire *metics* or *xenoi* so as to undertake *trierarchy*.
Moicheia Adultery.
Naukleroi Ship-oweners (*naukleros* in sing.).
Naupegos He was in charge of the technical matters of the ship which included repairs and fixes when these were required.
Neoria Shipyards (*neorion* in sing.).
Neoroi Known also as the *guardians of neorion*, were those officials responsible for the security of the Athenian ports.
Neosoikos A *trireme*'s shipshed (pl. *neosoikoi*).
Nine Archons The highest magistrates of Athens known as *archons*. They were: the *eponymous archon*, the *archon basileus*, the *polemarchos*, and the *six thesmothetai*.
Nomophylakes Public magistrates responsible for the protection of legal documents (which contained that state laws) from destruction and forgery. For this purpose, they had full access to the *Metroon* known also as *nomophylakion*. Any of these magistrates was known as the *nomophylax*.
Nomothetai Annual group of judges aimed to oversee whether there were duplications, contradictions, ambiguities between the laws in force, or whether in the legal system still existed inactive laws.
Nympheutria An older woman who was guiding the bride and assisted her through the marriage ceremony.
Obol A subdivision of the drachma (1/6 of a drachma).
Oikonomos Household manager
Oikos House, dwelling place; household.
Olkades A kind of a merchant ship. Merchants ships which carried wheat were known as *sitagoga* ships.
Opisthodomos The conventional name for the backyard of the Temple of Athena on the Acropolis where the chambers that hosted the treasuries of TTAGs and the AF were located.
Pedagogue A private tutor hired by the wealthy families.
Paideia Upbringing and educating children. Aside from education as a technical procedure of gaining knowledge, *paideia* comprised a whole range of further arrangements that aimed at shaping the moral character of youth from early childhood to adolescence.

Palaestra A wrestling private school or private arena of wrestling or boxing. *Palaestrae* (in plural) functioned both independently and as a part of public *gymnasia*; a palaestra could exist without a *gymnasium*, but no *gymnasium* existed without a *palaestra*. The guardian or the director of a *palaestra* was known as the *palaestrophylax*.

Panathenaea The most famous multi-day ancient Greek festival held annually at Athens. Its main purpose was both Athenians and non-Athenians to celebrate the Goddess Athena.

Pankration A mixed martial art invented in Sparta and spread around the known Greek world.

Pantopoleia Grocery stores (sing. *pantopoleion*).

Pentecoste A general tax on imports (2% tax on the value of the good). Tax collectors of this relative tax were called *pentecostologoi*.

Pentecontarchos An officer of a trireme. he had the duties of secretary, treasurer, and caretaker, as well as being responsible for all types of supplies.

Penteconter A type of warship before the introduction of the *triremes*.

Peplos Veil.

Pezonautai Athenian *hoplites* fighting as 'marines' in the *triremes*.

Phalanx The most well-known and practiced military formation in Ancient Greece from the Archaic to Hellenistic times. Its members were called *hoplites*.

Phanera ousia 'Disclosed property'. By contrast, 'hidden property' (to avoid taxation), categorized as *aphanes ousia*.

Phylae Tribes (sing. *phyle*).

Philotimia A sense of honor.

Phratry It was considered any socio-political group of people who was made up of relatives who had a common ancestor - progenitor, and were characterized by common values, standards and rules of behavior, formally included in a set with specific purposes (*phratriae* in plural).

Pistis Trust (in commercial affairs).

Plethron A subdivision of the *stadium* or *stadion*. A *plethron* corresponded to 100 ancient Greek *podes* or to 1/6 of the *stadion*, roughly 30 meters.

Pnyx A hill in central Athens, where the popular assemblies in Classical Athens were taking place since 507 BCE, and later on.

Poletai (Board of *poletai*). A group of public magistrates responsible for the leases of state land for exploitation by individuals or entrepreneurial consortia through auctioning processes on behalf of the state. These leases included the highly profitable silver mines. *Poletai* and the Council were entrusted with the supervision of the whole procedure of these leases.

Polis (in plural, poleis) Literally means 'city(ies)' in Greek. It also meant the body of citizens under a city's jurisdiction.

Probouleumata Bills prepared by the Council proposed for approval, rejection or modification by the Assembly.

Prorates An officer that he stood at the bow, reporting (to keleustes and kybernetes) in case he observed something of importance.

Proxeny A measure (mostly) for traders who travelled to other Greek poleis, to protect them from the risk of having themselves or their property seized. *Proxeny* could also be bestowed on *metics*.

Prytany (also known as *prytaneia*). The executive branch of the Council. Each *prytany* consisted of 50 councilmen who were originating from the same Athenian tribe, known as *prytaneis*. About one-tenth of the year, each of the ten *phylae* (tribes) presided in turn over the Council and the Assembly through a *prytany*.

Prytaneion (also known as *Tholos*). A luxurious and expensive government building where the *prytaneis* exercised their duties and dined with other high-ranking officials and foreign dignitaries.

Pyxis Vessel for perfumes, balsam.

Seisachtheia Debt abolishment, introduced by Solon in 594 BCE.

Sitophylakes A body of magistrates who were responsible to guard the wheat warehouses. Five of them were located in Athens and five in the twin city of Piraeus. They had similar duties with the *sitonai*.

Strategoi Literally meaning generals, being the highest military commanders of Athens (sing. *strategos*). They were gathered altogether in a specific place located in the Agora, known as the *Strategeion*. They were given specific assignments, such as the *strategos epi tin choran* for the defense of Attica and *strategos of the trierarchy*, being responsible for the efficient implementation of the *trierarchy* institution annually.

Stratiotikon It was a forth c. BCE fund, responsible for supporting financially the military expenditures of the state. It had a treasurer in charge known as *tamias epi ton stratiotikon*.

Sophronistai The *ten sophronistai*, together with the *ten kosmetai*, were responsible for educating young Athenian *ephebes* in the performance of their military duty (19-20 years of age). They were appointed by the Athenian *demos* instead of being elected by lot. These two groups of magistrates had similar duties.

Symbola (in singular: symbolon) Permanent bilateral treaties, introduced during the fifth c. BCE, created to regulate litigation between citizens of different states providing each party with a form of protection.

Symmories (singular, symmoria) Distinct taxation groups of wealthy citizens being liable i) to pay the *eisphora* war tax (ii) to cover the expenses of the *trierarchy*.

Symposion A banquet, such as the famous Platonic Symposium.

Synteleis Rich Athenians organized in groups by the state, being responsible for covering the expenses of the *trierarchy*. Each group of such, known as *synteleia* included 5 out of the 1,200 well-to-do citizens. As a result, 240 *synteleiai* were created in total.

Syntrierarchy Joint *trierarchy*.

Tamia Treasuries.

Tamiai (sing. *tamias*). Treasurers of the *Treasuries-Temples of Athena and the Other Gods* and other money managing authorities. They collected funds, paid bills, overlooked the operations of the treasuries and reported to higher authorities for reasons of accountability and transparency.

Talent The largest subdivision of drachma. A *talent* was equal to 6,000 drachmae.

Tetradrachm Four drachmae.

Theorica Monetary compensation of two *obols* provided by the state to citizens for the purpose of attending theatrical performances financed by a *liturgy* known as *choregia* under the auspice of the state.

Theoricon The fourth century fund which was responsible for the *theorica* payments. It had a treasurer in charge known as *tamias epi ton theoricon*. He was assisted in his duties by ten magistrates (*hoi epi to theoricon*).

Thetes The lowest-income social group according to the reforms of Solon.

Thesmothetai A board of six *archons* whose duties were to review the laws annually, to determine whether there were inconsistencies, duplications, or invalid laws in force and, if so, to inform the *nomothetai* to rectify the situation.

Trapeza Bank.

Treasuries-Temples of Athena and the Other Gods Quasi-state institutions, functioning as banks which mainly leased the state when in need.

Trierarch The commander of a *trireme* warship.

Trierarchy The most expensive type of *liturgy* where both wealthy Athenians and *metics* were charged with the running expenses of a *trireme* warship for one year.

Trieraules He used a flute and was responsible for the rhythm of rowing.

Trireme The main Greek warship of the Classical period which was rowed by three banks of rowers on each side.

Xenoi Foreigners.

References

Modern Authors

Acemoglu D, Robinson J (2013) *Why nations fail*. New York: Crown Business.
Achen CH, Bartels LM (2017) *Democracy for realists*. Princeton: Princeton University Press.
Acton PH (2014) *Poiesis: Manufacturing in Classical Athens*. Oxford: Oxford University Press.
Akerlof G (1970) The market for lemons: quality, uncertainty and market mechanism. *Quarterly Journal of Economics*, 84: 488-500.
Alesina A, Perotti, R (1996) Income distribution, political instability, and investment. *European Economic Review*, 40(6): 1203–1228.
Allen DW, Lantinova V (2013) The ancient Olympics as a signal of city-state strength, *Economics of Governance*, 14: 23–44.
Altman D (2019) *Citizenship and Contemporary Direct Democracy*. Cambrdge: Cambridge University Press.
Amemiya T (2007) *Economy and economics of ancient Greece*. London and New York: Routledge.
Ammous S (2018) *The Bitcoin sandard: The decentralized alternative to Central Banking*. Hoboken, New Jersey: Wiley.
Andreades AM (1933) *A History of Greek public finance*. Cambridge MA: Harvard University Press.
Angelakis AN (2016) Evolution of rainwater harvesting and use in Crete, Hellas through the millennia. *Water Science and Technology: Water Supply*, 16(6): 1624–1638.
Aperghis GG, (1998) A reassessment of the Laurion mining lease records. *BCIS*, 42: 1-20.
Arrow K (1950) A difficulty in the concept of social welfare. *The Journal of Political Economy*, 58(4): 328-346.
Arrow KJ ([1951], 1963) *Social choice and individual values*. New York: Wiley & Sons.
Arvanitidis P, Kyriazis, N (2013) Democracy and public choice in Classical Athens. *Peace Economics, Peace Science and Public Policy*, 19(2): 213-248.
Ault BA (2007) Oikos and Oikonomia: Greek houses, households and the domestic economy. *British School at Athens Studies*, 15: 259-265.
Avil´es D, Mirhady DC (2013) Law courts. In: Beck H (Ed.), *A companion to ancient Greek government* (pp. 205-218). Malden MA: Willey-Blackwell.
Austin MM, Vidal-Naquet P (1980) *Economic and social history of Ancient Greece*. London: Batsford Academic and Educational Ltd.
Barber BR (2003) *Strong democracy: Participatory politics for a New Age*. New York: MacMillan Press.

E. M. L. Economou, N. C. Kyriazis, *Daily Life in Classical Athens*, Frontiers in Economic History, https://doi.org/10.1007/978-3-031-58541-8

Baumol WJ (1972) On taxation and the control of externalities. *American Economic Review*, 62(3): 307–322.

Beaumont L (2012) *Childhood in ancient Athens: iconography and social history*. Abingdon, New York: Routledge.

Beck H, Funke P (2015) (eds) *Federalism in Greek antiquity*. Cambridge: Cambridge University Press.

Bergh A, Lyttkens CH (2014) Measuring institutional quality in ancient Athens. *Journal of Institutional Economics*, 10(2): 279-310.

Besley T, Ghatak M (2017) Public-private partnerships for the provision of public goods: Theory and an application to NGOs, *Research in Economics*, 71(2): 356-371.

Bitros GC, Karayiannis AD (2006) The liberating power of entrepreneurship in ancient Athens. In: Y Cassis, I Pepelasis-Minoglou (eds), *Entrepreneurship on theory and history. Country studies* (pp. 11-24). London: Palgrave.

Bitros GC, Karayiannis AD (2008) Values and institutions as determinants of entrepreneurship in ancient Athens. *Journal of Institutional Economics*, 4(2): 205-230.

Bitros GC, Karayiannis A (2010) Morality, institutions and the wealth of nations: Some lessons from ancient Greece, *European Journal of Political Economy*: 26: 68-81.

Bitros GC, Karayiannis A (2011) Character, knowledge and skills in ancient Greek paideia: Some lessons for today's policy makers, *Journal of Economic Asymmetries*, 8: 195-221.

Bitros GC, Karayiannis, AD (2013) *Creative crisis in democracy and economy*. Berlin, Heidelberg: Springer-Verlag.

Bitros, GC, Economou, EML, Kyriazis NC (2020) *Democracy and money: Lessons for today from Classical Athens*. London and New York: Routledge.

Bitros GC (2021) From the Athenian silver to the Bitcoin standard: Private money in a state-enforced free banking model. Available at: https://papers.ssrn.com/sol3/papers.cfm?abstract_id=3836037

Blamire A (2001) Athenian finance, 454-404 B.C. *Hesperia: The Journal of the American School of Classical Studies at Athens*, 70: 99-126.

Bresson A (2007) *L' economie de la Grèce des cites. Les structures et la production*, vol. 1. Paris: Armand-Colin.

Bresson A (2014) Capitalism and the ancient Greek economy. In: Neal L, Williamson JG (eds), *The rise of capitalism: From ancient origins to 1848*, vol. 1. Cambridge: Cambridge University Press.

Bresson A (2016a) *The making of the ancient Greek economy: Institutions, markets, and growth in the city-states*. Princeton, NJ: Princeton University Press.

Bresson A (2016b) Aristotle and foreign trade. In: Harris EM, Lewis DM, Woolmer W (eds), *The ancient Greek economy: Markets, households and city states* (pp. 41-65). New York: Cambridge University Press.

Bresson A (2019a) The Athenian money supply in the Late Archaic and Early Classical Period. *Journal of Ancient Civilizations*, 34(2): 135-153.

Bresson A (2019b) The choice of electrum monometallism: When and why. *White Gold*, 477–496.

Buchanan JM, Tullock G (1962) *The calculus of consent: Logical foundations of constitutional democracy*. Ann Arbor: University of Michigan Press.

Burke EM (1992) The economy of Athens in the Classical era: Some adjustments to the primitivist model. *TAPA*, 122: 199–226.

Burke EM (2010) Finances and the operation of the Athenian democracy in Lycurgan era. *American Journal of Philology*, 131(3): 393-423.

Buttrey TV (1979) The Athenian Currency Law of 375/4 B.C. In: Mørkholm O, Waggoner N (eds), *Greek numismatics and archaeology: Essays in honor of Margaret Thompson*. Wetteren: Belgium, 33-45.

Buttrey TV (1981) More on the Athenian Coinage Law of 375/4 B.C. *NumAntCl*, 10: 71-94.

Camp J (2003) *The Athenian Agora: A short guide to the excavations*, Athens. Princeton, NJ: American School of Classical Studies at Athens.

Camp J, Kroll JH (2001) The Agora mint and Athenian bronze coinage. *Hesperia*, 70(2): 127-62.
Canevaro M (2010) The decree awarding citizenship to the Plataeans ([Dem.] 59.104). *Greek, Roman, and Byzantine Studies* 50: 337–369.
Canevaro M (2018) What was the law of Leptines' really about? Reflections on Athenian public economy and legislation in the fourth century BCE. *Constitutional Political Economy*, 29: 440–464.
Cartledge P (1977) Hoplites and heroes: Sparta's contribution to the technique of Ancient warfare. *The Journal of Hellenic Studies*, 97: 11-27.
Cartledge P (1987) *Agesilaos and the crisis of Sparta*. London: Gerald Duckworth and Company.
Cartledge P (2002) The political economy of Greek slavery. In: Cartledge C, Cohen EE, Foxhall L, (eds), *Money, labour and land* (pp. 156-166). London and New York: Routledge.
Cartledge P (2011) *Ancient Greece: a very short introduction*. Oxford: Oxford University Press.
Cartledge P (2018) *Democracy: A life*. Oxford: Oxford University Press.
Cartledge P (2020). *Thebes: The forgotten city of Ancient Greece*. London: Picador.
Cartledge P (2022) Greece's finest hour? The democratic implications of the Battle of Salamis. In: Economou EML, Kyriazis NC, Platias A (eds), *Democracy and Salamis. 2500 years after the battle that saved Greece and the western world*, (pp. 55-74). Cham: Springer.
Christ RM (2006) *The bad citizen in Classical Athens*. Cambridge: Cambridge University Press.
Christesen P (2003). Economic rationalism in fourth-century BCE Athens. *Greece & Rome*, 50(1): 31-56.
Christesen P (2012). *Sport and democracy in the ancient and modern worlds*. Cambridge: Cambridge University Press.
Christopoulou-Aletra H, Togia A, Varlam C (2009) History of medicine. *Archives of Hellenic Medicine*, 27: 259-263.
Cline RS (1977) *World power assessment: A calculus of strategic drift*. Colorado: Westview Press.
Cohen EE (1973) *Ancient Athenian maritime courts*. Princeton, New Jersey: Princeton University Press.
Cohen EE (1992) *Athenian economy and society: A banking perspective*. Princeton: Princeton University Press.
Cohen EE (2000) *The Athenian nation*. Princeton: Princeton University Press.
Cohen EE. (2002) An unprofitable masculinity. In: Cartledge P, Cohen EE, Foxhall L, (eds) *Money, labour and land* (pp. 100-113). London: Routledge.
Congleton RD (2012) *Perfecting parliament: Constitutional reform, liberalism, and the rise of western democracy*. Cambridge: Cambridge University Press.
Copeland DC (2014) *Economic interdependence and war*. Princeton: Princeton University Press.
Corbet S, Lucey BM, Urquhart A, Yarovaya L. (2019) Cryptocurrencies as a financial asset: A systematic analysis. *International Review of Financial Analysis*, 62: 182–199.
Coase, RH, (1960), The problem of social cost. Journal of Law and Economics, 3(1), 1–44.
Costouros GJ (1978) Auditing in the Athenian state of the Golden Age 500-300 B.C. *The Accounting Historians Journal*, 5: 41–50.
Cox CA (2007) The 'astynomoi', private wills and street activity. *The Classical Quarterly, New Series*, 57(2): 769–775.
Craddock, PT, (1995), *Early Metal Mining and Production*. Edinburgh: Edinburgh University Press.
Crosby, M (1950). The leases of the laureion mines. *Hesperia: The Journal of the American School of Classical Studies at Athens*, 19(3), 189–297.
Cronin TE, (1999) *The politics of initiative, referendum, and recall*. Cambridge MA: Harvard University Press.
D'Amato R, Salimbetti A (2011) *Bronze Age Greek warrior 1600-1100 BC*. Osprey, Warrior, 153. Oxford: Osprey Publishing.
Davies JK (1967) Demosthenes on liturgies: a note. *Journal of Hellenic Studies*, 87: 33–40.
Davies JK (1981) *Wealth and the power of wealth in Classical Athens*. New York: Amo Press.

Davidson J (1997) *Courtesans and fishcakes; The consuming passions of Classical Athens*. London: Fontana Press.

Dawkings R (1976). The selfish gene. Oxford: Oxford University Press

De Romilly J (1994) *Pourquoi la Grèce?* Paris: Le Livre de Poche.

de Ste Croix GEM (1981) *The class struggle in the Ancient Greek world from the Archaic Age to the Arab conquests*. Ithaca, New York: Cornell University Press.

De Vries J, van der Woude A (1997) *The first modern economy*. Cambridge University Press, Cambridge.

Diamond L (2007) A quarter-century of promoting democracy. *Journal of Democracy*, 18(4): 112–126.

Diebolt C, Haupert M. (eds) (2019) *Handbook of Cliometrics*. Cham: Springer Nature.

Diebolt C, Haupert M (2016) Clio's contributions to economics and history, *Revue d' Economie Politique*, 126(5): 971–989.

Diebolt C, Haupert M (2020) How cliometrics has infiltrated economics – and helped to improve the discipline. *Annals of the Fondazione Luigi Einaudi*, LIV: 219–230.

Downs A (1957) *An economic theory of democracy*. New York: Harper & Row.

Dwyer GP (2015) The economics of Bitcoin and similar private digital currencies. *Journal of Financial Stability*, 17: 81–91.

Economou EML (2020) *The Achaean federal state in Ancient Greece. History, political and economic organization, warfare and strategy*. Cham: Springer.

Economou EML (2023) Applying a 'turn to the sea' strategy and the transformation of the Athenian economy (508-322 BCE). *Munich Social Science Review*, 6: 95–118.

Economou EML (2024). *The economy of Classical Athens. Organization, institutions and society*. London and New York: Routledge.

Economou EML, Halkos G, Kyriazis NC (2023) Environmental economics in Classical Athens. *Journal of Institutional Economics*, 19(1): 102–118.

Economou EML, Kyriazis, NA (2021a) Achieving sustainable financial transactions under regimes without a Central Bank-An intertemporal comparison. *Sustainability*, 13(3):1071.

Economou EML, Kyriazis NA (2021b) An intertemporal comparison of monetary policy strategies in extraordinary times. The COVID-19 and the Athenian plague during the Classical times. *Archives of Economic History*, XXXIII(1): 29–45.

Economou EML, Kyriazis NC (2015a) Ancient Greek democratic federations: A comparative study with the European Union. In: Peukert H (ed) *Taking up the challenge! Festschrift für Jürgen Backhaus* (pp. 289-306). Marburg: Metropolis-Verlag.

Economou EML, Kyriazis NC (2015b) The Aetolian Federation, the EU and Pakistan: An interactive analysis of federations. *Asian Journal of Humanities and Social Studies*, 3(2): 124-131.

Economou EML, Kyriazis NC (2015c) The Arcadian Federation: A benchmark for the further EU integration. *Journal of Social Science Studies*, 2(2): 294–308.

Economou EML, Kyriazis NC (2016a) The emergence and the development of the Achaean federation. Lessons and institutional proposals for modern societies. *Evolutionary and Institutional Economics Review*, 13: 93–112 (Springer Verlag).

Economou EML, Kyriazis NC (2016b) Choosing peace against war strategy. A history from the ancient Athenian Democracy. *Peace Economics, Peace Science and Public Policy*, 22(2): 191–212.

Economou EML, Kyriazis NC (2017) The emergence and the evolution of property rights in ancient Greece. *Journal of Institutional Economics*, 13(1): 53–77.

Economou, EML, Kyriazis, NC, Metaxas, T, (2017), Ancient Athenians, Californians and modern Greeks: A comparative analysis of choice set under direct democracy procedures. *Homo Oeconomicus*, 34, 47–65.

Economou EML, Kyriazis NC (2018a) Ancient Greek Achaeans, modern Germans and EU integration: An interdisciplinary analysis of federations. In: Holler MJ, Tridimas G, (eds) *German-Greek yearbook of Political Economy*, Vol. 1 (pp. 137-160). München: Holler-Verlag.

Economou EML, Kyriazis N (2018b) Is Greek debt sustainable? Analyzing three different scenarios for the forthcoming 2018-2022 period. *The Journal for Markets and Ethics (Zeitschrift für Marktwirtschaft und Ethik)*, 6(2): 171-182.

Economou EML, Kyriazis NC (2019a) *Democracy and economy: An inseparable relationship since ancient times to today*. Newcastle: Cambridge Scholars Publishing.

Economou EML, Kyriazis NC (2019b) The evolution of property rights in Hellenistic Greece and the Ptolemaic Kingdom of Egypt. *Journal of Institutional Economics*, 15(5): 827-843.

Economou EML, Kyriazis NC (2019c) The social position and the rights of women in ancient Greece: A response to Barbara Klose-Ullmann's 'Medea on Stage.' In Holler MJ, Tridimas G (eds), *German-Greek yearbook of Political Economy*, Vol. 2 (pp. 143-156). München: Holler-Verlag.

Economou EML, Kyriazis NC (2022a) 'Asymmetric information, social choices and democracy', in: EML Economou, NC Kyriazis, Platias A (eds.). *Democracy in times of Crises. Challenges, problems and policy proposals for today's and future societies*, (pp. 147-164).-Cham: Springer Verlag.

Economou EML, Kyriazis NC (2022b) The emergence of democracy: A behavioural perspective. In: Economou EML, Kyriazis NC, Platias A (eds), *Democracy and Salamis. 2500 Years After the Battle that Saved Greece And the Western World* (pp. 237-268). Cham: Springer.

Economou EML, Kyriazis NC, Metaxas T (2015) The institutional and economic foundations of regional proto-federations. *Economics of Governance*, 16(3): 251-271.

Economou EML, Kyriazis NA, Kyriazis NC (2021a) Managing financial risk while performing international commercial transactions. Intertemporal lessons from Athens in Classical times. *Journal of Risk and Financial Management*. 14(11): 509. https://doi.org/10.3390/jrfm14110509

Economou EML, Kyriazis NC, Kyriazis NA (2021b) Money decentralization under direct democracy procedures. The case of Classical Athens. *Journal of Risk and Financial Management*. https://doi.org/10.3390/jrfm14010030

Economou EML, Kyriazis NC, Platias A (eds) (2022a) *Democracy in times of crises. Challenges, problems and policy proposals for today's and future societies*. Cham: Springer.

Economou EML, Kyriazis NC, Platias A (2022b). Introduction. In: Economou EML, Kyriazis NC, Platias A (eds). *Democracy and Salamis. 2500 years after the battle that saved Greece and the western world* (pp. 1-34). Cham: Springer.

Eichengreen B (2011) *Exorbitant privilege: The rise and fall of the fdollar*. Oxford: Oxford University Press.

Engen DT (2005) Ancient greenbacks, Athenian owls, the law of Nicophon, and the Greek economy. *Historia*, 54(4), 359-381.

Engen DT (2010) *Honor and profit: Athenian trade policy and the economy and society of Greece: 415-307 BCE*. Ann Arbor: University of Michigan Press.

Fawcett P (2016) When I squeeze you with eisphorai: Taxes and tax policy in Classical Athens. *Hesperia*, 85(1): 153-199.

Fayol H (1949) *General and industrial management*. London: Pitman.

Fayol H. (1967) *General principles of management*. London: Pitman.

Feld PL, Savioz MR. (1997). Direct democracy matters for economic performance: An empirical investigation. *Kyklos*, 50, 507-538.

Figueira TJ (1986) 'Sitopolai' and 'sitophylakes' in Lysias' 'Against the Graindealrs': Governmental intervention in the Athenian economy. *Phoenix*, 40: 149-171.

Figueira TJ (1998) *The power of money: coinage and politics in the Athenian Empire*. Philadelphia: University of Pennsylvania Press.

Figueira TJ (2011) The Athenian naukraroi and archaic naval warfare. *Cadmo*, 21: 183-210.

Figueira TJ, Jensen SR (2019). *Hegemonic finances. Funding Athenian domination in the 5th centuries BC*. London: Bloomsbury.

Figueira TJ (2022) Salamis as inflection point: Militarization, politicization, and democratization', in Economou EML, Kyriazis, NC, Platias A (eds), *Democracy and Salamis. 2500 years after the battle that saved Greece and the western world* (pp. 75–98). Cham: Springer Verlag.
Finley MI (1973) *The ancient economy*. Berkeley: University of California Press.
Finley MI (1979) *The Bucher-Meyer controversy*. New York: Arno Press.
Finley MI (1983) *Economy and society in Ancient Greece*. New York: Penguin Non-Classics.
Finley MI (1985) *Ancient history: Evidence and models*. London: Chatto & Windus.
Fisher N (1993) Review of 'Apollodorus Against Neaira: [Demosthenes] 59' (edite by C. Carey), *Greece & Rome*, 40(2): 218–220.
Fisher N (1998) 'Gymnasia and the democratic values of leisure.' In P. Cartledge, P. Millett, & S. von Reden (eds), *Kosmos: Essays in order, conflict and community in Classical Athens* (pp. 84-104). Cambridge: Cambridge University Press.
Fishkin JS (2011) *When the people speak: Deliberative democracy and public consultation*. Oxford: Oxford University Press.
Flacelière R (1959) *La Vie Quotidienne en Grèce au Siècle de Périclès*. Paris: Librairie Hachette.
Fleck RK, Hanssen, FA (2009). Rulers ruled by women: an economic analysis of the rise and fall of women's rights in ancient Sparta. *Economic Governance*, 10(3): 221-254.
Forsdyke S (2005) *Exile, ostracism and democracy. The politics of expulsion in ancient Greece*. Princeton and Oxford: Princeton University Press.
Franklin B (2005) *The Autobiography of Benjamin Franklin*, ed. P. Conn, Philadelphia: University of Pennsylvania Press.
Friedman M, Schwartz, AJ (1986). Has government any role in money? *Journal of Monetary Economics* 17: 37–62.
Frier, BW, Kehoe DP (2008) 'Law and economic institutions.' In: Scheidel W, Morris I, Saller RP (eds), *The Cambridge economic history of the Greco-roman world* (pp. 113-143). Cambridge: Cambridge, University Press.
Fröhlich P (2013) Governmental checks and balances. In Beck H (ed), *A Companion to Ancient Greek government* (pp. 252-266). Malden MA, Willey-Blackwell.
Fukuyama F (1992) *The end of history and the last man*. New York: The Free Press.
Fuller JFC (2001) *Decisive battles of the Western world*. London: Cassell and Company.
Gabrielsen V (1994) *Financing the Athenian fleet: Public taxation and social relations*. Baltimore: John Hopkins University Press.
Gabrielsen V (2013) 'Finance and taxes.' In H. Beck (Ed.) *A Companion to Ancient Greek government* (pp. 332-348). Malden MA: Willey-Blackwell.
Garland R (2008) *Daily life of the Ancient Greeks*. Westport, Connecticut and London: Greenwood Press.
Gauthier L (2022) Putting Clio back in Cliometrics. *History and Theory*, 61(21): 289-311.
Gibbons R (1998) Incentives in organizations. *The Journal of Economic Perspectives*, 12(4), 115–132.
Georgiou M, Kyriazis NC, Economou EML (2015) Democracy, political stability and economic performance. A panel data analysis. *Journal of Risk and Control*, 2(1): 1-18.
Gill A (2008) Chattering' in the baths: The urban Greek bathing establishment and social discourse in Classical antiquity. Proceedings of the 36th International Conference, Budapest, April 2–6, 2008. Available at: https://proceedings.caaconference.org/files/2008/CD27_Gill_CAA2008.pdf
Gilpin, P (1981), *War and change in world politics*. Cambridge: Cambridge University Press.
Gilleard C (2003) Old age in Byzantine society. *Ageing & Society*, 27, 623–642.
Gough JW (1936) *The social contract*. Oxford: Clarendon Press.
Grossman GM, Helpman E (1991) *Innovation and growth in the global economy*. Cambridge: MIT Press.
Günther J, Hahn F (2019) Choregia and trierarchy as profit-oriented entrepreneurships. *Constitutional Political Economy*, 30: 177–193.
Habicht C (1999) *Athens from Alexander to Anthony*. Cambridge Massachusetts and London: Harvard University Press.

Halkos G, Kyriazis N (2010) The Athenian economy in the age of Demosthenes. *European Journal of Law and Economics*, 29: 255–277.

Halkos G, Kyriazis NC, Economou EML (2021) Plato as a game theorist towards an international trade policy, *Journal of Risk and Financial Management*, 14(3): 115. https://doi.org/10.3390/jrfm14030115.

Halkos G, Economou EML, Kyriazis NC (2022) Tracing the optimal level of political and social change under risks and uncertainties: Some lessons from Ancient Sparta and Athens, *Journal of Risk and Financial Management*, 15, 416.

Hallof K. (1990). Der Verkauf konfiszierten Der Verkauf konfiszierten Vermögens von der Poleten in Athen. *Klio*, 72: 402–26.

Hammond NGL (1994) *Philip of Macedon*. Baltimore: Johns Hopkins University Press.

Hammond NGL (1997) *The genius of Alexander the Great*. North Carolina: University of North Carolina Press.

Hansen MH (1974) *The sovereignty of the people's court in Athens in the fourth century B.C.* Odense: Odense University Press.

Hansen MH (1976) The Theoric fund and the graphe paranomon against Apollodorus. *Greek and Byzantine Studies* XVII: 235-246.

Hansen MH (1977) How often did the Ecclesia meet? *GRBS* 18: 43–70.

Hansen MH (1980) Seven hundred Archai in Classical Athens. *GRBS*, 21: 151–173.

Hansen, MH (1991) *The Athenian democracy in the age of Demosthenes*. Bristol Classical Press: London.

Hansen MH (2006) *Polis. An introduction to the ancient Greek city-state*. Oxford: Oxford University Press.

Hansen, MH (1991) *The Athenian democracy in the age of Demosthenes*. Bristol Classical Press: London.

Hanson VD (1994) *The western way of war. Infantry battle in Classical Greece*. Berkeley, Los Angeles & London: University of California Press.

Hanson VD (1999) *The other Greeks: The family farm and the agrarian roots of Western civilization*. Berkeley, Los Angeles and London: University of California Press.

Hanson VD, Heath J (2001) *Who killed Homer: The demise of Classical education and the recovery of Greek wisdom*. New York and London: Encounter Books.

Harris, EM, (1991), When did the Athenian Assembly meet? Some new evidence. *A JP*, 112(1991), 329–345.

Harris EM (1993). Apotimema: Athenian terminology for real security in leases and dowry agreements. *The Classical Quarterly*, 43(1): 73-95.

Harris EM (2002) Workshop, marketplace and household. In Cartledge P, Cohen EE, Foxhall L. (eds), *Money, labour and land* (pp. 67–99). London: Routledge.

Harris EM (2013) *The rule of law in action in democratic Athens*. Oxford: Oxford University Press.

Harris EM (2016) The legal foundations of economic growth in ancient Greece: the role of property records. In: Harris EM, Lewis DM, Woolmer M (eds), *The ancient Greek Economy: Markets, Households and City States* (pp. 116-147). New York: Cambridge University Press.

Harris EM, Lewis DM (2016) Introduction: Markets in Classical and Hellenistic Greece. In: Harris EM, Lewis DM, Woolmer M (eds), *The ancient Greek economy: Markets, households and city states* (pp. 1-40). New York: Cambridge University Press.

Harris EM, Lewis, DM, Woolmer M. (eds) (2016) *The ancient Greek economy: Markets, households and city states*. New York: Cambridge University Press.

Hayek FA (1960) *The constitution of liberty*. Chicago: University of Chicago Press.

Hayek FA (1973) *Law legislation and liberty. Rules and order*, Vol. 1. Chicago: University of Chicago Press.

Hayek FA ([1976], 1990) *Denationalization of money*. London: Institute of Economic Affairs, 3rd ed.

Hodgson G (1997) The ubiquity of habits and rules. *Cambridge Journal of Economics*, 21: 663-684.

Hodgson GM (2003) The enforcement of contracts and property rights. Constitutive versus epiphenomenal conceptions of law, *International Review of Sociology*, 13(2): 375-391.
Hodgson GM (2015a) *Conceptualizing capitalism: institutions, evolution, future*. Chicago: University of Chicago Press.
Hodgson GM (2015b) Much of the 'economics of property rights' devalues property and legal rights. *Journal of Institutional Economics*, 11(4): 683 – 709.
Humphreys SC (1974) The nothoi of Kynosarges, *The Journal of Hellenic Studies*, 94:88-95.
Izdebski A, Słoczyński T, Bonnier A, Koloch G, Kouli K (2020) Landscape change and trade in Ancient Greece: evidence from Pollen Data. *The Economic Journal*, 130(632): 2596–2618.
Jaeger W ([1939], 1967) *Paideia: The ideals of Greek culture*. Oxford: Oxford University Press.
Jacobsen J (1943) Primitive Democracy in Ancient Mesopotamia. *Journal of Near Eastern Studies*, 2(33): 159-172.
Johnstone S (2011) *A history of trust in ancient Greece*. Chicago: The University of Chicago Press.
Jovanovic, B (1982), Favorable selection with asymmetric information. *Quarterly Journal of Economics*, 97, 535-539.
Kallet-Marx L (1993) *Money, expense and naval power in Thucydides' History 1-5.24*. Berkeley: University of California Press.
Kallet L (2007) The Athenian economy. In: Samons LJ II (Ed.), *The Cambridge Companion to the Age of Pericles* (pp. 70-95). Cambridge: Cambridge University Press.
Kapparis KA (1999) *Apollodorus "Against Neaira" [D.59]*. Berlin and New York: De Gruyter.
Katz M (1992) Ideology and the status of women in ancient Greece. *History and Theory*, 3(4), 70-97.
Kennedy P (1989) *The rise and fall of the Great Powers*. New York: Vintage Books.
Kleiner FS (1975) *Greek and Roman coins in the Roman Agora*. Princeton New Jersey: The American of Classical Studies at Athens.
Knorr K (1956) *The war potential of nations*. Princeton: Princeton University Press.
Koutsoyiannis D, Zarkadoulas N, Angelakis AN, Tchobanoglou G (2008) Urban water management in Ancient Greece: Legacies and lessons. *Journal of Water Resources Planning and Management - ASCE*, 134(1): 45–54.
Koutsoyiannis D, Mamassis N (2015) The water supply of Athens through the centuries. 16th conference Cura Aquarum, Athens, https://doi.org/10.13140/RG.2.2.24516.22400/1. Retrieved from: http://www.itia.ntua.gr/en/docinfo/1543/
Krentz P (1985) The nature of Hoplite Battle. *Classical Antiquity*, 4(1): 50-61.
Krentz P (2002) Fighting by the rules: the invention of the hoplite agon. *Hesperia*, 71(1): 23-39.
Kroll JH (2011) The reminting of Athenian silver coinage 353 B.C. *Hesperia*, 80: 229–259.
Krueger AO (1974) The Political Economy of the rent-seeking society. *American Economic Review*, 64(3): 291-303.
Krugman PR, Obstfeld M, Melitz M (2023) *International Economics: Theory and policy*, 12th Edition. New York: Pearson.
Kuznets S (1966) *Modern economic growth: Rate, structure, and spread*. New Haven and London: Yale University Press.
Kyle DG (1987) *Athletics in ancient Athens*. Leiden: E. J. Brill.
Kyriazis NA (2019) A survey on efficiency and profitable trading opportunities in cryptocurrency markets. *Journal of Risk and Financial Management*, 12, 67.
Kyriazis NA (2020) Herding behaviour in digital currency markets: An integrated survey and empirical estimation. *Heliyon*, 6 (2020), e04752.
Kyriazis NA, Papadamou S, Corbet S (2020) A systematic review of the bubble dynamics of cryptocurrency prices. *Research in International Business and Finance* 54: 101254.
Kyriazis NC, Zouboulakis M (2004) Democracy, sea power and institutional change: An economic analysis of the Athenian naval law. *European Journal of Law and Economics*, 17(1): 117–132.
Kyriazis NC (2006) Seapower and socioeconomic change. *Theory and Society*, 35: 71–108.
Kyriazis NC (2007a) Economic democracy and decision making for public goods. *Archives of Economic History*, XIX(2): 19–34.

Kyriazis NC (2007b). Democracy and institutional change. *European Research Studies*, X(1–2): 65–82.

Kyriazis NC (2009) Financing the Athenian state: Public choice in the age of Demosthenes. *European Journal of Law and Economics*, 27(2): 109-127.

Kyriazis NC, Metaxas T (2010) Bounded rationality and institutional change. *Evolutionary and Institutional Economic Review*, 7(1): 1–19.

Kyriazis NC, Karayiannis A (2011) Democracy, institutional changes and economic development: The case of ancient Athens. *Journal of Economic Assymetries*, 8(1): 61-93.

Kyriazis, NC (2012) *Why ancient Greece? The birth and development of democracy.* Athens Psychogios.

Kyriazis NC, & Economou EML (2013) Social Contract, public choice and fiscal repercussions in the Athenian Democracy. *Theoretical and Practical Research in Economic Fields*, 1(7), 61-76.

Kyriazis NC, & Paparrigopoulos X (2014) War and democracy in ancient Greece. *European Journal of Law and Economics*, 38(1): 163-183.

Kyriazis NC, Paparrigopoulos X, Economou EML (2014) The glue of democracy: Economics, warfare and values in Classical Greece. In: Bitros GC & Kyriazis NC (eds), *Essays in contemporary economics. A festschrift in memory of Anastasios D. Karayiannis* (pp. 197-214). Heidelberg: Springer Verlag.

Kyriazis NC, & Economou EML (2015a) Macroculture, sports and democracy in Classical Greece. *European Journal of Law and Economics*, 40: 431-455.

Kyriazis NC, Economou EML (2015b) Democracy and education: A history from ancient Athens.' In: Backhaus J (ed.), *The University according to Humboldt. History, policy, and future possibilities* (pp. 75-84). Heidelberg: Springer.

Kyriazis NC, Economou EML (2016) 'The memoranda trap and the near fall of Greece.' In: Caldwell D, *Greece: Economic crises and management* (pp. 75-93). New York: Nova Publishers.

Kyriazis, NC, Metaxas, T, Economou, EML, (2018) War for profit: English corsairs, institutions and decentralized strategy. *Defence and Peace Economics*, 29(3), 335–351.

Kyriazis NC, Economou, EML (2019) The ancient Athenian economy: A review. In Dellis JG, Paipetis SA (eds), *The influence of Hellenic philosophy on the contemporary world* (pp. 56-67). Newcastle upon Tyne: Cambridge Scholars Publishing.

Kyriazis NC, Economou EML (2021) An intertemporal comparison of democracies: Athens, the Aetolian Federation, Greece and the EU. In Gkortsos C, Hrysohoou D., Passas A, Hatzopoulos V (eds), *European governance in times of uncertainty* (pp. 3-14). Athens: Nomiki Bibliothiki.

Kyrtatas D (2011) Slavery and economy in the Greek world. In: Bradley K, Cartledge P. (eds), *The Cambridge world history of slavery,* Vol 1. *The ancient Mediterranean world* (pp. 91-111). Cambridge: Cambridge University Press.

Laffont JJ, Tirole J (1991) The politics of government decision making. A theory of regulatory capture. *Quarterly Journal of Economics*, 106(4): 1089-1127.

Lambert S (2012) *Inscribed Athenian laws and decrees 352/1–322/1 BC.* Leiden and Boston: Brill.

Landau AY (2010) *The Philistines and Aegean migration at the end of the Late Bronze Age.* Cambridge: Cambridge University Press.

Lane FC (1973) *Venice. A maritime republic.* Baltimore, Maryland: The Johns Hopkins University Press.

Langdon M (1994) Public auctions in ancient Athens.' In: Lewis DM, Osborne R, Hornblower S (eds), *Ritual, finance, politics. Athenian democratic accounts presented to David Lewis* (pp. 253-268). Oxford: Oxford University Press.

Lanni AM (2006) *Law and justice in the courts of Classical Athens.* Cambridge: Cambridge University Press.

Larsen JAO (1968) *Greek Federal States. Their Institutions and History.* Oxford: Clarendon Press.

Lauk TC (2014) *The triple crisis of western capitalism: Democracy, banking, and currency.* London: Palgrave Macmillan.

Lazos C (1998) *Engineering and technology in Ancient Greece.* Athens: Aeolos Editions.

Lee HM (1988) The first Olympic games of 776 BC. In: Raschke W (ed), *The Archaeology of the Olympics* (pp. 110-118). Wisconsin: The University of Wisconsin Press.
Lefkowitz MR (1996) *Black Athena revisited.* North Carolina: The University of North Carolina Press.
Lefkowitz MR (1997) *Not out of Africa: How "Afrocentrism" became an excuse to teach myth as history.* New York: Basic Books.
Lefkowitz MR (2008) *History lesson. A race Odyssey.* New Haven and London: Yale University Press.
Leese, M. S., (2017), Kapêloi and economic rationality in fourth-century B.C.E. Athens. Illinois Classical Studies, 42(1), 41–59.
Leese MS (2021) *Economic decision making and money-making dtrategies in Ancient Greece.* Ann Arbor: University of Michigan Press.
Levine ME, Forrence JL (1990) Regulatory capture, public interest, and the public agenda. Toward a synthesis. *Journal of Law Economics & Organization*, 6: 167-198.
Lewis DM (1997) *Selected papers in Greek and Near Eastern History.* Cambridge: Cambridge University Press.
Licht H (2000) *Sexual life In Ancient Greece.* London and New York: Routledge.
Lindenlauf A (2004) Dirt, cleanliness and social structure in ancient Greece. In: Gardner A (ed), *Agency uncovered: Archaeological perspectives on social agency, power and being human* (pp. 81-104). London: UCL Press.
Lipset SM (1959) Some social requisites of democracy: Economic development and political legitimacy. *American Political Science Review*, 53(1): 69-105.
Livio, M (2002) *The golden ratio: The story of Phi, the world's most astonishing number.* New York: Broadway Books.
Loomis WT (1998) *Wages, welfare costs and inflation in Classical Athens.* Michigan: Michigan University Press.
Lyttkens CH (1994) A predatory democracy: an essay on taxation in classical Athens. *Explorations in Economic History*, 31: 62–90.
Lyttkens CH (1997) A rational-actor perspective on the origin of liturgies in ancient Greece, *Journal of Institutional and Theoretical Economics*, 153: 462-484.
Lyttkens CH (2006). Reflections on the origins of the polis. An economic perspective on institutional change in ancient Greece. *Constitutional Political Economy*, 17: 31–48.
Lyttkens CH (2010) Institutions, taxation, and market relationships in ancient Athens, *Journal of Institutional Economics*, 6(4): 505–527.
Lyttkens CH (2011) Health, Economics and Ancient Greek Medicine, *The Journal of Economic Asymmetries*, 8(1): 165–192.
Lyttkens CH (2013) *Economic analysis of institutional change in ancient Greece. Politics, taxation and rational behaviour.* London and New York: Routledge.
Lyttkens CH, Henrik G (2018) Understanding the politics of Perikles around 450 BC. The benefits of an economic perspective. In: Canevaro M, Erskine, A, Grey B, Ober J, (eds), *Edinburgh Leventis Studies, Ancient history and contemporary Social Science* (pp. 269-292). Edinburgh: Edinburgh University Press.
Lyttkens CH, Tridimas G, Lindgren A (2018) Making direct democracy work: a rational-actor perspective on the graphe paranomon in ancient Athens. *Constitutional Political Economy,* 29(4): 389-412.
Lyttkens CH, Gerding H. (2022) Coping with chronic warfare. The Athenian experience. In: Economou EML, Kyriazis NC, Platias A (eds), *Democracy and Salamis. 2500 years after the battle that saved Greece and the western world* (pp. 181-200). Cham: Springer.
McArthur M (2021) Athenian Shipbuilders. *Hesperia*, 90(3): 479-532.
MacDowell D (1975) Law-making at Athens in the fourth century BC. *Journal of Hellenic Studies*, 95: 61-74.

Mackil E, van Alfen PG (2006) Cooperative coinage. In: Kroll JH, van Alfen PG (eds), *Agoranomia: Studies in money and exchange presented to John H. Kroll* (pp. 201-246). New York: American Numismatic Society.

Mackil E (2013) *Creating a common polity: Religion, economy, and politics in the making of the Greek Koinon*. Berkeley and Los Angeles: University of California Press.

Manville B, Ober J (2003). *A company of citizens*. Boston, MA: Harvard Business School Press.

Marcaccini C (2015) The treasurers of Athena in the late 5th century B.C.: When did they take office? *Hesperia: The Journal of the American School of Classical Studies at Athens*, 84(3): 515-532

Matsusaka GJ (2005a) Direct democracy works. *The Journal of Economic Perspectives*. 19(2): 185-206.

Matsusaka GJ (2005b) The eclipse of legislatures: Direct democracy in the 21st century. *Public Choice*, 124: 157–177.

Mauro P (1995) Corruption and growth. *The Quarterly Journal of Economics*, 110(3): 681–712.

Mayor A (2014) *The Amazons: Lives and legends of warrior women across the ancient world*. Princeton: Princeton University Press.

Mayor A (2018) *Gods and robots: Myths, machines, and ancient dreams of technology*. Princeton, NJ: Princeton University Press.

McAuley A (2013) 'Officials and office-holding.' In Beck H (ed), *A Companion to Ancient Greek Government* (pp. 174-190). MA: Willey-Blackwell.

Mendels D (1982) Polybius and the socio-economic revolution in Greece (227-146 BC), *AC*, 51: 86-110.

Michels R (1915) *Political parties: A sociological study of the oligarchical tendencies of modern democracy*. New York: The Free Press.

Migeotte, L (2009), *The economy of the Greek cities. From the archaic period to the early Roman empire.* Berkeley, Los Angeles, London: University of California Press.

Miller S (2003a) The organization and functioning of the Olympic Games. In: Philips DJ, Pritchard D (eds), *Sport and Festival in the Ancient Greek World* (pp. 1-41). Swansea: Classical Press of Wales.

Miller S (2004) *Ancient Greek athletics*. New York and London: Yale University Press.

Miller TS (2003b) *The orphans of Byzantium: Child welfare in the Christian empire*. Washington DC: The Catholic University of America Press.

Milne A (2017) Cryptocurrencies from an Austrian Perspective. Social Science Research Network, 2017. Retrieved at: https://ssrn.com/abstract=2946160 or https://doi.org/10.2139/ssrn.2946160.

Moreno A (2007) *Feeding the democracy: The Athenian grain supply in the fifth and fourth Centuries BC*. Oxford: Oxford University Press.

Moreno-Jimenez JM, Polasek W (2003) E-democracy and knowledge. A multicriteria framework for the new democratic era. *Journal of Multi-Criteria Decision Analysis*, 12: 163-176.

Morris I (2004) Economic growth in ancient Greece. *Journal of Institutional and Theoretical Economics*, 160: 709–742.

Morrison JS, Coates JF (1986) *The Athenian trireme*. Cambridge. Cambridge University Press.

North D (1981) *Structure and change in economic history*. New York: W.W. Norton and Company.

North D (1990) *Institutions, and economic performance*. Cambridge University Press, Cambridge.

North DC, Thomas RP (1973) *The rise of the western world: A new economic history*. Cambridge: Cambridge University Press.

North D, Wallis JJ, Weingast BR (2009) *Violence and social orders. A conceptual framework for interpreting recorded. human history*. Cambridge: Cambridge University Press.

Ober J (1985) *Fortress Attica. Defense of the Athenian land frontier, 404-322 B.C.* Leiden: E.J. Brill.

Ober J (2008) *Democracy and knowledge. Innovation and learning in Classical Athens*. Princeton: Princeton University Press.

Ober J (2011) Wealthy Hellas. *Journal of Economic Asymmetries*, 8(1): 1-39.

Ober J (2015a) *The rise and the fall of Classical Greece*. Princeton: Princeton University Press.

Ober J (2015b) Classical Athens.' In: Monson A, Scheidel W (eds), *Fiscal regimes and the Political Economy of premodern states* (pp. 492-592). Cambridge: Cambridge University Press.

Ober J (2017) Inequality in Late-Classical democratic Athens. Evidence and models. In: Bitros GC, Kyriazis NC (eds), *Democracy and open economy world order* (pp. 125-146). Heidelberg: Springer-Verlag.

Ober J (2022) Herodotus on rationality and cooperation before Salamis. In: Economou, EM L., Kyriazis NC, Platias A (eds), *Democracy and Salamis. 2500 years after the battle that saved Greece and the western world* (pp. 33-56). Cham: Springer.

O' Halloran B (2018) *The Political Economy of Classical Athens: A naval perspective*. Leiden: Brill.

Olson M (1965) *The logic of collective action*. Cambridge: Harvard University Press.

Olson M (1982) *The rise and decline of nations: Economic growth, stagflation, and social rigidities*. New Haven: Yale University Press.

Olson M (1991) Autocracy, democracy and prosperity.' In R. J. Zeckhauser (Ed.), *Strategy and Choice* (pp. 131-157). Cambridge: MIT Press.

Olson M (1993) Dictatorship, democracy, and development. *The American Political Science Review*, 87(3): 567-576.

Osborne R (1985) *Demos: the discovery of classical Attika*. Cambridge: Cambridge University Press.

Osborne R (1993). Competitive festivals and the polis: A context for dramatic festivals at Athens. In: Sommerstein A, Halliwell S, Henderson J, Zimmermann B (eds), *Tragedy, comedy and the polis* (pp. 21–38). Bari: Levante Editori.

Osborne R (2013) Democracy and religion. In: Arnason JP, Raaflaub KA, Wagner P (eds), *The Greek polis and the invention of democracy: A politico-cultural transformation and its interpretations* (pp. 274-297). Malden, MA: John Wiley & Sons, Inc.

Osiander A (2007) *Before the state: systemic political change in the West from the Greeks to the French Revolution*. New York: Oxford University Press.

Paipetis S (2010) *The unknown technology in Homer*. Heidelberg, London New York: Springer Dordrecht.

Prichard DM (2015) *Public spending and democracy in Classical Athens*. Austin: University of Texas Press.

Papadamou S, Kyriazis NA, Tzeremes P, Corbet S (2021) Herding behaviour and price convergence clubs in cryptocurrencies during bull and bear markets. *Journal of Behavioral and Experimental Finance*, 30: 100469.

Papazarkadas N. (2011). *Sacred and public land in ancient Athens*. New York: Oxford University Press, Inc.

Patriquin L (2015) *Economic equality and direct democracy in Ancient Athens*. Basingstoke and New York: Palgrave Macmillan.

Philips DJ, Pritchard D (eds) (2003) *Sport and festival in the ancient Greek world*. Swansea: Classical Press of Wales.

Platias A, Trigkas A (2022) Themistocles: Leadership and grand strategy? In: Economou EML, Kyriazis, NC, Platias A (eds), *Democracy and Salamis. 2500 years after the battle that saved Greece and the western world* (pp. 99-130). Cham: Springer.

Pleket H (1975) Games, prizes, athletes and ideology: Some aspects of the history of sports in Greco-Roman World. *Stadion*, 1: 49-89.

Pleket H (2005) The Olympic Games in antiquity. *European Review*, 12(3): 401–413.

Pomeroy SB (1995) *Goddesses, whores, wives and slaves*. Women in Classical antiquity. New York: Schocken.

Pomeroy SB, Burstein SM, Donlan W, Roberts JT (1999) *Ancient Greece. A political, cultural and social history*. New York: Oxford University Press.

Pritchard D (2003) Athletics education and participation in Classical Athens. In: Philips DJ, Pritchard D (eds), *Sport and festival in the ancient Greek world* (pp. 293-351). Swansea: Classical Press of Wales.

Pritchard DM (2012) Costing festivals and war: spending priorities of the Athenian democracy. *Historia*, 61(1): 18-65.

Pritchard DM (2013) *Sport, democracy and war in Classical Athens*. Cambridge: Cambridge.

Pritchard DM (2014) The public payment of magistrates in fourth-century Athens. *GRBS*, 54: 1–16.

Psoma S (2011) The law of Nicophon (SEG 26·72) and Athenian imitations, *RNB*, CLVII: 27-36. Retrieved at: www.numisbel.be/2011_2.pdf

Putnam RD (1976) *The comparative study of political elites*. Englewood Cliffs (NJ): Prentice-Hall.

Quinault R (2001) Churchill and democracy. *Transactions of the Royal Historical Society*, 11: 201-220.

Qvortrup M (2007) *The politics of participation: From Athens to e-democracy*. Manchester, Manchester University Press.

Raaflaub, KA, Ober J and RW Wallace (2007). *Origins of Democracy in Ancient Greece*. Berkeley, Los Angeles and London: University of California Press.

Reibig A (2001) The Bücher-Meyer controversy: the nature of the ancient economy in modern ideology. Ph.D Thesis. University of Glascow. Available at: http://theses.gla.ac.uk/4321/1/2001ReibigPhD.pdf

Renfrew C (1967) Cycladic metallurgy in the Aegean Early Bronze Age, *American Journal of Archaeology*, 71, 1–20.

Rhodes PJ (1972) *The Athenian Boule*. Oxford: Oxford University Press.

Rhodes PJ (2005) A *history of classical Greek world: 478-323 BC*. Oxford: Blackwell Publishing.

Rhodes PJ, Osborne R (2003) *Greek Historical Inscriptions 404-232 BC*. Oxford: Oxford University Press.

Richard, CJ (2009). *Greeks and Romans bearing gifts. How the ancients inspired the founding fathers*. Lanham: Rowman and Littlefield Publishers, Inc.

Rodrik D (2000) Institutions for high-quality growth: What they are and how to acquire them. *Studies in Comparative International Development*, 35(3): 3-31.

Rodrik D, Wacziarg R (2005) Do democratic transitions produce bad economic outcomes? *American Economic Review*, 95: 50–55.

Robinson, EW, (2011) *Democracy beyond athens: Popular government in the Greek classical age*. Cambridge: Cambridge University Press.

Roselli DK (2012) *Theater of the people. Spectators and society in Ancient Athens*. Austin: University of Texas Press.

Ross SA (1973) The Economic Theory of Agency: The Principal's Problem, *The American Economic Review*, 63(2): 134–139.

Rostovtzeff M ([1941], 1953) *The social and economic history of the Hellenistic world*. Oxford: Clarendon Press.

Rothschild M, & Stiglitz J, (1976), Equilibrium in competitive insurance markets: An essay on the economics of imperfect information. *The Quarterly Journal of Economics*, 90(4), 629–649.

Rothstein B (2011) *The quality of government. Corruption, social trust, and inequality in international perspective*. Chicago and London: The University of Chicago Press.

Runciman D (2015) *The confidence trap: A history of democracy in crisis from World War I to the present*. Princeton: Princeton University Press.

Rutishauser B (2019) The wealth of metics and Athenian naval power. In Figueira, TJ, Jensen, SR (eds), *Hegemonic finances. Funding Athenian domination in the 5th centuries BC*, London: Bloomsbury, 233–258.

Samons LJ (1993) Athenian finance and the treasury of Athena. *Historia: Zeitschrift für Alte Geschichte*, Bd. 42(2): 129-138.

Samons LJ (2000) *Empire of the owl: Athenian imperial finance*. (Historia Einzelschriften) Stuttgart: Franz Steiner Verlag.

Samuelson PA (1938). Note on the pure theory of consumer's behaviour. *Economica*, New Series, 5 (17), 61-71.
Samuelson PA (1948). Consumption theory in terms of revealed preference. *Economica*, 15(60), 243-253.
Schaps DM (1979) *Economic rights of women*. Edinburg: Edinburg University Press.
Schaps, DM, (2008), What was money in ancient Greece?, In: W. V. Harris (Ed.),*The Monetary Systems of the Greeks and Romans* (pp. 38–48). Oxford: Oxford University Press.
Scheidel W, Morris I, Saller, RP (eds) (2008) *The Cambridge economic history of the Greco-Roman world*. Cambridge: Cambridge, University Press.
Schumpeter JA (1934) *The theory of economic development. An inquiry into profits, capital, credit, interest, and the Business Cycle*. Cambridge, MA: Harvard University Press.
Schumpeter JA ([1942], 2013) *Capitalism, socialism and democracy*. London: Routledge.
Schwartzberg M. (2004) Athenian democracy and legal change. *American Political Science Review*, 98(2): 311-325.
Selgin GA (1988) *The theory of free banking: Money supply under competitive note issue*. Totowa, NJ: Rowman & Littlefield.
Sherwood AN, Nikolic M, Humphrey JW, Oleson JP (2020) *Greek and Roman technology. A sourcebook of translated Greek and Roman texts*. London and New York: Routledge.
Sinclair RK (1991) *Democracy and participation in Athens*. Cambridge: Cambridge University Press.
Snell B (1982) *The discovery of the mind. The Greek origins of European thought*. Cambridge, Massachusetts: Harvard University Press.
Snow NC (2005) *The shield*. Bloomington, Indiana: Authorhouse.
Snow, NC (2014) *Last Love*, Bloomington, Indiana: Authorhouse.
Spears B (1984) A perspective of the history of women's sport in Ancient Greece. *Journal of Sport History*, 11(2): 32-47.
Stager LE (1988) The impact of the Sea Peoples in Canaan (1185–1050 BC). In: Levy TE (ed), *The archaeology of society in the Holy Land*. London: Leicester University Press.
Stigler G (1971) The theory of economic regulation. *The Bell Journal of Economics and Management Science*, 2:3-21.
Strauss B (2004) *The Battle of Salamis: The naval encounter that saved Greece-and western civilization*. New York: Simon and Schuster.
Stroud RS (1974) An Athenian law on silver coinage. *Hesperia*, XLIII(2): 157–188.
Stroud RS (1998) *The Athenian grain-tax law of 374/3 B.C.* (Hesperia Supplements). Princeton, New Jersey: American School of Classical Studies at Athens.
Sullivan B (2018) In the shadow of Phoenicia: North Syria and 'Palestinian Syria' in Herodotus. *The Journal of Hellenic Studies*, 138: 67-79.
Taylor FW (1911) *The principles of scientific management*. New York and London: Harper and Brothers.
Temin P (2013) *The Roman market economy*. Princeton, Oxford: Princeton University Press.
Thorley J (1996) *Athenian democracy*. London and New York: Routledge.
Thornton B (2000) *Greek ways. How the Greeks created Western civilization*. San Fransisco: Encounter Books.
Tridimas G (2011) A political economy of direct democracy in ancient Greece. *Constitutional Political Economy*, 22: 58–82.
Tridimas G (2013) Homo Oeconomicus in ancient Athens: silver bonanza and the choice to build a navy. *Homo Oeconomicus*, 30(4): 435–458.
Tridimas G (2017) Constitutional choice in ancient Athens: the evolution of the frequency of decision making. *Constitutional Political Economy*, 28(3): 209–230.
Tridimas G (2019) The debate about the nature of the ancient Greek economy: 19th century German scholarship and modern economic theory. In: Holler M, Tridimas G (eds), *German-Greek yearbook of Political Economy*, vol. 2 (pp. 3-25). München: Holler-Verlag.

Tridimas G (2020) Modelling the quest for status in Ancient Greece: Paying for liturgies. *Homo Oeconomicus*, 37: 213–236.

Tridimas G (2022) Religion without doctrine or clergy: The case of Ancient Greece. *Journal of Institutional Economics*, 18(4): 677–691.

Tridimas G (2023) Choice of slavery institutions in Ancient Greece: Athenian chattels and Spartan helots, *Journal of Institutional Economics*, 19: 820–836.

Tsakirgis B (2007) House, settlement and society in the Aegean and beyond. *British School at Athens Studies*, 15: 225-231.

Tullock G (1989) *The economics of special privilege and rent seeking*. Boston: Kluwer Academic Publishers.

Tylecote RF (2002) *A history of metallurgy*. London: Maney Publishing.

Van Alfen PG (2011) Hatching owls: Athenian public finance and the regulation of coin production. In: de Callatay F (Ed), *Quantifying monetary supplies in Greco-Roman times* (pp. 127-149). Bari: Edipuglia.

Van Wees H (2013) *Ships and silver and taxes and tribute. A fiscal history of Archaic Athens*. London, New York: I. B. Tauris.

Vaxevanopoulos M, Blichert-Toft J, Davis G, Albarede F (2022) New findings of ancient Greek silver sources, *Journal of Archaeological Science*, 137, 105474.

Verboven K (2021) *Complexity economics. Building a new approach to ancient economic history*, Cham: Palgrave MacMillan.

Vlassopoulos K (2007) Free spaces: Identity, experience, and democracy in Classical Athens. *The Classical Quarterly*, 57 (1): 33–52.

Vlassopoulos K (2009) Slavery, freedom and citizenship in classical Athens: beyond a legalistic approach. *European Review of History: Revue Europeenne d'Histoire*, 16(3): 347-363.

von Reden S, Kowalzig B (2022) 'New Institutional Economics, economic growth, and institutional change.' In: von Reden S (ed), *The Cambridge companion to ancient Greek economy* (pp. 347-359). Cambridge: Cambridge University Press.

von Reden S (ed.) (2022) *The Cambridge Companion to ancient Greek economy*. Cambridge: Cambridge University Press.

Walbank F (1983) Leases of Sacred Properties in Attica, Part IV, *Hesperia*, 52: 207–31.

Weber M ([1922], 1978) *Economy and society: An outline of interpretive sociology*. Berkeley, California: University of California Press.

Weingast BR (1997) The political foundations of democracy and the rule of law. *The American Political Science Review*, 91(2): 254-263.

White L ([1984], 1995). *Free banking in Britain*. London: Institute of Economic Affairs, reissued 2nd edition.

Woodhead AG (1952) The state Health Service in Ancient Greece. *Cambridge Historical Journal*, 10(3): 235-253.

Woolmer M (2016) Forging links between regions: Trade policy in Classical Athens.In: Harris EM, Lewis DM, Woolmer M (eds), *The ancient Greek economy: Markets, households and city states* (pp. 66–89). New York: Cambridge University Press.

Zelnick-Abramovitz R (2005) *Not wholy free: The concept of manumission and the status of manumitted slaves in the ancient Greek world*. Leiden and Boston: Brill.

Zittel T, Fuchs D (eds) (2007). *Participatory Democracy and Political Participation. Can participatory engineering bring citizens back in?* London and New York: Routledge.

Index

A
Adikia, 93
Aeschines, 4, 34, 38, 39, 63, 86, 90–92, 94, 120, 165, 183, 214–219, 236, 243, 245, 246, 266, 267, 269–271, 279, 305–308
Agathoi, 26
Agora, 2, 16, 17, 24, 25, 29, 30, 34, 38–40, 46, 51, 53, 54, 57, 69, 70, 78, 105, 115–130, 135, 137, 138, 141–143, 153, 163, 166, 167, 172, 174, 181, 191–194, 196, 197, 199, 220, 223, 236, 251, 252, 256, 273, 274, 289, 314, 318, 319, 323, 330
Agoranomia, 123, 157
Agoranomoi, 97, 123, 124, 135, 320, 328
Agoranomos, 123
Amphorae, 56, 139, 140, 169, 191, 192, 204, 280, 290
Anasaximon, 174
Andocides, 20, 22, 39, 65, 82, 125, 174
Andron, 15, 29, 30, 105, 132, 139–142, 214, 218, 253
Antidosis, 26, 51, 177, 179, 190, 244
Aparchai, 222, 223
Apeleuthere, 102, 259, 267
Apeleutheroi, 17, 46, 47, 49
Apocheirotonia, 93, 94, 328
Apodektai, 97, 175
Archai, 10, 90, 95–98, 165, 318, 323, 326
Archon
  basileus, 80, 86
  eponymous, 69, 80, 111, 174, 183, 221, 291, 301–303, 305
Areopagos, 79–80, 82, 93, 94, 117
Argyramoibos, 46
Argyrocopeion, 119, 141–145, 173, 181
Aristotle, 18, 25, 31, 32, 38, 40, 42, 43, 46, 47, 49, 50, 59, 60, 74, 77, 78, 81, 88, 90, 92, 93, 95–97, 106, 109, 112, 121, 123, 126, 156, 166, 173, 174, 225, 236, 237, 242–244, 247, 258, 267, 279, 285, 298, 329, 330
Asclepieia, 286–288
Assembly
  approval or rejection by the, 75
  Athenian (popular), 3, 38, 67, 71–75, 80, 83, 89, 94, 112, 143, 149, 173, 199, 215, 225, 241–249, 306, 325, 330
  of Citizens, 3, 10, 71, 74, 75, 82, 142, 144, 227, 323, 325
  Council and the, 79, 323
  decisions made by the, 84, 144
  laws to be submitted to the, 77
  local municipal, 63
  meetings of the, 51, 74, 85, 248
  proposals in the, 9, 72, 84, 85, 87, 225
  workings of the, 74, 219, 329
Asty, 30, 61, 62, 96, 135, 311
Astynomoi, 96, 106–108, 123
Asylia, 164, 278
Athens
  Acropolis of, 50, 211, 312
  Agora of, 40, 115–118, 120, 141, 142, 163, 181, 191–194, 197, 199, 207
  ancient, 2, 7, 118
  citizens of, 31, 43, 86
  city-state of, 3, 118, 129, 137, 159, 226, 277

E. M. Economou, N. C. Kyriazis, *Daily Life in Classical Athens*, Frontiers in Economic History, https://doi.org/10.1007/978-3-031-58541-8

Athens (*cont.*)
- classical, 1, 3, 6, 10, 11, 13–27, 80, 110, 120, 125, 162, 179–190, 227, 249, 263, 265, 281, 319, 322, 324, 325, 329–332
- daily life in, 7, 244
- *Metics* at, 43, 44
- Slaves in Athens, 44–51
- Sports at, 278–279
- The demos of, 10, 249
- the polis of, 34, 44, 73, 242
- the state of, 59, 62, 80, 220
- women in, 262, 266

Atimos, 70, 94, 174, 190, 270

Attica
- the coastal area of, 61
- defense of, 253
- drachma, 141
- nearby fortresses of, 3, 247, 253
- the people in, 52

Aulitrides, 258, 261, 262

Aulitris, 218, 257

B

Balaneia, 106

Banausos, 25

Boule, 10, 75

Bouleuterion
- New, 78, 79, 117, 119
- Old, 78, 117, 119

Bouleutes, 70

Boulomenos, 84, 85

C

Chalkoi, 146, 194

Chalkos, 146

Cheirotonia, 90, 165

Cheirotonoi, 90, 329

Choregia, 182, 185, 282

Choregos, 4, 282, 301–303

Clientelism, 12, 13

Citizen initiatives, 87, 109, 324, 325

Clepsydra, 80, 112, 243

Council
- and the Assembly, 79
- annual body of the, 76
- Athenian, 63, 64, 70, 77, 78, 86, 93, 94, 97, 173, 194, 237
- of the Five Hundred, 10, 19, 20
- membership in the, 76
- *prytanic*, 78

Councilmen, 19, 64, 70, 75–78, 91, 92, 95, 96, 98, 143, 280, 285, 306

D

Demarchs, 63–65, 284

Deme(s), 10, 16, 18, 23, 39, 51, 57–59, 61–67, 70, 77, 86, 89, 92, 96, 97, 109, 120, 123, 143, 171, 172, 175, 177, 185, 219, 229, 236, 247, 263, 267, 268, 275, 284–287, 329, 331

Democracy
- direct, 8, 9, 11, 12, 14, 144, 244, 249, 324
- economic, 14

Democratic
- deficit, 13
- elitism, 9, 13
- government, 59

Demos, 3, 10, 73–75, 86, 186, 225, 236, 249, 291, 317

Demosion, 221, 222, 225

Demosthenes, 4, 10, 18, 20–26, 31, 33, 35, 38, 47–51, 62, 65–67, 81, 85, 87–89, 92, 106, 109, 120–124, 126, 159–165, 167–169, 180, 183–186, 190, 198, 229, 235, 242–244, 246, 256, 259, 263–268, 270, 279, 284, 285, 297, 299, 303, 305–309

Diapsephismos, 62

Didaskaleia, 246

Dikai emporikai, 90, 160, 165–166

Dike
- *emporike*, 157
- *epitrierarchematos*, 184

Dioikesis, 95, 326

Dokimasia, 20, 76, 77, 94, 166, 327

Dokimastai, 141, 152–156, 320, 328

Dokimastes, 141, 155, 191

Douloi, 44

Drachma, 36, 43, 47, 61, 66, 70, 72, 74, 75, 82, 85, 94, 99, 102, 103, 121, 125, 137, 139–156, 172, 180, 181, 184, 189, 193–195, 197, 198, 216, 217, 224, 251, 253, 258, 259, 266, 268, 276, 280, 282, 285, 286, 312, 320

E

Ecclesia
- *of the Demos*, 3, 10, 73–75, 317
- *Kyria*, 71, 74, 75, 93, 327
- *synkletos*, 74

Ecclesiasticon, 74, 216

Ecclesiai synkletoi, 74

Economic
- activity, 14, 46, 113, 119, 125, 170, 173, 216
- analysis, 4, 6, 7
- democracy, 14

development, 7, 62, 160, 167, 331
freedoms, 14, 114, 152
growth, 23, 88, 126, 211, 245, 299, 318, 319, 322, 326, 332
history, 6, 7, 125
institutions, 2, 5, 7, 11, 14, 60, 162, 318, 331
liberalism, 5, 150
life, 6
performance, 11, 12, 125, 332
and political institutions, 7
principles, 5
prosperity, 8, 14, 125, 153, 226
recovery, 3, 213, 226, 242, 299
reform, 3
stagnation, 6
theory, 6, 19, 99, 107, 125, 160, 163
Eisangelia, 87, 93, 94, 327
Eisphora(*i*), 182, 183, 216
Enktesis, 52, 164, 278
Ephebeia, 15, 35, 96, 221, 231, 236–237, 255, 276, 330
Ephebes, 99, 236, 247, 248, 276, 330
Epiblema, 53–55
Epicleroi, 36, 93
Epimeletai tou emporiou, 97, 138, 320, 328
Epimeletes
(epi) ton ydaton, 90, 97
of the triremes, 184
tes koines prosodou, 90, 219–221, 226
Epistatai, 96, 99, 143
Epistates, 48, 78, 172, 241, 242
Ergasimon, 174, 175
Ergasteria, 122, 199
Eubulus, 3, 87, 119, 215, 219, 220, 225–227, 259
Eunomia, 98, 169
Euthyna, 94, 221, 327
Exeleutheroi, 46

G
Glauke, 142
Grammateia
leleukomena, 174
lexiarchika, 62
Grammateus
epi ta psephismata, 82
epi tous nomous, 82
of thesmothetai, 87
tois thesmothetais, 79
Grammatists, 247
Graphe
nomon me epitedeion theinai, 85, 87
paranomon, 75, 81–87, 306
xenias, 63, 66, 259
Gymnasia, 106, 182, 270, 278, 279, 281, 287
Gymnasiarchai, 281, 282
Gymnasiarchy, 182
Gynaikonites, 29, 30, 33, 35, 40, 41, 53, 54, 105, 251

H
Hegemon, 7, 80, 183
Heliaia, 10, 63, 64, 70, 77, 79–81, 85, 92–95, 98, 117, 118, 165, 184, 194, 257, 305, 323, 328
Heliastai, 80
Hellanodikai, 276, 277
Hellenotamiai, 97, 221–222
Helots, 44
Hemiobol, 146, 147, 149
Hestia, 237, 255, 291, 313
Hestiasis, 182
Hetaera(*e*), 3, 33, 42, 66, 105, 202, 256, 258–259, 266–268, 298
Hiereiae, 40
Himation, 55, 193
Hippeis, 61, 91, 231
Hippotrophia, 182
Homonoia, 23, 24, 217, 227, 228, 284
Hoplite
phalanx, 3, 58, 61, 321
type of weaponry, 59
Hydria, 37, 134, 214, 303

I
Impossibility Theorem, 13
Information asymmetry, 13
Institutional changes, 6–8, 227, 320, 321, 326
Isegoria, 73, 322
Isocrates, 18, 26, 31, 35, 49, 51, 80, 125, 190, 198, 217, 219, 244, 245, 299, 305
Isonomia, 90, 91, 164, 329
Isopoliteia, 164, 278
Isoteleia, 66, 306

K
Kalos kagathos, 15–27, 43, 58, 77, 169, 227, 329, 330
Kapeleion, 197, 199
Kitharistae, 247
Kleroterion, 81
Klerotoi, 90, 329

Klope, 92
Kollyboi, 146, 194
Koprologoi, 106–108
Kosmetai, 90, 248, 330
Kylix, 134, 216, 257
Kyrios, 22, 38, 47

L
Liturgies, 43, 64, 169, 179–190, 226, 245, 281, 282, 301, 321, 328
Liturgist(s), 3, 179–181, 184, 185, 189
Logodosia, 91, 94, 166
Logoi, 226
Lycurgus, 3, 16–18, 25, 48, 87, 198, 213–221, 225–227, 229, 231, 237, 241, 243, 244, 248, 299, 302, 305, 306
Lysias, 20–22, 25, 26, 33, 34, 37, 39, 44, 47–49, 62, 66, 74, 76, 77, 80, 90–92, 120–122, 124, 153, 159–162, 184, 190, 265, 267, 269, 284, 285, 303

M
Macedonia, 134, 180, 229, 231, 235, 241, 242, 284, 307, 323
Medimnoi, 61, 137, 139
Medimnos, 61
Mesogeia, 17, 57, 61, 132, 172, 179, 215, 255
Metic(s), 2, 4, 16, 17, 23, 25, 31, 34, 36, 38, 43–44, 46, 47, 49–52, 64, 105, 106, 120, 134, 140, 159, 161, 166, 175, 177, 181, 183, 186, 190, 193, 199, 231, 232, 259, 268, 279, 289, 290, 302, 306, 330, 331
Metoikion, 43, 46, 193
Metronomoi, 97, 123, 124, 320, 328
Metroon, 71, 79, 81, 82, 117, 119, 155
Minae, 121
Minas, 121, 285
Misthosis, 186
Myrioi, 136

N
Naukleroi, 203
Nautodikai, 165
Neoria, 73
Neorion, 73, 96, 98
Neosoikoi, 12, 73, 126–128, 180, 186, 202, 220, 230
Neosoikos, 126, 127, 129
New Institutional Economics (NIE), 6, 7, 332
Nine archons, 67, 77, 79–80, 86, 87, 173
Nomophylakes, 81–87
Nomophylakion, 81
Nomophylax, 71
Nomothetai, 81–87

O
Obol(s), 74, 81, 99, 124, 146, 147, 149, 172, 194, 219, 266, 285
Oikonomos, 24, 38
Oikos, 2, 3, 15–27, 29–35, 37–46, 48, 49, 51, 53–57, 61, 101–114, 116, 121, 132, 134, 140, 142, 161, 173, 192, 195, 197, 202, 213, 214, 251–253, 255, 262, 263, 265, 275, 291, 295–298, 311, 312, 314
Oligarchic
  government, 66
Olkades, 203
Open access society, 13, 14
Opisthodomos, 222–224
Ousia
  aphanes, 169
  phanera, 169

P
Paideia, 75, 218, 219, 241–249, 270, 321, 329
Panathenaea
  Great, 4, 182, 225, 280–281, 289–293
Pankration, 3, 247, 273, 274, 276–279
Pantopoleia, 38
Paralia, 61
Parliamentarism, 8, 13
Pedagogues, 194, 246
Penteconters, 189
Pentecoste, 125, 140, 175, 216, 329
Pentecostologoi, 125, 175
Peplos, 29, 55, 293
Phalanx
  Athenian, 230
  formation, 238, 321
  (The) *hoplite*, 3, 58, 61, 231–236, 321
  Macedonian, 180
  oblique, 232
  spartan, 232
Philotimia, 23
Phratries, 23, 59, 62, 65, 70
Phylae, 18, 61–63, 67, 119
Phyle, 61, 63, 215, 253
Pistis, 196
Plakountes, 132, 134

Plato, 26, 31, 34, 40, 42–44, 46, 48, 50, 81, 112, 192, 194, 218, 219, 228, 236, 242, 244, 245, 248, 252, 264, 269, 270, 279, 286, 287, 299, 312, 329, 330
Plethron, 16, 58, 59
Pnyx, 11, 74, 116, 131, 220, 243, 307
Poletai
  board of, 173–175, 222
  ten, 97, 173, 174, 176
Polis, 2–4, 8, 10, 12, 17–20, 22–26, 30, 31, 34, 40, 43, 44, 46–52, 57–59, 61–67, 69, 70, 72–74, 76–78, 82, 83, 87, 89, 91, 96, 98, 104, 105, 108, 109, 111, 116, 118, 124, 140–142, 149, 153, 159, 161, 166, 167, 170, 171, 174, 184–186, 196–199, 232, 235, 237, 241, 242, 244, 247, 248, 255, 259, 268, 270, 273, 275, 278, 280, 284, 285, 289, 293, 303, 305–307, 311, 321, 323, 330
Politico-economic
  model, 320
  regime, 14, 48, 227
  system, 13, 317
Principal-agent problem, 13, 323
Public-private partnership (3P), 107, 125, 143, 173, 247, 286, 321, 328
Probouleuma(ta), 75, 96, 306
Proxeny, 164
Prytaneion, 25, 69, 78, 79, 117, 119, 185, 221, 280, 281
Prytaneis, 76, 78–79, 84, 242, 317
Prytany, 74, 143, 241, 242

R
Recall, 25, 306, 324, 327
Referenda, 324, 325
Regulatory capture, 9, 12
Rent-seeking, 13
Rome, 14, 44, 45, 50, 51, 106, 123, 133, 199, 210, 212, 331, 332

S
Sarissas, 230, 232, 238
Seisachtheia, 60, 160
Sitagoga, 203
Sitonai, 124, 320, 328
Sitophylakes, 97, 124, 320, 328
Sitopolai, 124
Socioeconomic
  analysis, 1
  character, 45
  classes, 18, 55
  and cultural life, 7
  institutions, 2
  issues, 7
  nature, 2
  stratification, 60
Sophronistai, 90, 248, 330
Sparta, 36, 41, 44, 50, 84, 113, 123, 201, 217, 226, 241, 242, 280, 281, 283, 284, 323
Stadia, 57, 58, 63, 220, 278
Stadion, 58, 278, 280, 282
Strategeion, 119
Strategoi, 89–90, 95, 183
Strategos
  epi tin choran, 343
  Leosthenes, 299–300
  of the trierarchy, 180
Stratiotikon, 90, 97, 221, 225–226, 306
Symbola, 164, 278
Symmories, 179, 180, 183–184, 216
Symposion, 3, 16, 39, 40, 42, 58, 105, 213–218, 226, 229, 255–257, 264, 269, 270, 295, 296, 312, 313
Synteleia(i), 179–181, 183–184
Syntely, 180
Syntrierarch(y), 179, 183–185

T
Talents, 36, 47, 82, 83, 99, 125, 143, 145, 181–184, 189, 190, 209, 215–217, 220, 224, 226, 227, 235, 266, 299
Tameion ton Stratiotikon, 82
Tamia, 223
Tamiai, 213, 223
Tamias, 64, 221, 285, 329
  (treasurer) of the *deme*, 64
  epi tes dioikeseos, 338
  epi to Stratiotikon, 97
  epi to Theorikon, 97
  tes koines prosodou, 219–221
  tois adynatois, 285, 329
  ton koinon prosodon, 338
  ton stratiotikon, 225
Ten euthynoi, 70, 92–94
Ten logistai, 70, 92, 94
Ten synegoroi, 70, 92, 94, 99
Tetradrachm, 142, 145, 146, 149, 156, 239
Theorica, 64, 215, 216, 218–219, 225, 227, 285, 330
Theoricon, 97, 219, 221, 225–226, 306, 307
Thesmothetai, 80–87, 92
Thete(s), 61, 63, 64, 72, 215, 216, 231, 247, 285

Thucydides, 8, 24–26, 35, 40, 59, 69, 73, 82, 83, 108, 121, 125, 181, 185, 201, 203, 224, 232, 235, 246, 322
Trapeza, 167
Treasury-temple of Athena, 222–224
Treasury-temples of Athena and the Other Gods (TTAGs), 83, 97, 108, 213, 221–224
Trierarch, 3, 179–181, 184, 185, 188, 190, 229–231
Trierarchies, 26, 89, 107, 179, 180, 182–186, 189, 190, 215–217, 222, 229, 230, 301
Trireme(s)
  adephagai, 189
  Athenian, 126, 188
  epimeletes of the, 184
  rams of the, 73

X
Xenophon, 20, 23–25, 31, 32, 34, 35, 37, 38, 40–42, 44, 47, 48, 89, 103–105, 120, 136, 172, 176, 190, 215, 237, 247, 270, 274, 314

Z
Zeugitai, 61

The manufacturer's authorised representative in the EU is Springer Nature Customer Service Centre GmbH, Europaplatz 3, 69115 Heidelberg, Germany. If you have any concerns regarding our products, please contact ProductSafety@springernature.com

Printed and bound by CPI Group (UK) Ltd, Croydon, CR0 4YY
28/09/2026
02224062-0003